BESTSELLING
BOOK SERIES

Investment Clu...
For Dummies

M000301893

Checklist for Starting Your Investment Club

- Research investment clubs thoroughly so that you understand what you're getting into.
- Request membership information from the National Association of Investors Corporation (NAIC), or get it online at www.better-investing.org.
- Prepare a brief informational packet or letter explaining to prospective members how a club works.
- Invite prospective members to an introductory meeting.
- Explain the investment club concept and member responsibilities at the initial meeting.
- Schedule future meetings with those interested in starting a club.
- Agree on your club's investment philosophy.
- Choose your club name.
- Choose a time and location for regular monthly meetings.
- Decide on the dollar amount of initial, monthly and maximum club contributions.
- Elect club officers.
- Select the legal form of your club, such as a general partnership or a limited liability company.
- Review, revise, adopt, and sign your club's Operating Agreement and Operating Procedures (or By-laws).
- Apply for your club's Tax ID number (officially called the "Employer ID Number," or EIN) from the IRS.
- Make business filing (also known as a "DBA" or business certificate) at your local county clerk's office and also with state office, if required.
- Register your club for NAIC membership.
- Research and open your club's bank or brokerage accounts.
- Research and purchase stock selection and club accounting software.
- Create a schedule for your club's educational program.
- Explore online club communication and stock research options.
- Sign up for local NAIC classes, if available, or use materials online to start your club's investment education.

See Chapters 4, 5, and 6 for details.

Investment Club Resources on the Web

National Association of Investors Corporation (NAIC)

Official site of the nonprofit organization dedicated to providing investment education to investment clubs and individual investors. A vast source of helpful information, including listings of regional classes, a wide selection of online education resources, and stock selection and club accounting tools.

www.better-investing.org

For Dummies: Bestselling Book Series for Beginners

Investment Clubs For Dummies®

Securities and Exchange Commission (SEC)

Rules that investment clubs must follow, plus other resources written specifically for clubs.

http://www.sec.gov/investor/pubs/invclub.htm

Internal Revenue Service (IRS)

Official site of the IRS. Lots of detailed regulations and useful information when starting or managing an investment club.

http://www.irs.gov/prod/forms_pubs/pubs/p5500110.htm

ICLUBcentral

Providers of NAIC's official club accounting software and online club accounting resources. Also offers club web sites, message boards, and portfolio tracking.

www.iclub.com

Ways to Keep Club Morale High

- ✔ Follow your club's rules to the letter to avoid conflict. If club rules aren't working, change them.
- ✔ Encourage members to get to know one another better by providing a chance to socialize before or after each meeting.
- ✔ Provide refreshments at each club meeting.
- ✔ Avoid major club battles by tabling any topic for a bit when discussions get too heated. You can return to it when emotions settle.
- ✔ Reward yourselves for hard work by changing your meeting location to someplace fun one month — meet at a restaurant for dinner, invite family members to come to an all-club barbecue, or go on a club field trip.
- ✔ Assign new members a mentor to help them become a productive part of the club more quickly.
- ✔ Continually adapt your education program as your members become more sophisticated investors.
- ✔ Explore online resources for club communication and investment education.
- ✔ Keep your expectations reasonable. Remember that a club experience should be both enriching and *fun!*

Hungry Minds™

For Dummies: Bestselling Book Series for Beginners

TM

BESTSELLING BOOK SERIES

References for the Rest of Us!®

Do you find that traditional reference books are overloaded with technical details and advice you'll never use? Do you postpone important life decisions because you just don't want to deal with them? Then our *For Dummies*® business and general reference book series is for you.

For Dummies business and general reference books are written for those frustrated and hard-working souls who know they aren't dumb, but find that the myriad of personal and business issues and the accompanying horror stories make them feel helpless. *For Dummies* books use a lighthearted approach, a down-to-earth style, and even cartoons and humorous icons to dispel fears and build confidence. Lighthearted but not lightweight, these books are perfect survival guides to solve your everyday personal and business problems.

"More than a publishing phenomenon, 'Dummies' is a sign of the times."

— *The New York Times*

"...you won't go wrong buying them."

— *Walter Mossberg, Wall Street Journal, on For Dummies books*

"A world of detailed and authoritative information is packed into them..."

— *U.S. News and World Report*

Already, millions of satisfied readers agree. They have made For Dummies the #1 introductory level computer book series and a best-selling business book series. They have written asking for more. So, if you're looking for the best and easiest way to learn about business and other general reference topics, look to For Dummies to give you a helping hand.

Investment Clubs

FOR

DUMMIES®

by Douglas Gerlach and Angele McQuade

Foreword by Donald E. Danko

Hungry Minds™

Best-Selling Books • Digital Downloads • e-Books • Answer Networks • e-Newsletters • Branded Web Sites • e-Learning

New York, NY ◆ Cleveland, OH ◆ Indianapolis, IN

Investment Clubs For Dummies®

Published by:
Hungry Minds, Inc.
909 Third Avenue
New York, NY 10022
www.hungryminds.com
www.dummies.com

Library of Congress Control Number: 2001097470

ISBN: 0-7645-5409-3

Printed in the United States of America

10 9 8 7 6 5 4 3 2 1

1O/QV/RS/QR/IN

Distributed in the United States by Hungry Minds, Inc.

Distributed by CDG Books Canada Inc. for Canada; by Transworld Publishers Limited in the United Kingdom; by IDG Norge Books for Norway; by IDG Sweden Books for Sweden; by IDG Books Australia Publishing Corporation Pty. Ltd. for Australia and New Zealand; by TransQuest Publishers Pte Ltd. for Singapore, Malaysia, Thailand, Indonesia, and Hong Kong; by Gotop Information Inc. for Taiwan; by ICG Muse, Inc. for Japan; by Intersoft for South Africa; by Eyrolles for France; by International Thomson Publishing for Germany, Austria and Switzerland; by Distribuidora Cuspide for Argentina; by LR International for Brazil; by Galileo Libros for Chile; by Ediciones ZETA S.C.R. Ltda. for Peru; by WS Computer Publishing Corporation, Inc., for the Philippines; by Contemporanea de Ediciones for Venezuela; by Express Computer Distributors for the Caribbean and West Indies; by Micronesia Media Distributor, Inc. for Micronesia; by Chips Computadoras S.A. de C.V. for Mexico; by Editorial Norma de Panama S.A. for Panama; by American Bookshops for Finland.

For general information on Hungry Minds' products and services please contact our Customer Care department; within the U.S. at 800-762-2974, outside the U.S. at 317-572-3993 or fax 317-572-4002.

For sales inquiries and resellers information, including discounts, premium and bulk quantity sales and foreign language translations please contact our Customer Care department at 800-434-3422, fax 317-572-4002 or write to Hungry Minds, Inc., Attn: Customer Care department, 10475 Crosspoint Boulevard, Indianapolis, IN 46256.

For information on licensing foreign or domestic rights, please contact our Sub-Rights Customer Care department at 212-884-5000.

For information on using Hungry Minds' products and services in the classroom or for ordering examination copies, please contact our Educational Sales department at 800-434-2086 or fax 317-572-4005.

Please contact our Public Relations department at 212-884-5163 for press review copies or 212-884-5000 for author interviews and other publicity information or fax 212-884-5400.

For authorization to photocopy items for corporate, personal, or educational use, please contact Copyright Clearance Center, 222 Rosewood Drive, Danvers, MA 01923, or fax 978-750-4470.

Hungry Minds™ is a trademark of Hungry Minds, Inc.

About the Authors

Douglas Gerlach, a true Internet pioneer, founded one of the earliest financial Web sites, Investorama.com, in 1995. Since then, he has helped hundreds of thousands of people get started on the road to financial freedom, through books, Web sites, magazine articles, frequent media appearances and speaking engagements.

Gerlach's interest in investing and investment clubs began in 1993, when he helped found the Blue Chip Posse investment club in New York City. He also joined the world's first online club, the Pioneer OnLine Investment Club (POLIC), in 1994. Between the two clubs, he has served terms as president and treasurer.

Gerlach is closely involved with the National Association of Investors Corporation (NAIC), the leading non-profit organization committed to investment clubs and investment education. He is the co-creator and consulting editor of the NAIC Web site, and has served on the NAIC Computer Group's Advisory Board since 1995. In 1996, Gerlach received the Distinguished Service Award (known as the Dutch Shoes Award) from NAIC's Investment Education Institute in recognition of his pioneering efforts using the online medium to teach people how to invest in the stock market. This prestigious award, typically given for lifetime achievement, is an indicator of the impact that the Internet has had on NAIC's outreach to investors and of Gerlach's role in those efforts.

Gerlach is the author of several books, including *The Investor's Web Guide* and *The Armchair Millionaire*. In addition, he has written for *Individual Investor, Better Investing, Computer Life,* and *PC World* magazines, and is *Mutual Funds* magazine's Consulting Editor for online investing. His advice column for investment club members, "The Investment Club Therapist," appears regularly on ICLUB.com.

Angele McQuade joined the Terrace Investment Group investment club in 1996 not long after she first started investing, and soon discovered the enormous educational opportunities that investment clubs can provide. Since that time, she has been committed to finding innovative ways to teach investing and personal finance to others who might find Wall Street an intimidating foe.

As one of the original organizers of the online Investor's School of the National Association of Investors Corporation (NAIC), McQuade has helped to develop Web-based, interactive investing seminars and chats designed for both new and experienced investors. Her efforts have contributed to a popular on-going series of weekly educational offerings with a broad and continuously growing international audience.

In addition, she writes the monthly Book Value column as well as feature articles for NAIC's *Better Investing* magazine, read by the organization's members and sold on newsstands. McQuade also wrote extensively for the Investorama.com personal finance Web site.

Following a recent out-of-state move, McQuade withdrew from her investment club. She's now in the planning stages of starting a club in her new hometown of Ithaca, New York. She hopes to create a club that will include a unique twist, serving as a mentor to a youth club at her local high school. She envisions a club where the members will meet with the teen investors on a regular basis, and where the teens can visit and even participate in her club's meetings whenever they wish. She also hopes that when her own two children reach high school age, they'll be as enthusiastic about the benefits of club investing as she is and want to join the youth club themselves.

Dedications

Angele: To Monique and John Theriault, who have given me a lifetime of parental love and support (especially during this past chaotic year). To Will and Madeline, who are the end of my rainbow, my pot of gold. And most of all to my one true love, Tyler. Je t'aime.

Doug: To my mother, for her support through the years, and for demonstrating the true meaning of fortitude.

Authors' Acknowledgments

Many thanks to the team at Hungry Minds for their patience and perseverance in guiding this book to completion, including Norm Crampton, Mark Butler, and Neil Johnson, and also to Jonathan Malysiak for his initial interest in the project.

We're also indebted to the whole crew at ICLUBcentral, Inc., for lending their considerable expertise regarding the intricacies of club accounting. Thanks to Robert Brooker, Bryce Klempner, Ann Schiff, Matt Stoller, Stuart Schechter, Russell Malley, Greg Bixler and Rich Beaubien. Several of NAIC's leaders were also helpful in providing research and advice about the direction and content of the book, including Kenneth Janke, Sr., Don and Nancy Danko, Mark Robertson, and Sue Peterman.

We're very grateful to the ten investment clubs you'll find profiled throughout this book. All were incredibly generous with detailed information about their club operations, in the hope that future clubs could benefit from their real-life experiences. Thank you to Karen Phillips and the Coast to Coast OnLine Investment Club, Joyce Richards and the Fortune 2000 Investment Club, Jack Ellison and the GaAs Valley Group, Kenneth Theis and the Greenback Investors, Inc., Nataki Reynolds and the Heart & Soul Investment Club, Judy Fortlage and the Primetimers' Investment Club, Glen Hansen and the Totem Investment Club, Bob Torche and United Equities, Claudia Knauss and the University Place Investment Club, and Lori Muse and the Unlimited Potential Investors.

Thank you to all the other investment clubs who shared their information with us: the SEMO Investors, the Women in Secure Equities, Stock It Up, the Eastern Shore of VA Investment Club, the Top 2 Investment Group, the Rainy Day Investors, the GEE Investment Group, Ltd., the Totally Awesome Rewards Through Stocks Investment Club, the Monroe Money Maven Investment Club, the Lucky Ladies, the Original Calhoun County Investment Club, the Rose City Ladies Investment Club, and the Williamson County Ladies Investment Club.

None of this book would be possible without all the lessons, good and sometimes not so pleasant, we've learned from our own investment clubs, past and present: the Blue Chip Posse, the Terrace Investment Group, and the Pioneer On-Line Investment Club.

Finally, Angele has a few words of acknowledgement of her own: "I would like to thank Pat Smith for her constant encouragement and support, David, Paul and Joseph for giving me all the brotherly love I can handle, Lisa and Bridgette for being the sisters I never had, little Cade just for being himself, and Dr. Sam/Sal Iaquinta for his writer's empathy (and blessed lack of medical advice). I also owe my eternal gratitude to all the NAIC volunteers I've worked with and learned from through the years. I was once convinced that I'd never be able to understand anything about investing, but with their unflagging enthusiasm and unconditional welcome, I overcame my fear and embarked on the education I continue today."

Publisher's Acknowledgments

We're proud of this book; please send us your comments through our Online Registration Form located at www.dummies.com.

Some of the people who helped bring this book to market include the following:

Acquisitions, Editorial, and Media Development

Project Editor: Norm Crampton

Acquisitions Editor: Mark Butler

Copy Editor: Neil Johnson

Technical Editor: Mark Robertson

Editorial Manager: Pam Mourouzis

Editorial Assistant: Carol Strickland

Cover Photos: © PhotoDisc 2001

Production

Project Coordinator: Dale White

Layout and Graphics: Betty Schulte, LeAndra Johnson, Brian Torwelle, Jeremey Unger

Proofreaders: John Bitter, Valery Bourke, Andy Hollandbeck, TECHBOOKS Production Services

Indexer: TECHBOOKS Production Services

General and Administrative

Hungry Minds Consumer Reference Group

Business: Kathleen Nebenhaus, Vice President and Publisher; Kevin Thornton, Acquisitions Manager

Cooking/Gardening: Jennifer Feldman, Associate Vice President and Publisher; Anne Ficklen, Executive Editor; Kristi Hart, Managing Editor

Education/Reference: Diane Graves Steele, Vice President and Publisher

Lifestyles: Kathleen Nebenhaus, Vice President and Publisher; Tracy Boggier, Managing Editor

Pets: Kathleen Nebenhaus, Vice President and Publisher; Tracy Boggier, Managing Editor

Travel: Michael Spring, Vice President and Publisher; Brice Gosnell, Publishing Director; Suzanne Jannetta, Editorial Director

Hungry Minds Consumer Editorial Services: Kathleen Nebenhaus, Vice President and Publisher; Kristin A. Cocks, Editorial Director; Cindy Kitchel, Editorial Director

Hungry Minds Consumer Production: Debbie Stailey, Production Director

Contents at a Glance

Cartoons at a Glance

By Rich Tennant

"My portfolio's gonna take a hit for this."

page 321

"Honestly, I just think she's too Prada for our investment club."

page 5

page 241

"I'm suggesting our investment club pursue more aggressive growth funds. You know, really aggressive— funds with muscle, funds with respect, funds that don't take any lip..."

page 49

"...and Denise—did you have a chance to research the wig and novelty hairpiece industry for stock tips?"

page 135

Cartoon Information:
Fax: 978-546-7747
E-Mail: richtennant@the5thwave.com
World Wide Web: www.the5thwave.com

Table of Contents

Foreword

• •

I was 43 years old when I was invited to my first investment club meeting in 1985. I remember it well because all I could think about was how much I'd be able to help these fellas and show them how to really profit from the stock market.

It didn't matter that the club, started in 1940, was two years older than I was. It had somehow survived the war years when its members were in the service overseas and had to ante up their monthly 10 bucks via the mails. They had staying power, I thought, and with me they'd have professional investing power, too. After all, I'd be bringing a lot to the table — an MBA, the highly respected CFA designation, and years of institutional investment management experience with a top equity investor.

I was sure right about one thing. A lot of learning took place. Funny thing, though, I was the student, not the teacher. This group of supportive buddies soon showed me why I could leave behind much of what I had learned through my profession. They didn't want it. They didn't need it. These members of the Mutual Investment Club of Detroit built their million-dollar portfolio (today it's multimillion) by having far more valuable resources at their disposal — a few rules to go by, a desire to learn and earn, a willingness to lean on one another, and a commitment to have fun along the way.

This club experience turned out to be one of the most enjoyable, educational, and financially rewarding experiences of my life. You may feel similarly inspired when you read the information Doug Gerlach and Angele McQuade present with such panache in *Investment Clubs For Dummies*.

Whether you're 23, 43, or 63, this book will put you on the right path today. It's a path on which people and relationships count as much as numbers and profits. And they really do.

Donald E. Danko, CFA
Editor, *Better Investing*

Introduction

What happens when you mix finance, friendship, and education? For hundreds of thousands of Americans, what happens is that you create an investment club. Individuals are members of investment clubs for two main reasons: to learn to invest; and then, they hope, to see their investment in the club grow and grow. But along the way, club members often find a third benefit — fun.

Another great reason to get involved with an investment club is that it doesn't take a fortune to get started in the stock market. Many clubs have monthly dues of just $20, making it possible for almost anyone to take part.

Sure, there's work involved. But when all of your club's members contribute a bit of effort each month, researching stocks and building a portfolio becomes very manageable. Can you spend a few hours a month on club homework and research? If so, you can be a valued member of an investment club.

We've filled this book with guidelines, advice, and cautions to keep in mind as you start your very own investment club. But we can almost hear you asking, "Will this work in reality?" Our resounding answer is "Yes! Of course it will!" If you and your fellow club members are willing to put in a dedicated effort and carefully structure your investment club along the common sense lines we introduce to you, then your club can join the thousands of other successful investment clubs.

But rather than just tell you how clubs work, we share stories with you about real clubs all across the nation. We hope that hearing their stories will lead you to appreciate how rewarding and how much fun investment club membership can be. Not all of the clubs that we profile have been around for decades or beaten the market every single year. Not all of them have huge portfolios or twenty expert investors as members. But they all have demonstrated that a commitment to education, a hearty work ethic, and enjoying one another's company while learning about investing can be just as rewarding as a 25 percent annual return!

Whether you join an existing club, or start a club from scratch with your friends, family, and co-workers; whether your club meets in your living room or out on the Internet, you can reap the rewards of being a member of an investment club. But you'll never receive any of the benefits unless you get started today!

Getting the Most from This Book

We've organized this book into five parts that cover all aspects of starting, joining, and running an investment club. You can read the entire book from start to finish, or you can jump in at any point for answers to particular questions.

Part 1: Flying Over Club Country

Do you know what an investment club is? We explain the basics of clubs and how they usually operate, and help you decide if a club is right for you. Whether you're starting a new club, or joining an existing club, we outline just how important it is to have reasonable expectations about the work that's involved if you want your club to be a success.

Part II: Starting an Investment Club

Starting an investment club will take some work, so this part provides all the details you need. It's especially important that you get your club off on the right foot from the very first meeting, so take the time to address all the necessary legal and financial issues that we explain in this part.

Part III: Running an Investment Club

Starting a club is a one-time endeavor, but running a club presents challenges every month. Your monthly meetings are the core of your club's operations, and we've got tips for you on keeping your meetings well organized and running smoothly. We also review the basics of club accounting and give you plenty of strategies for making your club's educational efforts a top priority.

Part IV: Finding the Right Investment Approach

Investing in an investment club is a bit different from investing on your own (unless you frequently debate with yourself on the merits of selected stocks). This part deals with the process of investing, starting with how to pick stocks and continuing all the way to building and managing a successful portfolio.

Part V: The Part of Tens

The two short chapters in The Part of Tens cover some of the most important things you need to consider when your club is thinking about buying or selling a stock. You can use the 10-part checklists when your club is discussing the purchase or sale of any stock.

Icons Used in This Book

Throughout this book, icons in the margins emphasize specific bits of advice, or caution you about potential pitfalls.

This icon highlights our most tried and true strategies for operating a successful investment club with a minimum of problems.

This icon points out sticky situations and potential complications you should watch for. Look for trouble down the road if you ignore these!

This icon notes Web sites, books, and other recommended resources for you to explore if you want more details on a particular topic.

One of the reasons you choose to become an investment club member (we hope) is to enjoy social interaction with other members. This icon prompts you to focus on the fun every now and then with suggestions to keep your club a happy club.

This icon reminds you of the reasonable expectations we encourage you to have throughout your club experience. Every club flies through turbulence at one time or another. Reality Check reminds you to keep things in perspective.

This icon indicates essential information you absolutely must know about investment clubs. If you're tempted to skim these important points and run into problems later, don't say we didn't warn you!

Part I
Flying Over
Club Country

The 5th Wave   By Rich Tennant

"Honestly, I just think she's too Prada for
our investment club."

In this part . . .

*B*efore you start or join an investment club, you need a clear idea of what you're getting into. What *is* an investment club, anyway? Why would you want to be a part of one, and what can you expect to gain from the experience? This part answers those questions and more, and gives you an overview of what to look for if you decide to join a club instead of starting one of your own.

Chapter 1

Getting Acquainted with Investment Clubs

*I*t's hard to read about any kind of financial topic these days without stumbling across references to investment clubs. Pick up your favorite personal finance magazine, and you'll probably see a story about a traveling troupe of trapeze artists who spend their time on the ground debating methods of stock selection in their family investment club. Or a class of precocious third-graders whose teacher helped them form a club that regularly outperforms the best Wall Street analysts. Or even the retired firefighters in their 90s who meet in their nursing home's recreation room to douse a small hot spot in their portfolio before it rages out of control.

What's so special about investment clubs? Why do you want to be part of one? Thanks for asking. Luckily for you, we have some answers, even if you're not a circus performer and you graduated from elementary school long ago. All that you need to be an investment club member is some enthusiasm and a deep desire to find out more than you ever imagined about investing while having much more fun than you expected. Do you fit the bill? Great. Pull up a chair and we'll fill you in on everything you need to know to get started in an investment club of your own (fire hose not required).

Defining Investment Club

Simply stated (which we assume you prefer), an investment club is a group of people whose membership regularly meets, either in person or online, to study and then purchase individual stocks using a pool of money to which each member has contributed. Put another way, you and a bunch of your friends get together once a month to help each other learn about investing in stocks, and you collectively invest in those stocks that you decide have the best potential for future growth. Boiled down to its mathematical formula (always appropriate when discussing finances), that would be:

Study + Stocks + Socializing = Investment Club.

Don't try reproducing that on your financial calculator.

Investment clubs can take many different forms. Some are clubs made up of co-workers, family members, or high school students. People interested in starting a club may recruit people from their social clubs, their place of worship, or even complete strangers they meet at an investing event or by placing an ad in the local newspaper. Some clubs meet for an hour or two once a month. Some meet less frequently but then spend a weekend together. Other clubs never meet face-to-face at all.

Roots in Motor City

Investment clubs have been around in one form or another for the last century or so. The modern investment club movement traces its roots back to World War II. A group of young men near Detroit began a club to invest in stocks; something that would've been prohibitively expensive if they'd tried to do it on their own. The club continued through the war years, as members in the service stationed overseas sent their contributions to the club members still at home, who'd research and then purchase stocks for the entire club. When the war was over, the club returned to normal operating procedures.

This club, one of the longest-lasting clubs in investing history, is the Mutual Investment Club of Detroit. Founded in 1941, it's still active today and its portfolio is worth millions of dollars. This club and many others that have lasted for decades are tangible proof that a group of novice investors can band together to educate themselves about investing. Using this education, they select and invest in quality stocks with excellent growth potential. By doing so regularly, year after year, they take advantage of compounded growth and watch their portfolio grow over the long-term. With a little discipline and determination, you and your fellow club members can do the same thing.

Yes, being in an investment club and never meeting your fellow members is possible, even if you're all active club participants. Online clubs take advantage of the miracle of the Internet, and conduct all their club activities using e-mail, Web sites, and real-time chat to communicate. Completely online clubs are growing in popularity, as more investors become dependent on the Web for financial information gathering.

Online clubs also are perfect for students or others who move frequently and therefore can't commit to a traditional club because they know they'll soon be living in a different county or state. Many extended families use online investment clubs as a way of keeping family members connected even though they may live far apart. Holidays and family reunions provide the perfect time for semiregular club meetings, while monthly business is conducted by e-mail or on a Web site. We explain more about online clubs and ways to incorporate some of the better online tools into your traditional club in Chapter 5.

Measuring the Payback from Joining a Club

The most important reason for choosing to be a part of an investment club is that you're committed to discovering more about investing in the stock market and you'd prefer having a few other people join you on your journey. There's safety in numbers, of course. If you know you're not the only club member who's clueless about *price-earnings ratios* or *estimating future growth rates,* you probably won't be as self-conscious about asking questions and struggling to understand new investing concepts. Investment clubs offer you a number of specific benefits:

- ✔ A mixed bag of personal perspectives on stocks
- ✔ A speed bump to slow your headlong rush into the market
- ✔ Earnings that may outperform the market
- ✔ An investment program that you can afford
- ✔ Group purchasing power

Perspectives

By their nature, investment clubs often inadvertently pull together people with diverse opinions of the world. That means a wide variety of perspectives adding to the mix when discussing the pros and cons of your monthly stock study, which benefits your club. When you listen to your fellow club members share their thoughts about a stock, regardless whether you agree with them, you're gaining knowledge about how other people make judgments that you'd never get reading a book at home alone.

Safeguards

Sometimes, making decisions in a group keeps you from making mistakes when you're buying and selling stocks. Convincing yourself that you've found the absolute best, most perfect, guaranteed-to-rise-in-price stock that's come along in the history of the stock market is all too easy. In a club setting, however, your believing the stock will be a winner isn't enough — your fellow club members must also be convinced. Frequently, someone else in the club finds a reason (or two or three) why the stock may not be such a terrific buy after all. The club's collective brain often is smarter than the brain of an individual member.

Performance

The club approach seems to work well when it comes to investing in the market. According to annual surveys conducted by the National Association of Investors Corporation (NAIC) of the stocks most widely held by investment clubs, club holdings outperform the overall market. For instance, for the five years ending February 28, 2001, the annualized total return on NAIC clubs' Top 100 holdings has been 19.1 percent versus 15.9 percent for the S&P 500.

Affordability

Another great benefit of investment clubs is that your minimum monthly membership contribution usually is relatively small. So, even if you're living on a shoestring salary and can't put away much money toward retirement, for example, you can probably afford $20 to $40 a month for club dues. You're immediately putting that money to work for you, and someday when you have even more money to invest, you'll be able to use the investing skills you develop with your club to build up your own personal portfolio.

Purchasing power

By participating in an investment club, you're pooling your small investment with those of many other people, enabling all to make investments you probably couldn't make on your own, and keeping your commission costs much lower than if you'd been investing all by yourself. The higher the percentage your commissions are of the total amount invested, the less money you're actually able to invest. If you don't have thousands of dollars to start investing on your own, you usually can buy stock much more inexpensively on a percentage basis through an investment club than you can by yourself.

Deciding Whether an Investment Club is Right for You

We know you'll have a hard time believing that we're actually saying this, but not everyone is cut out for investment club membership. Clubs can be time-consuming and involve a great deal of study time outside of the regular meetings. Your investments may not always grow in value, leaving you discouraged about the wisdom of investing in stocks at all. Of course, you can't rely on any guarantees that your personal portfolio will perform well, either.

Save yourself the heartache of devoting hours of your life to starting or joining a club only to later doubt your commitment and have to decide whether to quit. Even one unmotivated member can be incredibly destructive to the morale of an otherwise healthy investment club. You don't want to have to hide your face as you walk around town to avoid being pointed out as "the one who destroyed Grandma's investment club," do you?

Measuring the fit between you and a club

If you're questioning whether you'd benefit from an investment club experience, we've commissioned a highly scientific diagnostic test to determine your investment club membership potential. Grab a Number-2 pencil and proceed. Your time begins . . . now!

Okay, you caught us. Just because this really is only a simple true and false quiz doesn't mean that it can't help you decide whether you're cut out for investment club nirvana. The more questions you answer *true,* the more likely you'll enjoy participating in a club with other enthusiastic investors.

- ✔ I always enjoyed group study projects in school.
- ✔ I have at least four hours a month to devote to stock research and my continuing financial education.
- ✔ My schedule is open enough that I can attend 80 percent of my club's monthly meetings every year, whether online or in person.

> ✔ I have sufficient savings to be able to make my club contribution on time every single month without causing financial distress.
>
> ✔ I'm willing to serve enthusiastically as a club officer every few years, according to the requirements of my club's by-laws.
>
> ✔ I'm prepared to attend stock study and other classes as available in my area, and report back on what I've learned to my club.
>
> ✔ If I'm a new member, I'm willing to be mentored by a more experienced member until I improve my stock analysis skills. If I'm an existing member, I'm willing to mentor someone new.
>
> ✔ I have a deep desire to learn more about investing and apply my new knowledge to my personal portfolio.
>
> ✔ I'm prepared to be a long-term investor and won't be tempted to cash out my club membership if the market falters.
>
> ✔ I'm looking forward to learning from my fellow investors and sharing my personal insights with them as well.

Are you ready for club membership?

So how did you score? We're hoping that taking this quiz opened your eyes at least a little to what you can expect as a member of an investment club. If you were hesitant about answering true to any of the questions, spend some time thinking hard about what it is you're looking for from a club before you join or start one of your own. Successful clubs only get that way through the hard work of a club full of dedicated members.

When you become a club member, you're entering into a legal arrangement with your fellow club members. Filling out all the paperwork and spending time getting acclimated to life as an active club member isn't necessary, if you know deep down that you're not in it for the long haul. Figure out what it is about the club environment that you can't fully embrace. If you still find that you want to be a club member at some point in the future, continue your financial education on your own while you work on whatever you need to do to accept the realities of club membership.

Networking Nationally through NAIC

If you're still reading, we assume that you've passed the self-test and you're committed to pursuing membership in an investment club, whether it's one that you join or start yourself. We give you all the information that you need to do both in Chapter 3 and Part II. Right now, however, we want to introduce you to a not-for-profit organization that can greatly increase your chances for investment survival if you choose to take advantage of all that it has to offer.

The single most useful resource any investment club can turn to (not counting the book you're currently holding, of course) is the National Association of Investors Corporation (NAIC). NAIC was founded in 1951 by members of four investment clubs in Michigan, including the Mutual Investment Club of Detroit. One of those club members, Tom O'Hara, still serves as NAIC Chairman. O'Hara is a lifelong advocate of investment club membership. Because of his leadership and the talents of thousands of NAIC volunteers nationwide, more than 34,700 NAIC-affiliated investment clubs operating in the United States now sport an estimated 545,000 members.

Full disclosure by the authors

You may have noticed in the Introduction or author biographies that we're both affiliated with NAIC in various capacities. Among other roles, Doug is member of NAIC's Computer Group Advisory Board, the creator and consulting editor of NAIC's official Web site, occasionally contributor to NAIC publications and frequent guest speaker at NAIC events nationwide. He is also the Investment Club Therapist at ICLUB.com, official provider of NAIC's club accounting software and online service. Angele writes a monthly column and occasionally other articles for Better Investing, NAIC's monthly member magazine. She is also one of the original organizers of NAIC's Online Investor's School, which offers free online investment classes through NAIC's Web site. We are both frequent contributors to some of NAIC's many e-mail lists, such as the I-Club-List, as well.

If you're concerned that by writing this book we're hoping to give NAIC some free publicity, well, in a way you're right. NAIC is the only organization of its kind offering high-quality investment information at a low cost for both investment clubs and individual investors. Not only that, it's a non-profit organization run mainly by hundreds of dedicated volunteers throughout the country, volunteers who so strongly believe in the value of what NAIC

teaches that they're willing to spend countless hours helping their fellow investors learn to invest their money more profitably.

We know this because we live it. Beyond any compensation either of us receives for articles we may write, we are strictly NAIC volunteers like all the other volunteers. Doug receives no speaking fees for his many educational presentations, just as a small example. We've both dedicated countless hours of our own over the years in the desire to give back just a little of what NAIC has taught each of us.

So if we introduce a few more people to a fantastic resource by mentioning NAIC frequently throughout this book, it's not because we'll somehow later profit from our relationship with NAIC. Our motive is simply to expose you, the reader, to the one organization that provides the most services and the most valuable information to anyone interested in being an investment club member. We don't hesitate to mention other quality organizations or investment club resources throughout the book. It just happens that NAIC offers more of what investment clubs need than anyone else out there. We hope that as you refer to this book, you'll be as impressed with NAIC as we still are, many years after our first encounters.

Who are NAIC's members? They're people just like you: 54 percent are female, 46 percent are male. 73 percent hold college or advanced graduate degrees, and the median age of NAIC members is 54 (although members are as young as 5 and as old as 95).

The average investment club is 4 years old with a portfolio of $106,000. Among all clubs, 54 percent are all female, 8 percent are all male, and the remaining 38 percent enroll men and women. (One interesting note: NAIC has found that all-women clubs tend to perform better than the all-men and mixed clubs.)

If the size of the average club portfolio seems daunting to you at first glance, don't fret. Remember that every investor started out with an empty portfolio and a few dollars. The average investment club has 11 members who each invest just $84 a month and, overall, commit an average of $927 to purchase stocks each month.

These investments, however, begin to add up, considering that the estimated total value of the portfolios of all NAIC clubs and their members is an astonishing $197 billion. Each month, NAIC clubs invest $247 million into the market.

Although it now also welcomes individual investors as members, NAIC began as an organization geared toward serving investment clubs. As the number of investment clubs steadily rises each year, NAIC continually provides a support system for new and established clubs. Membership in NAIC is an important investment that your new club can make. Annual dues are around $40 per club, plus $15 or so per member. Some clubs decide to skip NAIC membership because they don't want to pay the annual dues, but we consider that a shortsighted mistake. NAIC's dues are a nominal cost for the benefits you can receive, so be sure to take advantage of NAIC membership for your club.

NAIC offers support for investment clubs new and old and can provide a sample partnership agreement, brochures and manuals about starting and operating a club, and other materials designed with the unique needs of investment clubs in mind. Here are a few of the major benefits of NAIC membership:

- ✔ **Better Investing magazine.** Included with each member's annual dues is an annual subscription to *Better Investing,* a monthly magazine that features articles about time-tested investment strategies, stock studies, investment club issues, investor education and portfolio management, and other investment ideas.

- ✔ **A proven investing approach.** The NAIC has a unique, time-tested method of investing in stocks and building portfolios. The *Stock Selection Guide* (SSG) helps investors evaluate stocks and analyze companies to ensure they're worthy of adding to your portfolio. NAIC also sells books, manuals, and software to help you use the SSG. NAIC software also helps you analyze and screen company data files on CD-ROM, improving yours and your club's investment decisions. NAIC also offers a recordkeeping program for individual portfolios and membership in a computer group that features a subscription to *BITS,* its monthly newsletter.

✔ **Local opportunities to explore.** NAIC has more than 110 regional chapters throughout the United States where you can attend low-cost classes taught by talented volunteer educators, ranging from the basic stock selection through more advanced portfolio management and financial recordkeeping techniques. Classes are great for beginners. Many clubs require members to attend classes, but even if you're not a member, some chapters conduct model investment club meetings in public for others to see how clubs operate. And most chapters present annual investor fairs featuring public companies, educational workshops, and informative speakers, giving your entire club the chance to pick up some good investment tips and share experiences with members of other clubs.

✔ **National opportunities to advance your education.** If you'd like to combine travel with your inner journey toward investing mastery, consider one of NAIC's annual national conferences. CompuFest, for example, is a weekend of classes focusing on investment research and analysis using your computer. You can meet with representatives of public companies and attend educational seminars at the annual Congress and Investment Expo.

✔ **Online classes.** For investors who enjoy learning online, NAIC's Online Investor's School offers educational topics ranging from stock and mutual fund analysis to author chats and even the monthly meetings of a model online investment club. NAIC's Web site (`www.better-investing.org`) is a well-organized treasure trove for individual investors and investment club members, featuring workshops on stock analysis, e-mail mailing lists for stock study discussions and club treasurers, and transcripts from past Investor's School classes. Thousands of investors participate each week. NAIC also sponsors a forum on CompuServe (`go.compuserve.com/NAIC`).

✔ **Club accounting tools.** To ease the club treasurer's burden, NAIC publishes an accounting manual, endorses accounting software, and provides paper forms, all tools that are essential for keeping accurate records of members' dues and investment transactions and for the overall successful operation of your club. Every club treasurer needs to be using software of some sort to track club transactions (we cover this in detail in Chapter 10). The official NAIC-endorsed software is available to install on your computer or to be used online. The online accounting version enables all club members to check their club's portfolio and valuation statement online. More information about NAIC Online Club Accounting can be found at `www.naic-club.com`.

✔ **Performance comparisons.** How's your club doing? NAIC offers to clubs the chance to calculate and compare their performances with the S&P 500 Index and with other clubs of the same age and geographic region. For a nominal fee, NAIC determines the rate of return of your club's portfolio and issues a certificate with the results. Participating clubs are eligible to win national prizes for being the best performing clubs.

✔ **Low-cost Investment Plan.** NAIC's Low Cost Investment Plan enables your club to build a portfolio at its own pace with minimal charges. You start by buying a single share in any of 140 companies directly from NAIC and then by making additional purchases directly through the companies without a broker and usually without fees or commissions. Dividends are reinvested in additional shares, helping your club to grow slowly but surely.

✔ **General liability, bond coverage.** We hope you'll never need it, but your NAIC membership includes general liability insurance. Although the chances of your club being liable for injury or property damage are slight, a member could be injured during a meeting or damages could occur to the facility where your club meets. NAIC's policy covers your club for up to $2 million per year and $1 million per occurrence. Purchasing a similar policy can cost between $250 and $500. Another benefit of club membership is reasonably priced fidelity bond coverage, insurance that your club can purchase to protect against theft of club assets by any member. Protecting against this rare but possible risk is a good idea.

You can discover more about NAIC programs and materials that can help you and your club, including a youth investing program, instructional videotapes, an investor advisory service, and a club study program by calling its toll-free number (877-275-6242) or visiting its Web site at www.better-investing.org or service@better-investing.org. The NAIC mailing address is: National Association of Investors Corp., P.O. Box 220, Royal Oak, MI 48068.

It's Not a Perfect World: The Trouble with Investment Clubs

As wonderful as learning to invest with a great big bunch of friends or family can be (and it is a pretty wonderful thing), problems definitely arise from time to time. As we caution you in Chapter 2, almost all these problems can be avoided if your club is deliberate during initial planning and carefully creates and follows, a partnership agreement, organizational by-laws, and an investment philosophy. We detail exactly how to prepare these important documents in Chapter 6, and you can find samples from real-life clubs throughout the book.

Other common sources of club problems are control issues and personality conflicts. You may have every intention of being a perfect club member, but that doesn't mean your fellow participants are always going to be on their best behavior. Investment clubs by definition mean decision by consensus, or at least majority vote. Some people can't let go of their opinions enough to abide by the group's decision, and their disapproval can lead to discord and dissatisfaction. You also may have some club members with strong personalities who dominate every discussion and intimidate others who may choose to vote differently.

Dealing with overbearing members

If your club dynamic starts to suffer from the consequences of having overly dominant members, don't sit around waiting for the situation to resolve itself. Things aren't going to get better all on their own. Your club president may need to tell the offending member to tone it down (if your club president is the dominant one, you'll need the vice president to step in). If members don't feel comfortable about voting because of confrontations with opposing members, you may try a secret ballot rather than an open show of hands for a while. We offer more problem-solving strategies in Chapter 12, but the underlying message is that investment clubs are real-life. Sometimes you need to deal with difficult people or situations, but you can't allow your club experience to be ruined by them. Be proactive and persistent in shutting down annoyances as soon as they spring up.

Another problem with investment clubs is that they demand the participation of their members. Many club members lose interest after a year or two. If disinterest invades your entire club, and no one wants to do any work, then your club is doomed to fail. By the same token, because you're in a club, you can spread the work around so that no one is overburdened with responsibilities. Clubs are only as strong as their collective members.

Revisiting the Beardstown Ladies

You may have heard about the controversy surrounding the Beardstown Business and Professional Women's Club, authors of the 1994 bestseller *The Beardstown Ladies' Common-Sense Investment Guide*. Two years after the book was published, an investigative reporter discovered that the rate of return trumpeted on the book's cover, 23.4 percent a year, would have been impossible for the Ladies to achieve.

Eventually, the truth was revealed. After computerizing their club's records, switching from manual bookkeeping to NAIC's accounting software, the club's treasurer misinterpreted the rate of return calculated by the program. The 23.4 percent investment return wasn't for the life of their club; it was only for the prior two years. In truth, the club's performance was closer to 9.1 percent a year, hardly the handiwork of "investment geniuses" (as their publicists proclaimed), and much lower than the S&P 500's record of 14.9 percent for the same period.

Nevertheless, the resulting media hoopla all but ignored the fact that it was an honest mistake, that the ladies never had knowingly tried to deceive anyone, and their many books did far more good than harm.

The number of new investors the Beardstown Ladies turned on to the joys of stock study, investment clubs, and NAIC is hard to calculate, but we've talked to many people who've said that their first exposure to investing came courtesy of the ladies' homespun wisdom. And no amount of media backlash, deserved or not, can erase the sense of joy the ladies seem to derive from their club and each other's company.

Dismissing their books and philosophy as naïve or unsophisticated is easy, but we prefer to focus on the simple, rational stock selection criteria that they've championed from their beginnings along with their encouraging words aimed at inexperienced investors. Any club would do well to emulate the ladies' emphasis on the creation of community and generosity of spirit over a solitary focus on monetary gains. Some things you just shouldn't attempt to measure solely by annual return.

Oh, and perhaps the better of the lessons to be learned from the Beardstown Ladies? *Read the manual.* Whether you're using new software, learning to invest, or starting a club, it pays to read the instructions before you begin.

Chapter 2

Looking Before You Leap

In This Chapter

▶ Determining your motivation for starting a club

▶ Keeping your expectations realistic

▶ Building a blueprint for a successful club

*W*e won't mislead you. Starting an investment club isn't easy. In fact, the actual setup can be incredibly frustrating and time consuming if you don't begin with a good attitude and a great plan. But if you spend just a little bit of time thinking about what you hope to accomplish and then plan your strategy before starting your club, you can greatly reduce your frustration. You'll also greatly increase the chances that your club will be successful and long-lived. Isn't that what you're really hoping for in the first place? This chapter takes you through the important assessment process and brainstorming that you'll need to do before you even take the first step toward gathering up potential members.

Examining Your Motives

Knowing that you want to start an investment club is one thing, but knowing *why* is even more important. If you're interested in starting a club for all the wrong reasons, chances are the club will fail and any friends or family members you pulled into the club with you may not be as friendly at the end of the day. If you're still not really sure what's motivating you, know that having some elusive ideas about making money isn't enough.

Forming an investment club is a serious legal undertaking, so you must take it seriously! You need to spend at least a few minutes writing down your goals and desires for your as-yet-unformed investment club. That way you'll not only have a much clearer idea of why you want to take on this adventure, you'll also be that much more persuasive when convincing other people to join you on the journey.

Got that scribbled-on piece of paper in hand? We're about to amaze you with our skill as mind readers. If you're still excited about starting an investment club after all this introspection, we can safely assume a few things about you and your motivations. In the list that follows are some of the more common reasons people decide to start an investment club. We're willing to bet that you have more than one or two of them on that list in front of you.

- ✔ You want to learn more about investing and use the knowledge that you gain to invest in an investment club and on your own.

- ✔ You know that the sooner you start learning and then investing, the better off you'll be down the road.

- ✔ You'd like to make your money grow by investing in the stocks of successful companies.

- ✔ You want the whole experience to be much more fun than sitting in a library studying investment texts.

- ✔ You want to learn with a group of friends instead of muddling through on your own.

- ✔ You're excited at the prospect of creating a successful investment club to help you learn, start you investing and keep you socializing with fellow club members.

And finally, we assume that you'd like all your hard work setting up a club not to go to waste — you want your club to last more than just a few years or even months. Maybe you'd like to get your family involved, or some co-workers or neighbors. Maybe it doesn't matter to you whether the rest of your club consists of strangers, just as long as they're motivated and willing to work as hard as you are to make the club a success. If most of this rings true, you're well on your way to forming an investment club with the elements essential for long-term survival.

Starting Out Smart — 20-Year Plans

Regardless of your age or the length of your investing horizon, you need to approach the planning process as though you expect your investment club to be around at least 20 years. Sure you'll have to make changes to your operating agreement and bylaws from time to time, but the more effort you put into getting them right the first time, the happier you and your club members will be in the future. Many clubs have failed within a year or two because of an initial lack of organization; however, doing a fabulous rather than a half-hearted job is not that much harder.

According to NAIC, roughly a third of new investment clubs don't survive their first year. But if your club makes it that far, the outlook for long-term survival is much brighter.

Although any number of causes can be blamed for early club failures, the more important ones — and the ones among the easiest to avoid — are unrealistic expectations and lack of formal club structure and operating guidelines. Luckily for your club's longevity, the following section explains exactly how you deal with these issues before they cause problems.

Keeping your expectations down to earth

In the beginning, as you decide what you need to start an investment club, focusing on reasonable expectations is the most important thing you can do. Set your sights on the stratosphere and you'll find yourself tumbling miles without a parachute before you realize that your club cannot live up to your lofty ideals. Don't doom your club to failure before you choose your first stock. What *should* you expect from your investment club? Thinking about what you shouldn't expect may be the easier route to take.

Once you make sure that your motivations are appropriate for the task ahead of you, getting your expectations in line is next on the list. The most important expectations that you need to keep in mind are simple and make a great deal of sense once you think about them. If you can embrace the views explained under the next nine headings and convince your club members to embrace them, too, you'll be well on your way to a great beginning for an investment club of your own.

Don't expect everyone who's interested in your club to join or be a good member

Some people quit early on after they discover that they're expected to contribute in a substantial way. Being a part of an investment club is no free ride, and you want to spell that out to potential members at the first meeting. Most people you approach agree that planning for their financial future is important. An even smaller number express an interest in actually taking a step toward accomplishing what they've planned. Even fewer of these people will agree to consider the possibility of starting a club with you, and only a handful will actually attend the initial planning meeting.

No matter how clearly you spell out member responsibilities, you can still expect to lose *at least* 10 percent to 20 percent of your original members for a variety of reasons within the first two years. But if your club makes it past that two-year milestone intact and still full of enthusiasm, your chances for long-term survival are dramatically improved, even if you occasionally lose some members. And once you get past that initial "shaking out," you'll discover how to identify troublemakers or slackers before they ever join, enabling you to focus your club's attention on the prospective members with the greater potential for a mutually beneficial club experiences.

Don't expect smooth sailing from the beginning

As is true with any new venture, operating issues must be ironed out and diverse personalities must be combined. Unless you recognize and even expect a few such speed bumps as you get under way, problems in either of these areas can quickly threaten the life of your club. That is one reason why having reasonable expectations is so important right from the start. Make sure you know that everyone is on the same page by discussing these expectations with potential club members at your first planning meeting.

Discussing financial expectations is especially important, because new members must realize that an investment club can't be their only source of retirement savings and that they may, in fact, lose rather than gain money in club holdings. You can't guarantee that your club's investments will be successful, but you can avoid a lot of hurt feelings by making that clear from the beginning.

Another important factor to make clear is that your club offers no free rides. All members are required to do their fair share of work. Such upfront statements scare off most problem members before they ever join, so don't skip this crucial step!

Expect your club to invest only in stocks

Mutual funds, real estate, junk bonds, and lottery tickets need not apply! You're forming an investment club to learn to invest in common stocks, not any other investment vehicles. Some kinds of securities, like options, are notoriously difficult to successfully invest in. Others, like bonds, won't likely give your club the long-term return that it hopes to achieve. And can you imagine shopping for and managing a rental property with your fellow club members? Strike real estate off your list, too.

Mutual funds are the investment vehicle of choice for many people, but we suggest that your club avoid them. Why? Although we don't have anything against mutual funds, the techniques for selecting mutual funds are much different than those for choosing stocks, and believe us, you'll have your hands full just learning about buying and managing a portfolio of stocks. Besides, most people don't have many choices other than owning mutual funds in their retirement plans or other accounts. Introducing mutual funds into a portfolio of stocks also introduces the potential for other problems. For instance, a fund you own may hold stocks that are the same or similar to the ones you hold in your portfolio. That overlap can distort your *diversification plan.* (See Chapter 13 for more about mutual fund matters.)

As you find out more about analyzing stocks and building a diversified portfolio, you'll essentially be creating your own diversified, growth mutual fund. When you invest in a mutual fund, you must be right about the fund that you choose and the fund's managers must be right about the stocks they pick for the fund. When you buy stocks yourself, you must only worry about your own decisions and not anyone else's, even if they *are* supposed to be professionals. In any given year, fewer than 20 percent of all mutual funds beat the Standard & Poor's 500 Index (S&P 500 — a stock market index of 500 of the biggest and best companies in the United States, chosen to represent every kind and size of business).

Some clubs do invest in mutual funds. If your club feels a strong need to invest in a particular sector or region that's difficult for investors to analyze, like financial or international stocks, then maybe a mutual fund is your best bet (see Chapter 13 for more on this topic). Otherwise, feel free to invest in funds in your personal portfolio, but stick to a *stocks-only philosophy* in your investment club.

Expect to delay the purchase of your first stock for at least six months

You'll need at least six months to finish the initial bureaucratic paperwork, get to know your fellow club members a little better, and figure out your club's investment philosophy. Then you'll need to start educating yourselves so that you'll have at least a rudimentary understanding of stock analysis before making your first pick.

An education program is the cornerstone of your investment club. You want to spend as much time as possible bringing all club members up to a level at which everyone feels comfortable doing at least rudimentary stock analysis. Even if a few members still are reluctant or unsure of their skills, they need to at least know where to find the information they need to do a stock study (we discuss this subject in more detail in Chapter 14).

Watch out for *analysis paralysis.* That's what happens when you spend so much time analyzing potential investments that you become indecisive, never getting around to making any purchases. Buy your first stock as soon as you reasonably can after the education program begins. You may want to take advantage of low-cost ways of buying a small number of shares, such as through NAIC's Low Cost Investment Plan or through a direct stock plan with the company itself. That first experience at least speeds up your learning curve. Just keep in mind that you may decide later that your first purchase wasn't so smart, so if it wasn't, deal with it, and then move on.

And that's okay! This is, after all, a process, and you shouldn't expect to be investment gurus right off the bat. Sometimes there's something to be said for plunging in and taking a risk, especially if it nudges your club toward even more investment education. Don't plunge in at your first meeting, though. As we just said, waiting until you have at least a general idea of what you're doing is better. Most clubs make their first investment decisions three to nine months after starting.

If you're celebrating your club's first anniversary, however, and you're still in the "education phase," make an initial investment in a well-established company that you're all familiar with just to get your feet wet. Otherwise you'll soon watch your club members drift away and your club disintegrate because of a lack of interest. Because clubs are built on the premise of learning by doing, your educational progress will be severely stifled unless you actually start investing.

Don't expect positive investment returns immediately

Start-up expenses may take a chunk out of your starting capital, and that puts your club in the red immediately. When you actually start investing, you may find that your portfolio value declines even further, especially if you're all beginners. Even if you aren't, your first stock picks may not perform as well as stocks you choose later on when you've got some experience under your belt. Plus, when you own only a few stocks, you don't receive any of the benefits of the diversification found in a well-rounded portfolio. So, seeing the small gains that your holdings may be making may be difficult.

Sure, watching your portfolio lose money every month is hard, but don't let any of that discourage you. The learning curve is pretty steep when you first start investing. It may take members of your club more than a year to really feel like they understand what they're doing. Everyone learns best when actually doing what he or she is learning, not just by reading and studying.

Consider any losses as well-spent tuition in your quest for investment knowledge. Always keep in mind that your club experience is more of an educational adventure than an investment plan. Your goal is to learn as much as you can so that you can apply your stock selection skills to your personal portfolio, where you'll really see the difference.

As you think about starting a club, our best advice for you is not to expect the club to be your road to instant riches. Of course you hope that your investments are profitable, but more than anything, your club experience should help you become a better investor overall. Part of your club's mission is education, so go into the experience with the idea that you'll soon be gaining plenty of practical investing skills that you then can apply to your personal stock portfolio. We hope that you find monetary gains through your investment club, but that should be the cherry at the top.

Expect the first few months to feel a little nonproductive

Be patient and don't rush your first investment. You'll have a plenty of "busy work" writing your partnership agreement and bylaws, electing officers, and starting your education program. Hurrying through all this to get to the good stuff may be tempting, but planning is the foundation of your club's future. Skim over it, and not too far down the road, you'll find yourself wondering what went wrong when club members start fighting about the attendance policy, how to invest, or even who was supposed to bring the snacks. Trust us when we say that if you pay attention to the small details in the beginning, ensuring that everyone agrees with them, your club will have much greater potential for a long and productive life.

Expect every member to contribute

Expect each member of your club to participate, and we're not talking strictly financial contributions. Instituting a *no slackers policy* is one way to ensure your club's success. Your bylaws must be clear on that point. In addition to making monthly financial contributions, every member should be expected to:

✔ Regularly attend meetings.

✔ Present at least one stock analysis a year.

✔ Serve as an officer at some point.

✔ Contribute to the club's education program, doing any homework that's assigned between meetings.

✔ Live up to whatever other standards your club sets.

You can discover much more about member responsibilities in Chapter 8.

If a member starts missing meetings or always has excuses for not fulfilling club responsibilities, don't get caught up in club politics or personal feelings. Instead, this is one time that you want everything to be all-business, so a bit of tough love may be necessary. Give the member in question a warning, and then if things don't improve, give him or her the boot. Even if the offending member is your mother-in-law — we're serious about this, one rotten member can spoil the whole club barrel. That's why making sure everyone understands what they're getting into before they join the club is so important. With everyone on the same page, enforcing requirements is easier and less stressful. If you're having a hard time being tough, check out Chapters 8 and 12 for ways to say goodbye to problem members.

Don't expect it to be easy

Worthwhile things rarely are easy. You're going to spend a great deal of time learning before the club experience all starts to make sense, but the rewards can be incredibly valuable. Don't be discouraged and don't quit even if everyone else out there seems to be doing better than you are. Investors love to crow about their winners but rarely mention their losers. Have faith in yourself and the process and pay attention to your own benefits.

Above all, expect to laugh!

Remember that one reason you chose to learn about investing in a group rather than by yourself was because you wanted to have fun. In the middle of all the tedious work setting up your club and learning about stock analysis, be sure to take time every month to enjoy each other's company and get to know a little more about each other. Check out the tips in Chapter 11 and at the end of this chapter to ensure that you're meeting your club's fun quota.

Staying flexible as you settle into a routine

Unfortunately, you must deal with more than just short-term expectations. Even after your club gets over initial start-up hurdles, you need to keep the big picture in mind and expect that you'll still experience the normal highs and lows of any adventure. The sections that follow discuss a few more things to keep in mind as your club matures. Some may already seem familiar because they factor into your club's short- and long-term planning.

Expect your club meetings and operating dynamic to evolve

As your collective knowledge about investing grows, your club's educational needs and operating procedures will mature, too. Be open to changing your club's bylaws whenever you find that you need to do things differently. Some clubs decide that they didn't know enough about investing when they developed their investment philosophy, so they refine theirs after the first year. Other clubs won't realize until a member first asks to leave that their withdrawal procedures are poorly defined. So they'll discuss how they'd like to change the specifics and then rewrite that section of their bylaws to avoid problems the next time they're faced with a withdrawal.

Your club must welcome the chance to adjust its procedures to better fit its members' evolving knowledge of investing and club operations. Introspection and regular self-assessment are signs of a healthy, growing club. Make it a goal to re-evaluate and possibly revise your club bylaws every year, and then don't be surprised if your club ends up lasting for decades.

Expect your membership responsibilities to evolve, too

Many clubs realize after a year or so that their membership participation requirements aren't as comprehensive or appropriate as they need to be. If changes are made to this part of a club's bylaws, the members almost always choose to make the responsibilities *more* rather than less detailed. This usually is because of bad experiences with members who aren't pulling their weight, or worse, who are pulling the entire club down with their nonparticipation.

Don't wait while a member responsibility problem gets worse. Add a discussion of member responsibilities to the agenda of your next meeting and get the topic out in the open. Then revise that section of your bylaws, adding penalties for members who fail to fulfill them (including expulsion from the club if it comes to that). You can read more about member responsibilities and dealing with problem members in Chapter 8.

Expect your membership roster to change, perhaps drastically

You and other charter members will start your club fully expecting to stay involved for years. But life happens. People move away, financial circumstances change, and sometimes people decide that they really don't want to be in an investment club after all. Whatever the reason, at some point you'll lose some members. You may even lose several members. Unless you decide that you like your club's smaller size, you'll soon want to find new members to replace those who leave. In Chapters 3, 5, and 8, we tell you what characteristics to look for in a prospective member. Don't skip any of the screening steps, and make sure your new members understand exactly what is expected of them so there won't be any misunderstandings later.

While saying goodbye to your departing members can be hard, be comforted in the knowledge that new members often add a renewed sense of energy and enthusiasm to an existing club. Educational benefits also come from bringing a new member up to speed with everyone else, or from a new member who already is experienced bringing a fresh perspective to your club's traditional way of doing things. Although having a long-term stable club membership is preferable, in time you'll come to appreciate the benefits that can come from welcoming new members and their new ideas to your group.

Don't expect to show a profit in the first few years

We covered this earlier in the short-term expectations section of this chapter, but it holds true for the long-term, too. Your club must be committed to a buy-and-hold investment strategy. You need to expect to own the stocks you buy for at least five years, thus giving them time to do what you chose them to do. Realistically, as much as you'd like for it to be true, you cannot expect every stock that you buy to be a winner.

And if you happen to start your club in the thick of a bear market, reaching positive territory may take two years or longer. So if your portfolio value falls rather than rises during your club's first few years, have patience and don't sell any of your holdings unless something fundamentally has changed with one of the companies (more about when to sell can be found in Chapters 16 and 19).

Expect your portfolio returns to ebb and flow

Your club's portfolio will have good years and bad years, just like the stock market as a whole. You can't expect or even hope for exceptional returns every year, so be patient and above all consistently follow your club's investment philosophy.

What makes a good year? Most clubs compare their returns to the returns of the S&P 500. When you use good club accounting software, checking your club's annual return and comparing it to the S&P 500 is easy. Through the years, the S&P 500 has grown about 11 percent to 12 percent a year, although it *has* fallen or risen 30 percent or more in some years. NAIC suggests that clubs aim for a 15 percent annual return, which means they'd outperform the S&P 500 by a nice margin.

If every year is a good year, congratulations! Your club clearly has discovered the Holy Grail of investing, and your book and movie deal will follow shortly. If every year is a bad year, your club probably needs to revamp its education strategy and have a few refresher courses in basic investment strategy (see Chapters 14 and 15 for some hints).

Expect to deal with personality conflicts and basic misunderstandings

Even if you bring your best friends in the world together to start your investment club, at some point you'll have disagreements. The issue can be something as small as when or where to conduct your meetings or as serious as a yelling and screaming match about whether to buy a particular stock. Disagreements or disputes aren't necessarily a sign that your club is doomed to failure, but rather just an example of the unpleasant side of human nature at work.

We certainly hope all your problems are minor and easily resolved, but you need to be prepared at some point to encounter the kind of conflicts that spring up in every type of group situation. Chapter 12 offers some strategies for dealing with club problems in case your club needs help.

Building Your Clubhouse: The Four Elements of Success

You've laid the foundation. Now your well-thought-out motivations and reasonable expectations will give your investment club the solid basis you need even before starting the real construction. So it's time for you as the club architect to pull out the blueprints and start building your own investment clubhouse. Okay, so it's a corny analogy, but it works. What you're building is a clubhouse in every sense of the word. You're constructing a virtual meeting place for you and your club members, with four sturdy walls to protect you and give you a safe place to practice your new investment expertise.

Are you still willing to move ahead with your plans for starting your own investment club but with more reasonable expectations? Excellent! You're not alone — tens of thousands of clubs exist in the United States, with more forming every month. Of course, some are more successful than others. For every club that's lasted decades, probably hundreds won't even make it to their first anniversary. What makes these clubs so different from each other? Is it the members, the education plan, the economy in general, or even the meeting location? What matters most when starting a brand-new club?

Although it can be misleading to generalize, we have isolated four characteristics that successful clubs share:

- ✔ A solid education curriculum
- ✔ A strong investment plan
- ✔ A thoughtful operations strategy
- ✔ A sense of fun

Leave one of these elements out, or give it less attention than the other three, and you may as well quit before you conduct your first planning meeting. After all, what good is a club if you're not there to learn and apply that learning by researching and then purchasing stocks? And if it isn't going to be fun, then what's the point?

Before you start pulling prospective members together, spend some time brainstorming exactly what it is that you hope to accomplish by starting an investment club and how you plan to incorporate each of these four elements into your overall plan. Of course you won't be making all these decisions on your own. But as the primary mover in getting this club off the ground (because you're the one who's reading this book), your fellow club members naturally are going to turn to you in the beginning for this type of philosophical guidance.

Solid educational plan

One of the best things about starting an investment club is that absolutely no previous knowledge of investing is necessary. In fact, it actually can be a real benefit to start from scratch, with no preconceived ideas or faulty philosophies to unlearn. All that's required is an open mind and a willingness to learn as much as you can.

Educational curriculum

Your club's educational program needs largely to focus on all your planning efforts. Neglect the education and your club won't last. If you and your fellow members are serious about investing in the stock market, you'll first need to invest in yourselves, spending some time learning all that you need to know to make smart investing decisions. For a deeper discussion of club education, beyond what we cover in the next few sections, check out Chapter 11.

NAIC classes and events

The first place we'd start with any club educational program is the local NAIC Chapter. NAIC offers a wide variety of low-cost classes around the country. Attend a few with your club members and boost your investment IQ.

If you're in one of the few locations that doesn't have a local chapter (or even if you have a chapter nearby), be sure to look at all the educational offerings you can read at the NAIC Web site (www.better-investing.org). Many clubs print these simple yet valuable lessons and go over them together at their meetings.

Guest speakers

Consider bringing in guest speakers from your community to deliver an educational presentation. Many clubs invite brokers, bankers, financial planners, and even experienced members of other local clubs. Don't feel pressured to purchase any product or service from a financial professional. If they're truly professional, they won't blatantly troll for new clients in the middle of their lectures.

Member presentations

Member-to-member education can be an effective educational tool for your club. Assign each member to research a topic of particular importance to the club, then take turns leading the education segment of each meeting. You don't need to be an expert in the subject you're presenting. In fact, preparing a presentation on a topic you don't know much about is a great way to teach yourself. Some clubs also pay to send members to NAIC classes or other investing events on the condition that the members share what they learn at the next meeting.

Education evolves as membership changes

As yours and your club members' investing knowledge grows, your educational strategy will grow as well. You may find yourselves reading books about intermediate or advanced investment topics, or attending one of NAIC's national conventions for more advanced classes than are offered locally. Members still can share this information with other club members, either by presenting a book report, demonstrating new stock analysis software features, or supplying other such information at your club meetings.

New member education

When each new member enters the club, be sure to explain in detail the club's expectations for their self-education. They should at least attend a local NAIC stock analysis class or read some detailed investment information before they're ready to jump in with the rest of you, but don't leave them hanging on their own.

Mentor relationships

Many clubs use mentor relationships to ease new members into the investment club realm. The mentor tutors the new member one-on-one as needed and offers personalized attention when he or she needs it most. Your club needs to discuss whether to assign a mentor whenever a new member joins. We think you'll find these unique relationships will prove beneficial to both participants.

Strong investment plan

You're starting an *investment* club, not a folk music appreciation or a gourmet cooking club. The name says it all. So you shouldn't be surprised to hear that you'll be required to actually invest money as part of your club activities. Whether you pool your money with other club members or choose a *self-directed investment structure* (we discuss them fully in Chapter 4), be prepared to set aside money for monthly investments. You wouldn't want to let all that great education and research to go to waste, would you?

Choosing an investment philosophy

Determining how you'll choose your investments is one of the first things your club should do. The decision must be unanimous. If any club member doesn't agree with the chosen philosophy (and, after all, you can't force them to), you're going to run into problems later. We discuss how and why to choose a philosophy in Chapter 5.

Carefully researching your options

Take as much time as you need to understand your club's stock analysis to the best of your ability. Some clubs research each purchase for a full three months to ensure that they've investigated that particular company as fully as they possibly can. Most clubs, however, spend about a month analyzing and then discussing the pros and cons of their study choices before deciding whether they'd like to buy any of them.

Faithfully following your buy-and-sell guidelines

As part of your investment philosophy, your club will establish detailed guidelines by which you'll decide whether to buy or sell a specific stock. Doing so ensures that your club won't make hasty or emotional decisions. The guidelines protect you from your club's own indecision or laziness and require that you carefully think through each stock transaction. Don't sabotage your own good planning by ignoring these guidelines for every buy or sell decision.

Tracking your portfolio

Once your club actually owns something, your work has just begun. You need to follow those stocks on a regular basis and manage your portfolio as a whole. Most clubs assign a member to watch each stock and regularly report on company news and earnings. The stock watcher also is responsible for deciding whether the stock is a candidate for future reinvestments, or, less often, whether it should be sold.

The club treasurer, or another designated member, should watch the portfolio as a whole, keeping an eye on that "bigger picture." Your club members need to receive a portfolio valuation every month detailing how each stock is performing. Regular portfolio and individual stock updates must be an integral part of your club's investment strategy. We tell you exactly how to track both in Chapters 15 and 16.

Thoughtful operations strategy

Money management is important to your club's success and so is member management. Don't neglect the day-to-day (or month-to-month) workings of your club after you write an operating agreement and decide on bylaws. Little issues can quickly turn into huge disagreements if not dealt with quickly and fairly.

Strong agreement and bylaws

Your club's operating agreement and operating procedures are the road map by which you and your fellow members forge your path toward financial knowledge. Chapter 6 provides great detail on what to include in these two documents. But remember that they're not carved in stone. You should be willing to tweak and adjust them as time passes to better fit your club's circumstances.

Tweaking aside, your operating agreement and bylaws are only as strong as your club's will. If you frequently disregard the guidelines that you all previously agreed upon, look forward to being part of a club in turmoil. Simply put, don't disregard the guidelines. Perhaps you made a mistake when you drafted them, or were too inexperienced to know how to deal with an issue. Fine. That happens to clubs all the time. Just change that particular section so that it better fits your club's circumstances and then move on. But if you find your club couldn't care less about following the rules, start figuring out what you're going to do with all your free time after your club disintegrates into chaos.

Sticking to the rules . . . but still having a heart

Flexibility matters as your club evolves. As we mention above, playing by the rules is an important absolute that you've decided upon. Real life, however, has a way of creeping in, and you may decide to change your club's rules after a few months or years of experience.

In that situation, most clubs tend to leave their operating agreement intact because it's mostly just the legal framework and not that much needs to be revised. Changing the agreement requires collecting signatures from all club members, and, therefore, generally is a big hassle. That's why you want your club bylaws to be the heart of your club's operations. Bylaws are more of a living document, requiring simply a majority vote at a club meeting anytime changes are suggested. Don't be afraid to make changes if it turns out that late payments or absent members have become a problem, for example, or you need to add new penalties or strategies to deal with nonparticipating members.

As you do make changes, especially those that deal with member problems, always keep in mind that club membership takes a backseat to your members' personal lives. If someone suddenly becomes chronically late in paying dues or no longer attends meetings, don't assume they're no longer interested in being a club member. Such members may be laid off from work or experiencing health problems or other troubles that they don't want to share with the club. Before jumping into any punitive measures dictated by your bylaws, a quick phone call by a club officer offering *inactive status* for a few months may be all such members need to get their lives in order before heading back into full-fledged membership status again. Be true to your club's bylaws, but always stay open-minded, fair, and flexible.

A sense of fun

At the risk of sounding completely obnoxious, we're going to repeat this one more time. Please pay attention so we don't have to do it again. Why go through all the work of starting and running an investment club if you're not going to have at least a little fun doing it? If all you're looking for is a business-like environment in which to have serious economic discussions with other stodgy and curmudgeonly investors, you've picked up the wrong book. March right back to where you bought it and exchange it for a copy of *Investment Clubs For Grumps!*

That doesn't mean that an all-business club can't be successful. They exist, and even do quite well. Our point is that life's too short, and if you're going to meet with club members once a month for the foreseeable future, why not throw in a few smiles when you can? You may not be looking for your next best friend when you all get together (whether it's in person or online), but there's no reason why you shouldn't be comfortable and relaxed in an atmosphere of collegial companionship as you get to know each other better.

Becoming a true team

Your club should serve as a safe place where people feel comfortable learning something new as they try their hand at investing. Trust, familiarity, and a sense of working toward a common goal are characteristics that your club needs to develop over time. You can't and shouldn't expect trust to materialize overnight. Adding a little social interaction to your club helps you get there that much faster as club members get to know each other better.

Turning work into play

You want fellow club members to look forward to the meetings. If they're not excited about attending, they won't be excited about doing the work required to keep the club going, either. One way to keep motivation high is to liven up club interactions a little.

Match your members up into pairs or other small groups to complete work assignments between meetings. Teaming fosters friendly interaction between members who may not know each other well. It also makes the work much easier and is a great way to help newer or less experienced club members learn, by partnering them up with more experienced members.

Educational games or activities during the club meetings can also be a great way to mix business with fun. Some clubs play stock-picking games, the winners of which win a share of stock or another prize. We talk more about ideas like these in Chapter 11.

Networking for fun and profit

Other investment clubs more than likely are in your area. If you can make contact with them, consider doing a "club cultural exchange" once or twice a year, getting together for a joint educational project. Your local NAIC Chapter can help you find other clubs in your area and may even provide an instructor!

Meeting with other clubs is a great way of sharing ideas and brainstorming solutions to any problems your club may be having. As different as individual club members may be, club problems tend to be universal. Your partner club may just be able to help you figure out a new education strategy, or you may help them work on their member participation problems.

Field trip, anyone?

Every now and then, meet someplace different or attend an NAIC event together as a club. Tour a local publicly owned company as part of a stock study, visit a brokerage for an inside look at how they do business, or even attend the shareholder meeting for one of the companies whose stock you own. Find ways to share educational experiences with your club members and you'll soon realize the rewards of a communal renewed interest in the club.

Don't forget the tasty treats

You've heard the saying, the club that eats together, stays together. Okay, maybe it isn't a real saying, but it should be! One of the better ways to ensure that your investment club keeps its eye firmly focused on an important goal is to keep its collective stomach focused, too.

Don't laugh — tasty treats can go a long way toward ensuring your club's longevity. Regardless of whether members take turns stopping for donuts or other mass-produced bakery items before each meeting or you all gather for a sit-down gourmet meal at someone's home every month, sharing some kind of food is a surefire way of breaking the ice.

Some clubs use administrative fees to buy the food while others assign "snack duty" to a different member each month. Other clubs actually meet in the banquet room of a local restaurant and conduct their meetings either before or after eating a full meal together. As long as the food doesn't get in the way of important business, be creative and come to your meetings hungry. (Sorry. If you're in an online club, you'll have to raid your own refrigerator every week.)

Getting crazy once a year

Once a year, probably on your club's anniversary month, consider ditching the business part of the agenda and celebrating a successful year with a purely social meeting. Some clubs go out to dinner at a nice restaurant, others play host to a more casual event like a barbecue or a picnic and include club members' families. You can combine the festivities with your club's annual meeting, officer elections, and accounting audit, or simply take the time to savor all you've accomplished by just enjoying each other's company in a different way than you usually do.

Dealing with the spoilsports

As you begin incorporating a little fun into your club interactions, some members may be slightly uncomfortable with the social stuff, especially if they're shy or don't know other club members well. Be sensitive to their feelings and keep things low-key until you're all more at ease together. In the unlikely event that they just can't relax socially, and end up leaving the club as a result, their withdrawal will probably turn out to be a blessing in disguise. Teamwork is one of the more important aspects of your investment club, and you can't have teamwork without a solid team of willing participants.

Getting the balance right

After all we've said to convince you to find room for fun in your club, we'd be remiss if we didn't remind you to find a balance. Don't go overboard with the social aspects at the expense of your club. A good way to ensure the right mix of fun and formality is to set aside an established time just for chitchat either before or after each meeting so that it doesn't interfere with the important part of you club's work. The time that you set aside is perfect for enjoying your tasty treats along with the conversation.

Just because you have a set time for socializing outside of the meeting doesn't mean you can't incorporate fun into the meeting, too. Experiment a little, see what works for your club, but keep it all in balance, and you'll be well on your way to success! After all, if you and fellow club members don't enjoy your meetings and your meetings aren't productive, why bother going?

Chapter 3

Finding and Joining a Club

. . . .

. . . .

*B*efore joining an investment club, you need to recognize the characteristics that separate a healthy, thriving, successful club from a maladjusted, sickly, ineffectual one. But don't jump the gun — first you need to find a club that has an opening for a new member like you. In this chapter we give you plenty of leads to make the process of finding and evaluating a club as simple as possible. We also detail the most important traits of a successful club so that you can do your homework and find the best fit to suit your investment and educational needs. Once you're familiar with these qualities, we explain how to evaluate and join a club.

Finding a Club to Join

If you don't know anyone you'd like to start a club with, or you just don't want to deal with all the work involved with starting one from scratch, you'll need to find an established club that's looking for new members. Maybe you were thinking that's as easy as looking up "investment club" in the phone book. We hate to be the ones breaking it to you, but it just doesn't work that way. As much as it pains us to admit it, we're not exaggerating when we tell you that finding a quality club to join may just be the hardest part of your entire investment club experience.

No national directory of investment clubs is out there helping clubs look for members; no comprehensive Web site is just waiting to match you up with the perfect group of investors the next city over. Clubs that are looking for new members aren't likely to advertise with a flyer on your grocery store bulletin board, either. If you ask friends and neighbors about local clubs, expect a lot of blank stares in return. But don't let that dissuade you from trying.

Most investment clubs are made up of people who know each other or have some type of organization in common. They can be friends, co-workers, or family members. Or they may even be members of the same church congregation, trade union, or local service group. And, worse yet, they may not want an outsider like you for a member!

Once you're really sure that you want only to join an existing investment club instead of starting your own, you'll need to understand what you're getting yourself into and why finding a club is so hard in the first place. Then you have to figure out the best places to go for finding exactly the kind of club you're looking for.

You gotta follow the rules . . .

Rules? You mean investment clubs have rules and regulations to follow? Don't act so surprised. If money is involved, you'd better believe your local and federal governments have an interest in how your club advertises and operates. If it helps you to put these regulations in context, keep in mind that the rules protect you and the rest of the nation's investors from fraudulent and unscrupulous people who'd just as soon try to scam innocent or uneducated investors with bogus investment club opportunities.

Even with that in mind, you'd think the United States Securities and Exchange Commission (SEC) might have more important things to worry about than small-time investment clubs. However, a handful of securities laws regulate whether and how clubs can advertise for members. You don't need to worry about knowing all the nitty-gritty details, so here's the basic scoop.

Because investment clubs aren't required to register with the SEC (as long as they operate within boundaries discussed in Chapter 12), they're discouraged from publicly soliciting for new members. If a club does advertise for members and it happens to meet some other conditions (for instance, if it has more than 100 members), the SEC may interpret that action as a "public offering of a security." That's when things can get sticky.

Although it's unlikely that an investment club would be in defiance of any securities laws if ever it took out an ad in a local paper looking for new members, most clubs aren't willing to take that risk. Because of this legal complication, you'll rarely see investment clubs publicly soliciting new members. But that doesn't mean club members can't tell people about their club or ask them to become members. They probably don't want to try to attract new members by promising great returns or other financial benefits. In fact, if you find an investment club that advertises "guaranteed returns" or makes other outlandish claims, you need to steer clear of it.

Seeking help from your local NAIC Chapter

The best way to find a happy and healthy club is hanging out in the same places that club members like to visit. As the only organization in the U.S. supporting investment clubs, the National Association of Investors Corporation (NAIC) provides just the right environment to meet members of investment clubs. Details about the benefits of this nonprofit investment organization are provided in Chapter 1.

What NAIC can and can't do to help you find a club

More securities laws prevent NAIC and its network of 118 local chapters from playing matchmaker between clubs and potential members. Even though 37,000 clubs are members of NAIC, the organization is not allowed to provide individuals with referrals to specific clubs. The SEC says that providing a referral to a club can be construed as recommending a security. Only licensed broker-dealers or registered investment advisors can give investing advice, which leaves NAIC and its local chapters out in the cold.

Another huge roadblock is NAIC's possible liability if this kind of a match resulted in an unhappy relationship and either party turned the blame on the organization that got them together. Understandably, NAIC chooses not to get involved in actively linking clubs and individuals. So do most other investment associations and Web sites. That makes it more difficult for you to find a club but not impossible.

Hobnobbing at local events

If you have an NAIC chapter nearby (you can find out if you do by visiting NAIC's Web site at `www.better-investing.org`), your best bet is showing up at monthly meetings, classes, workshops, investor fairs, or other events. Even though NAIC can't directly link you up with a club, they do the next best thing. Most chapters make some sort of announcement at the beginning of their events asking whether people are looking for clubs or clubs are looking for members. Interested parties stand up and then look for each other after the program is over.

Another common tactic is providing lists or bulletin boards for clubs or individuals to post their contact information. The chapter destroys the lists after each event to avoid any potential for conflict with the SEC, so you'll need to attend the event.

Even if the chapter doesn't offer a specific opportunity to match clubs and members, you still can use the time to your advantage. Ask the local volunteers if they know of any clubs that are looking for members. Chat up the people around you to let them know you're looking for a club. NAIC events are the perfect place to find other serious, long-term investors, exactly the kind of people you want as fellow club members. Just remember that you want to make a good impression, too, so that anyone whose club has an opening considers you prime club material. Be friendly, engaging, and show your commitment. If you don't find a club after attending one meeting, don't give up. As you become a familiar face at your local chapter events, you'll become a more attractive candidate. Finding a club may take time, but it can be worth the effort.

Some NAIC chapters also run *model clubs,* clubs whose members invest real money and conduct monthly meetings in public. These meetings are open to any individual interested in a better understanding of how clubs work and in learning a little about stock selection strategies at the same time. If you're fortunate enough to have a model club in your area, be sure to take advantage of the opportunity and attend at least a few meetings. You're likely to find other investors with similar goals, or club members hoping to fill some vacancies in their memberships. Actually, some model clubs are often open to new members, and you may be just the type of person they're looking for.

Last resorts to finding a club

If you don't have an NAIC chapter nearby, you still have some alternatives. One is as simple as putting a classified ad in your local newspaper or posting a flyer in a public place. Although doing so certainly isn't the best choice or even one that we recommend, it has worked for some people looking for clubs. Be forewarned that you'll need to closely screen any club that responds to make sure the club's investment philosophy aligns with your own. We give tips for choosing a club later in this chapter — don't skip any of them if you go this route.

The main thing to remember about finding an investment club is that if you don't personally know anyone in the club before you join, proceed slowly and carefully. Attend a few meetings as a visitor and don't begin the joining process until you're completely comfortable with the club and how it operates.

Another possible but much less likely way to find a local club is by looking online. The Web is a fantastic place to find tons of investing information, but relatively few clubs have Web sites, and the chances of one of those clubs being in your local area are rather slim. The best way to find a club, remember, is to go where club members go. If you've tried that with no success in your area, get acquainted with club resources on the Internet and even consider joining an all-online club.

NAIC has a stock-study-discussion e-mail list called the I-Club-List. You can find a link on NAIC's home page (www.better-investing.org). Join the list and observe the discussion for a while as part of your investment education. Among the wide variety of topics are frequent conversations about investment club operations. Posting messages that you're looking for a club isn't allowed on the I-Club-List, but you may find someone from your area on the list and can ask that person privately if he or she knows of any club.

Online clubs eliminate the need to find a club within driving distance of your home because all club activities take place on the Internet. Online clubs are discussed in depth in Chapter 5. If you look for information on the Web, you can search for an online club that's seeking new members or visit message boards where people can post messages indicating that they're trying to find a local club (try the Motley Fool message boards at www.fool.com). Again, these methods won't yield the same results as will attending a local investing class, but if they're your last resort, then use them!

Look Hard Before Signing On

Groucho Marx once cleverly remarked, "I don't want to belong to any club that will accept me as a member." Although you'll ultimately have to decide for yourself whether you'd make a good member of any club that might have you as a member, some other points need to be considered when evaluating a club that has extended an invitation for you to join.

Once you find an existing club that's accepting new members, your work has only begun. Before signing on, you need to make sure that the club is right for you and that you're right for the club. If the club is worth joining, the members are going to want all kinds of information and promises from you. Don't be offended or scared away. Whenever a club willingly accepts you with little comment or knowledge of your commitment, that's when you should be afraid!

What should you look for in a club?

Although you may not be able to find a club that satisfies each and every one of your needs, that nevertheless should be your ideal goal. The most desirable and successful investment club:

- ✔ **Has a solid operating history.** If you're not going to start a club of your own, finding a club that's successfully made it through those first few potentially chaotic years is best. Optimally, you need to look for a club that's been around (and operating well) at least three or four years. That doesn't mean that a newer club won't perfectly fit your needs, but a club full of experienced members can really speed up your learning process once you join.

- ✔ **Operates under a formal agreement and bylaws.** You should consider only the clubs that have legal membership agreements. If the club is a general partnership (as most are), then the club's partnership agreement serves that purpose. Bylaws that cover operational procedures such as meeting structure and officer duties are crucial, too. If you encounter a club that chooses to operate without these basic but incredibly important documents, run away as quickly as possible without glancing back. We guarantee you'll never regret it.

✔ **Conducts its meetings on a regular schedule.** Look for a club that consistently meets monthly in person or online. If a club isn't disciplined enough to meet regularly or frequently cancels meetings at the last minute because no one can attend, you'll know there isn't much of a commitment on the part of its current members.

✔ **Meets at accessible times and locations.** Once you find a prospective club, you need to make sure that meeting times and locations are convenient for your schedule and lifestyle. A club that's perfect in every other way still won't meet your needs if you have to travel for hours to get there or the meetings are the same night your bridge club meets. Some clubs change their times or locations depending on the season. Make sure you have an accurate idea of how your chosen club decides these issues before you become a member of a club whose meetings you can't attend.

✔ **Provides an information packet to new or prospective members.** Not every club does this, so you've probably found a club worth a second (and third) look if they offer you some background materials before you even join. Most packets at the least contain the club operating agreement and bylaws so you can see exactly what you're getting into. You may also find information about the club's investing philosophy or its *investment policy statement,* details about its educational program, research about the companies it owns, and possibly stock selection guidelines.

If the club doesn't offer you these items, at least ask to see the operating agreement and bylaws before you decide to join. The importance of these documents is discussed in more detail in Chapter 6, so you'll have a better idea of what to look for when you read them.

✔ **Requires active participation by all members.** You want a club where most of the members attend most of the meetings. Trust us, if 30 members sign the operating agreement but only five people ever show up for monthly meetings, it's a bad sign. *Inactive* or *silent partners* create all kinds of problems with club dynamics and can lead to legal problems. According to the SEC, a club with passive membership can be construed as issuing securities, and that opens an entirely new can of worms.

✔ **Offers an investment education program.** Clubs should have a regular educational component to their meetings, especially if they have many members who are beginning investors. In many clubs, the vice president serves as the education coordinator and develops a full-fledged program for continually improving each member's knowledge of investing techniques and philosophies. Clubs that give education a top priority are the kind you definitely want to join, and you should be wary of clubs that put more emphasis on dollars than on learning.

✔ **Uses computerized recordkeeping.** True, using accounting software to keep accurate books isn't absolutely necessary. In fact, some club treasurers actually prefer doing the calculations by hand. Others create and maintain their own accounting spreadsheets. The problem with homegrown systems is that if something ever happens to the treasurer, other members can end up with a nightmare of paperwork and calculations on their hands, trying to keep the records straight.

NAIC offers excellent investment club accounting software, and other online services also are worth exploring. True, learning new software may take an untrained new treasurer a little bit of time, especially if the outgoing treasurer isn't available to help. However, with the written documentation that comes with the software program, plus the possibility of contacting the company directly for help, it certainly won't take as long to get up to speed as learning someone else's custom spreadsheet without instructions.

Frankly, with all the options out there for computerized accounting, including free online software, we wouldn't ever consider joining a club that still does its accounting by hand or with a personally designed spreadsheet. The risk for chaos in the event of unexpected treasurer turnover is just too great.

✔ **Requires reasonable initiation fees and contributions.** Many clubs charge new members a small initiation fee when they join, or require a set *buy-in contribution* that's higher than the regular monthly dues. Certainly, if either of these fees is so high that you simply can't afford them, then your decision is easy. But if the buy-in is excessively large, it may also be because the club requires equal contributions by all its members, and that can be problematic. (See the next item for more on this topic.)

✔ **Uses the valuation unit method of accounting.** Some clubs think that all members need to contribute equal dollar amounts every month, usually with the mistaken impression that it somehow makes the accounting easier. However, this method actually creates more problems. Look for a club that uses *valuation units*. As discussed in Chapter 7, this is similar to how mutual funds operate, and it's a far superior method of accounting.

✔ **Carries out an annual financial audit.** Even with club accounting software, making errors with the club's books still is possible. Although it's unlikely, it's still possible that a treasurer could illegally embezzle or otherwise misuse club funds. One way to make sure the club treasurer is doing the job correctly and that all transactions have been recorded properly is performing an audit every year. Few reasons exist, other than laziness, for a club to skip this routine.

✔ **Doesn't charge excessive penalties on withdrawals.** Many clubs levy a fee on withdrawing members to discourage them from leaving or from withdrawing funds too frequently. However, this fee should be no more than the actual costs of that withdrawal (such as any brokerage commissions or fees that might be paid) or 3 percent of the withdrawal amount. Avoid a club whose membership agreement includes a penalty that's greater than this amount.

✔ **Has a defined investment philosophy and purchase guidelines.** Any club worth joining has a set of requirements that must be met by any company whose stock the club is seriously considering. Needless to say, the club shouldn't merely *establish* guidelines; it should also follow them. Many clubs have a written document called an investment policy statement that details the club's chosen philosophy and strategy. For more about choosing a philosophy and creating an investment policy statement, see Chapter 6.

✔ **Includes a stable roster of members.** Ask how many members the club originally started with, and how many members have joined or withdrawn since then. If you notice a pattern of members coming and going frequently, you may want to look for another club. You at least need to investigate the reasons behind the membership turnover.

The cause may be something as innocent as club members unexpectedly moving out of town, but it also can indicate a club where expectations are not fully explained or followed up. Make sure you know the reasons before you join. Although not always complicated financially thanks to club accounting software, member withdrawals still take up your precious club meeting time with administrative details and stock selling or transfer decisions that need to be worked out.

✔ **Is a member of NAIC.** Membership of successful clubs in NAIC certainly isn't a given, But NAIC membership offers so many benefits (check out Chapter 1 for a detailed list) that it's hard to imagine a club that would pass up the opportunity to join just to save a few dollars in annual membership fees. Why reinvent the wheel when NAIC provides a huge range of tools designed specifically to help investment clubs, from stock selection guidelines to club accounting software and a wide variety of educational opportunities presented locally and online? Do yourself a favor and join a club that chooses to take advantage of the same resources that 37,000 other clubs do.

What should a club look for in you?

You're not the only one concerned that you and the club are a good match. The members of your prospective club have a great deal at stake when choosing new members, and need to interview you carefully before inviting you to join. Some of the important qualities they'll be looking for are:

✔ **Regular financial contributions.** No explanation needed here, right? If you aren't making regular capital contributions, you shouldn't be in a club. The club wants assurances that your contributions will be submitted in a timely manner each month and that you're expecting to invest the minimum amount (or more, if allowed). If you can't afford to join a club right now, you need to look instead for a stock study club where you can still learn while you build up your savings (see more about study clubs in Chapter 4).

✔ **Regular attendance at meetings.** If you won't attend the meetings, what good are you as a member? Everyone has an unavoidable conflict every now and then and has to miss a meeting. But if you're absent more times than you're present, you aren't showing a strong commitment to the educational mission of the club, and you may be asked to resign your membership. If you already know your schedule is busy or unpredictable, joining a club that meets in person may not be right for you. Instead, you may be better off looking for an online club.

✔ **Participation in all activities and operations.** It isn't enough just to come to the meetings, either. You need to be an active participant in stock discussions, even if you're only a beginner. You should demonstrate a desire to be an energetic member and have plans to bring enthusiasm and hard-core interest in investment education with you to every meeting. Your fellow club members will love you for it.

✔ **Commitment to long-term membership.** No club wants to go through the hassle of bringing you into its membership fold if you're planning to be around only a year or so. The paperwork, time, and effort required by club officers to add and withdraw short-term members, not to mention possible effects on the club portfolio, simply is not worth it.

Even if the club doesn't require a formal statement, you must be willing to offer a commitment of at least five years to prove how serious you are about entering the partnership. Of course circumstances change and you may be forced to withdraw earlier for personal reasons, but in your head you must be prepared to remain a member for many, many years.

✔ **Enthusiasm for learning.** Not only should you want to participate, you also should be eager for the education the club can provide. Expressing your desire to attend investing classes in your community or to help develop the club's education program makes you an attractive potential member. Even without local classes for you to attend, remember that the most novice investors still can make a huge contribution to a club by actively listening and questioning fellow club members.

Older and well-established clubs can become so entrenched in their operations through the years that some of the fun is lost in the process. A new member can provide an infusion of energy and bring a fresh feeling of enthusiasm to all the club members. If you truly feel this excitement on top of all the other necessary qualities we've discussed, any smart club would jump at the chance to add you to its membership.

Finally Ready to Make a Commitment?

You've found a club that's looking for new members and subjected it to a grilling that would make the FBI proud. And they've thoroughly checked you out, too. You've fulfilled many of the club's pre-entry requirements, such as attending a certain number of meetings or taking some investing classes. You've saved up the money you need for your initial investment and any administrative fees. Everything looks great, so all that's left to do is make it official.

Breathe a big sigh of relief at this point, because most of the hard work is behind you. The rest is just gravy as you embark on the exciting adventure of being part of an active, productive investment club. If you find yourself realizing that this description doesn't fit the club you're about to join, stop right here, say your goodbyes to this club, and for heaven's sakes reread this chapter before starting your search again. Few things can be worse than legally entangling yourself with a low-quality investment club. You stand a much greater risk of losing your money plus all the time you put into the club if they don't fit most of the characteristics we've just described.

If you did your research carefully and chose wisely, what you need to do now is finish up the paperwork, make your first investment, and start your education. At the next club meeting that you attend, you need to sign the operating agreement to legally become a member of the club. Some clubs also require you to sign the bylaws as evidence of your commitment to club responsibilities. You'll give the treasurer a check for your first capital contribution plus any administrative fees that you may be assessed as a new member. Then it's official. You're an investment club member!

You may be given educational resources such as stock study material or an NAIC manual. You should also receive a roster with contact information for everyone in the club, along with a schedule of meeting times and locations for the next few meetings. Above all, we hope you receive a warm and open-armed welcome from your new fellow club members, reminding you that no matter how many bureaucratic hoops you had to jump through to join, clubs are an awful lot of fun, too.

Totem Investment Club

Would you drive two hours to attend a club meeting? Some of the 12 members of the *Totem Investment Club* do! Formed in the Seattle area in 1996, the club's members are so committed that their long commutes don't deter attendance. All members are either current or former employees of the Allstate Insurance Company, which gives them a common background.

The Totem Investment Club conducts its monthly two-hour meeting at a restaurant so its members can combine dinner with the club business (and provide a bit of sustenance for those making a long drive home). Rather than making special arrangements with the restaurant, they all order from the menu and pay for their own meals. Members are required to attend no fewer than eight of the club's 11 meetings a year. Almost every meeting includes an educational presentation by the club's vice president.

The Totem Investment Club used to invest through discount brokerage E*TRADE, but now uses dollar cost averaging to invest in nearly all of its stocks automatically through FOLIOfn's (www.foliofn.com) innovative online investing service. The club uses accounting software to track its portfolio, which now proudly totals $311,000.

The minimum monthly contribution is $100, though members can contribute more. Members commit to tracking at least one of the club's 16 stocks, and present an updated Stock Selection Guide (SSG), Portfolio Evaluation Review Technique Worksheet A (PERT-A) and page two of the Portfolio Management Guide (PMG) to the rest of the club once a year.

Potential members must attend three meetings and read the prospective member packet and the NAIC investment manual before requesting to join the club. They also commit to attending all three SSG classes conducted by the local NAIC chapter, buying stock selection software, and making an SSG presentation to the club within six months of joining. The initial membership contribution is $3,000, which helps to ensure that new members take their club responsibilities seriously, even though it makes the club a bit less accessible for some potential new members.

Part II
Starting an Investment Club

The 5th Wave   By Rich Tennant

"I'm suggesting our investment club pursue more aggressive growth funds. You know, really aggressive— funds with muscle, funds with respect, funds that don't take any lip..."

In this part . . .

If you've decided you'd rather start an investment club of your own instead of finding one to join — you've got some work ahead of you! You need to find prospective members, hold your first few meetings, and carefully build your new club from the ground up. This part gives you all the information you need to create a well-organized, legally structured club, as well as the scoop on all the money management issues your new club must deal with.

Chapter 4

Laying the Groundwork for Your Club

. . . .

In This Chapter

▶ Scanning the pros and cons of starting a club

▶ Choosing the right type of club model

▶ Finding the right kind of club members

. . . .

*I*f you can't find an investment club to join, or you're not so sure you want to jump into a group that's already well established, perhaps it's time to form a club of your own.

Starting a club can mean a lot of work, but it's also a great deal of fun and has the potential for offering great rewards. In fact, starting your own club gives you the best potential for a successful club experience, and we recommend that you choose this route if at all possible. You don't need to devote your every waking hour to your club, and it doesn't have to take the place of other hobbies in your life.

By following the strategies we provide in this chapter, you should be able to get your club up and running with the least effort possible. Who knows, you may just have fun doing it, too!

It Isn't All Fun: Scanning the Downside

Starting your own investment club isn't a romp in the park. It can be hard work and time consuming, and you need to begin the process with your eyes wide open. So that you're prepared, we want to make sure that you know the pros and cons of starting your own investment club rather than joining one that's already been formed. (You already know our bias in favor of starting your own club — that's why we've rigged the lists, giving a slight advantage to the pros.)

First, the pros. When you start your own investment club, you can

- ✔ Choose people who fit your model-member profile
- ✔ Make a fresh start with no past problems to overcome
- ✔ Write the perfect operating agreement and procedures for your club
- ✔ Start your club's books from scratch with club accounting software
- ✔ Set the perfect meeting time and place
- ✔ Ensure that all members share the same investment philosophy
- ✔ Begin at the beginning in your club's education program
- ✔ Take advantage of your new members' natural enthusiasm

But those pros have a flip side, the cons. When you start an investment club, you have to:

- ✔ Find and screen potential members
- ✔ Find a location and set a meeting time that work for everyone
- ✔ Write your operating agreement and procedures from scratch
- ✔ Complete all the required legal paperwork to establish your club
- ✔ Find a brokerage that recognizes investment club accounts
- ✔ Buy the necessary stock selection and accounting software
- ✔ Get past the steep learning curve required for inexperienced investors

You can see that among the bigger drawbacks of starting your own club are the time and effort involved in finding potential members and doing the paperwork required to get the club up and running. Another is the initial cost involved, including the purchase of appropriate software to keep your club running as smoothly and as easily as possible. But if you have the enthusiasm and dedication to survive the setup process, starting a club can be incredibly rewarding.

Part of the problem is that joining an existing club, with its experienced investors, can be difficult because you're just beginning your own financial education. When you start a club of your own, members usually are at the same level of financial savvy; however, you should expect a few members to know how to invest and a few who don't even balance their own checkbooks.

It takes all kinds of people to form a successful investment club. You'll all lean on each other from time to time for different reasons. And even if the member who can't balance his checkbook never really masters the art and science of stock analysis, he may be the one club member who bakes really great chocolate chip cookies and asks the most questions, which can be positive attributes for your club, too.

Starting Out on Solid Ground

Just because you're ready to start an investment club of your own doesn't mean that you have to reinvent the wheel or go it alone. Once you've read this book and you're ready to take the first steps toward getting your new club off the ground, don't neglect the advantages to be gained from resources offered to investment clubs by the National Association of Investors Corporation (NAIC).

How NAIC can help you start a club

We go into great detail about the many reasons your club should join NAIC in Chapter 1. Review our list if you need a refresher. Otherwise, this chapter will focus on a few of the ways NAIC can be of service specifically to newer clubs.

Maybe you're lucky enough to live near a regional NAIC chapter. Many people are. You can find a list on NAIC's Web site at

```
www.better-investing.org/regions/regions.html
```

Local classes

NAIC chapters often offer classes about starting a club. These introductory-level classes are a great source of information as you begin the process and attending them can provide a perfect opportunity to find other people interested in starting a club. If the class doesn't offer a formal time to network with fellow attendees, be sure to chat up the people sitting next to you, and take full advantage of free time before and after the meeting and during any breaks.

This advice works well for any NAIC event. Chapters often post lists for clubs and prospective members to use in sharing contact information. However, the chapters are forbidden by Securities and Exchange Commission (SEC) rules to match up clubs with prospective members, so the lists often are destroyed after every event. You'll have to attend the meeting to make the most of the opportunity to connect with other would-be club members.

New club visits

Once you're serious about starting your own club, NAIC chapters can help even more. The local chapters often have volunteers who can attend a club's introductory meeting and explain the basics of starting and running a club. These volunteers are experienced with club issues and can be a tremendous resource to club members in the beginning stages of forming their club.

Problem solving

If you encounter problems after your club has been up and running for a while, NAIC volunteers can help with that, too. Most chapters provide either an in-person club visit (usually limited to once a year) or phone consultation, helping with issues like club accounting, stock selection education, or club member dynamics. Asking for help at the first sign of trouble can mean the difference between watching your club fizzle from the stress of unsolved problems or sizzle toward greater success after receiving guidance from a more experienced club expert. Take advantage of this great resource if it's available.

Educational opportunities

In addition to the personalized club visits, NAIC chapters also offer a wide variety of classes. Although most are general investing classes, which many clubs attend together as part of their continuing education plan, club-specific classes often are offered and can prove incredibly useful. Club accounting is a practical and helpful class for any club treasurer. This class helps explain software and processes that your club treasurer needs to follow for tracking your club's books.

Other relevant sessions that may be offered include classes about starting and running a club, keeping club members motivated, and, of course, the traditional investing classes that NAIC is famous for. Opportunities to talk with members from other clubs may arise at club officer networking events or during club operation panels. Become familiar with what your local chapter offers, and then make a point of attending regularly.

If you don't have a local chapter, you can find many wonderful NAIC educational resources online at www.better-investing.org. Look for the "Education" section. You'll find a bounty of goodies that your club can use during the start-up process as well as throughout the years. Chapter 11 has more information about using online resources in your club's education program.

Looking at other online resources

While we consider NAIC by far the best source of quality information for investment clubs new and old, you can also check out these other valuable references. Our favorites are online, so if you don't have a computer at home it's well worth a trip to your local library or Internet café to check them out.

About.com Guide to Investment Clubs

investmentclub.about.com/

About.com's human guides have pulled together information on 700 different topics, including a *Guide to Investment Clubs.* The site is regularly updated with its own articles and with links to other investment club-related sites. It also devotes an entire section to "Starting a Club."

The Motley Fool

    www.fool.com/InvestmentClub/

The Motley Fool is a popular financial site that aims to make investing fun and accessible for everyone. Its *Investment Club* section includes articles and message boards where you can talk about club issues. You can even ask the Fools to set up a discussion board just for your club.

ICLUB.com

    www.iclub.com/

Of course, we're a bit biased in recommending ICLUB.com, but this site has a collection of articles and ask-the-expert columns by Doug Gerlach (yes, the same Doug Gerlach who's a co-author of this book) that tackle unusual club problems. You'll also find ICLUBcentral's suite of online club resources, including a private message board, mailing list, and accounting tools just for your club.

World Federation of Investors

    www.wfic.org/

If you're outside the United States, don't think that you can't start a club. The World Federation of Investors was established in 1960 and now has member organizations in 20 nations. Each of these groups can provide you with more specifics about laws and regulations in their own countries. Check the WFIC Web site for links and contact information for your country.

Given the ever-changing nature of the Web, all the links mentioned here may change. New sites may appear with interesting and useful information, so check www.douglasgerlach.com/clubs/ for updates and additional tools.

Finding and Recruiting Members

No matter how much enthusiasm you have for the idea of starting a club, being a member of a club of one doesn't make much sense. You need some people to get involved — preferably a group of committed, hard-working, eager, and interested individuals who can work well as a team. The onus falls to you as the field general of your newly founded investing corps to find just the right mix of willing participants. Before starting your search, you have to know who you're looking for.

Key attributes of successful club members

Which personality type would you rather have as predominant in your club: grumpy, curmudgeonly hermits or friendly, curious team players? We don't know about you, but we'd much prefer to work with the second type, especially when money is at stake. A club is only as strong as its members, so finding the right people is important.

What makes a good member? We're not going to give you a complete psychological profile for an ideal club member, but some admirable attributes to look for in successful members are open-mindedness, curiosity, enthusiasm, dependability, and responsibility. They must be willing to accept compromise and take the initiative in helping the club make progress in all its efforts. Members also need to be willing to be active participants in all aspects of the club's operations, including attending meetings, conducting stock research, and serving terms as club officers.

Notice that we didn't include "has lots of investing experience" among our criteria. Although seeking out a diverse group of people is a good idea, don't fall into the trap of looking only for people with a head for business or those who already are active investors. Having an accountant, attorney, business owner, corporate executive, or diehard stock aficionado in your club may be great, but don't overlook potential candidates who may not seem the right type at first glance. Enthusiasm and dedication are more important than any amount of investing experience.

Recruiting only men . . . or only women . . . or only family

If you have a family investment club, then the job of finding members when you're starting up is certainly much easier, although your potential audience is probably much more limited than other clubs. Later on, finding new members for your club may depend on who's marrying into your family (for better or worse, indeed). Other types of clubs where you may have a limited population from which you'll attract members include those formed at work, church, a service club, or other organization.

Sharing your club's expectations and goals with prequalified members is even more important before they become members. If you start running into problems in your club, it may also wreak havoc around the office or during Thanksgiving dinner. If you want to avoid the potential for some incredibly awkward moments, be certain that anyone joining the club understands all the risks, responsibilities, and rewards before signing the operating agreement.

You also may've decided that your club will practice same-sex exclusivity. (That's another way of saying that your club will be made up of all women or all men.) Members of an all-women club may feel more comfortable asking questions and making decisions when they're in the company of their own. Or an all-male club may want or need to fulfill a distinct desire to "hang out with the guys" at their monthly meetings.

Choosing to form a club with members of only one sex has no particular disadvantages other than the fact that you'll be cutting your pool of potential members in half. Some research has been done on whether same-sex or mixed-gender clubs have better-performing portfolios and on whether all-male or all-female clubs come out ahead in the market. The results, however, are inconclusive.

Nevertheless, NAIC reports that all-women clubs in recent years have had the better performing portfolios, followed by mixed-gender clubs, with all-male clubs pulling up the rear. A study conducted by Terrance Odean and Brad Barber at the University of California at Davis concluded that men trade in their portfolios 45 percent more than women. Men's overconfidence and increased trading can be hazardous to the rates of return their portfolios earn. Women tend to take a more cautious, less active approach with their investments than men, so that often translates into higher returns.

But ladies, before celebrating this seeming victory in the investing battle of the sexes, be sure to note the results of another study carried out by Brooke Harrington at Brown University in 1998. Harrington showed that coed clubs tend to have better performing portfolios than either all-male or all-female clubs. Perhaps the natural tendencies of men and women are nicely counter-balanced in a club environment, the same way group investing helps put the brakes on many bad ideas of individual members.

This same study showed that clubs whose members have more professional or workplace relationships have better performing portfolios than clubs made up of friends or family members. Although that doesn't mean you have to keep friends and relatives out of your club, it suggests that diversity is good. A club with members who have different occupations, who are of varying ages, ethnicities, and religions, and who have had different experiences in the world can join together in your club to build a much better portfolio than each might be able to build on his or her own. (We know we've said that before, but it bears repeating as you begin the recruitment process.)

Looking for members in all the right places

Now that you know the right kinds of people to look for, where are you going to find them? Although you have plenty of places to look, you need to start with the places that you know best: your home, work, church, and other places where you regularly meet and socialize. Go ahead and make a list of all the people you think are good candidates for your club.

Ultimately, your club probably needs to have about a dozen members. That's a good size for most clubs and means you'll have enough people to do all the work but not so many that the group can't function cohesively. A dozen members enable your club to split up into three or four study groups or committees, and, at the same time, generate enough money in monthly contributions to make regular purchases through a typical deep-discount brokerage firm.

You may decide that your club's membership can be larger or smaller, and that's okay too. Just don't stop making your list when you reach your target membership number. Some of your candidates may not be interested or have time in their schedules, or they may have other reasons not to participate. And as you go through the club start-up process, you're bound to have some of them drop out along the way. Attrition may continue through your first few months' worth of meetings, so aim high for now so the chances are good that you'll end up with your target in the end.

When you're looking for members for your new club, your first recruits should include those who are more promising on your list of candidates. Although that may sound obvious, you'll also want your first few contenders to do some recruiting of their own, reaching out to their own best candidates and ultimately helping you to form a merry band that enthusiastically gets your club up and running.

Besides the people you know and the people they know, you may also want to expand your search into other avenues. This is especially true for existing clubs looking to rejuvenate through the addition of new blood. However, once you go outside your circle of acquaintances, you need to step a little more carefully. Investment clubs don't have to register with the Securities and Exchange Commission as long as they meet certain criteria. Announcing that your club is looking for new members is one of the things that can cause a problem with the SEC.

In most cases, as long as your club has fewer than 100 members, you can probably make public announcements that you're looking for members for your club without running into trouble with the SEC. However, you still need to avoid placing ads in newspapers or using other mass marketing tools, because they're probably too costly and won't reach the right target audience. As an alternative, you can consider placing an announcement in a newsletter or bulletin from your church or fraternal organization or posting a notice on the bulletin board at work or in other semipublic places. These sorts of announcements aren't public enough to run afoul of SEC regulations.

People who attend meetings and events conducted by your local NAIC chapter are one final source of new members. The same way as you may be able to find a club to join by hobnobbing with people attending at investor's fairs and workshops, you may also find people who are looking for clubs to join. People attending these events are demonstrating a commitment to learning about investing, so they can be among the better candidates for membership in your club. And if they're already happy members of a club or just not interested in joining yours, they may know other people searching for a club to join.

Producing a Club Information Packet

Once you have a list of candidates, start recruiting. Inviting someone to join your club with only a phone call isn't enough. Okay, that can be a great place to start, but you need to do more. Instead of wasting the candidates' time and yours when they realize at the first meeting that they're really not interested, be kind and give them the facts upfront.

What you need is an information packet for prospective members. The packets serve two purposes. They're a great introduction to the investment club concept for people who aren't that familiar with the idea and they state outright what a member's responsibilities are. With a detailed overview of what it means to be a club member, no one will be able to later use "but I didn't know!" as an excuse for not fulfilling member responsibilities.

You want to make your member packet as explicit as possible so there's no room for misunderstanding. Scaring potential members off with too much detail at the beginning is far better than to have them leave later, unhappy and disillusioned. If they're not willing to read through your materials, chances are they won't make a dedicated club member. Your prospective member packet is your first chance to gauge a prospective member's level of interest.

Some of the topics that you need to cover in your prospective member packet are taken directly from your operating agreement and bylaws and define and explain

- Investment clubs
- Reasonable expectations of what a club can and can't provide
- Attendance requirements
- Work requirements
- Education requirements
- Financial requirements
- Rotating officer duties
- Meeting frequency
- Stock selection (a brief overview) and what a stock study entails

Be sure that you don't guarantee any rate of return that your club portfolio will generate in the future. If your club has been in operation for a few years, you may want to quote your past performance, but always include a reminder (disclaimer) that no investment is guaranteed. If those reading your new member packet are new to investing, reminding them that their investment may go down as well as up is particularly important.

Choosing Your Club's Type

If you stop and ponder how investment clubs are structured (and we're sure you do this often), we're willing to bet that you'd never even consider an alternative to the traditional *shared account* setup. Although this is by far the most popular type of investment club, an alternative way to organize may better serve your needs. Looking at both types will help you see which one works best for your club.

Pooled assets club

Although it may sound unfamiliar or complicated, a *pooled-assets* investment club is nothing more than what you probably already think an investment club is. Specifically, pooled assets means that all the club members make contributions toward a common account, where their money is *pooled* before investing.

All members retain ownership of their own money, but it's held in the same brokerage account as everyone else's. The club treasurer, using club accounting software, keeps track of who owns what percentage of the club's portfolio and tracks individual members' investment returns as well as the return for the club as a whole. When a member decides to leave the club, the treasurer performs a withdrawal and pays out the amount of that member's ownership in either cash or stocks.

Advantages of pooling your assets

So, you may ask, "Why would I want to combine my money with everyone else's?" One of the biggest reasons is accountability. We're not talking about accounting, but rather the kind of accountability where you feel a commitment to the bigger group and you take your club responsibilities seriously out of loyalty to your fellow members. You've all put your money to work together, and the feelings of trust and a shared mission that come from this joint effort sparks a loyalty for your club that otherwise can be hard to find. If you're not contributing your money to the club each month, imagining that your sense of commitment might not be as strong is no stretch. There's something to be said for feeling obligated to others!

Another huge advantage of the pooled-assets model is a reduction of expenses associated with your club's investing. If you personally want to invest $50 a month in a stock that you've studied, the brokerage commission costs are quite prohibitive. Even if you trade online at reduced rates, a $15 commission takes quite a big chunk out of your available investment money. However, if you're in a pooled-asset club, with 14 other members also contributing $50, that same $15 commission represents a much smaller percentage of your $750 pooled investment. Similarly, expenses for club accounting software or educational materials are spread across the entire membership.

Reduced expense is no small matter for investors who can set aside only a minimal amount in savings each month. Small investors can accomplish much more while paying proportionally much less as a group than as a single small investor. That is one reason why investment clubs are such a popular way of getting your feet wet in the stock market.

Drawbacks of pooling your assets

We won't hide from the truth that a pooled-asset investment club also can be a huge pain, especially for the club treasurer. Shared investment accounts lead to more complicated accounting practices than you need for your own personal accounts. The club treasurer must be diligent about recordkeeping and preparing valuation statements for the club every month and tax forms annually. Luckily, club accounting software considerably lightens the treasurer's workload, but pooling assets nevertheless creates an additional layer of complexity.

The other main problem stems from dealing with monthly member contributions. Each member is required to make regular financial contributions, but you can always count on unorganized or uncooperative members turning theirs in late or not at all. That creates work and stress for the rest of the club because reminders, late fees, and sometimes forcible removal of the delinquent member all need to be dealt with promptly.

Self-directed investment (SDI) club

What if your club finds that it's made up of members who frequently move away (if you live in a college town, for example), or forming as an online club with people who currently are strangers? What if your new club members are extremely independent and prefer investing on their own? What if no one is willing to take on the role of treasurer? Is there any way to manage a club when it's facing the potential for troublesome accounting issues? Would we ask all these nosy questions if we didn't have an incredibly good option for you? Of course not because that's exactly what a less common model for structuring an investment club has to offer.

You've probably heard of self-directed retirement accounts where you can invest in individual stocks that you choose yourself. The idea is much the same for a *self-directed investment (SDI) club.* Sometimes these clubs are known as *study clubs* or *paper clubs,* because you invest only on paper. If your club is structured as an SDI, it functions in nearly the same way as a pooled-assets club. You and your fellow club members still meet regularly (in person or online) educating yourselves and making investment decisions while enjoying each other's company.

The big difference between SDI and pooled-assets clubs is in making an actual investment. As the SDI name implies, instead of giving the club treasurer a contribution every month, self-directed investment club members invest their money in their own individual brokerage accounts. After an investment decision is made, club members buy the chosen stock in their own accounts, managing their own portfolios.

Advantages of self-directed clubs

Look at the disadvantages of pooled-assets clubs in the "Drawbacks of pooling your assets" section earlier in this chapter and then imagine them all disappearing in a puff of smoke. No club accounting, no club operating agreement, no late member contributions, no valuation statements, no tax reporting, no member withdrawals — no need for a club treasurer at all! Self-directed clubs are more streamlined, enabling a greater focus on the education and investment part of your club's mission — not to mention that whoever would've been club treasurer can now spend more time baking those tasty treats your club so enjoys at its meetings.

The other huge advantage is pragmatic. Some clubs just can't function as well with a traditional pooled-assets approach. Youth investing clubs formed in a high school, for example, can be an accounting nightmare. Not only do underage investors have to deal with custodial accounts, they also tend to move in and out of a club after only a few years because of family moves and certain other unavoidable events (like graduation). Military club members also find themselves frequently on the move. And typical club accounting also can be problematic for purely online clubs.

These types of clubs, along with people who may be skeptical or suspicious of pooling their money with others but don't face any of the other SDI issues, are ideal candidates for a self-directed investment approach. Other investors may prefer the idea of a *study club* where education takes on a higher priority than investing. If any of these situations are familiar, you should strongly consider establishing your club with an SDI approach.

Drawbacks of self-directed clubs

We wouldn't be honest if we didn't warn you that SDI clubs can end up with much shorter life spans than pooled-assets clubs. The biggest disadvantage of choosing the SDI structure has to do with motivation. One big benefit of joining a club in the first place is the camaraderie that comes from being a part of a group. Although you still have a group of investors to learn with in an SDI club, you won't be tied to them financially.

Skipping a meeting or not doing your stock study homework is much easier when you don't feel obligated to the rest of the group. You're not "putting your money where your mouth is" in the same way you do in a pooled-assets club, and, unfortunately, that can make a difference in member attitudes unless it's specifically discussed when the club forms.

Another potential problem with SDI clubs is that nothing forces club members to actually invest their money on their own. If part of the reason for joining an investment club is to actually *invest* your money, then you have to follow through. Investing is automatic in a pooled-assets club because you risk being booted out of the club altogether if you don't pony up your contribution each month. SDI club members endure no such consequences because their finances are completely private. If you think you may be too scared to invest on your own, or simply too busy, you're probably a better candidate for a traditional club where fellow members keep you honest.

Be aware of two other accounting-type issues unique to SDI clubs. With SDI clubs, you aren't able to instantly spit out a figure for your club's annual rate of return. In fact, your club won't have a return at all. Because all members of an SDI club invest on their own, each member's return will be different, based on how much was invested in a particular stock and how many shares were purchased. And, as we mentioned above, doing business on your own is much more expensive because you're not spreading the costs among all your club members. True, you don't need to buy club accounting software, but you'll be applying a much greater percentage of your investment toward commissions.

If you join an SDI club, you and your club members may want to investigate services like Sharebuilder (www.sharebuilder.com) where you can invest small amounts of money at much lower commissions than even online discount brokers offer. You and your club members can also decide to focus on stocks of companies that offer low or no-fee DRIPs and DSPs as a way of holding down costs. (For more about these two alternatives to brokerage purchases, see Chapter 7.)

So should you think about SDI?

Although it appears that a self-directed investment club is the obvious choice, if only because of the lack of need for a club treasurer and all the legal paperwork, something must be said for the sense of camaraderie that comes from pooled ownership. With an SDI club, nothing holds you back from slacking off (no fees for late contributions) or avoiding club meetings and responsibilities altogether. (It's much harder to do a "forcible withdrawal" when there's nothing to withdraw.)

On the other hand, the SDI club structure is perfect for online clubs, youth clubs, military clubs, family clubs whose members are far flung, study clubs, or virtually any situation that makes traditional club accounting a hassle or an impossibility. If your club fits these parameters and your fellow members have worked out a solution to motivational problems, we bet you'll love the SDI format. See Table 4-1 to compare the differences in the two types of clubs. Seriously discuss those differences with your fellow club members to determine what is best for your situation.

Table 4-1	Differences between Pooled Assets/SDI Clubs
Pooled-assets Club	**Self-Directed Investment Club**
Investments are pooled	Investments are made individually
Traditional club accounting	Individual recordkeeping
Standard operating agreement	No operating agreement
Standard treasurer role	No treasurer or software needed
Standard member withdrawals	No need for withdrawals
Stronger group commitment	Potential for less group loyalty

Defining Your Club's Mission

Not surprisingly, your club's best chance for a long and prosperous life depends on a shared goal. You club's members all need to be working toward roughly the same goals (education, camaraderie, investment success) for roughly the same reasons. Dress up these "goals" in formal eveningwear and your club has a mission.

Among the things that you may want to include in your club's mission statement are the same elements that we talk about in Chapter 2. The key aspects of a successful club, things like education, socializing, building a profitable portfolio, all should be covered in your mission statement. But the statement can be short and informal, something as simple as:

The Blue Chips and Salsa Investment Club was formed to educate its members about investing in a safe and enjoyable environment, and to enable those members to invest the club's money in a well-researched portfolio of individual stocks.

Agreeing on a mission for your new club isn't enough; you all need to commit to faithfully abide by it. If your mission says that you'll follow a certain set of guidelines before you purchase a stock, make sure you don't skip any of them. Once you start compromising on one of your shared principles, compromising on all of them will become easier and easier.

Similarly, if your mission sets out a plan for continuing education, don't abandon it if your members start thinking they're too experienced and don't need to learn anything new. If your club cares enough about something to put it into its mission statement, then it clearly is important. Respect your earlier motivation and keep the commitment that you all made to each other and your club.

That doesn't mean your club can't evolve and change its mission over time. You may find that your investment guidelines aren't as specific as they need to be, or maybe they're *too* specific. You may also find that you wish that you'd focused more on the educational aspect of your club experience. You can, of course, make adjustments to your mission, if your club feels the need. But be judicious in the choices you make, and always keep in mind the ultimate goal is a long-term, successful, and *enjoyable* club.

United Equities

Even if they tried, members of *United Equities* (an online investment club) aren't likely to meet in person anytime soon. As soldiers in the United States military, club members are stationed around the world. This unusual circumstance, however, doesn't stop them from learning more about investing together. They take full advantage of the Internet to research and present potential stocks for purchase, to e-mail the monthly club newsletter and financial statements, and to communicate about club business. They invest through discount broker E*Trade and use software to keep track of the 17 stocks in their $242,000 portfolio.

United Equities was formed in 1985 by ten soldiers of different ranks, who each initially contributed $100. The regular monthly contribution is $25, but members can invest more if they desire. Members have come and gone through the years, but the club membership now totals 21, ranging in age from 30 to 50 and varying in rank from sergeant to colonel. Among the more unique provisions in this club's operating agreement is the stipulation that no member can be in the chain of command of any other member.

New members are required to read the potential member packet, which includes an introductory letter containing important details about the club's operations. The letter clearly states that although the goal of the club is to learn and invest together, club members are soldiers first and their primary priority remains above all to protect the freedom of the United States and her allies. The club keeps a strict boundary between on- and off-duty status, and members are asked to limit discussions of club business to off-duty or informal gatherings.

When club discussions take place, members focus on their continuing investment education. Any member who wants to recommend a potential stock for purchase must first demonstrate why the stock is worthy of study. One member is then assigned to research it and prepare a Stock Selection Guide (SSG) for the rest of the club. Member participation sometimes can be interrupted by long deployments, so above all, the members of United Equities remain flexible when determining member responsibilities.

Chapter 5

Building a Structure for Your Club

*Y*ou've gotten together a group of people who may be interested in forming an investment club. And you've distributed packets of information so each potential member has the same understanding of what is expected. The work they'd be doing hasn't scared them away (whew!). Next comes the big step — getting everyone together in one place and actually meeting to discuss your club's formation. Hold on tight. The fun begins here!

As the process of building your club from scratch begins, you'll have two different types of meetings ahead of you — introductory meetings and your first regular monthly meetings. The introductory meetings are with people who are interested in finding out more about investment clubs but haven't yet decided whether they really want to participate. These are the meetings where you'll lay out all the responsibilities and benefits of club membership, just to be certain that everyone is on the same page.

Once you have a group of people who are committed to the work involved in starting and maintaining a club, you'll conduct the first of your monthly club meetings. You'll want to begin with one or two meetings devoted solely to club planning, organization, and all the other details that are discussed in this chapter. Then, once your club structure is in place and officers have been elected, you'll be ready to start on the fun stuff as you set your education program in motion and begin investing.

Planning Your Introductory Meeting

The details about a few of the more important things that you need to do before you conduct your first introductory meeting are provided in this section. Do them step by step and you'll be well on your way to success.

If you're forming an online club rather than a traditional face-to-face group, you still want to follow the same steps described in this section. Of course, you'll want to substitute online alternatives in many cases. For instance, instead of finding a place to hold monthly club meetings, you'll research chat rooms or e-mail list services. You can adapt the rest of the items in this section to fit your group's specific online needs in the same way. Additional tips for online clubs are available in the "Conducting meetings online" section near the end of the chapter.

Finish looking for possible members

Assuming that you're hoping for a core group of about 15 members, you probably want at least 20 to 25 qualified potential members at your first introductory meeting if you can find them. You can expect to lose a few after the first meeting and a few more as your planning meetings get underway and people begin fully comprehending the scope of the commitment they're being asked to make. This weeding out is natural and, in fact, it's a good thing. Better to lose these people now than in a few months, after they've already signed an operating agreement, made a few contributions, and then decided that they really don't want to be in a club after all. Don't work too hard convincing people to come to your planning meeting, either. If they're skeptical or uninterested, they probably won't want to be a club member anyway. If you can get together a roomful of enthusiastic candidates, you'll be in much better shape than if your recruits are lackadaisical about the idea of an investment club.

If you need a few more people for your first meeting, contact the people who already have agreed to attend, asking them to bring along a well-chosen friend or two. Don't forget to review the tips for finding members in Chapter 8 and consider using some of those options to round up a few more potential club members.

Choosing a meeting place and time

Look over the list of potential places for monthly club meetings in Chapter 9 and decide whether any of them will work for your first meeting. Whenever possible, choose a public place (like a library meeting room) as opposed to a conference room at your place of business. A public location may be less intimidating to any strangers, unless all your potential members happen to be your co-workers. Then it makes sense to meet at work.

If you can, poll the people whom you think may attend to determine whether an evening or weekend meeting time is more convenient. Plan on about two hours for the first meeting. You don't want it to go much longer; otherwise, you'll lose your audience's attention. You need to cover all the important topics in two hours and still have enough time to take a short break.

Once you've decided on the time and place, notify everyone you already know is interested. You can also make a few flyers with the meeting specifics to post at work, school, or church, if you're still hoping to find a few more people. While we don't recommend creating flyers once your club is up and running — because you can run afoul of Securities and Exchange Commission restrictions on advertising a club — using this approach to finding people who are interested in *starting* a club, probably is okay.

Preparing your meeting materials

As the meeting approaches, you want to put together all the handouts that you'll need for the meeting. Although you don't want to overwhelm people with too much information, you nevertheless want to make sure everyone has the same understanding of what it means to be in an investment club. If possible, you may even want to distribute some of the information prior to the meeting so potential members have a chance to review the material beforehand. That way they can formulate questions and, in general, come to the meeting better prepared to talk about what comes next.

Some of the items that you'll most likely want to have available at your introductory meeting include

- ✔ **An agenda.** Prepare a short, simple agenda with all the items that you plan to cover, so that your meeting attendees have a better feel for what to expect. An agenda reassures them that the meeting won't last forever.

- ✔ **A list of reasonable expectations.** You may want to make copies of the expectations that are explained in Chapter 2. You can read parts of it out loud to the group, thus ensuring that everyone understands what investment club membership can and cannot offer them. When everyone has similar expectations, you can head off possible future misunderstandings. Be sure to ask whether anyone has any questions when you reach this point in the meeting.

- ✔ **Prospective member packets.** We discuss in detail what these packets need to contain in Chapter 4. Whenever possible, you may want to give a packet to potential members before the introductory meeting so they can read through it at their leisure.

Conducting Your Introductory Meeting

This first meeting is your chance to get to know prospective club members and to introduce everyone to the basic expectations and responsibilities of investment club membership. Use the agenda provided in this section as a framework for your introductory meeting. Be sure to ask someone to take minutes so that you'll have a record of what was discussed.

Sample introductory meeting agenda

Follow this step-by-step agenda at your first exploratory meeting, and you're bound to have a good meeting — and maybe even an investment club!

1. **Welcome and introduction**

   Briefly introduce yourself to the group, providing a little background about why you've arranged the meeting before going over the agenda so that everyone knows what's in store for them.

2. **Overview of reasonable expectations**

   Be sure to read parts of your club's expectations out loud to the group. Doing so ensures that everyone understands what investment club membership can and can't offer. As long as you all have similar expectations, you can head off any possible future misunderstandings before they have a chance to mess things up. Be sure to ask whether anyone has questions when you reach this point in the meeting.

3. **Overview of planning process**

   Explain how the process works from here on. In other words, after the introductory meeting you'll have one or two planning meetings to settle all the details before "officially" starting your club. Provide details about what people can expect during this process.

4. **Break**

   At this point, letting people stop and chat for a few minutes is a good idea. They can do so while enjoying the tasty treats that you've brought. Ten or 15 minutes is probably enough time to break the ice.

5. **Attendee self-introductions**

   Go around the room, asking people to introduce and share a little about themselves and their motivations for being a part of a club. A little more about the importance of this exercise is discussed in the next section.

6. **Discuss whether to form a club**

   Don't spend too long on this. You'll find out pretty quickly whether you have enough people interested in going ahead to the next step — your first club-planning meeting.

7. **Discuss the logistics of your next meeting**

   Set the time and location of your club's next meeting, and discuss any homework assignments. Ideas for appropriate homework are discussed in the next section. Whenever possible, choose a meeting date about two weeks away. That gives people time to think realistically about whether they have the time and motivation to be an active club member. If you wait too long, however, you'll lose momentum and possibly potential members. You want to take advantage of the natural enthusiasm that is certain to bubble up after your introductory meeting.

8. **Adjournment**

Officially call the meeting to a close but let people know that they can stay and chat. When you reserve your meeting room, make sure to leave enough time for informal socializing at the end of the meeting. This is a great opportunity for potential club members to get to know each other better.

Making the commitment

Your introductory meeting is going well. You've got a room full of people interested in forming an investment club. What do you do now? You all need to be brutally honest with yourselves. You've had a chance to read the prospective member packet and to ask questions. You've gotten to know each other a little better, and, it is hoped, all of you are excited at the prospect of forming a club.

Now is the time to let people show their commitment. Taking a quick break is the best way to do this is — as is addressed by the sample agenda in the previous section. Before the break, make a general announcement letting people know that if the reality of joining a club isn't what they expected, they're welcome to leave during the break. That way people who aren't quite sure about the idea can leave without feeling self-conscious.

People leaving during the break is, without a doubt, a good thing. Trying to convince people that they want to be in the club, or intimidating them into thinking they've come too far to back out, is the last thing that you want to do. If they aren't instantly enthusiastic about the idea of a club, they likely won't be motivated to do the necessary work.

In fact, it's okay to blatantly ask people why they want to be in an investment club and what they think they can offer the club. In fact, that is exactly what you *should* do right after the break. Go around the room, asking all the potential members what they'd like to get out of the club experience as well as what they're willing to contribute.

By the time you reach the last person, you'll all know even more about each other, and you'll have a good idea of who'll end up being your fellow club members. So set a time and location (the same place, if you can) in the next two weeks or so for your first planning meeting, and then congratulate everyone taking their the first steps toward forming an investment club before thanking them for their time and saying goodbye.

Don't forget to pass around a sign-in sheet for those interested in meeting again. You'll want to have contact information (name, address, phone number, e-mail address) collected in one place in case you need to get in touch with anyone before the next meeting.

Handing out homework

Prior to your next meeting, anyone who's interested in starting a club needs to at least read through the prospective member packet and familiarize themselves with NAIC. Doing so puts everyone on the same footing when you get together at your next meeting. Other homework can include reading through relevant chapters of this book and coming up with a list of things each new member would like to learn about investing. If everyone prepares a list, the topics on those lists can form the basis of your club's educational program. Focus on one or two of them at each meeting, and you'll be well on your way.

Getting Down to Business — Your First Regular Meeting

At your first real club meeting, be prepared to officially form your club, choose a name for it, and even settle on when and where you're going to meet. You had no reason for bringing these topics up at your introductory meeting because you weren't sure who was going to stick around to form the club. But now that you have a set of committed members, you need not worry that you should've done any of this before. By the time you adjourn your first regular meeting, you'll have decided on all these things plus more.

You'll see that the following list of sample agenda items for your first planning meeting is much more detail-oriented than the list of agenda items for the introductory meeting. Again, make sure that someone takes complete and accurate notes. You'll all be making a lot of important decisions during this meeting. The planning meeting agenda needs to include

1. **A welcome**

   After brief opening remarks, welcome those in attendance and then go around the room, having people introduce themselves.

2. **A review**

   Bring everyone up to speed with a quick overview of what was discussed at the previous meeting. Briefly go over the agenda for this meeting so that everyone knows what to expect.

3. A decision on your club's investment policy

This is one of the more crucial discussions that your new club ever will have. Don't even dream of forming a club unless *all* members are in agreement on the investment philosophy. (We talk about investment policy statements in more detail later in this chapter and in Chapters 13 and 14.)

4. A choice of club's name

You may decide a formal, businesslike name is best, but you can also have little fun with it. Create a clever name based on your geographic area, a shared interest, or anything else that works. Choose one or two alternate names in the unlikely event that another club already has registered your first choice.

5. A break

Stop the business portion of the meeting for a brief break, because you'll need it after the previous discussions. Members need to mingle and get to know each other better. The break also is a good time for asking members to write down all their contact information for the club roster. In addition to their own addresses, phone numbers, and so on, be sure to ask members to list an alternate contact (such as a local friend or relative). Your club may one day need this information if a member moves without providing the club with a new address. (See Chapter 12 for more about "missing members.")

6. An election of officers

After discussing the responsibilities of each office (see Chapter 6), conduct your first official election. Although elections may seem premature at this early stage, selecting officers now helps your club get up and running as quickly as possible (in addition to giving club members a sense of loyalty and ownership).

7. A review and discussion of the sample operating agreement and procedures (bylaws)

You won't formally adapt or adopt your own operating agreement and bylaws until the next meeting, but taking a "sneak peek" at places where you'll want to customize these legal guidelines will greatly streamline the process.

8. A decision setting the amount of your club's financial contribution

You'll need to decide on initial and regular monthly investments. Agree to start contributing at your next monthly meeting if possible.

9. A decision setting the time and location of your club's meetings

You can set meeting times and locations for the next two or three months or as far in advance as a year, depending on your members' needs. More of the specifics to consider when selecting meeting times and locations are discussed in Chapter 9.

10. **A homework assignment for all members**

    In preparation for the next meeting, ask one member to arrange for refreshments and then set up some goals for your club officers. Among other duties, your president needs to set an agenda, the vice president should outline a proposed education program, your treasurer should investigate accounting software, banks and brokerages, and your secretary should contact NAIC for membership materials and make arrangements for future meeting locations. All club members need to read Chapters 13 and 14 for an introduction to investing so that the club can start its educational process immediately.

11. **Adjournment**

    Time to congratulate yourselves for another productive meeting. If members have time, enjoy more refreshments and socialize a little before saying goodbye and farewell until next time.

    As you can see, this agenda is more than enough work for your first planning meeting. You don't want to burn everyone out by trying to get everything done all at once. At your next meeting you can firm up the details of your operating agreement, bylaws, and education program.

In fact, your next few meetings will be a combination of paperwork and education. Your club still has a lot of work ahead of it, but you're now beyond the biggest hurdles. Check out Chapter 6 for assistance in completing your operating agreement and bylaws, Chapter 9 for tips on running your meetings, and Chapter 11 for help in setting up your club's education program.

Defining Your Investment Approach

Your club needs to create an *Investment Policy Statement*. This fancy sounding document is nothing more than putting down on paper your club's most basic rules about investing. Following a consistent set of rules helps your club avoid misunderstandings and conflicts between members.

You all must agree to abide by your club's stated investment philosophy, but you also should establish more specific guidelines that stocks must meet before the club can agree to purchase them. A sample of such a statement is included at the end of Chapter 6. Chapters 13 and 14 go into great detail about what to look for in a stock, so we recommend starting there for ideas about forming your club's own Investment Policy Statement.

If your club wants to incorporate socially responsible investing, for example, the Investment Policy Statement is the place to detail what all your members mean by socially responsible and what guidelines you'll use to screen potential companies.

Putting this philosophy and your purchase guidelines in writing (your operating procedures/bylaws would be the perfect place) is important. Not only does this focus your club on a long-term strategy based on buying quality companies with excellent growth potential, it also prevents disagreements whenever a member pushes for the purchase of a substandard stock. Having your club's pre-established checklist to measure any nominated stock against may help eliminate hurt feelings. After all, your club isn't rejecting the member, it's only a stock that's doesn't meet your requirements.

Some of the more common elements that clubs include in their Investment Policy Statements are

✔ That members must complete a Stock Selection Guide and other appropriate research before presenting a stock to the club. Buying on tips or hunches is not allowed.

✔ That stocks are purchased for the long-term (your club may want to define exactly what is meant by "long-term"). Neither day trading nor market timing is permitted.

✔ That all stock dividends must be reinvested.

✔ That the club's portfolio will contain a only a certain number of stocks. Decide how many stocks your members can reasonably track, and then don't stray above that number.

✔ That members each will take a turn researching and presenting stock proposals. You may want to detail exactly how often they are required to do so.

✔ That the club will wait to purchase a stock until enough money has accumulated so that commission costs are kept below 1 percent to 2 percent of the investment amount.

You don't have to create an investment policy statement right at the start, especially when you're new to investing. But keep it in mind as you begin building a portfolio and putting down your club's own rules on paper as your portfolio begins to crystallize.

Forming an Online Investment Club

Online investment clubs aren't new. The world's first recorded online investment club celebrated its tenth anniversary in the fall of 2001. The Pioneer OnLine Investment Club (POLIC) was started on CompuServe in 1991 by a group of investors who didn't know each other. It has been going strong ever since. (In fact, Douglas Gerlach, one of the co-authors of this book, has been a member of the Pioneers since 1995.)

Ask most people who belong to online investment clubs what's so different between their clubs and clubs that meet in living rooms and basement rec rooms, and the answer likely will be, "Not much!" Online investment clubs have many more similarities than differences when compared with traditional, face-to-face clubs. Members of online clubs may never actually meet in person, but they still can create viable, working, successful investment clubs.

Think of it this way: Sending a memo, taking a meeting, transmitting a fax, making a phone call, and sending an e-mail message all are ways of communicating. Each has its advantages and disadvantages when compared with other methods. You probably know people who are more productive when they spend the day on the telephone, while others communicate more efficiently by letter or memo. The same is true of online clubs. The rules basically are the same, except the mechanics of communicating are just different.

When club operations and investing are mentioned throughout this book, the same information goes for either type of club. Many of the online tools that are available to clubs work for online clubs as well as offline clubs. However, keep in mind that some special considerations relate to online clubs.

Clearly the biggest difference with online clubs is in the way that members communicate. Online clubs do everything by computer — distributing club information, researching stocks, and even conducting meetings. Club members need either to own or have easy access to a computer with an Internet connection; otherwise, they won't be able to participate in club discussions or decisions. Once you get past the computer-related issues, however, you'll find that online and face-to-face clubs operate in pretty much the same manner. Almost everything in this book can easily be adapted strictly for use by online clubs . . . well, everything except sharing those tasty treats. We haven't yet figured out a way to do that online, so you're on your own to figure out a solution.

Online clubs are invaluable for people who, for whatever reason, simply can't meet in the same physical location. The Pioneers have members across the United States and even a member in Japan, so getting together for a regular meeting is out of the question! Even people who *do* live close enough to meet in person may choose to form an online club purely out of convenience. If you're trying to decide whether an online club may be the best option the benefits of taking club communications and education online are discussed in Chapters 9 and 11.

Setting up online

Almost everything your club needs to accomplish can be done using e-mail. Besides the service at ICLUB.com (www.iclub.com), which has all the tools most online clubs ever could need, you can set up an e-mail list through a service like Yahoo! Groups (http://groups.yahoo.com/) or Topica (www.topica.com) so that any message you send is automatically distributed to all club members. Agendas, meeting minutes, monthly valuation statements, Stock Selection Guides and research reports all can easily be sent through e-mail. E-mail also is great for discussions about a stock before it's purchase. Even the vote for or against purchasing a stock can be conducted online!

If your club has someone with the appropriate talents, you can even set up a Web page where club documents can be archived and updates posted. Although a club Web page is not essential, it can be a useful tool, especially when club members want quick answers to questions and all the information they need is up on the club's site. If you want to post your club's portfolio or valuation statements but club members are worried about privacy, just set up a password so that only club members can reach the site.

Another useful tool is a chat room, or a place that club members can gather online for meetings in real time. This is useful when your club members all are awake during the same hours of the day. Yahoo! Clubs offers free chat areas that can be restricted only to club members (http://clubs.yahoo.com). Some online clubs use special software to connect to IRC (Internet Relay Chat) forums online. (Go to www.irchelp.org and www.mirc.com for more detailed explanations of IRC.) If the logistics of finding and using chat rooms becomes overwhelming to your club, you'll be relieved to know that although they can certainly add a great deal to your club's interactions, they're in no way a necessity.

Setting up a club site at Yahoo! Groups enables your club to communicate via a message board if you want. Message boards, like e-mail lists, offer members a chance to send (or post) messages in a way that everyone else in the club can easily access them. Again, a message board can be a wonderful aid to communication but is by no means essential.

An online club can accomplish everything necessary for its operations with only an e-mail list. You should, however, explore all your interaction options to find out what best meets your club's needs, bearing in mind that the Internet is constantly evolving. So, keep your ears open for news about new technology or resources to aid your online club.

When your online club drafts its operating agreement and bylaws, be sure to include all the details that are unique to the structure of your online club. Set in writing your meeting time and location, specifics about club communications such as e-mail lists, attendance and participation requirements, and anything else that may differ from how a traditional face-to-face club operates. In addition to establishing these guidelines in writing, going through the bylaws carefully help you think through all the logistics of your online club.

One area that can prove to be more work in an online club than it is in a face-to-face club is fostering interpersonal interactions between club members.

Trust is an important issue in a club where it's possible that none of the members have ever met "in real life." Misinterpreting someone's comments in an e-mail or a chat room can be easy when you're not as familiar with their personality. Take things slow and get to know each other well.

If you form an online club with people you've never met, the possibility exists that you may *never* meet them in person. But you can still develop friendships and have a lot of fun learning and socializing together, even from afar. You'll definitely want to write and share biographies when you start the club. You can even exchange pictures online so that you have a face to go with the personalities you'll be getting to know so well. You may find opportunities to conduct a "reunion" of sorts at some point, and meet some old friends for the first time!

Because getting to know and trust people online can take awhile, online clubs can be the perfect place to use the nonpooled assets or Self-Directed Investment (SDI) approach where members choose stocks together but then invest in their own individual accounts. You can find out more about the SDI structure in Chapter 4.

If your online club chooses to use the traditional pooled assets approach, we highly recommend purchasing NAIC's Fidelity Bond to protect your club's investments from an unlikely yet possible instance of treasurer fraud. Like any dealings online, club members need to take the necessary precautions to ensure privacy and security. We're certainly not suggesting that you can't trust people you meet online, just that you shouldn't put blind faith in anyone you've just met or barely know. You wouldn't do it in a face-to-face club, so don't be lulled into a false sense of safety online.

Conducting meetings online

The first thing that your online club must decide is whether you even want to conduct actual meetings. Some clubs meet at a specific time every month using Internet chat rooms. Others, on the other hand, just have continuous conversations via e-mail or message boards. If your club members are scattered across various time zones, arranging a time when everyone can congregate in a chat room can be difficult. Your online club can be successful with or without meetings, so choose whatever choice is best for your members.

If you conduct meetings, remember that following a solid meeting agenda is just as important for online clubs as it is for face-to-face clubs. You need to establish formalities for deciding who speaks when and develop strategies for delivering the education program lessons. Setting a strict ending time for the meeting is a necessity, too, but be sure to let people know they're welcome to stay and chat after the meeting is adjourned. Just like in a traditional club, the better you all get to know each other, the more smoothly your online club operates.

You don't need to accomplish all your club business during the meeting. You can do preliminary work ahead of time, like screening stock presentations and bringing only the best to the meeting for a vote. By taking advantage of your e-mail discussions, you can bring only the most important business to your actual meeting. You'll probably find that you can accomplish almost everything outside the meeting and save your limited real-time interactions for those agenda items that benefit most from chat-room discussion. No matter what you discuss, remember to have someone keep detailed minutes or log a chat transcript for later distribution.

Helping Kids to Start an Investment Club

One of the more important things we investors can do is pass on our knowledge and enthusiasm for investing to the younger generation. A great way to do this, if you can, is to help children (your own, or someone else's, it doesn't matter) learn to invest through a youth investment club. In addition to the regular club education topics, youth clubs should also cover some basics of money management and responsibility. Lessons need to be simple and aimed toward the young investors' age and interest levels. Be sure to take advantage of stock selection software and the wide variety of online resources that are available to clubs.

One easy way to involve children in a club is by starting a family investment club and letting youth invest right alongside you. You also can help start clubs at school, in Scout or 4-H groups, or through other social organizations. NAIC has some wonderful resources for youth clubs, including a textbook called *Investing in Your Future,* which explains all the basics of money management and stock selection. NAIC's youth investing Web page is worth exploring at:

`http://www.better-investing.org/youth/youth.html`

Because children younger than 18 are not allowed to invest on their own, parents must set up custodial accounts for them. Because of the complexity of club accounting for youth clubs, where member turnover inevitably will be high as children move or change schools or simply grow up, choosing a Self-Directed Investment (SDI) structure probably is best. The benefits and details of setting up an SDI structure are covered in Chapter 4.

Chapter 6

Taking Care of the Legal Stuff

· ·

In This Chapter

▶ Choosing the right legal entity for your club

▶ Creating operating procedures to keep it running smoothly

▶ Establishing your club's investing philosophy

· ·

*W*hile it may not rank up there with bungee jumping or rock climbing, starting an investment club can be plenty of fun and exciting, too. As you recruit potential members, arrange your first few meetings, and start thinking about all the money that you're hoping to make in the stock market, who wouldn't be excited?

But when the time arrives for you to make it all official, things aren't quite as fun anymore. You and your soon-to-be fellow club members have a zillion questions. How do you make your club legal? What kind of paperwork does your new club have to file with local authorities? What kind of documentation is needed to provide to open an account at a brokerage firm?

Take a deep, cleansing breath and relax. Starting an investment club is not really that complicated, provided that you follow the guidelines we set out for you in this chapter. We call this the "legal stuff" for two reasons. First, you don't want your club to violate any local, state, or federal laws. Fines or other penalties can be leveled against you for failing to comply with any applicable regulations. Second, you don't want your club members to break any of the rules that you've worked so hard to create for your club. Making everything legal is where you start.

Step One: Making the Club Official

One of the first decisions that your club has to make is which legal entity you'll adopt for your club. Just like a business, your club must make itself official to begin operations. In fact, in the eyes local, state, and federal authorities, not that much differentiates an investment club from a beauty salon, construction company or bakery. Of course, in your club you'll be dealing with stock splits, not split ends; building a portfolio, not houses; and looking for hot buys, not hot buns.

Business entity is the term that's used to describe the various forms under which any individual or group of individuals can set up shop. Investment clubs generally organize as one of the following six common business entities:

- ✔ General Partnership
- ✔ Limited Partnership
- ✔ Limited Liability Partnership
- ✔ Limited Liability Corporation
- ✔ Corporation
- ✔ Voluntary Cooperative Association

No matter which entity you choose you'll probably be required to inform certain local and/or state agencies about the formation of your club. That means filing some paperwork and paying a fee of anywhere from $10 to $400, depending on the entity you choose. Laws vary widely among localities and states, so it's hard for us to provide specific instructions for your own area. Your local chapter of the National Association of Investors Corporation (NAIC) can provide that information for you. Find your closest chapter on the NAIC Web Site, www.better-investing.org. Find contact information for state regulatory agencies at www.douglasgerlach.com/clubsfordummies.

Each type of entity has advantages and disadvantages, but your choice probably won't be too difficult to make once you understand the differences between them.

General partnership

Most investment clubs form as general partnerships. In fact, NAIC recommends the partnership format as the easiest and least expensive way to form your club. No limitations apply to the number of members who can be a part of a partnership, and you generally don't need an attorney's services to create a partnership agreement for your club. NAIC provides a sample partnership agreement that you can adopt for your club. If your state or county requires general partnerships to file their agreements (not all states or local governments do), then you may have to pay a $25 or $50 fee, and perhaps even an annual renewal fee.

Besides the low start-up and operation costs and the simplicity of a partnership, this business entity has tax benefits, too. A partnership doesn't have to pay any taxes itself, but that doesn't mean that club members escape taxes. Any taxes that are due on the club's income or gains pass through the partnership to the individual partners, and then are recorded on the partners' own tax returns. The partnership must file an informational return each year with the IRS but won't have to pay any additional taxes itself.

The biggest problem with a general partnership is that you and your fellow members, the *general partners,* become legally joined at the hip. One member's actions can potentially bind the entire partnership to some financial transaction that may cost everyone vast sums of money. According to NAIC, however, no known cases of that happening have been recorded, and their suggested partnership agreement clearly delineates allowable and forbidden actions of partners. In the past 50 years, tens of thousands of investment clubs have formed as partnerships with no such liability problem, so it's a natural choice for most new clubs.

In many states, general partnerships don't have to register with the secretary of state or division of corporations. If yours requires it, you'll have to make an initial filing by completing a form and making a payment. You may have to renew your registration each year, as well.

If you start an online club with members from many states, or if you live near a state's border and your club has members in two states, you'll probably be able to choose which state to call home. Take the time to research the filing requirements and costs in any state in which your club can register and then make the decision. Be extra careful to determine whether you may be required to register your general partnership or make annual tax filings in *any of the states* in which your partners reside — regardless of whether that's the state in which your club officially operates. New York and Missouri now have such regulations in place. If that's the case and you have a choice between registering in more than one state, you may want to consider making the state with the more restrictive filing requirements your official home. That way, you'll only have to file one return, not two.

Regardless of whether you must register your partnership with the state, you'll almost certainly be required to make a *fictitious name filing* with the office of your county clerk. Sometimes known as a *dba certificate* (for *doing business as*) or an *assumed name certificate,* this registration is designed to protect the citizenry from people running an unscrupulous business under a fake name. With this system, anyone can make a quick trip to the county clerk's office to uncover the fact that Joe's Bar and Grill isn't actually owned by Joe but by Bob. Counties typically charge $10 to $20 as a one-time filing fee, payable at the county clerk's office when you submit your completed forms.

Limited partnership

Limited partners have no say in the operation of the partnership — the entity's general partners make all the decisions for the business. The limited partners only provide investment capital. You may have heard horror stories about investors who lost bundles investing in limited partnerships in the 1980s.

For most clubs, the limited partnership structure is inappropriate, because all the members of your club need to be involved in the club's decisions.

The only exception is if your club is well established, well funded, and wants to enable its members to invest in individual retirement accounts within the club. Because of the laws that govern IRA accounts, a qualified custodian (such as a bank or brokerage firm) must be a member of your club to oversee those accounts. Within a club structure, you accomplish this by forming your club as a limited partnership. You and your club members are the general partners, and a willing bank is a limited partner, serving as the IRA trustee. You may find it difficult to find a bank that's willing to serve your club in that capacity; if so, contact NAIC and it can refer you to a bank that's more familiar with these types of arrangements.

A limited partnership also is created by means of a partnership agreement similar to NAIC's recommended general partnership agreement; however, it also includes provisions for limited partners who are to serve as trustees of IRA accounts. NAIC can provide you with a sample limited partnership agreement to use.

Limited liability partnership

In the past few years, nearly all states have passed laws allowing the formation of two kinds of businesses, the limited liability partnership (LLP), and the limited liability corporation (LLC). Although these two forms are quite similar and share many of the same tax and liability advantages, there are some differences.

An LLP is similar to a general partnership, with the main advantage being that an LLP limits its members' potential liability, except in the case of "gross or willful misconduct." In some states, liability for debts incurred by the entity may not only be limited. Nay, it may be eliminated entirely. Remember how members of a general partnership are theoretically liable for the actions of other members? The LLP is designed to eliminate that concern.

As is true of a partnership, an LLP helps its members avoid the double taxation problem faced by corporations. Tax liabilities pass through to the LLP members, and the LLC must file an informational tax return with the IRS each year, just like a partnership.

Still with us? Whew. We hate to torture you with this amount of detail, but because it's rather important, we will. Take another one of those deep cleansing breaths and stick with us to the bitter end.

The downside of forming as an LLP is that it can be expensive to establish. You'll probably pay the state an initial registration fee of between $200 and $300, and you'll likely need an attorney to help you draw up your *articles of organization* (sometimes known as *articles of formation*) and your operating agreement. Although your attorney can probably create your paperwork for less than $500, the filing and legal fees may total up to nearly $1,000, which makes a significant dent in your start-up kitty. Similarly, renewal fees may eat up another $200 or $300 each year after that.

Some states may limit the number of members in an LLP to a certain maximum, typically between 35 and 75. And some states, like California, restrict the LLP membership to professionals like attorneys and accountants, so adopting the LLP entity may not hold potential for your club. In that case, investigate the limited liability corporation as an alternative.

Limited liability corporation

The limited liability corporation shares most of the same advantages and disadvantages of the LLP when compared with the general partnership. LLCs are more expensive and complicated to start and maintain than partnerships, and LLCs with two or more members are presumed to be partnerships, not corporations, for tax purposes.

If your state doesn't allow you to form a LLP, then you may want to consider an LLC. If you have a choice between an LLP and LLC, make sure you determine whether your state offers LLP members *full-shield* or *partial-shield* protection from personal liability. In some states, members of LLPs still may have some liability for debts incurred by the entities (partial-shield protection); in others, members have no such liability (full-shield protection). If you live in a state that offers only partial-shield protection for LLPs, then the LLC is preferable.

Corporation

Although the prospect of having an "Inc." at the end of your club name may make your group sound official, choosing that route probably isn't the best choice for most clubs.

Corporations come in a couple of flavors, more common are the *C Corporation* and the *S Corporation,* which take their names come from definitions in Subchapters C and S of the Internal Revenue Code.

In a C Corporation, the legal entity is separate and distinct from members (the owners) of the corporation. The main advantages of C Corporations are that they protect the liability of individual shareholders and they can have an unlimited number of members. However, the corporation is liable for paying taxes on its own share of gains and income. Each year, a corporation files its own tax returns and pays its own taxes. Any of the corporation's income that is paid out to its shareowners must be reported as taxable income on their personal tax returns. In effect, that means the owners of a C Corporation are taxed twice on the same earnings.

Besides double taxation, C Corporations are expensive to set up and usually must pay annual registration fees of between $100 and $300 to the state. You may also need an attorney to help draft the appropriate paperwork and incorporation documents.

Using an incorporation service is an alternative to retaining an attorney that helps you establish a corporation at a cut-rate cost by providing all the documents and instructions you need to complete them in each state. Two such services on the Internet help you set up either a corporation or an LLC: www.mycorporation.com or www.corporate.com. Be forewarned, however, that the unique nature of an investment club may present complications that don't fit the boilerplate documents offered by these companies.

Because of these complications, clubs rarely choose to form as a C Corporation. On the other hand, forming as an S Corporation may be a reasonable choice for some clubs. S Corporations also are expensive and complicated to organize, but they allow income and losses to pass through to the individual owners, avoiding the double-taxation of C Corporations. Only U.S. citizens or residents can be members of S Corporations, and most states permit no more than 75 shareholders — which shouldn't be a problem for most clubs.

As with C Corporations, consulting an attorney for assistance is probably best when creating an S Corporation. However, for the most part, an LLP offers the same advantages as an S Corporation, so make sure that you thoroughly explore the LLP before deciding to incorporate. In either case, if you form your club as a corporation, your operating procedures are laid out in your articles of incorporation.

Cut to the chase: Become a general partnership

For most new clubs, the decision about which entity to choose comes down to picking either a general partnership or a limited liability partnership. The liability issues that arise with a general partnership concern some people, while the start-up costs of an LLP/LLC worry others. One pragmatic way to approach the dilemma: In most states, converting an existing partnership to a limited liability partnership or corporation is easy.

So start your club as a general partnership, and make plans to reconsider at some point down the road the issue of continuing as a partnership or converting to an LLP/LLC. You may consider writing a provision into your bylaws to annually reconsider converting to a LLP or LLC, or to trigger reconsideration when your club assets reach a certain dollar amount. That way, when your club is just getting started, you won't be whacked with a thousand dollars of start-up costs, digging you into a hole that may take years for your club to climb out of. Once your club is more established and has more assets, you'll have more at stake, and swallowing the steep expense of registering as a limited liability entity will be easier.

Don't pretend you're a nonprofit organization

Let's get one thing straight! Your club must definitely subscribe to the profit motive. Sure, you're not a *business* in the traditional sense of the word, but you're also not a nonprofit organization as the IRS sees it. Some clubs try to qualify for special rates or fee waivers at local banks, or request free meeting space at their public library, on the basis of being a *nonprofit* or community group. Although taking advantage of any perks or discounts you can negotiate for your club is fine, taking advantage of privileges reserved for truly charitable and educational groups isn't. The IRS recognizes partnerships as being tax-exempt entities (because the partnership itself doesn't actually pay taxes), but your club has no legal basis on which to claim that it's a charitable organization.

Voluntary cooperative association

Finally, one last, somewhat obscure entity under which a club can form is the voluntary cooperative association. It often is employed by organizations that band together to acquire and distribute certain products or services, such as energy, food, or housing, to the group's members. Many of the country's rural telephone and utility companies started out as cooperative associations — groups of farmers who banded together to form small independent companies to oversee the delivery of electricity or phone services to their homes.

Cooperative associations are not usually intended to generate profits for the association itself. Members pay dues that cover the operations of the cooperative and the services that they receive, usually at a discounted rate, and profits generally have to be distributed back to the membership.

For tax purposes, the Internal Revenue Service normally considers a cooperative association as subject to the same filing requirements as a general partnership as long as the association's operating procedures resemble a partnership. For instance, a club that makes all its business and investing decisions as a group, as is true of a general partnership, would likely be considered a partnership by the IRS. All tax liability, therefore, flows through the association to its individual members. If the club authorized a board of directors to act on its behalf, then the IRS may consider the cooperative association to be more like a corporation and taxable on its own.

If you form a voluntary cooperative association, your operating procedures are outlined in your *articles of association,* the formal document that describes how your club is organized.

Some states require cooperative associations to have a minimum number of members, such as five or more. If your club is smaller than that, you won't be able to use this entity in those states.

The National Cooperative Business Association (www.cooperative.org) sells manuals, forms, and other materials related to cooperative associations. The NCBA doesn't have materials relating specifically to investment clubs, but if you'd like to explore the option of forming your club as a cooperative association, it can provide a framework for your articles of association.

For more details about on the more common business entities, the Small Business Guide on *Business Week* magazine's Web site includes a great deal of helpful legal information (businessweek.findlaw.com/book/).

Creating Rules and Procedures

Like your school principal explained to you once upon a time, rules are meant to protect you, not to put a damper on your fun. Your club needs rules, too — not to curtail the thrills of investment clubbing but to prevent misunderstandings and make sure that all members are held to the same standard. Your club's rules ensure that all situations are handled in a consistent and fair manner.

The main mechanisms for setting your club's rules and guidelines depend on the business entity you choose for your club. If you form as a partnership, then the partnership agreement lays out your operating procedures in general terms. If you form as an LLP or LLC, then the operating agreement serves the same purpose.

Besides your partnership agreement, your club must also draft bylaws. Your partnership agreement needs to be general in scope, because you don't want to deal with the hassle of creating a new partnership agreement every time you change a minor detail about the way your club works. That's where your club bylaws come in.

Bylaws supplement the partnership agreement by providing specific details about your club's operations. For instance, your agreement may stipulate that "Periodic meetings shall be conducted as determined by the partnership." Your bylaws specify: "Meetings are to be conducted on the third Monday of each month at 7 p.m." Now, if you want to change your meetings to the second Thursday because a club member now has a bowling league on Mondays, you don't have to execute a new partnership agreement — just amend the bylaws.

In practice, the decisions you make at your monthly meetings determine how your club runs. The only thing you can't decide as a group is to contradict any point made in your partnership agreement. You can clarify or specify points made in your agreement, but you can't go against the grain of the procedures included in that document. So laying down the rules so that everyone understands how the club works is important. And the bylaws are the rulebook of your club. Every few years, you may decide to revise your partnership agreement, and that's your opportunity to make more permanent changes.

But what exactly must your agreement and bylaws cover? How detailed do you need to be? When you're starting a club for the first time, predicting all the possible problems that might arise in your club's lifetime is difficult, and that makes knowing what rules to include tough, too. But without firm rules, you're looking for trouble whenever a problem springs up. That's why covering all the bases is so important.

During your club's first organizational meetings, you'll need to create your own documents. Some fledgling clubs appoint committees to make recommendations to the entire group; other clubs talk through the proposals point by point, soliciting input from every member.

Your club's agreement and bylaws are yours to make — you and your club members set the policies and procedures. Don't go overboard with crazy rules governing what types of snacks are allowed or what color socks members are required to wear, yet be sure to include as many specifics as necessary to tailor the documents to your club's particular needs.

Drafting your club's partnership agreement

Ready for some fun, finally? Well, at least it's more fun than that discussion of legal entities. Now you can get down to the business of drafting your partnership agreement. NAIC's sample agreement is the actual document created by one of the oldest investment clubs in the U.S., the Mutual Investment Club of Detroit. In the 1940s, the founders of the Mutual Investment Club didn't have the benefit of NAIC's guidance (or this book) when they started their club. In fact, a number of the Mutual club members went on to found NAIC in 1951 to put their experiences to use helping other people start their own investment clubs.

But they were flying blind in 1940, so they had to put a lot of research into creating their partnership agreement. They apparently received some good legal advice at the time — the partnership agreement has remained relatively intact since then and has served as a model for tens of thousands of investment clubs through the decades. You can download a copy of the Partnership Agreement from NAIC's Web site (www.better-investing.org).

When you begin to draft the partnership agreement, an easy working method is to download the NAIC model to your computer screen (better-investing. org, then select "Site Search" and type in "general partnership agreement"). That way you can edit the language on screen to suit your needs. As a guide, we break down the Detroit agreement in the next section by interspersing our comments and suggestions.

Partnership Agreement of the
Mutual Investment Club of Detroit

THIS AGREEMENT OF PARTNERSHIP, effective as of (date) by and between the undersigned, to wit: {names of partners}

NOW, THEREFORE IT IS AGREED:

1. Formation. The undersigned hereby form a General Partnership in accordance with and subject to the laws of the State of Michigan.

2. Name. The name of the partnership shall be Mutual Investment Club of Detroit.

3. Term. The partnership shall begin on (date) and shall continue until December 31 of the same year and thereafter from year to year unless earlier terminated as hereinafter provided.

4. Purpose. The only purpose of the partnership is to invest the assets of the partnership solely in stocks, bonds, and other securities ("securities") for the education and benefit of the partners.

5. Meetings. Periodic meetings shall be held as determined by the partnership.

Paragraphs 1–5. These paragraphs are pretty self-explanatory. State your new club's name, and that you're forming a general partnership in your state on the date of the agreement. You'll also state that the purpose of your club is to invest in securities, and that you'll be conducting regular meetings.

6. Capital Contributions. The partners may make capital contributions to the partnership on the date of each periodic meeting in such amounts as the partnership shall determine; provided, however, that no partner's capital account shall exceed twenty percent (20%) of the capital accounts of all partners.

Paragraph 6. You and your club members will make regular payments to the club known as *capital contributions*. The agreement states that members must make these regular contributions on the date of each meeting, but it doesn't state the amount (that will be covered in the bylaws). Most clubs also limit the amount that any one member can contribute to the club to minimize the influence of a single member when a weighted vote (a vote counted according to the percentage of the club owned by each member) is taken. The limit also protects the club from a majority-owning member withdrawing from the club, forcing a large portion of the portfolio to be sold or transferred. Clubs typically limit a single member to 15 or 20 percent ownership.

It's important to note that this agreement allows members to contribute varying amounts to the club. Many new clubs get hung up on the idea that each member must kick in exactly the same amount to the club. On the surface, it seems like an easy way to keep everyone equitable and to make recordkeeping easier. However, it actually creates more problems and accounting complications down the road. (We talk more about the equal ownership conundrum in Chapter 7.) For now, avoid requiring equal contributions. Set your maximum ownership here in the agreement and let each member decide how much to contribute above the minimum amount that you'll set in your bylaws.

> 7. Value of the Partnership. The current value of the assets of the partnership, less the current value of the liabilities of the partnership, (hereinafter referred to as the "value of the partnership") shall be determined as of a regularly scheduled date and time ("valuation date") preceding the date of each periodic meeting determined by the Club.

Paragraph 7. Each club member needs regular updates on the club performance and how much their accounts are worth. This paragraph simply states that the club has a set schedule for presenting valuations to its members. In your bylaws, you'll specify exactly when the valuation reports will be created and distributed.

> 8. Capital Accounts. A capital account shall be maintained in the name of each partner. Any increase or decrease in the value of the partnership on any valuation date shall be credited or debited, respectively, to each partner's capital account on that date. Any other method of valuing each partner's capital account may be substituted for this method, provided the substituted method results in exactly the same valuation as previously provided herein. Each partner's contribution to, or capital withdrawal from, the partnership shall be credited, or debited, respectively, to that partner's capital account.

Paragraph 8. Hey, here's a simple one! As each member of your club makes *capital contributions,* his *capital account* will be credited. As a member withdraws funds from the club, his capital account is debited.

> 9. Management. Each partner shall participate in the management and conduct of the affairs of the partnership in proportion to his capital account. Except as otherwise determined, all decisions shall be made by the partners whose capital accounts total a majority of the value of the capital accounts of all the partners.

Paragraph 9. Vote tabulation ranks right up there with the equal ownership issue as one of the more contentious issues for new clubs. Although you won't have to worry about hanging chads or Supreme Court rulings when your club holds a vote, you'll need to decide which of the two opposing schools of thought your club will choose regarding voting methods.

The first is *one person, one vote,* by which each club member has an equal say in the club, no matter how big (or little) that member's piece of the club portfolio is. This is democracy in action, say its proponents, where the richest and the poorest have equal rights and opportunities.

The second voting method is *by ownership percentage,* in which each member votes the number of shares he or she owns in the club. This is how corporations cast votes — each shareholder in a public company has a vote equal to the number of shares he or she owns. Votes by this method give members of the club who own a greater number of shares a larger voice in the club's decisions. That's one reason clubs often restrict the amount that any individual can invest in the club — so that no one member can exert too much control of the club's decisions.

Sure, when you're tallying votes at a meeting, counting hands raised in the air rather than adding up every member's percentage of the vote is easier. But when you simply give each person an equal say in the club's operations, you're shortchanging those members who have more invested in the club. Long-time members who have significant assets invested in the club may not enjoy giving up control of the club's portfolio to upstart new recruits who have little at risk. Most veteran club members would balk at joining a club that didn't employ weighted voting as described in Paragraph 9. Your bylaws may include other specific voting methods. It's also possible to switch between the methods in certain circumstances

> 10. Sharing of Profits and Losses. Net profits and losses of the partnership shall inure to, and be borne by, the partners, in proportion to the value of each of their capital accounts.

Paragraph 10. Your club will have profits, and it will have losses. Paragraph 10 acknowledges that gains and losses will be shared by all members in proportion to their capital accounts. According to NAIC, the IRS frowns on any other methods of spreading profits and losses within the club.

> 11. Books of Account. Books of account of the transactions of the partnership shall be kept and at all times be available and open to inspection and examination by any partner.

> 12. Annual Accounting. Each calendar year, a full and complete account of the condition of the partnership shall be made to the partners.

Paragraphs 11 and 12. Your club must keep records of all its transactions and prepare an annual accounting for all members. We cover accounting in great detail in Chapters 7 and 10.

13. Bank Account. The partnership may select a bank for the purpose of opening a bank account. Funds in the bank account shall be withdrawn by checks signed by any partner designated by the partnership.

14. Broker Account. None of the partners of this partnership shall be a broker. However, the partnership may select a broker and enter into such agreements with the broker as required for the purchase or sale of securities. Securities owned by the partnership shall be registered in the partnership name unless another name shall be designated by the partnership.

Any corporation or transfer agent called upon to transfer any securities to or from the name of the partnership shall be entitled to rely on instructions or assignments signed by any partner without inquiry as to the authority of the person(s) signing such instructions or assignments, or as to the validity of any transfer to or from the name of the partnership.

At the time of a transfer of securities, the corporation or transfer agent is entitled to assume (1) that the partnership is still in existence and (2) that this Agreement is in full force and effect and has not been amended unless the corporation has received written notice to the contrary.

Paragraphs 13 and 14. Your club definitely needs a brokerage account and you may or may not need a bank account (many brokerage firms will accept checks from your individual partners and enable you to write club checks from the club's money market account, meaning you can skip the bank account completely). These paragraphs enable your club to open accounts at firms that you select. The sample agreement also prohibits any broker from being a member of your club, a provision that the Mutual club later dropped from its own documents.

Because the securities industry is regulated, some complications arise from having a broker or anyone employed at a financial services company as a member of your partnership, but they're not insurmountable. You'll have to let your own brokerage firm know that you have a partner who works in the industry, for instance, and the broker-member may have to keep his employer notified of purchases made in the club.

But more important, will having a broker as a member of your club affect your club's education efforts? Will members defer to the broker-member when making decisions, perceiving him or her as having superior insight because of his or her job in the industry (which may or may not be the case)? If your club is made up of beginners, adding a broker-member to the mix may get in the way of each member learning to make sensible investing decisions.

Additionally, Paragraph 14 allows brokerage firms to accept the authority of any member of your club that you designate. Your bylaws will detail exactly who that will be (usually it's the Treasurer).

> 15. No Compensation. No partner shall be compensated for services rendered to the partnership, except reimbursement for expenses.

Paragraph 15. No member of your club should be paid for rendering any services on the club's behalf. Some investment clubs appoint a member who functions as the investment manager for the club, paid by the club with either a fee or by an additional share of profits. This practice defeats the point of being in an investment club, where each member participates in the decision-making process and becomes educated about investing as a result. Other legal issues may be involved with a member who is paid to serve as an investment manager, so run, don't walk, from any club that uses this structure.

> 16. Additional Partners. Additional partners may be admitted at any time, upon the unanimous consent of the partners, so long as the number of partners does not exceed twenty five (25).

> 16A. Transfers to a Trust. A partner may, after giving written notice to the other partners, transfer his interest in the partnership to a revocable living trust of which he is the grantor and sole trustee.

> 16B. Removal of a Partner. Any partner may be removed by agreement of the partners whose capital accounts total a majority of the value of all partners' capital accounts. Written notice of a meeting where removal of a partner is to be considered shall include a specific reference to this matter. The removal shall become effective upon payment of the value of the removed partner's capital account, which shall be in accordance with the provisions on full withdrawal of a partner noted in paragraphs 18 and 20. The vote action shall be treated as receipt of request for withdrawal.

Paragraph 16. New members can reinvigorate your club, bringing fresh perspectives to club meetings and providing eager hands to complete club tasks. You'll want to allow new members to join, but you'll also want to limit the total number of members in your club.

So how many members does a good club make? The answer depends on how much each member is willing to commit to making the club successful, but not on the number of people who belong. A successful club may have two members, or ten members, or even 100 members. On the other hand, some clubs may think that four members are too few, or that 50 are too many.

Your partnership agreement is where you'll specify the maximum number of members who may belong to your club. You'll have to figure out what number makes the most sense for your club so that you can balance the workload and still have productive meetings. Between 12 and 15 active members is an optimal number.

Does that mean you need to cap your club membership at 15? Not necessarily. What happens if potential member 16 comes along and wows you with her interest in and knowledge of the market? If your agreement stipulates that you have no more than 15 members, then you'll have to politely tell the candidate that you have no room right now to accept new members. Many clubs maintain a waiting list of people who are interested in joining if a spot becomes available.

If you decide that 15 is an ideal number of members, then maybe you'll have your partnership agreement stipulate that you can have as many as 20 members. That gives you a bit of a fudge factor, so that you can reduce the risk of being forced to reject a new member you may otherwise want to welcome into the family. At the same time, you and your members may have an understanding that your goal is to have no more than 15, even if you are allowed to have 20.

Another case in which you may want to allow for more members is if some members of your club aren't quite as active in club business because of some circumstance. If many members of your club frequently travel on business, for example, or have unpredictable work schedules, like doctors who must be on call, those members may not be able to attend every club meeting. Your club members may feel somewhat short-handed with only nine or ten members present at any particular meeting, so you can allow for some extra members, knowing that you won't likely be overwhelmed by having too many people at a meeting.

One legal consideration affects the size of an investment club. According to the Securities and Exchange Commission, an investment club must register with the commission as an *investment company* if it makes or proposes to make a public offering of its securities, and has more than 100 members. The commission further explains that an announcement that a club is looking for new members may be construed as a "public offering of a security." If your club membership remains fewer than 100, then you'll have nothing to worry about.

Obviously, a number of differences exist between how a club of 80 members operates and how a 15-member club works. For instance, a large club probably can't meet in your living room (unless you've got a house the size of Bill Gates' palatial residence!) and discussions about stock purchases can turn chaotic if every member wants to have his or her say.

On the other hand, a small club may find it has too much work and not enough people to do it, so don't set your maximum membership limit too low, either. Remember, you and your members always have the chance to vote on new candidates, so you can decline to admit a new member even if your agreement allows it. Your bylaws will contain more information about the process a new member must follow to join the club.

Paragraph 16A. For members who want to use a living revocable trust as part of their estate planning tools, transferring their investment club account to a trust can be advantageous. This paragraph enables such transfers. No disadvantage results from permitting these transfers, so even if your members are young and not yet thinking about trusts and estate planning, you can keep this provision with no downside.

Paragraph 16B. Unfortunately, your club may someday be in a situation in which you may want to invite a member to leave your club. Your agreement needs to establish that your partnership has the authority to remove members. Your bylaws can then provide for the specific reasons why a member may be removed.

17. Termination of Partnership. The partnership may be terminated by agreement of the partners whose capital accounts total a majority in value of the capital accounts of all the partners. Written notice of a meeting where termination of the partnership is to be considered shall include a specific reference to this matter. The partnership shall terminate upon a majority vote of all partners' capital accounts. Written notice of the decision to terminate the partnership shall be given to all the partners. Payment shall then be made of all the liabilities of the partnership and a final distribution of the remaining assets either in cash or in kind, shall promptly be made to the partners or their personal representatives in proportion to each partner's capital account.

Paragraph 17. While some clubs carry on for decades, others end their operations a bit sooner than that. What are the procedures for terminating your partnership? Is a simple majority vote enough to end your club? Identify those points here.

18. Voluntary Withdrawal (Partial or Full) of a Partner. Any partner may withdraw a part or all of the value of his capital account in the partnership and the partnership shall continue as a taxable entity. The partner withdrawing a part or all of the value of his capital account shall give notice of such intention in writing to the Secretary. Written notice shall be deemed to be received as of the first meeting of the partnership at which it is presented. If written notice is received between meetings it will be treated as received at the first following meeting.

In making payment, the value of the partnership as set forth in the valuation statement prepared for the first meeting following the meeting at which notice is received from a partner requesting a partial or full withdrawal, will be used to determine the value of the partner's account.

The partnership shall pay the partner who is withdrawing a portion or all of the value of his capital account in the partnership in accordance with paragraph 20 of this Agreement.

Paragraph 18. Eventually, members of your club will choose to leave your club, or desire to withdraw a portion of the funds in their capital accounts. Either way, you'll want to make sure that you clearly lay out the terms of full and partial member withdrawals. A club member should be able to leave the club at any point, but your agreement needs to outline the terms of that departure — how a member announces his intention to withdraw, the valuation date that's used to determine the member's ending balance, and so on.

19. Death or Incapacity of a Partner. In the event of the death or incapacity of a partner (or the death or incapacity of the grantor and sole trustee of a revocable living trust, if such trust is partner pursuant to Paragraph 16A hereof), receipt of notice shall be treated as a notice of full withdrawal.

Paragraph 19. In the event of the death of a member, your club should immediately take action as if the member had requested a full withdrawal.

20. Terms of Payment. In the case of a partial withdrawal, payment may be made in cash or securities of the partnership or a mix of each at the option of the partner making the partial withdrawal. In the case of a full withdrawal, payment may be made in cash or securities or a mix of each at the option of the remaining partners. In either case, where securities are to be distributed, the remaining partners select the securities.

Where cash is transferred, the partnership shall transfer to the partner (or other appropriate entity) withdrawing a portion or all of his interest in the partnership, an amount equal to the lesser of (i) ninety-seven percent (97%) of the value of the capital account being withdrawn, or (ii) the value of the capital account being withdrawn, less the actual cost to the partnership of selling securities to obtain cash to meet the withdrawal. The amount being withdrawn shall be paid within 10 days after the valuation date used in determining the withdrawal amount.

If the partner withdrawing a portion or all of the value of his capital account in the partnership desires an immediate payment in cash, the partnership at its earliest convenience may pay eighty percent (80%) of the estimated value of his capital account and settle the balance in accordance with the valuation and payment procedures set forth in paragraphs 18 and 20.

Where securities are transferred, the partnership shall select securities to transfer equal to the value of the capital account or a portion of the capital account being withdrawn (i.e., without a reduction for broker commissions). Securities shall be transferred as of the date of the club's valuation statement prepared to determine the value of that partner's capital account in the partnership. The Club's broker shall be advised that ownership of the securities has been transferred to the partner as of the valuation date used for the withdrawal.

Paragraph 20. Members making full or partial withdrawals must be paid, and your agreement must outline the terms upon which your club writes a check or transfers shares to settle the withdrawal. In addition, your club may want to charge the withdrawing member a fee to cover brokerage commissions and other costs. NAIC's sample agreement enables the club to charge a withdrawal fee of 3 percent or the actual costs, whichever is greater. With today's discount brokerage commissions at an all-time low, your costs may be much less than 3 percent. You may still want to keep that fee in place for one good reason — to make members think twice about withdrawing funds from the club on a regular basis. If your club starts to function like a bank account for your club members, where they make frequent deposits and withdrawals, your treasurer will quickly become overwhelmed, and you'll be robbing your club of the working capital it needs to invest.

Some clubs impose steep penalties on withdrawing members in an attempt to stifle departures. This is a pretty unfair practice, because members have plenty of legitimate and unavoidable reasons why they may have to withdraw from the club. A member may be transferred to a new city, for instance, or simply become financially strapped and need to tap into his or her club account. Or a member may simply lose interest in the club and become inactive. Either way, these members are almost certainly going to go away at some point in the future, so it's in the club's best long-term interest to allow such members to withdraw sooner rather than later, and a stiff penalty only delays the inevitable. Better to be reasonable and make the departing member responsible for paying any actual costs related to the withdrawal, such as brokerage commissions.

21. Forbidden Acts. No partner shall:

a. Have the right or authority to bind or obligate the partnership to any extent whatsoever with regard to any matter outside the scope of the partnership purpose.

b. Except as provided in paragraph 16A, without the unanimous consent of all the other partners, assign, transfer, pledge, mortgage or sell all or part of his interest in the partnership to any other partner or other person whomsoever, or enter into any agreement as the result of which any person or persons not a partner shall become interested with him in the partnership.

c. Purchase an investment for the partnership where less than the full purchase price is paid for same.

d. Use the partnership name, credit, or property for other than partnership purposes.

e. Do any act detrimental to the interests of the partnership or which would make it impossible to carry on the business or affairs of the partnership.

Paragraph 21. Outlining the forbidden acts in which partners must *not* engage on behalf of the partnership is extremely important. These clauses define behavior that can put the club in jeopardy, and they help to limit the personal liability of the club's members.

The Detroit agreement ends this way:

This Agreement of Partnership shall be binding upon the respective heirs, executors, administrators, and personal representatives of the partners.

The partners have caused this Agreement of Partnership to be executed on the dates indicated below, effective as of the date indicated above.

Partners: {Signatures of partners}

Signed, sealed, delivered

According to NAIC, its sample agreement has been cleared in all 50 states. You don't need to make many changes in the sample partnership agreement to be able to get your club up and running. In fact, you should resist any urge to make the partnership agreement any more specific than the original — you can do that in your bylaws. That way, your agreement is better able to stand for many years without requiring revision.

Once you've decided on the details, draw up a final copy of the partnership agreement and have everyone sign it. Then make a copy of the signed agreement for each member. Your secretary needs to file the original for future reference.

Creating your club's bylaws

Your club's bylaws go hand in hand with its partnership agreement. Here's where you'll get down to the nitty-gritty of your club's operations. You can easily modify your bylaws as you go along, so if something isn't working for your club, take a vote and make the change. Here's an overview of the points you ought to cover in your club's bylaws.

Duties of officers

Your club needs leadership. That doesn't mean you must hire a CEO or investment manager — you and your fellow club members are perfect candidates for the jobs in your club.

The club's operating documents need to outline all the officers and their duties. Most clubs operate with four officers: a president, vice president, secretary, and treasurer. In some clubs, the officers respectively are known as presiding partner, assistant presiding partner, recording partner, and financial partner. The jobs are the same, only the names are different.

Some clubs also elect an assistant treasurer (or assistant financial partner) to help with the duties of collecting cash and keeping the books. The assistant treasurer is considered the *treasurer-in-training,* who subsequently will be elected to the position of treasurer. The assistant also learns the principles of club accounting, including how to use club accounting software, and may even keep a parallel set of the club's books, for training purposes and to serve as a backup if the treasurer's records ever become lost, damaged, or destroyed.

Some clubs recommend that each officer select or appoint an assistant. These nonelected assistants are responsible for helping out as needed, by carrying out administrative tasks, making phone calls, or taking care of paperwork.

Just like in Congress nowadays, term limits are a hot topic in investment clubs. Many clubs limit the number of consecutive terms that any member can serve, or enforce provisions that keep members rotating through the officer positions. Some clubs insist that all members eventually serve a term in each position at some point during the lifetime of the club.

Here are overviews of the duties that each officer of a club commonly assumes:

If you're the president . . .

If you're the president, you're responsible for setting the agenda for and presiding over each meeting. During your club's monthly meetings, you hold the gavel, keeping discussions moving along, making sure that motions are made and seconded properly, conducting votes, and refereeing disagreements. You're responsible for helping your club reach a consensus and making sure that each member has an opportunity to be heard.

If you're the vice president . . .

If you're the vice president, you're responsible for assuming all the duties of president in his or her absence. In most clubs, the vice president also is education czar, the member who leads the educational component of each club meeting. (We provide ideas for a fun and enlightening education program in your club in Chapter 11.)

If you're the secretary . . .

If you're the secretary, you keep the official minutes of your club meetings. You'll record motions and their seconds and the results of votes during club meetings. You'll also distribute (or make sure that the president distributes) the agenda for each meeting. Distributing the agenda, along with the proposed minutes of previous meetings, before members arrive is a good idea. Doing so gives them a chance to read and review the minutes beforehand, instead of taking up precious club meeting time on administrative business. E-mail is a great way of distributing agendas, minutes, and announcements. The secretary is also responsible for keeping the club archives — copies of the partnership agreement, bylaws, any vital correspondence, official forms and filings, resignation letters, and other important documents.

If you're the treasurer . . .

If you're the treasurer, you probably have the most time-consuming and detail-oriented job of any member. If you make a mathematical or data entry mistake, the results can take a lot of time and energy to repair. The essence of your job is taking care of anything related to the club's money. You handle the club's accounts at the bank or brokerage firm, make deposits, reconcile statements, and write checks. You keep the books that track every financial transaction (ideally using software or an online service). You collect the monthly contributions from each member and levy fines when necessary. You provide reports to the club every month on the value of the club's holdings and each member's account. You file all statements and financial records, including copies of all reports. When members depart or withdraw funds, you provide reports and adjust the books accordingly. At the end of each year, you prepare and file reports for your club members, for the IRS, and for your state authorities (when required).

You may decide to appoint, select, or volunteer other jobs in your club, on permanent or temporary bases. For instance, some clubs have portfolio specialists who are responsible for overseeing the club's overall portfolio — not necessarily for analyzing individual stocks but for making sure the portfolio fits your club's allocation and diversification guidelines. The portfolio specialist may recommend that certain stocks be reviewed when they fall in price, or point out to the club that another holding has grown so much that the club's portfolio is out of balance. That's just one job that can be taken on by a member of a club. Use your imagination to create positions for others to help you accomplish your joint goals.

Your operating documents must specify when and how officers are elected. Your annual elections can be held on the anniversary of your club's formation, for instance. A better plan may be to elect officers at your annual meeting, perhaps sometime in February or March. Why February or March? That's when your treasurer finishes the tax filing and reporting procedures for the prior tax year. If you elect officers in December, your new treasurer has to file your club's tax return with the IRS in the first few months of the next year. That puts her at a disadvantage, because she wouldn't be as familiar with the books from the prior year as the outgoing treasurer.

Prior to your annual elections, your club should appoint a nominating committee whose job is to determine the willingness of each member to serve as particular club officers. The nominating committee can then create a slate of officers and present it to the club for consideration.

Some clubs have elected absent members as officers — providing quite a surprise for the newly elected officer when he gets word of the election results! That's a good reason to make sure that you don't miss any meetings at which elections are scheduled.

Guests

Inviting people to be guests at a meeting is a great way of introducing them to how an investment club works. Your club bylaws can outline rules regarding any advance notice that is required if you plan to invite someone to a meeting, or how many meetings a guest must attend before being considered for membership.

Meetings

Identify the schedule of your club's monthly meetings, such as the second Tuesday of the month. You can also identify the time and the place, if you know, or you can simply say that the secretary will notify all members at a certain point prior to the meeting.

Terminating a member

When it comes to terminating a member, your bylaws must identify the reasons that your club can boot a member. It isn't fair to any of your members if a majority of your club members decide that they just "don't like" a certain member any more and want to vote to expel him. Inactivity is a common reason for terminating a member. A member who fails to attend a certain number of consecutive meetings, or misses a certain number of meetings in a year, may be subject to termination.

Some agreements stipulate that any member who misses a certain number of meetings may be automatically expelled with no further action or voting by the members. Your club secretary may be required to send a warning letter to any member who's in danger of being terminated, and a letter informing that member of the meeting where her termination is on the agenda. For other offenses, the termination action must be brought to a vote by the club, and your agreement must stipulate the voting procedures to be used when considering the termination. For example, is a simple majority enough to expel a member, or must two-thirds of the club vote to discharge the member?

Member responsibilities and attendance requirements

Because a club's success depends on the participation of its members, it's a good idea to clearly lay out what is expected from each member, such as a minimum level of attendance at club meetings, the number of stock studies that a member must complete in a year, and how much a member must contribute to the club.

Adding new members

A new member who doesn't share your club's investment philosophy may turn out to be a troublemaker. That makes it important for you to make sure that new members understand your club and how it works and that you recognize whether a candidate is a good fit with your club's existing membership.

No, this doesn't mean that you must make new candidates run the gauntlet before joining your club. But your bylaws need to describe the process that a candidate must undergo to be considered for membership. Most clubs try to gauge the interest and commitment of new members by requiring them to carry out some formal series of tasks during an initiation period. Must the initiate attend a certain number of meetings before becoming an official candidate, make a presentation to the club, or complete a certain number of stock studies? An initiation process is intended to be self-selective — those who don't have what it takes will drop out before completing their assignments. We cover new members in more detail in Chapter 8.

Voting procedures

Clubs often set up voting procedures that are different when they vote to purchase or sell securities than they are for simple administrative decisions. Say your club has enough money to invest in two new holdings, but three members move to purchase three different stocks. How do you fairly decide which two stocks to buy? A solution is to allow a *point system ballot*. Based on three purchase proposals, each partner assigns three points to her most favored stock, two points to her second favored stock, with the least preferred stock receiving one point. The secretary tallies the points, and the stocks with the two highest numbers of points are purchased.

Although voting weighted by the values of the capital accounts of members is the fairest method of making decisions, it can be cumbersome for the secretary to tally votes in this fashion during a meeting. A good compromise solution is to specify that the *one person, one vote* method be used by default whenever a vote is taken. But then, allow any member to call for the vote to be tallied by weighted shares immediately following the vote. That way, your club meetings can run smoothly and accommodate the valid concerns of those who have more dollars at stake whenever your club makes decisions.

Member dues

Anyone who's learning how clubs work for the first time wants to know how much it costs to be a member. Your bylaws need to lay out the minimum amount that members contribute each month. It may be $20, or $50, or $100 — deciding how much is up to your club. You may also set a specific increment for contributions above the minimum amount, say $10, for instance. Doing so makes the treasurer's job a bit easier when he's recording dues and adding up deposits (although this is probably not a big issue if you're using software for club accounting).

Your club may also establish an initial investment amount for new members that is different from the monthly minimum, or levy an additional one-time *initiation fee*. Just don't set a *buy-in* amount that's excessively high — there's no reason to limit your club membership to people who already have a lot of money. Your club's objective is to help its members build wealth, so you ought to give new members a chance to start small.

Late payments and fees

Avoiding having to deal with late payments by members is impossible. Members occasionally will miss a meeting or forget their checkbooks, so there isn't much you can do about it. However, a member who makes a late payment may benefit from being tardy if the club's unit value declines by the time of the next valuation statement, and she's able to buy more shares at a lower price than if she'd been on time with her check. Given the overall tendency of the market to rise, it just as easily could have worked to the late member's disadvantage — the lump sum contribution could've purchased fewer units at a higher valuation than the other club members.

Yet allowing a late member to profit from being tardy still doesn't seem fair to the other members of the club. Many clubs deal with this issue by charging a late fee, usually $5, for each month that a partner's dues are late or missed. In some clubs, the $5 fine is deducted directly from a member's account so the treasurer doesn't have to worry about collecting the fee.

This fine wipes out any chance of a delinquent member profiting from his or her delinquency and removes the possibility that a member can manipulate payments, delaying them until the unit value was lower, and then making a large payment to buy shares at a more favorable price.

Club valuation and member status reports

Everyone in the club needs to be informed on a regular basis how well the club is performing and how much their accounts are worth. Each month, the club's treasurer needs to create a valuation statement and member status reports for distribution to the club's members. The valuation statement includes the total value of the club's portfolio and any cash it has in the bank. The member status reports simply state the value of each individual club member's account — how much they've contributed and how much their investments are worth on the date of the report.

While these reports should be provided to the club each month, it doesn't really matter *when* in the month they're prepared — but you need to be consistent. Your agreement should specify that the reports are created using prices on a set schedule. You may determine that valuations must be prepared using prices as of the end of day on the Friday just before the club meeting or on the last business day of the month before the club meeting. You probably should give your treasurer a couple of days to prepare the reports, so don't make the report date the day before your club meeting.

Handling club expenses

As your club operations continue, you'll incur certain expenses, such as subscriptions, software, postage, stationery, banking fees, and so on. You may want to ask each member to contribute an equal amount for certain fees, like your NAIC membership, or simply pay all club expenses from your capital accounts. Another approach that some clubs take is charging each member annual dues of $20 or $30. The dues are not used to purchase units in the club. Instead they're recorded as fees paid by the members. This method helps to distribute expenses a bit more equitably among all members.

Nailing Down Your Club Philosophy, Policies

Many Wall Street pros religiously follow this saying: "Consistency is more important than conviction." As much as you may like a stock, and believe deep in your heart that its price will rise, being consistent in your evaluation and selection of investments for your club's portfolio is more important. Making sure that all the members of your club understand and agree with the club's philosophy is even more important. If one member wants to buy IPOs, another is interested in high-dividend blue chips, and a third likes penny stocks, the resulting clash of investing styles is sure to doom the club's portfolio.

In fact, one of the more common reasons that clubs disintegrate is that they don't have or follow a consistent investment philosophy. Therefore, having guidelines in place before you start buying stocks is vital for your club. Stick with your plan.

Professional financial advisors and brokers often create an *investment policy statement* with their clients at the beginning of their working relationship. The document defines the investor's financial objectives, the investment methodology, and the strategy that will be used to reach those objectives.

Fortune 2000 Investment Club

When the all-male investment club in their housing community wouldn't open its membership to women, the future members of the *Fortune 2000 Investment Club* of Vass, North Carolina, didn't get mad and they didn't get even — they just started a club of their own. Now numbering 16, the members all live in the same adult community and enjoy golfing and playing bridge together. They wanted to learn more about investing and the stock market, so they formed their club in 1994 and turned to their local NAIC chapter for educational seminars.

As they found out more about investing, they started their portfolio with five stocks, requiring a completed Stock Selection Guide (SSG) for each purchase and assigning a member to follow the stock after it has been added to the portfolio. Because their portfolio now numbers 27 stocks, each member watches and reports to the club monthly on at least two of them. In addition, members update their stocks' SSGs on a quarterly basis and are expected (except for the treasurer) to serve three months on the committee that researches new stocks for potential purchase by the club.

The members of the all-female Fortune 2000 Investment Club require potential members to have lived in their community at least a year and have a strong interest in learning about investing. After attending one meeting, they're given a new-member fact sheet and invited to a future meeting where current members can interview her and answer any questions she may have. Unanimous approval by a secret ballot must be given before she is invited to join.

New members pay $200 upon joining, and all members contribute at least $50 monthly. Members cannot miss more than three meetings a year. Club officers serve for one year, and elections are conducted every November, with new officers starting their terms in December.

The Fortune 2000 Investment Club manages its $101,000 portfolio through TD Waterhouse, an online brokerage. It also uses club accounting software, consults online resources for stock research, and invites guest speakers from time to time to its two-hour meetings, which take place in a common room in their community. (No word yet on how Fortune 2000's portfolio has performed compared to that of their male counterparts!)

If your club is new, it may not have enough collective experience in buying and selling stocks to develop an investment policy statement. For the time being, that's okay. You can flesh out the details as you progress. Here's what we'd suggest as a starting investment policy for a new club, based on NAIC's guidelines:

> The club's objectives are to build a long-term portfolio of quality growth stocks. The club's portfolio should include stocks from a number of industries, as well as small, medium, and large company stocks.

Deciding whether you want to include your club's investment policy statement in your bylaws is up to you and your club's membership. Nevertheless, make it a point to put your investment philosophy *on paper* as soon as your club is ready. Then make sure that all new members get a copy of it before they join the club.

Chapter 7

Following the Money: Startup Costs, Accounting, Banking, Brokering

In This Chapter

▶ Estimating the startup costs of your club

▶ Understanding the basics of club accounting

▶ Choosing a bank and a broker

Money — when you get right down to it, that's what your club's all about, right? And hundreds of details affect the money that moves in and out of your club. If you're not careful, that's also hundreds of details that can lead to big headaches down the line.

But money management doesn't have to be a nightmare. In this chapter, we'll talk about the green stuff and how it comes in, where you'll spend it, how it'll be taxed, how you'll account for it, and where you can deposit and invest it.

One of the advantages of being in an investment club is that you don't need a wad of money to start building your portfolio. Your 20 bucks a month is likely to add up and grow over time until you wake up one day and realize that you've got quite a sizeable nest egg in place.

Covering the Initial Costs of Clubbing

When you're just starting out, you're likely to feel swamped by the size of some of the expenses that you'll need to cover to get your club up and running. Some of these costs, like the purchase of club accounting software or registering your club with your state, are one-time expenses. You won't have to worry about them every year. Others are recurring expenses that your club pays on an annual basis. Either way, at the start, those costs may pack an unexpected wallop.

Keeping costs in perspective is important, because although they may seem like a lot now, especially when your club is young, some are important investments in your club's long-term success. Even if they total a few hundred dollars, when you spread out those costs among your entire club's membership, they may amount to only $20 or so apiece. That certainly is a reasonable amount for each member to pay to give your club its best chance of survival.

The next few sections describe some of the expenses you can expect to pay to help get your club off the ground.

Becoming an NAIC member

We can't recommend membership in the National Association of Investors Corporation highly enough. We describe NAIC in much greater detail in Chapter 1. Sure, you'll find almost everything you need to get your club off and running right here in this book, but NAIC offers much more than we have room to write about. No other organization presents local events and workshops and provides a bevy of online resources for clubs and their members. Individual club membership is $40 a year, plus $14 per member. In return, each member receives a subscription to *Better Investing* magazine and all the benefits of individual membership.

Acquiring accounting manuals and software

Investment club accounting often is complex. You must be aware of tax laws and any number of possible scenarios that your club may have to deal with. Torturing your club treasurer by making her or him try to figure it out unassisted just doesn't make sense. So, NAIC offers you all the expertise and experience you need, with a club accounting manual and all the paper forms necessary to accurately keep track of your club's books.

But if your club is like most in the new millennium, you'll probably opt for the computerized approach to club accounting. That can mean the purchase of club accounting software, generally for less than $200. You may also use an online club accounting service, which can be free or offered for an annual subscription of $50 or so.

Educating the members

If you're going to be true to your club's mission of educating its members, then you'll probably want to invest in some manuals or other materials. For instance, NAIC sells a complete stock study course that one of your members can use to lead your club in monthly lessons on analyzing and selecting stocks. Or buying a copy of a book or two just like this one can help you get organized and make sure that you're not forgetting anything important.

Buying subscriptions to stock analysis tools like the *Value Line Investment Survey* or other monthly or quarterly periodicals also helps. We talk more about using Value Line, a popular investment resource, in Chapter 14. Be sure to read that section before your club chooses to purchase this more expensive educational tool. Buying Value Line isn't essential. You can go to your local library to use it for free, but your club may decide the convenience of having its own copy is better and then can split the cost among the members. All told, that's another $150 to $200 well spent, and even a little more if you purchase an additional educational tool like Value Line.

Paying for outside classes and workshops

Many clubs send members to workshops and classes conducted by their local NAIC Chapters. For instance, a club treasurer's workshop is timely training for your newly elected treasurer. Some chapters conduct regular workshops for club presidents, with tips and advice on running club meetings, keeping clubs organized and on track, and dealing with problems. Or perhaps your club's education officer can attend a workshop and then report back to your club on lessons he or she learned. Asking your club to pay the registration fees (typically under $50) for those types of events certainly is reasonable.

Paying for legal advice

If your club plans to form as a limited liability corporation, then you may want to engage an attorney to draft organizational documents. This can run between $200 and $500. You can shop around to find a lawyer who's willing to work for a reduced rate, or try to negotiate with your selected attorney. If the attorney practices estate law, you may want to suggest that he or she discuss estate planning, wills, family trusts, and other financial planning topics at a future club meeting. Chances are the opportunity to meet 15 interested potential new clients will serve as an inducement for charging a reduced rate for your club's initial legal needs.

Registering with state and local agencies

Depending on the form of organization your club chooses (general partnership or limited liability corporation), registering your club with your county and state can cost between $50 and $400. Each year thereafter, you may spend another few hundred dollars in renewals. We cover the registration requirements and potential costs in more detail in Chapter 6.

Paying the Tax Man

You're probably already dreaming about all the profits that your club is going to make in the years ahead. And even if you don't yet know the difference between a capital gain, a dividend, and an income distribution, you surely understand that wherever profits are made, taxes must be paid. Clubs handle tax issues somewhat differently than you do with your personal portfolio, and it's important that you understand the differences.

Your friends and family are watching your new club with interest, wondering how your portfolio will perform or maybe even if you and your fellow members will ever get around to buying that first stock without driving each other crazy. But someone else wants to know about your club, too — your dear old Uncle Sam and his pals at the Internal Revenue Service.

They're not alone. Your friends in your state's department of revenue also are keenly interested in your club.

Of course, these folks aren't looking over your shoulder for any protective or paternal reasons. They want to make sure that they get their fair share of any taxes that may be due, regardless whether they're paid by your club or its individual members.

One of the biggest reasons that clubs form as general partnerships or LLCs (more on this choice in Chapter 6) is that the tax liability "flows through" the club to its individual members. That means the club may not have to pay federal taxes or state taxes in many (but not all) states. However, each member of a club is responsible for paying his or her fair share of any taxes that may be due. Because individual members won't receive Form 1099 reports or account statements directly from the club's brokerage (information that the brokerage also provides to the IRS), clubs must file their own informational returns with the IRS and state and local (if required) tax agencies.

Getting your tax ID number

When opening an account at a bank or brokerage firm, your club must have its own *tax identification number (TIN)*. For individuals, this is usually a Social Security number. Businesses and organizations (including investment clubs) must request an Employer Identification Number (EIN) from the IRS. Don't be put off by the name "Employer Identification Number" — that's just what the IRS calls it. It's probably less confusing to refer to it as a taxpayer identification number, or TIN.

Do not use a member's Social Security Number instead of acquiring a TIN for your club. If you do, the IRS holds that single member liable for any taxes that may be due on the part of your club. The member providing the SSN would have to report all the club's income and gains on his or her own tax return, and then somehow directly collect the taxes due from each individual member. Furthermore, it may not be easy to change the tax ID number on a bank or brokerage account once you've set up the account — you may need to close the account and open a new one.

Receiving a TIN is a simple matter — the IRS is all too happy to provide a way to track down any organizations or transactions that may result in tax liabilities. To request a TIN for your club, you just need to complete **IRS Form SS-4, (Application for Employer Identification Number).** You can download a fresh, full-sized copy from the IRS Web site (www.irs.gov) or call your local IRS office to request one. (On the site, the form is provided in Adobe Acrobat format, which means you'll need to install the free Acrobat reader software on your computer to view and print the file. The IRS provides a link so that you can download this program.)

The form contains all the instructions that you'll need to fill in the blanks. You'll also need the official name of your club before you can complete the form, so be sure to register your club's name with your county and/or state before applying for a TIN. Your club also needs a mailing address, which can simply be in care of one of your partners (usually the secretary or whoever is also the official club contact for NAIC).

Once you've completed the TIN form, return it to the IRS, and you'll receive your number in a few weeks. To expedite the process, you can fax the form to your local IRS service center or request your number by phone using the agency's Tele-TIN service. If you use the automated phone service, you still need to have a completed form in front of you before you call.

For more information on TINs and EINs, refer to **IRS Tax Topic 755 (Employer Identification Number [EIN] — How to Apply),** or **Publication 1635, (Understanding Your EIN).** Both are available on the IRS Web site, (www.irs.gov).

Sorting through the taxes you may have to pay

Taxes are a confusing enough matter for most individuals, so it isn't surprising that they're just as incomprehensible at times for investment clubs, too. The specific tax filing requirements for your club vary depending on your state requirements and on the legal entity your club chooses to form under (check out Chapter 6 for the legal stuff). So we can't give you the specifics for your particular club, but what we can offer is an overview of the issues you can expect to encounter when it comes to dealing with investment club taxes and tax returns.

Recognizing the common "taxable events"

First, however, gaining an understanding of the relationship between investing and taxes is important. Here are common types of taxable events that investors and investment clubs can generate.

- ✔ *Interest income* is that money paid to you by a bank on the funds you keep on deposit with that institution. It also comes from loans that you make to other people or interest that is paid on savings bonds. While most interest income is taxable, the interest paid on municipal bonds may be tax-exempt. Investment clubs typically have interest coming in only from the cash that the club holds while waiting to make a stock investment. Most clubs steer clear of savings or municipal bonds in favor of stocks, which historically have higher returns.

- ✔ *Dividends* are a portion of a company's profits that are paid out to shareholders, usually on a quarterly basis. Not all companies that you'll invest in pay dividends. Even if you choose to reinvest your dividends in more shares of the stock, you'll still owe taxes on the full dividend amount for the tax year in which your club received them.

For most individuals, dividends and interest are taxable as ordinary income on your tax return, which means that you pay the same federal, state, and local taxes on this income as you do on your salary from work.

- ✔ A *capital gain* is the profit you make when you sell a security that has increased in price. Any commissions that you pay when buying or selling the security reduce your gains (or increase your losses) accordingly. You incur capital gains only when you sell a security — if you buy a stock for $10 and it increases in value to $12, you have a $2 gain on paper, but it isn't considered a capital gain until you actually sell the stock.

- ✔ A *capital loss,* on the other hand, is what you get when you sell a security for less than you paid for it. Before you pay taxes on any capital gains, you can deduct your capital losses from your gains, possibly eliminating your tax liability. If your losses exclude your gains, you can even use a portion of your losses to reduce your regular income on your federal tax return, and perhaps defer some of the losses to the next tax year.

Capital gains and losses come in two varieties. Short-term gains and losses come from a security that's been sold after being held for a year or less. Long-term gains and losses come from securities that are sold after being held for longer than a year. Short-term gains are taxed at a higher rate than long-term gains, so it works to your advantage to hold on to your winners for at least twelve months. The IRS details all the rules for calculating capital gains and losses in **IRS Publication 550 (Investment Income and Expenses),** available at your local tax office or at the IRS Web site, (www.irs.gov).

✔ Mutual funds make ***distributions*** on a regular basis, sharing any income with fund holders. A distribution can include dividends, interest, or capital gains or losses and is taxed according to the type of income it contains. Most investment clubs steer clear of mutual funds, preferring to choose their own investments.

Your club can incur any of these taxable transactions in its portfolio, and because the appropriate financial institutions report this information annually, you can bet that the IRS and your state tax authority know about them — and want to collect any and all taxes that are due.

Members pay taxes but clubs don't — except in Florida

The good news is that general partnerships, limited liability companies, and S Corporations generally don't have to pay taxes. That doesn't mean that your club can simply avoid the taxman. These entities allow for tax liabilities to *pass through* to individual club members who then must report their share of gains on their personal tax returns. (If your club is formed as a C Corporation, explained in Chapter 6, then your club has to file returns and pay corporate taxes.)

Florida is one notable exception from the rule that clubs don't have to pay taxes. Because Florida doesn't have an income tax, it has other taxes that generate revenue for the state, including an *intangibles tax.* This tax applies to investment assets held by an individual or business (including an investment club), as long as those assets exceed $20,000. Generally, the annual tax is $2 per $1,000 of assets. A club with a $40,000 portfolio pays $80 in intangibles taxes to the state. Check with your state department of taxation to see whether any similar regulations apply to your club.

But even though most clubs don't have to pay taxes, they do have to file informational returns with the Internal Revenue Service and usually (but not always) with their state's department of taxation. These informational returns give the details of the club's taxable events and names of members who are responsible for paying any taxes that may be due.

Form 1065 (U.S. Partnership Return of Income) is the federal partnership tax return that must be filed each year with the IRS. In addition, the club must provide each member with a **Schedule K-1 (Partner's Share of Income),** which details that member's share of all taxable transactions for the year. Copies of all K-1s are included with the Form 1065 that's sent to the IRS. Individual members then use the information on their K-1 to complete their own personal tax returns and pay any taxes due. You can download copies of both forms from the IRS Web site (www.irs.gov).

For more about the filing requirements for your club, check out **IRS Publication 541(Partnerships),** which covers regulations governing partnerships, and Publication 550 (discussed in an earlier section of this chapter), which deals with investment income and expenses. Both are available on the IRS Web site (www.irs.gov).

Your state will likely have a similar partnership return that must also be completed each year. And if your club has members from multiple states, then you may be required to file returns with each of those states. Contact your state's department of taxation to find out what's expected of your club. You can also contact your local NAIC Chapter, because it's likely to have experience with practices in your area.

If all this paperwork sounds like a big mess of, well, *paperwork,* you're absolutely right. Your club treasurer is responsible for keeping track of all the tax and investment information, so be sure that your club gives him or her all the support possible. Club accounting is not the place to try to skimp on or reduce expenses. Fortunately, club accounting software programs and Web sites can simplify the process of preparing all these forms for your treasurer. Pledge to make an investment in them, and you'll make your treasurer happy. And needless to say, a happy treasurer is an asset to any investment club. Check out Chapter 10 for all the details on computerized recordkeeping.

Keeping good records — a must!

Keeping records of all the transactions in your portfolio is important, not only to the IRS but also to your club. You can't forget the little details that accompany your club's forays into the market. When it comes time to sell a stock, for example, you'll need to document how much each investment costs you.

Although updating the stock prices in your portfolio can be fun, other tasks like preparing tax reports or creating monthly member reports aren't quite so exciting. You could record all your club's cash and investment transactions on ledger paper with a pen or pencil, as in olden times, or you can take advantage of the latest technology. Fortunately, today's software programs make the task of recordkeeping much more painless.

Even though some online brokers are moving toward electronic records and away from mailing printed trade confirmations and statements, you'll still have plenty of paperwork to file away. Not everything can be done on the computer. Because the club treasurer or secretary most often manages the task of filing, your club needs to buy them a portable plastic file box or other sturdy container to keep all the paperwork and files in a convenient, central location.

Here are some basic tips for keeping track of your club records.

   ✓ **File every document.** That includes all account statements, confirmations, year-end reports, receipts, and other documents that you receive in conjunction with your financial accounts. You need to set up a filing system to keep track of all paperwork associated with all your club's investment accounts. You'll need to be able to verify the purchase price of securities (to establish a basis) when you sell them, as well as any dividends on which you've already paid tax.

You'll also want your club's operating agreement, bylaws, and membership roster, plus minutes and other notes from each meeting, on file and easily accessible. Splitting your records up may make sense, giving the administrative files to the club secretary and the financial files to the treasurer.

✔ **Be complete.** You need to enter every transaction into your accounting system, whether you do it by hand or using a computer. All income and expenses must be recorded — no item is too small or insignificant. Club accounting software helps you keep track of even the smallest amounts.

✔ **Be accurate.** Software can be only as accurate as you are, so enter transactions carefully. Reconcile your accounts on a regular basis, making sure that your bookkeeping and that of your broker or mutual fund company are correct. You'll also want to run an audit of your club's financial books once a year. We take you through this process in Chapter 10.

✔ **Don't confuse recordkeeping with portfolio management.** While recordkeeping software can be an important tool, help you keep track of your holdings, a portfolio of stocks must be constantly managed. Your club should actively weed out losers and find replacement stocks as needed, determining whether a price drop is a good time to purchase more shares and making sure that the portfolio is adequately diversified. We cover portfolio management in detail in Chapter 16.

Introducing Your Club's Best Friend: Unit-Value Accounting

The first questions that most people have about investment clubs are all about club accounting. How do clubs keep track of who owns what stocks? How is each member's money tracked in the club? What happens to the profits?

Although clubs can manage their books a few different ways, we recommend a certain method of accounting called the *unit-value system*. It just may prove to be your club's best friend.

An easy way to describe the unit-value system is to compare it with the method of accounting used by mutual funds. In a mutual fund, investors contribute cash to the fund. That cash is used buy shares of the fund. If three investors want to buy $100, or $1,000, or $100,000 worth of shares on a single day, it isn't a problem for the mutual fund. The fund sells new shares to each investor, and each investor buys shares at the same price.

Sidestepping the *equal-shares* trap

Equality! That's the cry of many fledgling clubs as they consider the matter of money. That isn't surprising, either, because every investment club wants each member to have a fair say in the operation of the club. But fairness and equality aren't the same things, and in the case of financial contributions, the quest for equality will create only problems down the road.

Clubs that demand that each member's contributions be exactly equal to those of every other member — the *equal-shares method* of accounting — usually have two reasons for enacting such a rule. First, they want to keep their accounting simple. All they have to do is divide the club value by the number of members and voilà! They now know how much each member's share is worth. No fuss, no muss. With the use of the club accounting software or Web tools that now are available, however, keeping the club's books without imposing an equal-shares requirement is easy enough.

The second reason that new clubs may want to adopt an equal-shares method is that they believe it creates a more equitable environment within the club, particularly when it comes to voting. After all, isn't the concept of "one person, one vote" the foundation of democracy? But the concept of variable proportions of ownership doesn't have to mean confusing votes. Regardless of how club ownership is split up, most investment clubs stick to the "one person, one vote" system (except under unusual circumstances that we discuss in Chapter 6).

Forcing all members to contribute equal amounts to the club only creates headaches down the road. Clubs that insist on equal shares eventually come to an understanding that such a system ends up creating unfair situations where members end up being treated unequally after all.

The fund then invests in stocks, bonds, or other securities, and the value of the fund rises and falls. As the overall value of the fund changes, the price of a share rises and falls, too. When fund holders want to sell shares, it's no trouble for the fund, which simply buys back the shares from the shareholder at that day's price.

At least once each year, the fund distributes any profits it may've earned (after being reduced by any losses it recorded) to all shareholders in proportion to the number of shares each owns. This is the *unit-value system* in action. Your club operates in the same way.

All the stocks that your club owns are held in the name of the club in a single portfolio. This portfolio of cash and stocks or other securities can be held in a single brokerage account or in any number of bank and brokerage accounts.

Each member has a *capital account* in the club. This isn't a separate account. Instead, it's a bookkeeping term that means the club treasurer keeps track of each member's monthly contributions to the club, and how many units (or *shares*) that members buy with each dues payment.

Instead of setting the price of a single unit every day, like a fund does, your club sets the price of a share once each month on a specified date set by your club. This is called the *valuation date*. It can be the last business day of the month, or the last business day of the week prior to your monthly meeting, or some other date that is set in your operating agreement. Your club treasurer creates a statement that includes the value of the club's portfolio as of the valuation date. That club valuation then is used to determine the unit value for that month. And each month, regardless whether a member puts in $20 or $100, the single unit (or share) price is exactly the same for each member.

To figure out the value of your balance in the club, multiply the total number of units that you've purchased since becoming a member of the club by the current value of a single unit. You won't have to do this multiplication each month, because part of the treasurer's job is to create regular monthly reports that detail each member's contributions to date, contributions since the last meeting, the number of units owned by each member, and the value of those units. You can find many more about club-accounting details in Chapter 10.

The other accounting method that catches a considerable amount of attention with new clubs is the *equal-shares method*. But we don't think it's a good choice (see the sidebar "Sidestepping the *equal-shares* trap"). We strongly recommend the unit-value system. Here are a few reasons why:

- ✔ **Handling late payments.** The fact that some members of every investment club occasionally pay their dues late is inevitable. A member may miss a meeting because of illness, or travel, or because of family obligations, and won't be able to deliver a check in time for the monthly meeting. Even if that member makes a catch-up payment at the next meeting, is that fair to the rest of your club? After all, money has a time value — and the delinquent member has had the use of his or her funds for an extra month during which they could've collected interest in that member's bank account.

  Or what if your club decides to invest in a stock, but has less money to invest because of the missed contribution by the member? Because most clubs pay fixed commissions to their brokers, the club's commission would be a higher percentage of your total investment than it would've been with the late member's dues included. In the unit-value method, if your portfolio's valuation has increased since the last meeting (as we hope it will tend to do over the long haul), that member's money buys fewer units than money invested on time at the previous meeting. Thus crediting the late contribution according to the next month's valuation certainly is fairer to the rest of the club members who paid on time.

- ✔ **Accommodating larger member contributions.** Some members of your club may want to contribute more than your club's set monthly minimum dues. In an equal-shares club, such contributions are prohibited. Since the unit-value method welcomes increased contributions, your club has a larger chunk of change to invest, and commissions take a smaller bite out of your investment dollars. That can help boost your club's overall portfolio return.

✔ **Increasing the minimum member contribution.** As your club grows, what happens if you want to make investments more frequently or in larger amounts? In an equal-shares club, the only way to do that is to increase the minimum dues. But if a member can't afford the increase, must that member therefore be terminated? How fair is that?

✔ **Allowing member withdrawals for emergencies.** What happens when a member needs cash and wants to withdraw funds from his or her club account? In an equal-shares club, that member is forced to withdraw completely, because every member must own the same percentage of the club. Financial emergencies do occur, however, and so restricting these partial withdrawals or forcing a club member to leave completely is almost inhumane. With unit-value accounting, your club disregards the ownership percentage issues and just focuses on following your bylaws for the exact withdrawal procedure.

✔ **Difficulties in finding new members.** As your club grows through the years, the value of each member's account also grows. How will you handle accepting new members into your club if under the equal-shares accounting method, you must require an extraordinarily large buy-in to maintain equal ownership? How many people do you know who can afford to invest a lump sum of $5,000, or $10,000, or $20,000 just to join an investment club? By requiring equal shares, you limit your potential pool of new members to only a small group of people — if you can find them at all.

✔ **Voting unequal shares.** Many clubs opt for the equal-shares method of accounting because they believe it simplifies voting. In a unit-value system, voting is "properly" done by giving each member a weighted vote according to the number of shares each owns. A reasonable compromise that most clubs follow for simplicity's sake is to give each member a single vote (that old "one person, one vote" thing), but to allow all members the right to request a weighted vote at any time. This method allows club meetings to run more smoothly since you don't need to break out the calculator in order to tally each vote.

It is possible for an existing club to change from the equal-shares method of accounting to the unit-value system, but — to repeat — new clubs should strongly resist the urge to adopt the equal-shares system in the first place. It truly creates more problems than it avoids in the long run. If we still haven't convinced you, take a look at all the "No" entries under the "Equal-Shares" column in Table 7-1.

Table 7-1	Comparison: Valuation Units versus Equal-Shares Accounting	
Factor	*Valuation Units*	*Equal Shares*
Allows contributions of varying amounts	Yes	No
Accommodates late payments justly	Yes	No
Allows new members to easily join	Yes	No
Allows partial withdrawals	Yes	No
Allows fair and uncomplicated voting	Yes	Yes

Insuring Against Theft

Investment clubs have no shortage of tough jobs, but the treasurer's job undoubtedly is the most complicated. Not only is the treasurer entrusted with keeping track of the cash contributed by each member but also with maintaining the books and tracking the club's portfolio value. As you look around at your fellow club members, imagining any of them committing a crime any more serious than an illegal U-turn is probably pretty tough. But money *is* at stake in your club, and where money's involved, the possibility always exists that someone might succumb to temptation.

Call it embezzlement. Call it absconding with funds. Or just call it theft. It's all the same thing, and the day would be sad, indeed, if one of your partners ever made off with some or all of your club's portfolio. It doesn't happen frequently, but it has happened to some unsuspecting clubs and surely will happen again. Fortunately, you can protect your membership from this type of malfeasance by bonding your club.

 This type of bond is an insurance contract in which an insurer guarantees payment to an organization in the event of unforeseen financial loss through actions of a member or employee. You can purchase a bond from any insurance company, at least in theory. In practice, you may have trouble finding an insurer that's familiar with investment clubs and willing to bond your club. Fortunately, NAIC offers a *fidelity bond* to help protect your investment club portfolio against theft by a partner (yet another reason for your club to join NAIC).

Underwritten by a national insurance company, NAIC's fidelity bond is available to all NAIC member clubs. To qualify for coverage, your club must be organized and operated in accordance with NAIC's procedures and must conduct a self-audit each year to verify the accuracy of its books and records.

(We cover the audit process in detail in Chapter 10.) These practices help ensure that no member of your club is siphoning money away.

NAIC member clubs are invited to purchase a bond at the end of each calendar year. Rates are low and vary with the amount of coverage your club needs, and all policies have a $1,000 deductible.

In your first few years of operation, while your club is just getting started, you may choose to forego the bond. After all, your portfolio will take some time to grow, so you may decide that you don't need the protection. Like any insurance policy, it's only useful if it's in effect. But once your club has significant assets, or if you're starting a club with people you don't know well or you're part of an online club, then the fidelity bond is an absolute must. You may think that purchasing a fidelity bond is an unnecessary expense when the club is young and the portfolio is small. But we recommend including purchase of the fidelity bond in your club bylaws from the beginning, if only to avoid the potential for misunderstanding and hurt feelings that may arise if you bring up the subject a few years down the road.

Choosing a Bank

Unless you plan to buy a large piggy bank or a small safe, you'll need a secure place to keep your club's cash, where you can deposit member checks and pay the occasional bills. Sounds an awful lot like a bank, doesn't it? For most clubs, the answer *is* a bank. But finding the right bank for your investment club may not be easy.

Many banks today now require minimum amount on deposit to avoid monthly fees and service charges. Because your club's purpose is investing in securities, being forced to stash thousands of dollars in a low- or no-interest bearing account just to avoid service charges runs counter to your objectives. All that cash drags down your club's performance, especially during your start-up years. Your club merely needs a place to deposit checks from members, write checks for withdrawals or to pay expenses, and transfer funds to your investment accounts.

Finding a club-friendly, conventional bank

Unfortunately, banks recognize your club as a business, so you'll have access only to business bank accounts, which tend to be more costly than individual accounts. We offer the following suggestions to help you find a bank that meet your club's needs.

✔ Investigate all available types of checking accounts and associated fees, initial minimums to open an account, and monthly minimums to avoid service charges. Some banks may offer noninterest-bearing accounts with no monthly minimums in which you pay per check written instead of paying a monthly fee. Because fees and minimums vary from bank to bank, you'll have to shop around.

✔ If a member of your club has a relationship with a bank because of his or her business or personal banking, perhaps that member can introduce your club to the same bank and receive preferential treatment.

✔ Even if you don't have some sort of inside relationship, bank managers often have the ability to waive requirements, particularly at smaller, local banks. It pays to speak to the manager directly to explain your club and its needs.

✔ Explore savings banks, savings and loan associations, and credit unions. These bank alternatives often have lower minimums and fees than commercial banks, while offering the same services. If a member of your club belongs to a credit union, investigate whether your club can open an account at that institution. Most credit unions are happy to oblige and open a business or partnership account for you as long as one of your club members has an account or is eligible to join. That member may be required to be one of the signers on the account, however.

Don't feel compelled to seek out a bank that's in your neighborhood. You can mail deposits to the bank; the weeklong delay in getting funds in your club account is inconsequential in the long run. If you can get a better deal at a credit union with an office that's in the next town, any delay may be worth it if you can save on fees or get better services.

Doing your banking through an online brokerage

One of the great promises of the Internet is that it helps to make many tasks in our lives easier and more convenient. In the online world, that means that you can find many more services now offered by online brokers (see more about online brokers in the "Choosing a Broker" section later in this chapter) and you may be able to eliminate a conventional bank from your plans altogether.

A number of online brokerage firms now offer check writing as a part of their basic parcel of services. The firm provides you with a checkbook and allows you to write checks based on the balance in your brokerage account. Some firms offer the service at no charge to all customers; others require a certain minimum account balance (of stocks and cash) before you can request check-writing privileges. Other firms require that checks be written in amounts of

$100 or more, or restrict the number of checks you can write each month to a certain maximum.

Many clubs have found that opening an account with a club-friendly brokerage firm that offers check writing eliminates the need for a bank account altogether. If you can't find a bank in your area with reasonable terms, then you may want to make check writing privileges a high priority when you shop for a brokerage firm.

One important potential roadblock to this strategy, however, is that when you send money to a broker, the customary way is to send a check made out to the broker, like "Big, Wig & Fig Brokerage Co." That's called a second-party check — the second party is you, writing the check to your broker, and the first party (you got it!) is the broker. But if your investment club members make their monthly checks payable to the club, many brokers will not accept such checks because they are now "third-party" checks — payable initially to a third party, the club. The broker might accept checks for deposit into the account of the Abracadabra Investment Club only if they've been written on the account of the Abracadabra Investment Club at another financial institution.

However, one potential solution to the problem of depositing member checks is to ask the brokerage firm to accept checks written as payable to "Big, Wig & Fig Brokerage Co. FBO Abracadabra Investment Club." "FBO" is the abbreviation for "for benefit of," and it's standard financial nomenclature for indicating how funds are to be handled. Members or the club treasurer also need to note the club's account number on each check before they're sent for deposit.

One solution to simplifying your club's deposit process that you should never for a moment consider is having club members write their checks to the treasurer or another member rather than to the bank or brokerage. You don't want that designated member depositing all those contributions into his or her personal account just to be able to write one check for the club's monthly deposit to the financial institution. Although it may seem like a commonsense way to streamline part of the deposit process, club money should *never* be funneled through anyone's personal account. Not only could your club run afoul of IRS regulations, you'd just be asking for trouble if something goes wrong (and invariably it does if you choose to do something like this).

Opening an Account

If you decide that a bank is right for your club after all, and you've selected what you hope is the perfect bank, you'll need to complete an application form, providing a mailing address along with your club's Taxpayer Identification Number. You must also determine who in your club can sign checks and withdraw funds from the account. Usually the treasurer and one other officer are designated as the authorized agents for your club account. If your bank allows you to designate multiple check signers, you'll probably want to require two signatures on checks of more than a certain amount, say $1,000 or more. This security feature can help prevent malfeasance or errors when your club disburses larger sums.

When you open the account, the authorized representatives from your club must sign signature cards at the bank. That means a special trip, or scheduling an appointment to take care of the paperwork.

You'll need a small supply of checks, but your club will likely be writing only a few checks a year so ordering hundreds or thousands of checks, selecting a lovely genuine leather checkbook cover, or paying for designer checks isn't necessary. In fact, you can save a few dollars by buying inexpensive checks from a third-party check printer rather than from the bank. Some third-party check printers include:

- ✔ Checks In The Mail, www.citm.com
- ✔ Checks Unlimited, www.checksunlimited.com
- ✔ Deluxe, www.deluxeforms.com

You often can find advertising circulars for these check companies in the Sunday newspaper.

Choosing a Broker

If only stocking up on a few securities for your portfolio were as easy as running down to your local Home Depot! Instead, you'll need the services of a brokerage firm, where your club can buy and sell stocks and funds, and perhaps even access research and other services. Your brokerage firm can be local or online — either type gives your club great service.

Hundreds of brokerage firms operate in the U.S., so how can you choose the best one for your club? Before considering the most important factors in making your choice, you must understand the difference between the various types of brokerages: full-service, discount, and online firms.

Comparing full-service, discount, and online brokers

Before the early 1970s, no *discount brokers* existed. If you wanted to invest in the stock market, you needed to work with a full-service stockbroker, who provided advice (whether you wanted it or not, in many cases) — and charged you accordingly. These firms always seemed to have two names: Smith Barney, Dean Witter, Morgan Stanley, Paine Webber, and Goldman Sachs. In some cases, like Merrill, Lynch, Pierce, Fenner & Smith, they had even more — though the firm is now known as Merrill Lynch.

Many clubs that were established 20 or 30 years ago continue to work with full-service brokers. They trust their brokers and have a good relationship, so why change what works? In many cases, these clubs have been able to negotiate commission rates that they pay, reducing their costs below the standard fee schedule. Their brokers may offer the club research and occasionally attend meetings and participate in discussions. And many club members may choose to open their own individual accounts with their club's broker.

For a new club, a full-service broker probably is not the best choice. Negotiating a lower commission won't be as easy for a new club, because you won't have sizeable assets or an impressive track record with which to negotiate. A broker may offer good advice to your new club, but beware of a broker whose investment philosophy doesn't match your club's. For instance, a broker who just tries to sell you the "hot stock of the day" from his or her firm's research probably isn't looking out for your club's overall portfolio.

Although you may invite your broker to attend your club's meeting, many clubs prohibit brokers from being members. No legal requirements prevent a broker from officially joining a club, but many investment firms restrict employees from being a member. Chapter 8 describes the issues surrounding brokers being members in a club.

Following the establishment of one of the first discount brokerage firms (perhaps you're familiar with one of the early leaders, Charles Schwab & Co.), the investment business changed dramatically. These new *discount brokers* were legally permitted to buy and sell stocks on behalf of investors, but they were prohibited from giving specific investment advice to their customers. That didn't seem to matter to the thousands and thousands of investors and clubs who flocked to the new firms with the much lower commissions. These investors were *self-directed* — they made their own investment decisions and didn't want to pay a broker for services not required or rendered.

Next came the *deep-discount brokers,* firms that offered cut-rate commissions, often at a fixed rate of $30 or less per purchase, and bare-bones services.

In the early 1990s, many discount brokerage firms began offering online trading. By the end of the decade, millions of Americans had opened accounts and were buying and selling stocks online. The main attraction of Web trading? Commissions as low as $8 — even lower in some cases — as well as the convenience of online access. Online brokers also offer stock research, free check writing, and other features that make them attractive to investors and investment clubs.

Although nearly 200 firms offer online trading, the top 10 or 12 firms are the dominant players in the market, and all offer accounts for investment clubs. We list a number of deep-discount online firms in Table 7-2 later in this chapter.

For most new clubs the decision is fairly simple. Because you and your fellow club members are doing all the research and analysis for the stocks your club ultimately will purchase, you don't require those services from a stockbroker. All you need is a cheap and reliable company where you can place trades and hold your portfolio. An online, low-cost broker is your best bet.

Features of club-friendly brokerages

No matter whether you choose to work with a full-service broker or a local discount brokerage firm, or even if the online road is right for you, some important considerations for you and your club to understand are

- ✔ **Account insurance.** All brokerage firms are supposed to carry $500,000 of insurance through the Securities Investor Protection Corporation (SIPC). Similar to FDIC insurance offered by banks, this insurance protects you if an institution fails — not from losses in any investments that you make. Most brokerages also carry millions of dollars of additional commercial insurance on top of their SIPC coverage, so your club account is likely to be protected for a good long while. If a brokerage doesn't carry SIPC coverage, then avoid them at all costs.

- ✔ **Broker and firm reputability.** If you're working with an individual broker, you'll want to check that individual's license and any record of violations. For that matter, you can also check on any brokerage firm. NASD Regulation is the official regulatory arm of the National Association of Securities Dealers, which keeps tabs on people and companies in the investment business. You can search the DASD Regulation Web site at www.nasdr.com to find the record of any broker or brokerage firm.

- ✔ **Trading commissions.** While a firm may advertise the lowest commission they offer, that rate may not be available for all types of trades. Usually, the quoted minimum commission is for market orders (orders with no price limit) placed online. Some firms charge higher rates for limit orders (where you specify the maximum or minimum price for which the order can be executed), for orders placed using a touch-tone telephone system, or for orders placed through a live broker. Typically, firms also charge an additional commission for orders of 1,000 or 5,000 shares or more.

The brokerage firm should publish a commission schedule that includes all rates they charge. Study it carefully. While you don't want to pay more in commissions than you have to, the dollar amount of the commissions is important only when you compare it to the amount you expect to invest in each purchase of stocks. Keep in mind the *2-percent*

rule — your commissions should be less than 2 percent of each total investment. With many online brokerages, consider the *1-percent rule,* in which commissions eat up even less of your investments.

✔ **Fees and service charges.** Many online brokerages offer cheap trading, but charge for any other special services or features that you use. Often, these charges may be hidden away in the fine print, so make a point of uncovering all possible fees. Inactivity fees and charges for closing an account or issuing certificates are quite common. If you can't find a complete listing of all fees or charges on the firm's Web site, or if they won't send you one in the mail, avoid that brokerage!

✔ **Initial minimum.** How much does the brokerage require in cash or securities to establish an account? You may not be required to maintain this amount once you've opened the account, but the firm may want to have a check for at least this amount before it does business with you. If your top pick has a higher minimum, you may want to collect member contributions for a few months before opening your account to ensure you have enough to meet the requirement.

✔ **Free checking.** Some brokerages offer free check writing services to customers, but a higher minimum account balance may be required and the number of checks you're permitted to write each month may be limited. The amount of the checks that you write may need to be above $100 or some other minimum amount.

✔ **Dividend reinvestment.** Does the brokerage offer reinvestment of dividends without charging commissions? Some firms reinvest dividends only for purchases of whole shares, while others allow the purchase of fractional shares. This can build up your account slowly by keeping all your funds invested in the market.

✔ **Branch offices.** Some brokerage firms, such as Charles Schwab and TD Waterhouse, have local offices across the country, which is convenient and adds a certain extra measure of confidence to your relationship, knowing that you can just walk into a branch to resolve any problems that you may have.

✔ **Service and support.** Online brokerages in particular have taken the heat in recent years for sub par customer service, particularly during peak times of market activity. Ask friends and co-workers about their experiences with their online brokerages, or review the ratings at the Web sites listed at the end of this chapter. Call or e-mail the brokerages to find out how quickly and accurately they respond to questions. You don't want to deal with your firm's Web site being down when you need to make a trade or have to wait an hour or longer on hold to talk to a customer service representative.

✔ **Online security.** Brokerages should offer online access only via a Web browser that supports the Secure Sockets Layer (SSL). This ensures that all information moving between your computer and the brokerage's Web server is encrypted and protected from prying eyes.

✔ **Research.** Many online firms offer investment research that can be invaluable to your club. At some firms, the research may only be available to members who are authorized to trade. At others, all members may have access via a separate password. You can find quotes, charts, news, fundamental data, and stock screening tools at most online brokerages.

✔ **Dual passwords.** Some online brokerages offer two passwords, one for trading and one for account information access. This can be useful for clubs that want all members to have access to the brokerage account balances or research but restrict trading authorization to the treasurer or other officers. While dual passwords are by no means a necessity, they are a great perk if your brokerage firm offers them.

✔ **Duplicate or online statements.** Many clubs like to have copies of each month's statements sent to the club treasurer and secretary to double-check that transactions are properly recorded and to provide a backup set of all documents on file in case anything happens to the treasurer. Some firms don't offer this service, so ask whether it's available. Duplicate statements aren't necessary if your brokerage enables you to print or download statements online.

Table 7-2 is a selection of popular online brokerage firms with a summary of features that are of interest to investment clubs. These are all deep-discount firms, though commissions range from $5 to $30 per trade (and even free in some cases!). You can contact the firms directly for more information, account applications, and all the forms you'll need.

Table 7-2		Club Friendly Brokerage Firms			
Broker	*Initial Minimum*	*Minimum Commission*	*Free Checking*	*Dual Passwords*	*Free Dividend Reinvestment*
American Express					
finance. american express. com/ finance/ brokerage. asp	$2,000	$24.95	*	Yes	Yes
Ameritrade					
www. ameritrade. com	$1,000	$8.00	Yes	No	***

(continued)

Table 7-2 *(continued)*

Broker	Initial Minimum	Minimum Commission	Free Checking	Dual Passwords	Free Dividend Reinvestment
Charles Schwab					
www. schwab. com	$2,500	$29.95	*	No	Yes
CSFB Direct					
www. csfbdirect. com	$0	$20.00	No	No	Yes
Datek					
www. datek.com	$0	$9.99	**	No	No
E*Trade					
www. etrade.com	$1,000	$14.95	Yes	Yes	Yes
Fidelity					
www. fidelity.com	$5,000	$25.00	Yes	No	Yes
Financial Café					
www. financial cafe.com	$0	Free	Yes	Yes	***
JB Oxford					
www. jboxford.com	$5,000	$15.00	No	No	Yes
MSDW Online					
online. msdw.com	$2,000	$14.95	Yes	No	***
MyDiscountBroker.com					
www. mydiscount broker.com	$0	$12.00	Yes	No	Yes

Broker	Initial Minimum	Minimum Commission	Free Checking	Dual Passwords	Free Dividend Reinvestment
National Discount Brokers					
www.ndb.com	$2,000	$14.75	Yes	No	Yes
Net Investor					
www. netinvestor. com	$0	$19.95	Yes	Yes	Yes
Quick & Reilly					
www. quickandreilly. com	$0	$14.95	Yes	No	***
Scottrade					
www. scottrade. com	$500	$7.00	No	No	No
TD Waterhouse					
www. tdwaterhouse. com	$1,000	$12.00	Yes	No	Yes
Trading Direct					
www. tradingdirect. com	$0	$9.95	No	No	No
Wall St. Electronica					
www. wallstreete. com	$2,500	$14.95	Yes	No	No
Wang					
www.wangvest. com	$5,000	$8.00	Yes	No	***
Wyse Securities					
www.wyse- sec.com	$0	$4.95	Yes	Yes	Yes

*When minimum balances are met
** Not for investment club accounts
*** Whole shares only

For more about choosing a brokerage, check out these Web sites:

- ✔ Gomez.com's "Internet Broker Scorecard" (`www.gomez.com`)
- ✔ SmartMoney.com, "The Best and Worst Online Brokers" (`www.smartmoney.com/brokers/`)
- ✔ Don Johnson's "Discount Stock Brokers Ranked" (`www.sonic.net/donaldj/`)

Opening an account at a brokerage

When it's time to open an account at a brokerage firm, you'll have to complete an application form, of course, but you'll also have to jump through a few other hoops that are unique to investment clubs.

Bring on the paperwork

Most brokerage firms have a separate account application form just for clubs. They may refer to it as a *partnership application.* You'll need your club's tax identification number before you apply.

Your club must also decide which of your members are authorized to make trades and receive information on the club's behalf. Most clubs appoint two members or officers to act in that capacity, usually the treasurer and one other person to serve as a backup. Your brokerage may have a separate trading authorization form that also must be completed, enabling your club's selected representatives to deal with the firm.

Some brokerage firms ask for the personal investment experience and other financial information about the authorized contact person, including a bank reference, number of years of experience in the markets, a statement of annual income, and whether the member holds a 10-percent share of any public corporation. Some of these details may be specific to margin accounts (more on margin accounts later in this section); others are required for cash and margin account applications. Some club members may balk at answering these questions, so check with the brokerage to make sure you understand whether your club needs to fill in those blanks for the type of account you're opening. Then make sure your designees are comfortable with the questions.

The account application also requires a mailing address for your club. You don't need a P.O. box or separate address just for the club; you can use the home address of your treasurer, secretary, or any other club member. In fact, even if you have a P.O. box, you still need to provide a street address for the application, but you can request that mail be sent to the P.O. box. Some clubs have a member who arranges to use his or her work address to receive club mail. Besides monthly account statements, your club also receives proxy statements and quarterly and annual reports from each of the companies in your portfolio, so expect to receive some mail for the club at whatever address you choose.

Cash or margin?

The account application form also asks whether you want to open a *cash* or a *margin* account for your club. Margin accounts allow you to borrow money from your brokerage firm, usually to enable your club to invest in additional shares. This is known as *buying on margin*. Margin accounts are required if your club wants to trade options.

Most clubs want to avoid margin accounts for two reasons: They'll be investing only in stocks, not options, and they'll not want to take on the additional risks of margin trading. When you trade on margin, you must maintain a minimum account value in your portfolio at all times. If the market tumbles while your club is buying shares on margin, you'd either have to contribute more cash or sell shares from your holdings to bring your account value back up to the minimum (what's known as a *margin call*). Choose a cash account now, and you can always convert later if your club decides that it wants to open a margin account.

Some brokerages require that you fund your account when you open it, so you may need to send a check for at least the initial minimum amount required by that firm.

The application and trading authorization forms need to be signed by all your club's members, and you'll need to include a copy of your signed operating agreement with your application.

Skipping the broker — using DRIPs and DSPs

In some cases, investing in the stock market is possible without a broker. How? By buying shares directly from the company itself. More than 1,600 companies now offer Dividend Reinvestment Plans (DRIPs) or Direct Stock Plans (DSPs) that enable investors and clubs to invest in their stocks, in many cases at lower commissions than you'd pay at a brokerage firm — and in some cases with absolutely no commissions whatsoever.

Another advantage of DRIPs and DSPs is that investing much smaller amounts than you'd expect to invest through a brokerage firm often is possible. If your brokerage firm charges a $20 commission, your purchases must be $1,000 or more to keep expenses at or below 2 percent of your total investment. For a new club, it can take a long time to build a portfolio at a brokerage firm.

With DRIPs and DSPs, you purchase shares for your club's portfolio with as little as $50 to $250. When your club is starting out, that is a great way to begin building a portfolio a few shares at a time as you're learning the ropes about investing. You won't need to put thousands of dollars at risk at a time while you're learning about investing in stocks or delay making that first purchase because you're unsure about investing a large sum in the first stock your club chooses.

You can also invest smaller amounts on a monthly basis and take advantage of a method of investing known as *dollar cost averaging.* When you invest a fixed dollar amount each month in a stock, you automatically buy fewer shares when the stock is priced higher and more shares when the stock's price falls. As a result, your average per-share purchase cost is lower, which means your rate of return increases.

Direct stock investing doesn't have to completely replace the role of a broker-age firm. Many popular stocks don't offer direct plans, such as Microsoft, Cisco Systems, and Yahoo!, so you'd need a broker if your club wanted to buy shares of those companies. Many clubs begin building their portfolios using DRIPs and DSPs and then open a brokerage account at a later date.

For more about direct stock investing, including listings of companies that offer DRIPs and DSPs, see these web sites. You can search for plans that meet specific criteria, such as those with no fees or with low initial minimums, or you can learn more about how direct investing works at:

- ✔ DRIP Central, www.dripcentral.com
- ✔ NetStock Direct, www.netstockdirect.com

DSPs have a few disadvantages. When you own shares in a direct plan, you may actually have to hold stock certificates yourself. In a brokerage account, your stocks are held in *street name,* which means that the firm keeps the certificates and holds the shares on your behalf. The best place to keep certificates is in a safe or a bank deposit box. One of your members may volunteer to hold any certificates, but doing so makes those shares a bit harder to retrieve if you ever want to sell or transfer them. Depending on the specific plan, you may also find it harder to sell shares quickly. Many plans only buy and sell shares for customers once each month, something you can do instantly at a brokerage firm.

For every direct account that your club has, you'll receive a separate state-ment at least once each quarter. That means your treasurer must cope with many account statements and stacks of records.

Although enrolling in a DSP is easy — just send a check and application form to the company, enrolling in a DRIP isn't so easy. You first must own the required number of shares (sometimes only one share, others as many as 100 shares, depending on the company). Getting that first share can be an expen-sive problem. You can buy the shares from a brokerage, and then ask the broker to issue a certificate to your club. You'll probably have to pay a fee for issuing a certificate in addition to the initial commission, so this route may not be economical.

Buying that first share

Another approach is to use the services of a DRIP-starter program. You have two options. The first is First Share, a network of investors who've agreed to sell single shares of stock of companies that they already own to other members. First Share requires an annual membership fee to join, and you'll pay a referral fee and a commission for each stock that you want to purchase. Buying shares this way creates mounds of paperwork, because you must manually transfer shares. Once you own a single share, you still need to enroll in the company's DRIP before making an additional purchase. And for each stock that you purchase, you agree to transfer a single share at a later date to another member of the First Share collective.

For more information, contact First Share, 305 Mitchell Mountain Road, Westcliffe, CO 81252; phone 719-783-2929, fax 719-783-2909; Web site `www.firstshare.com`.

Another choice is the Low Cost Investment Plan offered by NAIC. Members can purchase a single share in any of 140 companies for a fee of $7. When you purchase a share through the Low Cost Plan, you'll automatically be registered in the company's DRIP, but it typically takes six to eight weeks for your initial purchase and enrollment to be completed. For more information, contact NAIC, PO Box 228, Royal Oak, MI 48608; phone 888-275-6242; Web site `www.better-investing.org`.

What if your club decides to start out in DRIPs or DSPs but you later decide there's too much paperwork or hassle to deal with? Simply request stock certificates for all the whole shares that you own (you can sell any partial share) and deposit the certificates into your brokerage account. If your brokerage allows free dividend reinvestment plus the purchase of partial shares through that reinvestment, the only difference you'll notice is much less paperwork. All your holdings then are conveniently consolidated onto one account statement. But you want to do this only if you're no longer planning regular contributions to the direct plan. Otherwise, you end up paying a tremendous amount in commissions to your brokerage after the transfer when you continue making small monthly contributions.

Part III
Running an Investment Club

The 5th Wave   By Rich Tennant

"...and Denise—did you have a chance to research the wig and novelty hairpiece industry for stock tips?"

In this part . . .

Your investment club is up and running, but your work is not done. You need to have productive meetings, keep your club members on top of their responsibilities, create an education program, and find ways to deal with any problems that may arise. This part touches all those bases, and it gives you important information about club accounting and recordkeeping.

Chapter 8

Managing the Ins and Outs of Club Membership

In This Chapter

▶ Reviewing the duties and obligations of club members

▶ Welcoming new members

▶ Saying goodbye — handling the withdrawal of a member

*M*embership in an investment club has its privileges, it's true, but it also has its responsibilities. In fact, without members who are willing to take their club duties seriously, your club is doomed, doomed, doomed.

Being well organized right from the start is essential for your club. Make it clear to all new members exactly what's required of them before they join — and reminding current members on a regular basis won't hurt, either! Your club has years, it is hoped, of productive work ahead of it, and slackers can't be tolerated.

We scared you off? Sure, an investment club is a great deal of work, but most club members find the *work* interesting, educational, and not at all tedious. As your club progresses and you begin seeing the fruits of your collective labors, the work part of it will become as comfortable as your favorite old sweater.

Member Responsibilities

Business is your number-one priority. Successful clubs find the exact mixture of fun and education to inject into the mix, too, but members must agree that focusing on the really important stuff is what matters. These clubs adopt clear rules about member responsibilities, stringently enforce them, and willingly take appropriate action against members who don't live up to their obligations. When the survival of the club is at stake, members must know when to help certain members hit the highway and then actually follow through by waving goodbye.

Laying out your expectations for all club members in your club's bylaws is good idea. You may also want to create a separate document that describes in detail what each member is required to do and use it when you are recruiting new members to quickly show exactly what their responsibilities will be if they choose to join.

So what should your members be expected to do? The following sections describe some of the more important membership tasks for your club to consider when deciding on member responsibilities. In the end, they all add up to one single word — commitment. In as many ways as you can, delineate the various ways that members must be committed to your club and its eventual success, and we're willing to bet that your members will rise to the challenge.

Attending meetings regularly

Because most of your club business transpires during regular meetings, members who can't attend meetings aren't going to contribute as much to the club's success. In fact, few things are more disheartening than a club meeting where only a handful of members show up. Sure, everyone will miss a meeting now and then, but chronic absenteeism just won't cut it.

Some clubs go so far as specifying the minimum number of meetings that a member must attend each year or quarter. Members who miss a certain number of meetings are placed *on probation,* and the club secretary writes them a letter asking them to reaffirm their commitment to the club. If the member doesn't respond or continues to miss meetings, he or she may become a candidate for termination.

Occasionally, because of changes in work, family, or school responsibilities, some club members may not be able to attend meetings on a consistent basis. Determining how to handle these situations is up to your club, but once you set a precedent for one member, you need to follow it in the future for all other members.

We hate suggesting that you follow a hard line with your members, but being fairly intolerant about irregular attendance is important because, among the SEC regulations that affect investment clubs is the stipulation they shouldn't have inactive members. By itself, having absentee members shouldn't be a problem, but if your club runs afoul of other regulations it can get into trouble.

Researching and presenting stocks

Every member of your club needs to be an active participant in the club's effort to find suitable stocks for your portfolio and then to research those stocks to determine whether they meet your club's goals. In the beginning, your club members may be inexperienced investors, but they'll never learn unless they put some effort into their education. Providing a supportive environment during meetings is far better for your club as it encourages neophytes to make presentations. They'll learn from their experience, and your more experienced members also will benefit from this reaffirmation of the important aspects of stock analysis.

Members also need to be expected to serve as a stock watcher for one or two holdings in the club's portfolio. Each month, stock watchers update your club on their assigned stocks, which requires them to devote some time to researching stock between meetings. The stock-watcher process is discussed in more detail in Chapter 16.

Your club may decide to require members to take the initiative to discover and then to present a certain number of stocks to the club for purchase consideration each year (including a completed Stock Selection Guide, the primary tool for stock analysis used by many clubs). Regardless of whether you include this requirement in your bylaws, be sure to emphasize that each member must contribute to the club's investment process in some way.

Doing their homework

Homework may bring back grade-school nightmares for many, but it is inescapable in your club. Every month, your best and brightest will come together to trade ideas, share research, and build a world-class portfolio of stocks. And then you'll all go off to come up with more ideas, follow up with more research, and make your portfolio even better.

One of the worst ways to spend a club meeting is hearing excuse after excuse from members who haven't done their assigned homework. Make it clear that those who volunteer for assignments must follow through, and members who don't finish their homework automatically get a failing grade. Too many failing grades, and they risk flunking themselves right out of the club.

Serving as officers

Some club members have natural leadership qualities, and others, well, they're natural followers. Some of your club's members will be organized and detail-oriented, while others will have a decidedly less methodical approach to the world. But all your members need to be ready to serve as club officers when called. Some clubs expect every member to eventually serve in every club officer's position, and even have term limits to make sure that members rotate through all the positions.

It's important to recognize that serving as an officer can be a time-consuming job. Clubs often don't expect their officers to be as active as other members in the club's investment research and portfolio management.

Making timely contributions

Money makes the world go 'round, and your club, too. But members who routinely don't pay up promptly have an adverse effect on your club portfolio. One of the basic rules about club investing is that you need to regularly invest in the stock market. If members aren't regularly adding to the club's capital account, the club can miss opportunities in the market. Even with today's discount brokerage commissions, you still can tweak your portfolio returns upward when you invest larger sums in your stock purchases, because that means commissions will eat up less of each investment.

Almost every club stipulates a minimum member contribution in its operating agreement or bylaws. But stipulating the penalty for members who either stop making contributions or are late with their monthly dues is equally as important. Many clubs levy a $5 fee every time members are late with their dues. They may allow for a grace period of a day or two after the meeting, but then that member has to pay the fine. If the member doesn't pay the late fee when making his or her late contribution, the club can choose to instruct the treasurer to deduct the fine from the tardy member's holdings automatically.

Recognizing your superstars

A little bit of positive reinforcement can go a long way toward fostering a spirit of teamwork in your club. While every member should be willing to serve the club as best he or she can, don't be afraid to let your members know when they've done an exceptionally good job, or put forth a solid effort no matter what the end result. And those members who go the extra mile need to be acknowledged.

Be imaginative. Why not give out awards at your annual meeting, showing your appreciation for club members? Think up categories such as Most Valuable Member, Most Improved Club Member, Best Investment Analyst, or Provider of Tastiest Snacks, and give out simple prizes. Your focus needs to be on emphasizing that everyone's contributions throughout the year are important to your club's continued success. Your president must also remember during meetings to point out any exceptional efforts made by members. Saying a nice word or two isn't hard, but doing so means an awful lot to those who have put in a lot of effort to ensure the club's success.

Members who miss meetings are probably not making their required monthly contributions, either. These members need to be handled the same as any delinquent member. For starters, all members need to realize that they don't have to contribute many dollars to their club, but they need to be consistent in their payments. Some clubs require all members to write 12 checks at the beginning of each year, one for each month. The treasurer then deposits each month's batch of checks, so that no member ever misses a payment. (Of course, members have to make sure that enough cash is in their personal bank accounts to cover the checks every month.)

Admitting New Members

No matter how successful or entertaining your club is, some of your founding members inevitably end up withdrawing from the club. Members may find their schedules changing, no longer leaving any time to contribute, or they may simply move away. In some cases, they just lose interest and decide that an investment club isn't right for them after all.

If you end up with vacancies in your club membership after members leave, it's time to think about recruiting new members. For most clubs, the process of admitting new members is fraught with contradictions. You want to be democratic and extend opportunities to people within your realm of acquaintances, but you don't want troublemakers. You want eager but not overbearing members. And, unfortunately, you can't evaluate members by how much investment knowledge they possess. In fact, too much "knowledge" can be a detriment in a club setting, yet an excited beginner can end up being one of the most productive members of your club. Just remember, new members can breathe new life into your investment club.

You want to be able to give any prospects a good long assessment and clearly outline member expectations that your club already has before inviting them to join your club. That's why clubs establish formal guidelines for admitting new members. New prospects also must establish their commitment to the club during a trial membership period by fulfilling certain requirements before becoming full members. Although this may seem like a trial by fire, it's more often a self-selecting endeavor. Once some prospects see how much work goes into running a club, they lose interest and decline to join.

The number of members that your club can have usually is set out in your operating agreement. Once you've reached the maximum, you can maintain a formal waiting list of prospects who are interested in the club. Then, as members withdraw from the club and spaces becomes available, the next entry on the waiting list is invited to begin the rites of initiation.

Your club needs to appoint one member to coordinate the member admittance process. This task can fall to your vice president, but because his or her role traditionally is overseeing the education program, you may want to create a new officer position or simply designate one member as membership coordinator. Some clubs simply turn these tasks over to the club secretary, whose task already is dealing with more of the nonfinancial club paperwork.

As your club decides on a procedure for bringing in new members, keep in mind the important new-member requirements described in the following sections.

Testing their commitment

The ultimate objective in assessing prospective members is determining that they'll be committed to the club. No single question you can ask provides an answer to this, but actions speak louder than words. In the right setting, you can evaluate candidates by their conduct during a period of initiation or trial membership.

Requiring a sponsor

In some clubs, a prospective member must be sponsored by a current member. Because clubs generally are close-knit groups, rarely does a candidate come along who is completely unknown to all the members in the club. But even if you actively search for new members outside of your members' business and social circles, you still can require an existing member to step up to the plate as a mentor or sponsor for the candidate. The sponsor can coach the prospect, provide advice, and guide him or her along the path to becoming a member.

Attending several meetings

Most clubs require their prospective members to attend between three and six club meetings before formally being considered for membership. This trial membership period provides an opportunity for the entire club to get to know the candidate and for the candidate to get a better feel for the club and how it operates. The candidate can silently observe meetings or else ask questions and join in discussions. The recruit who's willing to jump into the fray or ask questions, even at the most basic level, is giving you a good indication that you've found a great prospect.

Learning the club's investing strategy

Clubs that make education a priority often require that applicants demonstrate a similar commitment to education. Prospective members may have to agree to complete a Stock Selection Guide (SSG) class conducted by a local NAIC chapter or work with another member to learn NAIC's approach to investing. Other clubs may require new members to view NAIC's educational SSG videotape.

New members can demonstrate proficiency with the stock analysis methods used by the club in many ways. Requiring candidates to take steps toward learning the tools certainly helps cull the unlikely candidates. When they're unwilling to make the effort here, you can be sure they're not the type of member you want.

Making a presentation to the club

Nothing motivates you to work harder than speaking before a group of people that you're trying to impress! Clubs often require prospective members to prepare and present a complete stock study at a regularly scheduled meeting. Other topics may be acceptable for presentations, too. An applicant can present a brief talk about the status of an industry, or another educational topic, or just about any subject. The important thing is that they're willing to do their homework. They can develop the presentation under the guidance of the sponsor or mentor, or do it solo.

Completing a questionnaire

A simple questionnaire helps you evaluate a person who is interested in joining the club. You don't want to scare prospects away with a long form, but you do want to gather some details while giving them a little glimpse of your club's objectives. Examples of information requested in a questionnaire that combines personal contact information with questions about a candidate's goals and experience are

- Name.
- Address.
- Day and evening telephone.
- E-mail address.
- Why do you want to join this club?
- What do you hope to gain from being a member?
- What is your previous investing experience?

- ✔ What is your investment philosophy?

- ✔ How much time can you devote on average each month to researching and analyzing stocks for the club, preparing presentations for club meetings, handling the duties of a club officer if so elected, and fulfilling other responsibilities of membership?

- ✔ Are you willing to commit to the club for the long term?

- ✔ Are you financially able to meet the minimum monthly contribution amount, initiation fee, and initial buy-in?

- ✔ What other experience and skills can you offer the club?

Why brokers shouldn't be club members

Although NAIC's suggested partnership agreement states that no broker shall be a member of a club, no SEC regulations prohibit employees of a broker-dealer from being in an investment club or having a brokerage account at some other firm. So why does NAIC make this strong recommendation against permitting a broker to be a club member?

Part of the reason is the justified fear that the broker member, as a more experienced member, can dominate other, less knowledgeable members. They might turn to the broker member for guidance on every subject, which completely undercuts the entire educational purpose of the club. Thus members won't be as motivated to learn when they have someone else to lean on (and we're certainly not assuming that the broker is an expert when it comes to a long-term, buy-and-hold philosophy, either).

Another reason is the securities industry is highly regulated, with rules governing how employees of brokerage firms can buy and sell securities in the public markets. The rules are meant to prevent brokerage employees from personally benefiting from inside information to which they may have access because of their jobs. Some companies require regular disclosure by employees of their personal investment activities. Some won't permit employees to have a brokerage account at another firm, which can be a problem for any broker members of your club when the club's account is held elsewhere.

Although unlikely, your broker member can be granted an exemption by his or her employer as long as the member regularly submits detailed information on your club's activities. Interestingly, many brokerage firms permit their licensed brokers to have accounts at other firms or become members of investment clubs, yet they require the broker's spouse and immediate family members to hold accounts exclusively with their firms and forbid them from belonging to an investment club.

Although the brokerage firms' policies may seem hard to understand in certain situations, remember that they're a strong example of the self-regulation that protects us all from the misuse and abuse of information for the personal profit of those in the inner circle. Having those policies in place is also why the American financial markets are the best in the world. Not allowing brokers to be members of your investment club may not seem fair — and may even seem trivial, but like it or not, that's the way the system works.

Customize the questionnaire to suit your own needs but keep it as short and as relevant as possible. Potential members should submit a completed questionnaire before visiting your club for the first time. When it's clear that they don't share the same investment philosophy and aren't interested in adopting a new one, for example, you have no reason to invite them to your club meetings. They're not the kind of member you're interested in.

Creating a Prospective Member Packet

How can a prospective member find out more about your club when all the strategies we just outlined are designed to help your club learn about the prospective member? Well, one way is to create a prospective member packet that includes a collection of the club's documents, clearly and fully describing the process that a candidate must follow to be considered for membership. The packet also needs to provide plenty of information about the club in general. Here are some of the items your club should include in your packet:

- ✔ An introductory letter from your club president explaining the history and goals of the club.
- ✔ An outline of steps the candidate must take to be considered for membership.
- ✔ The current club operating agreement.
- ✔ The current club operating procedures or bylaws.
- ✔ The club's mission statement/investment philosophy.
- ✔ A recent valuation statement.
- ✔ A brief overview of member responsibilities (drawn from bylaws) for quick reference.
- ✔ A sample Stock Selection Guide, with resources for learning the SSG.
- ✔ A sample Stock Watcher report with description of responsibilities.
- ✔ A schedule of local NAIC classes during the next 6 months, if available.

It's a Go: Formally Requesting Membership

After completing all the requirements for membership, many clubs require prospective members to submit a letter to the president formally requesting membership. The letter doesn't need to be long or eloquent, it merely serves as a written confirmation that the candidate understands the club's goals and requirements and wants to become a member. Your club can create a template for prospective members to use when officially acknowledging that they agree with the club's goals and strategy and will work hard to help the club thrive. You can provide this sample letter in the prospective member packet. The signed letter then can be filed away with the club's permanent records.

Submitting to a membership vote

Once the potential member has run your club's gantlet and passed all the initiation rites with flying colors, it's time to put the matter of his or her membership to a vote. The president places the new member's candidacy on the agenda for an upcoming meeting, and the club should move, second, and discuss the item the same way it would any other item of business. If your club is informal, you may allow the candidate to remain in the room during a vote, but in most cases, the prospect is excused while the club discusses the candidacy and then votes.

Your club's operating agreement generally specifies how voting is to be carried out. However, as a practical matter, new members typically must receive a unanimous vote of current members, ensuring that they meet with the satisfaction of all the other members and reducing the chance of personality conflicts at some point down the road.

Signing the operating agreement

Once the prospect is duly elected as a member of your club, and after the last drop of champagne has been polished off, the new member can get down to business. One detail that must be taken care of right away is for the new member to sign the club's operating agreement. In some clubs, the member signs the actual agreement, while other clubs ask the member to sign and date a simple statement that's attached to the original.

Depending on state and local regulations, the addition of a member may require your club to file an updated operating agreement with local authorities. This can entail an additional filing fee, so check out the requirements in your jurisdiction and take action accordingly. (In practice, few clubs file every time they add or remove a member from their roster.)

Designing a New Member Orientation Packet — and a Routine

Once admitted to your club, you'll want to bring that new member up to speed as quickly as possible by providing him or her with an orientation packet. Much of the information already is included in the prospective member packet — if your club provides one as we recommend, so you need to give new members only the documents they don't already have, including:

- ✔ A letter from the club president welcoming the new member and stressing how happy your club is to have him or her on board.

- ✔ A brief reminder of the work ahead.

- ✔ A roster with the names, addresses, phone numbers, and e-mail addresses of each member. Some clubs include birthdays, names of spouses, and other information.

- ✔ A current operating agreement.

- ✔ A current operating procedures and/or bylaws.

- ✔ The club's mission statement/investment philosophy.

- ✔ A brief overview of member responsibilities (drawn from bylaws) for quick reference.

- ✔ A sample Stock Selection Guide, with resources for learning the SSG.

- ✔ A sample Stock Watcher report with description of responsibilities.

- ✔ A schedule of meeting times/locations for the upcoming year.

- ✔ A schedule of partner presentations set to be given at the next few meetings.

- ✔ A schedule of local NAIC classes over next 6 months, if available.

- ✔ A list of current officers.

Paying the initiation fee

The founding members of any investment club bear the burden of startup costs, including expenses for state and local registration fees, software, and educational materials. As new members join the club, they receive the benefits of those expenditures without ever directly having to pay for them.

As a result, some clubs try to make things a little bit fairer by requiring new members to pay an initiation fee, a one-time charge of $20 to $50, which is perhaps equal to the minimum monthly contribution set by the club. Recorded in the club's books as a member fee (not a payment), it doesn't buy units for the new member. Instead it offsets some of the costs incurred by the original club members. However, member fees slightly increase the unit value of the club since they increase the club's total value but don't trigger the issuance of any additional units. Therefore, fees benefit those members who have the larger capital accounts, not necessarily those who've been in the club the longest.

Some clubs set high initiation fees of $100 or more, usually in an attempt to discourage casual interest from prospective members. The problem with high initiation fees is that new members will probably show a loss in their account values for a long time and may become discouraged. Requiring a large initial contribution is better than a large fee that doesn't buy units for the new member. Keep your initiation fees reasonable.

Making an initial buy-in

The question of whether new members should "buy-in" usually comes from clubs that require all members to have equal ownership in the club. In Chapter 7, we explain why equal ownership often creates more problems than it solves and generally isn't a good idea for most clubs. One primary reason is that difficulties arise when equal membership clubs admit new members. If club members have built up large capital accounts over a number of years, the cost of a *buy-in* can be in the thousands of dollars.

When you set a financial membership requirement like this, you automatically reduce the size of your pool of qualified applicants, and thus may be overlooking some of the better candidates. Plenty of eager and committed members could be out there for your club, but investing thousands of dollars all at once is more than likely a difficult proposition for most of them.

That said, your club has no reason not to require an initial contribution that's modestly higher than your monthly minimum, especially if you require an initiation fee. The fee increases the new member's average unit cost, but initially shows up as an investment loss. As new members make their regular contributions each month, the percentage loss will likely become smaller and smaller as the club's unit value grows. Over time, new members finally break even. The bigger their contributions in the beginning, the quicker they'll reach profit territory in their personal accounts. In addition, the larger the new members' investments in the club, especially in the beginning, the more involved and committed they'll feel to their club.

It's up to your club to decide what's best: not to require a buy-in for new members and simply let them make their first monthly contribution, or to require an amount in addition to their regular contribution to encourage a stronger personal commitment. Both policies have benefits and drawbacks, so discuss this issue thoroughly before coming to a final decision.

Faithfully Executing the Duties of Office

Do you solemnly swear to faithfully execute any position as club officer, and, to the best of your ability, preserve, protect, and defend your club portfolio? You'd better!

As a self-governing association, your club needs to elect officers to carry out various administrative and management tasks. That means all members must be willing to serve when called upon. Hard-working officers are essential to your club's successes, and the extra bit of work they do each month is of utmost importance.

Officer responsibilities

Most clubs elect four officers: the president, vice president, secretary, and treasurer. In some clubs, these positions are known, respectively, as the *presiding partner, assistant presiding partner, recording partner,* and *financial partner.* Although the names are different, the jobs are the same.

President

Like the president of a country or a humongous multinational corporation, your investment club president sets the tone for your club's operations. When nominating candidates for this office, look for someone who's organized, dependable, and able to motivate your members and pull any laggards back in line when necessary. The president doesn't have to be your club's most knowledgeable investor or most brilliant stock analyst, either. Any member with a strong commitment to your club's continued success can make a marvelous president regardless of investment expertise.

The president sets the agenda for each meeting, by either polling members to see who'd like to present or assigning members to cover certain topics. The president also sets the agenda for the club's entire operation, interpreting its mission and putting it into practice.

The president's job is to run each club meeting. Chapter 9 includes plenty of tips and advice for making sure that meetings run smoothly, from understanding the basics of parliamentary procedure and *Robert's Rules of Order* to refereeing disagreements between members.

Think of how different our country's presidents have been during in the last 20 years, and you can see that many different presidential styles exist. Some run the club with a firm hand, and some move a meeting along by being quietly prepared and detail-oriented, while others are top-notch negotiators.

During the meeting, the president calls for motions to be made and seconded, and conducts the voting on those motions. Perhaps the most important skill in leading a meeting is knowing when a discussion should be concluded. Too often during club meetings, members engage in spirited debates but they end up rehashing the same old arguments in circular fashion. A good president knows when to move on after all have had their say and then puts the item to a vote or otherwise takes action.

In the end, an effective president almost always is a consensus builder. The president must be attuned to the club's discussions and the personalities of its members and be able to sense when a consensus is forming to take action in a certain direction. Likewise, if no consensus forms, the president must either move the club on to a new topic or explore compromises that can help members toward reaching an agreement.

The president has some fiduciary duties in the club, too. Some clubs require their presidents to cosign checks above a certain amount, or to authorize expenses that fall below a certain nominal amount, say $25. That way, the club doesn't spend its valuable time approving modest expenses such as for a few postage stamps. The president also may have trading authorization in the club's brokerage account, serve as a backup to the treasurer, and facilitate the transition to a new treasurer when the time comes.

Club members look for their president to direct them, give them instructions, and ask for their assistance. The president should never hesitate before asking for volunteers to help with the work or calling upon individuals directly when there's a job to do.

Vice president

Everything you've just heard about the president goes for the vice president, too! In most clubs, the vice president mostly is a benchwarmer who rarely gets any playing time. As the president's backup, the VP steps to the plate only if the president can't make it to the ballpark.

Instead of making the vice president's role mostly ceremonial, however, many clubs choose to make their VP the club's designated education officer. The VP then is responsible for the educational component of each meeting, whether it's a simple presentation or fun and games. Chapter 16 provides plenty of ideas for helping stoke the club education officer's imagination.

In some clubs, the vice president serves as the portfolio manager. That doesn't mean the VP makes decisions about trading in the club's portfolio, but rather he or she is responsible for keeping tabs on the portfolio's diversification and performance over time. The portfolio manager consolidates Stock Watcher reports, and then prepares reports and graphs about the club portfolio as a whole.

As mentioned in the section "Admitting New Members," earlier in this chapter, the vice president also may serve as the club's membership officer, responsible for recruiting, inducting, and mentoring new members. The membership officer maintains the club's prospective and new member packets and shepherds prospects through the club's initiation period.

There's no end to the jobs that your club can assign to the vice president — wait, here's another! Why not have the VP be responsible for meetings and special events, scheduling the location of each meeting, setting up and breaking down the meeting room, and organizing the club's annual meeting? Like we said, you can customize the vice president's job to your club's needs.

Be sure your club doesn't overwhelm the same vice president with *all* these duties. In larger clubs, multiple vice presidents may each be assigned a specific function, such as portfolio manager, membership officer, education officer, and meetings and events planner. Each has his or her own responsibilities but all would contribute a great deal to the success of your club.

Secretary

Although the secretary's job is largely clerical, an efficient secretary goes a long way toward streamlining every club meeting. The secretary's main role is keeping the official minutes of each club meeting, recording the wording of every motion, the name of the member who made the motion, who seconded it, and the results of the voting. The secretary summarizes discussions that occur during the meeting, announcements that are made, and items that are tabled. If any assignments are made for members to make presentations at future meetings, the secretary includes them in the minutes and reminds the chosen members a week or so before their presentations.

After every meeting, the secretary distributes copies of the minutes for every member to review prior to the next meeting. In some clubs, the president may first review the minutes before they're distributed to the membership. If it isn't possible to send out or e-mail the minutes prior to the next meeting, the secretary distributes copies at the start of the meeting. Most clubs try "to dispense with the actual reading of the minutes" by giving members the chance to review them between meetings or at the start of the following meeting. Members then can suggest corrections instead of sitting through the formal reading of the minutes. The secretary then makes any approved changes and files a copy in the club's permanent records.

One ace secretary we know brings his laptop to meetings and writes the minutes as the meeting goes on. When the meeting is over, he has a draft ready to be e-mailed for review. Appendix A includes sample club meeting minutes that you can use as a guide for your own club's minutes.

Club secretaries need to take advantage of e-mail whenever possible. Instead of mailing minutes, the secretary can quickly send copies electronically to all club members along with reminders about upcoming meetings and assignments. More about collaborative online tools and how they can help keep your club meetings running smoothly is explained in Chapter 9.

Your club secretary needs to assist the president in distributing the agenda prior to or at each meeting, serve as the club historian, and keep the club's official records, correspondence, forms, paperwork, applications, bylaws, and operating agreement. The secretary should make use of a simple filing system to keep these assorted documents in order.

Treasurer

Your club treasurer holds the combination to your club's vault. As the financial officer, the treasurer's job is filled with details, numbers, and reports. So much so, that we devote all of Chapter 10 to dealing with the treasurer's job. Some clubs split the responsibilities of the treasurer into two positions, electing or appointing an associate treasurer or co-treasurer. The most important aspects of the position are summarized in this section, regardless of whether the job is done by one member or two.

The treasurer is responsible for managing your club's financial books. Each month, the treasurer collects checks from every member, records them, and deposits them into the club's account. The treasurer pays bills, writes checks, and collects fees, in addition to placing stock trades and transferring funds.

During club meetings, the treasurer provides a report on the club's current financial condition and all recent transactions. Once a year, the treasurer must prepare the club's tax filings with federal and state authorities.

Club accounting software (as we describe in Chapter 10) is absolutely essential in helping your treasurer do his or her job precisely and with as little effort as possible. Don't make your treasurer suffer through the hard, tedious work of doing the accounting and recordkeeping by hand just to save the club the cost of the software. Using software enables the treasurer to prepare reports, reconcile accounts, and record all the club's transactions quickly, accurately, and easily.

Remember, a well-done treasurer's job is essential to your club's survival, so you'll want to keep your club treasurer as happy as possible. Buy the software, and you'll be rewarded with a content and smiling treasurer through the years.

Requiring each member to serve

Sometimes, merely expressing the desire that every member must serve as an officer isn't enough. You must put the rule of law behind it. In many clubs, the operating agreement or bylaws specifically state that each member shall serve as an officer, and that no member will serve more than one term as a particular officer until every other member has served.

Term limits

Unless your operating agreement calls for a dictatorship or a constitutional monarchy, your club will conduct elections each year to put in place a slate of new officers. Some clubs try to encourage every member to serve as an officer by prohibiting any member from serving successive terms as an officer, or by implementing term limits.

Instead of simply stating that no member can serve more than a set number of successive terms, your club may also specify a period of a few years during which a past-officer cannot serve in the same post. The point of these rules is to keep the club's leadership fresh and spread the responsibility around to all your members.

As an added bonus, term limits help prevent any single member from establishing his or her own little fiefdom by being re-elected year after year and becoming an oppressive, overwhelming force in the club.

Officer rotation

Another practical way to ensure that every member serves (and to prevent officer burnout) is to rotate officers each year according to a set schedule. Some clubs establish a formal procedure for nominating each year's slate of officers, chronologically moving through their membership lists according to the order in which each member joined the club. This year's secretary becomes next year's nominee for treasurer, the treasurer becomes vice president, the vice president becomes president, and so on. The next member on the list becomes new secretary, and the president goes back to the bottom of the list with a reprieve from serving as an officer for at least a few years depending on how many members your club has.

Sounds like musical chairs, doesn't it? The advantage of this method is its simplicity. All members know what will be expected of them and when, and officer responsibilities are assigned fairly and with a minimum of fuss. Your club may prefer conducting traditional elections, but this is one strategy that's worth a least a short discussion the next time election season rolls around.

Dealing with Member Withdrawals

As sure as members come into your club, members certainly will go. Some of your founding club members eventually will depart the club for one reason or another. And even if members don't leave, at some point they may want to withdraw a portion of their club accounts either to pay for college expenses for a child, buy a vacation home, or take care of some other large expenditure.

Withdrawals from accounts are perfectly acceptable — what good is any savings or investing account if the money is locked away forever? But your club wants to discourage members from making too many withdrawals, especially for nonessential reasons. If members constantly are pulling out money and redepositing it later, your entire club membership suffers the consequences. Your money won't be working for you in the stock market the way you'd like, and you may even be forced to let go of particular stocks that you'd much rather keep just to fund the withdrawals.

Your operating agreement (see Chapter 6) outlines how any withdrawal should be handled, regardless whether it's a partial or a complete withdrawal.

Complete withdrawals

Two types of complete withdrawals can be made, the same way that members can leave your club two ways: voluntarily and involuntarily. It is hoped that you'll never have to remove a member from your club, but your operating agreement must be prepared for that contingency in the event one of your members turns out to be the proverbial bad apple.

A member who wants to permanently withdraw from your club has to make such a request in writing and submit it to the club president. The request is read into the minutes of the next meeting, and the club members then decide how to pay the withdrawal (more on that later in this section). Usually, the amount of the withdrawal is determined by the unit value on the club's valuation statement created for its next meeting, and the club has 30 days to pay. These delays don't exist because the club wants to be difficult, but rather to allow enough time for it to raise the cash to pay off the exiting member, if there isn't enough cash in the club's account to fully cover the cost.

In most cases, it comes as no surprise when a member asks to leave the club. The member may already have expressed his displeasure to other members. He probably stopped making contributions and no longer attends meetings. Perhaps she failed to fulfill her responsibilities to the club, and therefore the provisions of the club's bylaws and operating agreement. The secretary or president needs to either ask the member for his or her resignation, or persuade the member to give it another try. But it's not worth pushing too hard. Members who half-heartedly agree to participate after a period of inactivity may never really come around. You can give them a second chance but don't expect miracles.

In other cases, members seemingly disappear from the face of the earth. They won't attend meetings, or return calls or e-mails. Before assuming that the member really wants to forget all about the club, an officer or designated representative of the club must try to reach the member personally. You may find that the member has had some serious life change such as a major illness or loss of job, so give him or her the benefit of the doubt before taking any action to remove the member from the club.

If you have reached the end of your rope after trying without success to reach out to the member, and if your club agrees that a member must be terminated, then you can proceed with an involuntary withdrawal. Your operating agreement should clearly state the reasons why a member can be removed, and you should exercise caution by carefully following the steps outlined in your agreement.

Partial withdrawals

A partial withdrawal is handled almost exactly the same as a complete voluntary withdrawal. The member's written request for the withdrawal of a portion of his or her account goes before club during its regular meeting. The unit value is set at the next meeting, and the member then is paid within 30 days. Club members decide whether to pay the member in cash or via a stock transfer.

Withdrawal fees and limits

When a member withdraws, the club may encounter some costs involved in raising the cash to pay off the member, including brokerage commissions to sell shares from the club's portfolio. For that reason, many clubs require members to pay a withdrawal fee whenever they leave the club or take out funds. Traditionally, this fee has been 3 percent of the amount of the withdrawal, or the actual costs, if they turn out to be higher. However, with today's discount brokerage firms, commissions usually are much, much lower than 3 percent.

Some clubs see the withdrawal fee as deterrence against too frequent withdrawals. If members know they'll have to pay a certain fee every time they take cash from the club, they're more likely to refrain from making too many withdrawals. You may decide that charging members only the actual costs (if there are any) associated with their withdrawal is fairer. If you're worried that members may make too many partial withdrawals, you can restrict them to one or two withdrawals per year, or give them one free withdrawal a year but apply a fee on any subsequent withdrawals during the same year.

Some clubs take a cue from a common practice in the mutual fund industry in determining the fees that members pay for a complete withdrawal. Some funds carry what is known as a *declining back-end load*. This is a fee (load) that you must pay when you sell (that's the back-end) a fund. The fee decreases each year that you own the fund. It may start out at 6 percent or 7 percent, and then decline a percentage point each year until it gets to 1 percent or even zero. This practice encourages shareholders to hold on to their shares for the long-term, and can work the same way for your club.

Your club sets its own withdrawal fee in its operating agreement. Try to be equitable, and don't make your withdrawal penalties so severe that they become overwhelming. If you charge a member hundreds of dollars upon making their withdrawal, you may end up with a club of inactive, uninterested members, hanging around only out of fear of the penalty they'll be assessed if they leave. Having an energetic group of members with a small portfolio always is better than having a large amount of money and many inert members.

Paying off a withdrawal

Partial and full withdrawals from your club can be paid off in three ways. You can either write a check, transfer shares of stock, or write a check and transfer shares.

The method your club chooses depends on a number of factors. Each has its advantages and disadvantages, so you may end up choosing the cash option in some circumstances and transferring shares in others. Your club should always consider both options, however, and then take a vote on how to proceed as is outlined in your operating agreement and bylaws.

The withdrawing member may have a preference for how he or she wants to receive the payout. But, remember that your club is under no obligation to satisfy this preference unless it also fits with your club's best interests.

Cash payoffs

The easiest way to pay off a withdrawal is to write a check. Of course, that means your club must have enough cash on hand in your bank or brokerage accounts to cover the check. If your club doesn't have enough of a cash reserve, you can solicit additional contributions from members to raise the necessary amount.

Some clubs refer to this as *buying out* a departing member, but that term is a misnomer, because the buyout is nothing more than members purchasing additional units in their own capital accounts and the club using the cash that's raised to retire the departing member's units. No actual transfer of units occurs, but rather it's merely a simultaneous purchase and disbursement.

If your members are unwilling or unable to commit more money to the club, then you can sell some of the shares in your portfolio to raise the cash, which isn't such a bad choice, because most club portfolios can use a little bit of pruning. However, if you decide to sell shares, sell only the shares that your club is holding at a loss. Your club thus records the capital loss, which is then distributed among remaining members as part of your year-end distribution. Members then report their losses on their personal tax returns.

Nearly every club has a loser or two in its portfolio, and even if you're convinced of a losing stock's long-term potential, you may still be better off selling the dog to raise cash. You can always buy it back. Just be sure to wait 31 days after the date of sale so that you don't violate the IRS's wash sale rule, which says that if you sell a stock to register a capital loss, you can't buy it back until 31 days later. This works just fine for your club; simply put the stock on the agenda for the next meeting and consider purchasing it back for your portfolio as soon as 31 days elapse and you raise enough new member contributions to fund the purchase.

As part of any withdrawal, the member receives a withdrawal earnings distribution report from the club treasurer, outlining each member's share of income, capital gains and losses, and expenses since they became a member. The withdrawing member reports those figures to the IRS on his or her personal tax return.

Unless it's unavoidable, you should try not to sell shares that have appreciated (that means they've gone up in price) in your portfolio since you purchased them. If you own only stocks that have gone up in price, then you're probably a most unusual club! A much better way of taking care of the withdrawal is by transferring the appreciated stock.

Stock payoffs

The second method of paying off a withdrawal is by transferring stock to the withdrawing member. Transferring shares is not particularly difficult, but it generally takes several weeks to complete.

If a brokerage firm holds your shares, you can request that certificates be issued to the club for the appropriate number of shares (usually for a fee of $25 to $50 that should be taken out of the departing member's payoff amount before the transfer is started). Once you have the certificate in hand, your club can transfer the shares to the member.

A company's transfer agent can provide your club with the details you'll need to know for transferring shares, or you can contact the investor relations office of the company for help. A standard *Stock Power* form is used to authorize the transfer, or the treasurer can simply sign the back of the stock certificate in many cases. The signature needs to be verified with a *Medallion Signature Guaranty* available at your local bank. Send the Stock Power and the certificate to the transfer agent, and ownership of those shares transfers into the departing member's name.

You can also ask the withdrawing member to open an account with the brokerage firm where the club has its account. Then your treasurer can simply instruct the brokerage to transfer the shares to the member's account. Most brokerages won't transfer shares to an account under a different name at another firm, so your member must open an account at the same company, even if only temporarily. The member can simply close it after the transfer is complete and send the shares to his or her primary brokerage account. Be aware, however, that some firms charge a transfer or account-closing fee.

Whenever you do decide to transfer shares, selecting one of the better performing stocks in your portfolio can work to your benefit. In fact, the bigger the gain is, the better for your club. A provision of the IRS partnership regulations allows securities to be transferred to withdrawing partners. In the case of a full withdrawal, that same law also allows the cost basis of the transferred shares (the amount that the club paid for those shares, which determines how much of a gain the club has realized) to be transferred to the member along with the stocks. If the club's cost basis in the transferred shares is greater than the member's basis in the club, then the member's basis in the stocks is adjusted to be the same as the member's basis in the club. Rather than pay taxes on gains from their withdrawal from membership when they file their next tax return (as they would if they had accepted cash), members receiving shares won't face any tax liability until they sell them. That gives departing members control over when and even how much tax liability is generated. Although that may sound complicated, it means that members and the club all come out ahead if they transfer shares of stock to pay off withdrawing members.

The favorable tax treatment is even better for the member. The holding period for transferred shares is set by the date when the club first bought those shares. If the club held the shares for more than one year before transferring them, the departing member can sell the day after receiving the shares and trigger only a long-term capital gain and not a short-term capital gain. Former members who give some of the shares to charitable organizations avoid capital gains taxes altogether on the donated shares yet still receive a tax deduction in the amount of the value of the shares on the date of the gift. If they give those shares to their children, they can also avoid taxes because the basis of the shares is passed along to the recipient. By accepting withdrawals in stock, members have more control and many more options when dealing with tax ramifications of the withdrawal.

For the club, the difference between its cost basis and the market value of the transferred shares is carried on the books indefinitely as *unrealized gains.* All capital gains are, in effect, stored away and the remaining club members can avoid ever having to pay taxes on those gains. If you have a choice, don't let this opportunity to avoid or control taxes in this way pass your club by!

Regardless of which way your club decides to make the withdrawal payoff, do *not* transfer shares of a stock that are worth less than when your club purchased it, because you don't want to abandon the capital loss. You're better off recording the loss by selling the stock, because doing so reduces every member's taxes. If you really want to get rid of a dog, sell it and use the cash to pay off the departing member.

Chapter 9

Holding Successful Meetings

. . . .

In This Chapter

▶ Organizing your club meetings

▶ Planning an agenda

▶ Keeping your meetings on track

. . . .

*Y*our investment club's work doesn't happen only during its two-hour monthly meetings. You and your club members will spend time during the weeks between your meetings on a number of duties — researching stocks, coming up with new investing ideas and managing (you hope) a growing portfolio. Some of these tasks you'll do on your own, others you'll do in small groups. Then each month, you'll share your findings together at your general meeting before making any final decisions.

You have only a limited time at your meetings to assimilate a great deal of information from your members. You'll need to report on the status of the club's portfolio, get a bit of investing education, decide on potential investments, and perform a handful of other tasks. Clearly you need to make the most of your meetings. That's why an organized meeting strategy is of utmost importance to having a successful club experience.

Planning for Smooth Meetings

Because your club is a democracy, every member gets to have his or her say on any matter under discussion. That's good, of course, because you want your members to be active participants. Sometimes, however, your little democracy can run amok with meetings that drag on for hours, decisions that divide your club, tempers that flare, and frustrations that build and build. Getting your meetings to run like a well-oiled machine may take some time, but a bit of planning in a few different areas goes a long way toward preventing potential disaster.

When to meet

Early in the planning process, you and fellow club members need to decide on a regular meeting time. You can maximize attendance by making sure that your meeting is scheduled at a time when all your members are available. If you schedule the meeting the same night as your secretary's standing mandolin lesson, for instance, your club may find itself conspicuously lacking meeting minutes every month.

Here are five important factors to consider when choosing a meeting time.

1. **Weekday or weekend?**

   Query your members about their schedules and you'll quickly realize which choice works best. If your club is made up of co-workers, everyone will more than likely want to meet during the week. If your fellow club members are mostly mothers with young children, a weekend meeting may make childcare issues easier to resolve.

2. **Day or night?**

   Can you meet over an extended lunch break or on a Saturday afternoon? Maybe a meeting over dinner or after work is more convenient. You may not have enough time to meet during a lunch break, particularly if your members need to eat. With the distraction of trying to complete their midday meals, your club may not have enough time to conduct all its important business.

3. **Always meet at the same time?**

   Some clubs have long, weeknight meetings during the school year, and then schedule shorter meetings, sometimes even at a different time than usual, during often-busier summer months. Although that may make meeting times a little trickier to remember, anything that ensures maximum attendance regardless of season is worth considering. Some clubs even alternate an extended weekend meeting (three hours or more) with a shorter weeknight meeting from month to month. Be flexible and go with what works best for *your* club.

4. **Face-to-face or online?**

   Some successful investment clubs never actually meet. If you form an online club, you can structure it so that you don't have a formal meeting time, but rather you maintain a continual dialogue with regular educational and potential stock purchase voting opportunities. Other online clubs choose to establish a scheduled meeting time, congregating in an Internet chat room at a specific time to conduct traditional club business. We talk more about online club operations in Chapter 5.

5. Availability of meeting location?

If you have a great place to meet but it's available to your club only at certain times, these open times, accordingly, dictate when your club can meet.

Once you decide on the best time to meet, putting the schedule in writing ensures that everyone's on the same calendar page. Your regular meeting schedule also needs to be included in your club's operating agreement. Regardless of whether you meet the second Monday evening of every month, or for breakfast on the third Thursday, or immediately following work on the second Tuesday, have your club secretary type up and distribute the schedule of meeting dates for the coming year at your club's annual meeting. Your members can put this on the refrigerator, next to their computer, or enter the schedule into their calendar program or personal digital assistant (PDA).

Where to meet

Unlike the schedule of meetings, determining the *location* of your club meetings may be more fluid. Some investment clubs meet in an established location each month. Others float from location to location. Your club may decide to meet in the banquet room of a local restaurant, in a meeting room provided free of charge by your library, bank or brokerage house, or in the homes of club members on a rotating basis.

Any of these choices can provide a fine meeting place, as long as it fulfills your club's needs. The more important characteristics of your club's meeting place are that it's comfortable and easily accessible. You want make sure that club members actually look forward to the time they spend at meetings instead of secretly dreading them because they have to search for parking spaces for half an hour first.

Here are six important factors to consider when choosing a meeting location:

1. Will your meeting location remain the same or rotate from month to month?

If your club meetings will be take place in members' homes, you'll need to set up a formal schedule far in advance so that members can plan accordingly. A written schedule with the phone number, address of and direction to each meeting location help ensure that your members make it to the right home on the right date.

2. How accessible is it?

Do your potential meeting places have ample parking? Are they easy to find and located in areas that are convenient for your members?

3. How available is it?

If you want to meet in a free room at the library, are you able to reserve it months in advance? Do the hours that the meeting place is available fit your members' schedules? Does the location offer enough flexibility to adjust meeting times on short notice if the need arises?

4. What kind of space is it?

If you're meeting in space provided by your local bank, will the bank allow you to bring in your tasty snacks? Will you need to be careful about keeping the noise level down as you debate your current stock purchase? Conversely, if you're meeting in a more social environment like a restaurant banquet room, will the location be too distracting to enable you to carry out your important club business? You don't want to be fighting obnoxiously loud music as you try to approve last month's meeting minutes.

5. Will you have all the resources you need?

Some facilities provide computers with Internet connections and overhead projectors for your club's use. Others offer only the basic four walls, a door, tables and chairs. Decide what your club needs before choosing a location — you won't need online computers if you don't use them during your meetings.

6. How much will it cost?

One benefit of meeting in members' homes is that paying a rental fee won't be necessary. Remember that your club can often find free meeting facilities at public libraries, restaurants (providing you all eat there), banks, and other financial businesses. Ask around and you'll probably be pleasantly surprised. Some clubs find it worthwhile to pay a small fee for a convenient, well-equipped meeting place. You cover the expense of any rental fee with whatever annual administrative funds your club requires of its members.

Encouraging regular attendance

No matter what meeting schedule and locations your club establishes, we guarantee that some members of your club will be susceptible to forgetfulness. They'll have just as much trouble remembering *where* your club is scheduled to meet as they will *when* it's supposed to meet. Announcing the date and location of your next meeting at the conclusion of every meeting keeps the dates and locations fresh in everyone's minds.

When your club secretary distributes meeting minutes (either by mail or e-mail), he or she can include an extra reminder about the next month's meeting. An e-mail reminder a few days before the meeting, along with a copy of the meeting agenda, can help remind everyone of the upcoming gathering. Although all members of your club theoretically should be responsible for remembering each meeting on their own, reminders never hurt. You want as many members as possible to attend each meeting, so do what you must to encourage them to show up.

Building the Right Meeting Structure

Despite our emphasis on indulging in tasty treats at club meetings, the key to running a successful investment club meeting — after making sure that everyone attends — is not refreshments but a solid structure. Setting the agenda for each meeting falls to your club's president, who then needs to take command during the meetings, making sure all club business is covered in the time that's allotted. If you're the president, don't sweat it — we'll tell you everything you need for preparing to run each month's meetings.

Running your club's first meetings

Your club's first few meetings can be particularly troublesome, seeming like they're going on for hours — and maybe they actually are! Although your members may have a great deal of enthusiasm and eagerness to get your club up and running as quickly as possible, remind them that your club has plenty of time. Take it slow in the beginning, and don't let your members become overwhelmed by all that needs to be done.

At early club meetings, the president and other officers can be helpful by doing a little extra work before each meeting and planning how everything will come together. Some investment clubs conduct officer meetings outside of the regular monthly meetings, and thus are able to streamline full membership meetings. Although you may not want to make a habit of conducting extra meetings, meeting a few extra times as your club starts out can really help. As you become more experienced, and your club settles into a regular routine, you may not have to spend quite so much time on preparation and administrative tasks, and you can all focus more on your club's portfolio.

Just say no to endless meetings

Your investment club meetings must keep members engaged, interested, and awake. For most clubs, two hours is plenty of time to cover all the necessary business, but your club will settle into its own pace and quickly discover what works best. Some clubs meet during their lunch hours, finishing the necessary business in record time. Other clubs meet over dinner so they can spend three hours or more conducting business and socializing. Whenever you have a special guest or an extended educational presentation by a member, your meetings may run a bit longer than usual. If your club regularly spends three hours every month just covering the basics, chances are good that your members are getting pretty exhausted by the time your meeting is over.

Keeping your club on task and not straying from its agenda helps prevent meetings from running on and on and on. The following are some other tactics to use for smooth-running meetings:

✔ If you have several new members, you may want to schedule your meeting in two parts, providing a special educational workshop specifically for those members just before your regular meeting. That way, your long-standing club members won't become bored while you're covering the basics for new members (although almost everyone can benefit from a review of the basics, particularly when it comes to investing).

✔ If your club members have trouble getting together to research stocks between monthly meetings, you may want to designate an hour before the start of the regular meeting as a work session. That way members of your stock selection committee can use the extra time to review their individual research and decide which stocks to discuss during the formal meeting.

✔ If discussions frequently drift off topic, remember that keeping meetings running efficiently ultimately is your club president's job. He or she can end discussions when they stop being productive, limit the length of discussion on certain items, postpone discussions until the next meeting (a practice known as "tabling" in meeting lingo), and otherwise keep matters moving right along.

Following the "Rules"

In 1876, General Henry M. Robert published the rules under which the United States Congress conducted its meetings. Over time, these rules of parliamentary procedure have become the overriding guidelines by which most meetings are held. Every time someone makes or seconds a motion, or a chairperson calls a meeting to order or tables a discussion, that's *Robert's Rules of Order* being put to use.

The advantage provided by *Robert's Rules of Order* is an instant structure for any meeting. As we said earlier in this section, a structured meeting is a good thing, and *Robert's Rules* can provide a good roadmap for the route your club meeting takes. But remember that a good strong dose of common sense also is important, along with a hefty quantity of reasonableness. If all your club members can act in a reasonable manner, then your club business gets done in the most effective manner.

Here's a summary of the applicable *Robert's Rules* your club may want to adopt, as well as our advice on putting them to use. Many investment clubs already follow these general guidelines without even knowing their source.

✔ In your club, every member should have the right to speak on any matter. Unlike the U.S. Senate, you need not allow obstructionist tactics like a filibuster to be used. Every question must be thoroughly discussed before taking action. If a member proposes a stock purchase, then you need to talk about it before putting the matter to a vote. That doesn't mean that you have to talk endlessly about it, but be reasonable. Whenever a member says nothing or chooses not to cast a ballot, it's assumed that he or she agrees with the actions about to be taken by the club.

✔ The club president controls the floor during the meeting. No, not with a mop and broom — whoever is speaking at any time during your meeting is said to *have the floor,* and only one person can have the floor at any time. The president must *recognize* a member before he or she can speak. In your club, discussions may occur spontaneously, and that's okay. However, one rule that may be useful, particularly when you have a talkative member, is this: No member is allowed a second shot at the same question until everyone else has had a chance to address it.

✔ If a number of members try to speak at the same time, or if an issue appears to have divided the club, then the president needs to take a more active role in establishing who has the floor. That can be as simple as reminding the club to speak one at a time, or as formal as setting the order by which members will speak ("Joe, you speak first, and then Pam, and then Herb"). Members can raise their hands or otherwise indicate their desire to speak.

✔ The club president also can *turn over the chair* to any other member. For example, when a member is making an educational presentation to the club, that member then controls who gets to speak during the duration of the presentation.

✔ A *question* is any item that requires a decision and is presented for discussion at the meeting. Examples include proposals to sell a stock or admit a new member. If you follow *Robert's Rules* to the letter, discussions about a question can't begin until a formal motion is made. In most clubs, a more casual approach works just fine — members discuss an item and then put it to a vote. Any member can make a motion but it requires a second from another member before it can be opened for discussion. The club secretary records the motion and the second in the minutes, using the exact phrasing of the motion and the names of the mover and the seconder.

✔ The mover can modify or withdraw the motion at any time; likewise, the seconder also can withdraw the second or accept or reject the modification.

✔ Once a motion is on the floor, no other business can be conducted until either a vote is taken or the motion is withdrawn or tabled.

✔ If no discussion takes place, or when discussion is completed, the question can be put to a vote as outlined in your operating agreement. The president needs to ensure that discussions don't go on and on. If members appear to be reaching a consensus, the president asks for any further discussion and then conducts a vote.

✔ If a consensus seems to be far off, the president can ask that the motion be tabled until the next meeting or at some other future point. A motion can be laid on the table only after a motion is made to that effect, seconded, and then voted on by the members. Removing the motion from the table, at the next meeting, for instance, also requires a seconded motion and vote.

In practice, the mechanics of laying a motion on the table and taking it up again seldom is practiced according to the letter of *Robert's Rules*. If the presiding officer observes that a simple consensus exists, he or she can move items to and from the table.

Your club doesn't have to follow *Robert's Rules* to the letter, or appoint an official parliamentarian to enforce the rules. We've outlined the basics for you, and they should provide enough structure for most clubs. But if someone in your club objects to a certain procedure, or doesn't think that your club is operating properly, you can always consult the official *Robert's Rules* for verification.

You can get a copy of *Robert's Rules of Order* at any bookstore, or at your public library. Web sites where you can find more information, and even the complete text of one early version of the book, are at:

> *Robert's Rules of Order* (Official Site)   `http://www.`
> `robertsrules.com`
>
> *Robert's Rules of Order* (1915 Version)   `http://www.bartleby.`
> `com/176/o`

In the end, it doesn't matter whether your club follows *Robert's Rules,* as long as you have a consistent set of rules in place for your meetings. Just remember that having the rules isn't enough . . . your club needs to be willing to enforce them, too.

Setting and Following an Agenda

The cornerstone of your monthly meeting is an agenda. Your club president sets the agenda for each particular meeting, and in many clubs, either the secretary or president distributes the agenda before the meeting.

Before your club's president sets the agenda, she must know what items to put on the schedule. Club communication is a two-way street, but making sure that each meeting's agenda has the right amount of business and that it can be covered in a reasonable amount of time ultimately is the president's responsibility.

At the end of each meeting, the president can call for volunteers to make presentations at the next meeting, or request (or even assign) a member to cover a topic. Or the president can e-mail or call members a week before each meeting to find out what items they'd like to present. Members also need to take the initiative, informing the president when they have ideas for presentations. If you want to make life really easy for your president, set up your educational presentation schedule far in advance.

Appendix A contains a sample agenda that can be rearranged, trimmed, and prioritized according to your club's needs. Many of these meeting elements can be adapted easily for online clubs. The remainder of this section examines each of the meeting elements in the order that it appears on the agenda.

1. Call to order

At the set meeting time, the president says to all in attendance, "The meeting will please come to order." This is official notice that the meeting has begun. In formal assemblies, the chair of the meeting bangs a gavel, so feel free to give your president a noisemaking device if he or she has trouble getting everyone's attention. If the president can't attend, then the vice president or any other officer in attendance can call the meeting to order.

2. Roll call and quorum

You don't really have to have all members say "present" when their names are read by the secretary, but the secretary needs to record attendance as part of club minutes. The secretary can help keep meetings moving by taking attendance as members arrive.

The secretary also must ensure that your club has a *quorum,* a minimum number of members (or representation of the minimum number of shares owned by all members in attendance) that must be present to approve any official business. Your club operating agreement or bylaws may specifically set the requirements for a quorum or it may set by default. For example, if your agreement states that a majority of members must agree before a stock is purchased, and fewer than half of your members are at a meeting, then you won't be able to put a stock purchase to a vote. The secretary must acknowledge to the president whether a quorum exists.

Another way that you can also ensure that you have a quorum is by using proxy statements. When members are unable to attend a meeting, they can send a signed statement to the club giving another member the authority to vote on their behalf. For the purposes of determining a quorum, the proxy counts as though the members actually are in attendance.

Appendix A includes a sample proxy that your club can adapt and use. But this proxy statement has a twist. Instead of assigning your proxy to a single person, this statement assigns your shares to all members in proportion to the percentage of their ownership in the club. The aim of this proxy is preventing any one member from gaining too much control of the club's vote during that meeting. By distributing your proxy in the manner by which all other members in attendance cast their ballots, you ensure that a quorum is in place and that the will of the club can still be exercised.

3. Introductions

Remember your manners and be hospitable. Prior to the start of the meeting, the president should meet visitors and welcome them to the club gathering. The president then can immediately introduce the visitors, or ask that members playing host to the guest make the introduction. You may want to have the guests say a few words (or not) after they've been introduced.

4. Reading of the minutes

Whatever you do, please avoid having the secretary actually read aloud the minutes from any previous meeting. The secretary can distribute the minutes for review a few days before the meeting, or at least give members a chance to review the official record as they arrive prior to the meeting. The president asks for corrections, then asks the secretary to make the changes and, after the corrections are made, calls for a motion and second to accept the minutes (or to accept the minutes as corrected), before putting the question to a vote. The approved minutes become part of the official record of the club, and need to be filed safely.

During the meeting, the secretary takes minutes of all discussions and actions taken during the meeting. The secretary should follow the agenda, and the minutes don't need to be explicitly detailed. They must, however, include the names of everyone making motions and seconds, the specifics of motions, summaries of discussions, and the official tally of votes that take place. The secretary distributes each meeting's minutes to all members for review, either before or at the start of the next meeting.

Appendix A contains sample minutes from a club meeting.

5. Treasurer's report

The club treasurer provides printed copies of reports for distribution at club meetings. At each meeting, he or she reviews the current Member Status Report and Valuation Statement. Chapter 10 provides details about these reports — they provide the current value of each member's account with the club and the value of the club's cash and portfolio. The treasurer also reviews the status of any approved purchases or sales made in the club's portfolio since the last meeting, as well as any expenses or income that were recorded.

As with the minutes, the treasurer's report must be corrected if necessary, and then approved and accepted into the record by a club vote.

6. Portfolio and stock watcher reports

Each of your club's members is responsible for following one or two of your club's holdings. At your monthly meeting, these *stock watchers* should be prepared to update the club on any important company news that's happened since the last meeting. Stock watcher reports should be brief and concerned only with any significant changes in the company's condition that warrant further analysis to determine whether the club should sell, hold, or buy more shares. Your club may wish to take action at this point on buying or selling shares, but many clubs push all portfolio decisions until later in a meeting following the presentation of any new stocks. That way all buy and sell decisions can be considered at once.

Chapter 15 includes a sample of a stock watcher's report that you can use for these updates.

7. Member stock presentations

At least once a year, stock watchers need to provide a full update on their assigned stocks, including a recently completed Stock Selection Guide (SSG) and a recommendation for purchasing more, holding or selling the stock, depending on the SSG.

As members discover new candidates for your club's portfolio, they'll present those stocks to the club for consideration. Chapter 14 describes how to find and analyze stocks for your club's portfolio. If your club thinks that they've found a winner, the stock can be put to a vote after all presentations have been made.

8. Educational presentations

As we've said time and again, successful clubs share one common trait — a focus on education. In your club's beginnings, you'll spend a considerable amount of time on this agenda item as you and other club members teach yourselves how to invest in the stock market. Guest speakers or members may present lessons on a selected topic.

Educational presentations don't have to be lengthy to teach your members something important. And no members have any excuses for *not* making a presentation to their club, regardless of their level of investing experience. Preparing a presentation for your club can make you a miniexpert on that topic, so you'll actually be doing you and your club a favor.

Chapter 11 is filled with more ideas for the educational component of each month's meeting.

9. Old business

If any business is left unfinished from previous meetings, here is where you need to discuss it again.

10. New business

Any questions that haven't been brought before the club can now be discussed. For instance, if you're sponsoring a candidate for membership, you can discuss that person's candidacy and put him or her to a vote.

The president needs to be notified prior to the meeting about any new business so that the specific item can be placed on the agenda in this category.

11. Announcements

During the announcements, the club can set — or remind the members about — the next meeting's location and date. You also can use this time to inform the club of any personal news.

12. Adjournment

The meeting ends by a vote or by general consent. The secretary notes the time of adjournment and specifics of the vote to adjourn.

While most clubs stick fairly closely to this agenda, you might find a different order works better for your club. Some clubs move partner stock presentations to an early position in the agenda, since these often take up lots of time and generate much discussion. Later in the meeting, members may be tired and find it harder to concentrate on those topics. By moving the presentations earlier, members may be "fresher" when they consider the important questions about buying or selling stocks in the club's portfolio.

Keeping Members Attentive and Cooperative

Keeping your meeting moving at a good clip isn't enough. The president also must ensure that meetings are interesting and maintain everyone's focuses on the matters at hand. The president shouldn't be afraid of stepping in to cut off long-winded members, regardless of how elegant they are. If your club can't ever seem to wrap up a conversation, try imposing a 10- or 15-minute time limit on discussion of any given motion. When time's up, the president calls for a vote and the matter is resolved.

You also want to watch out for members who tend to dominate all the discussions by virtue of their breadth of knowledge or heightened sense of authority. Domineering members may call for a stricter implementation of *Robert's Rules of Order*. By requiring that every member be given a chance to address a particular issue before anyone can readdress it, you make sure that everyone gets a fair shake.

The same thing goes for discussions that spiral out of control and become arguments. Healthy disagreement is good for your club, but bickering and heated disputes leave some members angry and others disgusted and, if left unchecked, eventually will destroy your club. Stepping in whenever common courtesy seems to be getting trampled is the president's job. That may mean speaking privately to a member outside of the meeting, or taking steps during the course of the meeting to minimize unnecessary arguments.

The president often helps by encouraging on-topic conversations and reminding members that everyone should aim to be reasonable. In any investment club, votes that don't go your way are bound to happen. All members just have to make sure that disputes don't become personal.

Bringing member presentations up to speed

Garrison Keillor, creator of the popular public radio program *A Prairie Home Companion,* often speaks about the trials and tribulations of shy people. He's even an advocate for the "shy rights" movement (because shy people tend not to speak up for themselves). For many shy people, the prospect of making a presentation to fellow club members can be pretty terrifying. Sure, anyone can prepare a talk on a topic, but they often go weak-kneed when time comes to present their work.

Fortunately, clubs often are informal enough so that even shy folks can muster enough courage to give a presentation. Preparation is key. Although some members are likely to have a natural, God-given talent for public speaking, others hate the prospect of opening their mouths in front of a group. Every member must at some point speak in front of the club, and that expectation must be conveyed upfront to all prospective members.

In reality, most members get through that first presentation just fine. And most clubs realize that a nurturing environment is better for the entire club, supporting the work of neophytes as well as the more experienced members. If members are having trouble preparing a presentation, arrange to have two members work together as a team, or have an experienced member serve as a mentor or coach.

You can set time limits for member presentations to keep them short and sweet. If a member knows that he or she is expected to present only a 10-minute lesson, it can be less stressful than being asked to fill a half-hour segment on the agenda.

Taking Your Club Communication Online

Although your club members will communicate face-to-face at each month's meeting (unless you're a completely online club), more and more clubs are taking advantage of online tools to help them communicate more effectively in between meetings. These online tools can help your meetings operate more efficiently, and your members to become better informed about the club's portfolio.

Of course, your members need access to computers and the Internet if they want to take advantage of these great tools. If some of your members don't have computers, you may want to consider a field trip to the home of a member who's online or to your local library to see what investment resources are available. In fact, a presentation about interesting and useful Web sites for investors can prove beneficial, especially during your club's meeting. You can start with some of our favorite Web sites (you can find a list of the best in Chapters 11 and 14).

Acquiring a club Web site

Building a Web site just for your club isn't the easiest job in the world. Sure, plenty of tools are available to simplify the technical aspects, but in the end, you'd be hard-pressed to build a site that's more useful than a few of the already available club-oriented sites on the Web. Two great starting places to get your club online quickly and easily are

✔ **ICLUB.com** (`www.iclub.com/`). ICLUB.com provides a suite of tools tailored just for investment clubs and approved by NAIC. Once you set up shop on ICLUB's Web site, you can keep track of your portfolio and accounting records, use your private discussion board and e-mail list to communicate with other members of your club, file important documents, and even vote on purchases and sales of stocks.

   While all these features are especially useful for online investment clubs, any club can use the site to help keep your club members informed about all kinds of club matters. Your club members will need a password to access your club information, so you won't have to worry about privacy. For most clubs, ICLUB.com has all the features you need for your club's online toolbox.

✔ **Yahoo! Clubs** (`http://edit.clubs.yahoo.com/create/naic.html`). The National Association of Investors Corporation (NAIC) has worked with Yahoo! to create a special area on the Web just for investment clubs. You can track your portfolio, schedule meetings and events on a master calendar, and talk with your fellow members on your discussion board. It's all private, too, unless you elect to make your club publicly accessible. The drawbacks are that your club members can't talk via e-mail, the way they can with ICLUB, and the site doesn't have a club accounting feature, either.

Using e-mail and mailing lists

E-mail is a quick and convenient way to communicate — just type up a message, address it to its intended recipients, click a button or two, and your thoughts almost instantly are delivered.

Although sending messages to a handful of people is easy enough, sending messages to all 15 people in your club at the same time becomes a little more complicated. Any time a member of your club wants to send a message to all the other members, he or she must remember to add the addresses of all members. If a member of your club changes his or her e-mail address, the other members must change their address books or else messages won't be delivered.

This is where *mailing lists* come in handy. An Internet mailing list uses special software on a server to manage a list of e-mail addresses. When a subscriber to a list sends a message to a special list address, the message automatically is sent to every member on the list. That means you have to remember only one e-mail address to reach all the members of your club.

A number of sites offer free mailing lists for private groups. ICLUB.com includes a mailing list feature as part of its package of tools, or you can sign up to create a list for your club at Topica.com (www.topica.com) or Yahoo! Groups (http://groups.yahoo.com). One member of your club serves as administrator, setting the list, with rights to invite and approve new subscribers. You can keep your mailing list completely private, so that only your club members have access. These sites also can save copies of your messages for future reference.

Once you've set up your club's list, you can do a great deal more than just chat about the weather. Here are a few of the ways that investment clubs use e-mail lists:

- ✔ The secretary sends reminders about the next meeting's date, time, and location.
- ✔ The president requests agenda item proposals for the next meeting, and then sends the agenda prior to the meeting.
- ✔ The treasurer sends a copy of the club's valuation statement and member status report a day before the meeting.
- ✔ The secretary sends a copy of the last meeting's minutes for review before the next meeting.
- ✔ A member who is unable to attend a meeting sends his or her proxy to the club.
- ✔ Members send updates about the stocks that they follow.

By getting information into your members' hands before the start of your monthly meeting, you can streamline the time you spend together conducting club business.

Chat and instant messaging

Although e-mail offers nearly instantaneous communication, you also can tap into the world of real-time online conversation. *Chat* is the term used to describe a group of people meeting online in a designated *chat room* for the purpose of discussion. Chat software enables your words to be displayed to all other guests in the room as soon as you type them on your keyboard, replicating the experience of sitting in a room with your club members.

Chat can be a useful way of conducting a meeting when members can't meet together in the same room. Some online clubs even use chat to get together periodically to talk about their portfolios or other club business. In your club, the stock study committee can discuss their research findings in one or two evenings, for instance.

Yahoo! Clubs offers a chat room as part of its service, so you can test chat with a few of your members after setting up your club on the Yahoo! site. If the Yahoo! chat room doesn't give you all the options that you need, your club can research more sophisticated chat options that are available online. *Instant messaging* is another way to communicate online. AOL.com's free Instant Messenger software enables you to chat with another person anytime the two of you are online. AOL's program also enables you to create a private chat room on the fly. Simply invite a small group of people to your chat, and you can talk to your heart's delight.

Setting a Social Agenda

Just like the saying, "All work and no play makes Jack a dull boy," if your club is immersed in business all the time, you're missing an important component of any social activity. Giving your club members a chance to have some fun can actually make your club stronger. Social interaction helps your members get to know one another better and leads to an increased level of trust among members.

Regular social activities keep motivation high and meetings fresh. An easy and natural way to make your club more sociable is by simply establishing a little chitchat time either before or after every meeting. That gives your members an opportunity to get together informally, spending some quality time with each other.

Make sure that club members know that a strict line exists between business and pleasure at each meeting. Keep things balanced — your members will regret having had too much fun if your portfolio suffers as a result.

Snacks also can be important. People invest better on a full stomach, so clubs often provide refreshments at their meetings. Tasty-treat duty can be rotated among all the members, or the member who's playing host to a meeting can be responsible for light refreshments. In many clubs, members compete informally to see who provides the tastiest homemade snacks or the most outrageously fun treats. Although some clubs pay for snacks out of their club's petty cash, most of the time members pay for the refreshments that they provide out of their own pocket.

Some clubs meet over lunch or dinner, either by necessity or because they truly enjoy sharing a meal as a group. Whether your club provides a full meal or light snacks, make sure that food doesn't interfere with your club meeting.

Coast to Coast OnLine Investment Club

In 1998, some members of NAIC's I-Club-List decided to start an investment club of their own. With sixteen current members ranging in age from 20 to 70, *Coast to Coast OnLine Investment Club* (CTCOLIC) conducts all of its business on the Internet. From the hour-and-a-half monthly meeting conducted using chat software to frequent communications on their e-mail list, CTCOLIC members constantly use online resources.

Potential members are required to familiarize themselves with CTCOLIC by reading the extensive background information found at the club's Web site (www.ctcolic.net). Anyone can attend the club's online meetings as a guest and follow the e-mail discussions, but only current and prospective members can participate by posting messages or "talking" during online meetings. Prospective members must go through a three-month probation period, proving their commitment by actively participating in the club's ongoing discussions. This waiting period also allows the current and potential members to get to know each other a little better, which is an important factor in a purely online club where members may never actually meet face-to-face.

CTCOLIC doesn't have a formal education program, but members are assigned to teams that make presentations to the entire club approximately every five months. All stock studies are conducted publicly on the club's e-mail distribution list so that every member can follow along. Presentations are archived on the club's site so members can easily access them as needed.

Club members contribute at least $20 a month. The club's portfolio of nine stocks, worth more than $37,000, is invested through discount brokerage TD Waterhouse. CTCOLIC also uses club accounting software to track the portfolio's return. Members are required to use stock analysis software to research and then watch the stocks that the club is interested in. Stock watcher reports also are posted on the club's site for easy reference. Like many purely online clubs, CTCOLIC relies heavily on the many research resources that can be found on the Internet and also clearly spells out operating procedures and member responsibilities to prevent any misunderstandings that may result from the lack of in-person interaction.

Some clubs create a *social chair,* an officer who's responsible for arranging activities and coming up with ideas for keeping the club experience entertaining as well as educational.

Whatever you do, don't ignore the social side of clubbing. With just a little effort, you can keep your meetings interesting, rewarding, *and* fun.

Holding Your Club's Annual Meeting

In many clubs, the annual meeting is a celebration of another year of progress toward each member's education and financial goals. Club members may bring their spouses and family members to a potluck supper or backyard barbeque, or they may meet at a nice restaurant for a leisurely meal.

Combining business and pleasure is par for the course at a club's annual meeting. This meeting also is a great opportunity for your club to elect officers for the coming year and to review the performance of the club in the year just gone by. Some clubs prepare a written report about the club's activities during the year, similar to the way mutual fund managers write an annual letter to shareholders.

The best time of the year for your annual meeting is in late March or early April. By that time, your treasurer has received all the tax documents from your financial accounts, and has had time to prepare the year's tax filing. If you elect officers in January, as some clubs do, the new treasurer will immediately be put to work preparing the club's partnership return, without having had the benefit of managing the books for the year. If, on the other hand, you elect officers in March or April, the new treasurer takes office after the tax returns have been prepared.

Chapter 10

Keeping the Books

In This Chapter
▶ Defining the treasurer's job
▶ Checking off those end-of-year tasks
▶ Using software to do your club accounting

*I*t's time to get down to the nitty-gritty, in fact, the nittiest and grittiest part of club operations. That can only mean one thing — it's time to talk about club accounting. Keeping the books isn't necessarily a tough job, but each of the hundreds of transactions that your club makes through the years affects your club in one way or another and needs to be recorded properly to keep the details straight.

Your members aren't the only ones counting on the treasurer to keep accurate and timely records. Many of the transactions that occur in an investment club have tax implications, so the IRS relies on your club to keep precise records of your investment expenses, income, and losses. And you can bet that if you fail to live up to those expectations, the IRS will happily assist you in making things right (in their own persuasive — and often expensive — way).

But why harp on bureaucratic concerns when your members have more immediate needs that your club treasurer must address. Every month, the treasurer is supposed to provide reports that show how much each club member has contributed, the value of each member's share of the club, and how the club's stocks have performed. In this chapter, we discuss how those reports are prepared and many other aspects of club recordkeeping.

The Treasurer's Job

Although the job of treasurer isn't easy, it also isn't impossibly difficult. In fact, any member of your club is qualified to serve as treasurer, and no special training or experience is required. Many clubs make special efforts to ensure that every member eventually serves a term in each office (president, vice president, secretary, and treasurer). Yes, that's right, even as treasurer. Fortunately, help is available for you to find the club treasurer hidden inside of you. With the aid of these resources, you'll be up and running in no time.

Resources for club treasurers

The bible for most club treasurers is the *NAIC Club Accounting Manual* published by the National Association of Investors Corporation. Available only through NAIC (http://store.yahoo.com/betterinvesting), for about $10, the manual is the product of 50 years of research and experience with investment clubs. It describes in great detail how you can manage the books of a club using paper and pencil. If you use software to perform your club accounting, you'll find the electronic version of the manual and its help screens are just as educational and useful as the manual.

NAIC also sells various blank forms, like the Journal Page, Valuation Units Control Ledger, and Individual Valuation Units Ledger, which you'll need to keep the books if you choose to ignore our advice to take advantage of the computerized tools that are available. You can order forms at (http://store.yahoo.com/betterinvesting).

If you're puzzled about any part of the job of treasurer, help is no further away than the Internet. NAIC operates a Club Treasurer Discussion List (http://lists.better-investing.org) where you can find answers to your toughest questions about club accounting from other treasurers. Once you subscribe, you can participate by e-mail or on the NAIC Web site. The NAIC Forum (http://go.compuserve.com/NAIC) likewise plays host to a Club Treasurer Chat message board exclusively for conversations about accounting issues.

In some clubs, the annual election for treasurer merely rubber stamps reelection of the person serving as "Treasurer for Life." Unless your club is comfortable with a member establishing sovereign rule in the treasurer's position, we think it's important that members take turns serving as treasurer. (The same can be said of other officer positions, for that matter.) That said, changing treasurers year after year sometimes is traumatic, because it may take a few months for an incoming treasurer to get up to speed. Often, the new treasurer masters the job right about the time his or her term is up! In some clubs, the answer is to appoint or elect an assistant treasurer.

The assistant treasurer

Before the advent of computer accounting tools, many clubs helped the treasurer do the job by electing or appointing an assistant treasurer. The two split some of the duties of collecting and recording member contributions, making bank deposits, placing trades with the brokerage, and filing away all the statements and paperwork that your club generates. However, with software now so readily available, you probably don't need an assistant treasurer just to handle monthly chores. Yet some clubs now look to the assistant treasurer as the treasurer in training. The assistant works in conjunction with the club treasurer; even going so far as managing a second, parallel set of the books for the club. Besides making sure that your club has a reliable candidate for the job of treasurer during the next year, your club has a backup of its data and records, if for some reason the treasurer becomes unavailable.

Understanding the Unit Value System

Chapter 7 summarizes the recommended method of club accounting, the *unit value system,* which essentially is how mutual funds operate. Every dollar invested is used to purchase a certain number of shares (or units) in the fund based on the current price of a unit. The price of a unit is set at the end of the day, based on the closing value of the fund's portfolio divided by the total number of units that were purchased prior to that day.

Here's how the units work in an investment club. Using round numbers to explain them, rather than value the portfolio once a day the way funds do, most clubs value their portfolios once a month. On the valuation date set by the club, the treasurer of the Blue Chips and Salsa Investment Club, for example, prepares the Valuation Statement by adding the current market value of the club's cash and stock holdings. In this case, she determines that the portfolio is worth a total of $1,000.

Next, the treasurer prepares the Member Status Report. Counting up all the units purchased by the 10 members of the club, she notes that the club has exactly 100 units outstanding. To date, each member has purchased 10 units. Dividing $1,000 by 100 units, the treasurer determines that the unit value of the club now stands at $10. Each member's value in the club is $100.

$1,000 ÷ 100 units = $10 value of one unit

At the club's next meeting, each of its ten members contributes $20. Because the value of each unit is $10, each member purchases two units with his or her contribution that month. Now each member owns 12 units out of 120 outstanding, and the club's total value is $1,200.

Prior to the next meeting, the treasurer determines the value of the portfolio once again and sees that the club's stocks have increased, so its total value is 10 percent more, increasing from $1,200 to $1,320. With 120 shares or units outstanding, what's the value of each unit? The treasurer divides $1,320 by 120 units to find out that each unit is worth 10 percent more, or $11.

$1,320 ÷ 120 units = $11 value of one unit

Each member who owns 12 units now sees that his or her interest in the club is worth a total of $132.

$$12 \text{ units} \times \$11 \text{ unit value} = \$132 \text{ value of member's capital account}$$

If a member withdraws before the next meeting, he or she receives $132, less any fees that your club may charge.

The value of a unit always is the same for every member of the club, but the number of units that each member owns can be different. Every time members make payments to the club, the number of units that they own increases (and decreases when they withdraw some or all their holdings from the club). The value of a single unit is tied to the total number of units and the club's overall value.

As it happens, a new member is joining the club this month. He writes his first check to the club for $20. How many units does he receive for his contribution? (Hint: the answer is not two units.) Because the unit value is $11, his $20 buys 1.818 shares.

$$\$20 \div \$11 \text{ per unit} = 1.818 \text{ units}$$

Because the club determines the value of its portfolio only once a month, a large window exists for when members can pay their dues and purchase units at the current unit value. Members who happen to miss a meeting can deliver their checks to the treasurer, who then can record the purchase at the unit value set at the last meeting. However, most clubs frown on late payments, because the late-paying member has an unfair advantage of having their money at their personal disposal for up to several weeks more than prompt-paying members. Many clubs establish late fees or set a policy that late payments are recorded at the unit value set at the next meeting. Some clubs do both.

Club Accounting, Task by Task

Regardless of how you keep your books, by hand or by computer, the job of club accounting comes down to the same tasks. The treasurer performs various tasks as part of his job, some every month, some occasionally, and some at the end of the year. Other more specific tasks are related to the initial start-up of your club. Here are six general types of tasks that investment club treasurers are called upon to perform in the course of operating your club:

- Start-up tasks
- Tasks before every meeting
- Tasks during every meeting

> ✔ Tasks after every meeting
>
> ✔ Occasional tasks
>
> ✔ Year-end tasks

Start-up tasks

When you start your club, you must take care of a few one-time tasks to get things going. Some, like getting your Tax ID number, may take a few weeks, so hop to it right away.

Getting your Tax Identification Number

Get your Tax Identification Number (TIN) from the IRS. Chapter 7 includes the details on acquiring and completing the proper form.

Acquiring club accounting software or service

Purchase club accounting software from NAIC and install it on your computer. Or, if you prefer, register with an online accounting service such as ICLUBcentral.com. Read through the manual or Web site help pages thoroughly so that you begin gaining a good understanding of how the program works. Depending on your club's bylaws and operating agreement, you may need approval from your club members or president before making this expenditure. You may also need to research what products are available and what costs are involved, before reporting back to the club with your purchase recommendations.

Collecting member data

Collect names, addresses, e-mail addresses, work and home telephone numbers, and Social Security numbers from all members. You need members' Social Security numbers to complete the year-end tax filings, and getting that information now is better than having to collect it in a rush at the end of the year. When new members join the club, get the information from them right away. One helpful tip: After inputting this data into club accounting software, you can print a *Member Information Listing,* a report that includes each member's contact information without Social Security numbers. Make copies of the listing and distribute them to your members to serve as your club's official contact directory. That way everyone knows how to reach each other.

Tasks before each meeting

Immediately before and after club meetings, treasurers must carry out the bulk of their assigned duties. At these times contributions are received, deposits are made, and reports are generated. With practice, these tasks shouldn't take more than 30 minutes or an hour a month to complete. These are your pre-meeting responsibilities.

Recording security transactions

Working with your brokerage and statements from other accounts where you hold securities (such as dividend reinvestment plans, or DRIPs, and direct stock plans, or DSPs), record any transactions that have occurred since your last club meeting. If your brokerage is online, you usually can log on to its site and obtain a list of transactions made since your last statement. Doing so helps ensure that your transactions are up to date.

For your securities, the transactions you'll see may include purchases, sales, dividends, reinvested distributions, stock splits, mergers, takeovers, or even spinoffs. If you hold money market funds in your brokerage account, don't worry about entering them as mutual funds. You simply treat them as cash and the dividends they pay each month as interest.

Recording other transactions

From your bank statement and register, enter any interest the club received and checks that you wrote during the month. Like your brokerage account, you may be able to visit your bank's Web site and download a list of recent transactions so that you're sure you've entered them all.

If you paid any miscellaneous expenses, record them now. The expenses your club can incur are either deductible or nondeductible. Deductible expenses are recognized by the IRS as being associated with investing in and running your club. Nondeductible expenses have nothing to do with investing, such as paying for snacks at your meeting.

The IRS recognizes the following as investment expenses:

- ✔ Club accounting software
- ✔ Postage and stationery
- ✔ Manuals, books or reference materials relating to investing
- ✔ Costs of copying, producing, and mailing meeting notices
- ✔ Dues paid to NAIC
- ✔ Rent paid for your meeting location
- ✔ Service charges
- ✔ Trips to investing conferences and fairs

You must record all these expenses in your club's books.

The following, however, are nondeductible expenses:

- ✔ Snacks, refreshments and meals
- ✔ Greeting cards
- ✔ Parties
- ✔ Flowers and gifts for members or others

The IRS doesn't consider the latter expenses to be relevant to managing your investments. Newer versions of NAIC Club Accounting Software enable you to enter these as nondeductible expenses in your regular accounts, but you can also use the *petty cash account.*

If you take up a collection to buy flowers for a member who's in the hospital, you can enter the contributions and expense in petty cash. Or if you collect a few dollars each month from your members to cover meeting refreshments, you can record the payments and the expenses in the petty cash account. What is important, however, is noting that the petty cash expenses are completely separate from your other expenses and don't affect the valuation statement or members' status reports. Petty cash transactions are additional optional expenses.

Reconciling account statements

After you've entered all the transactions, reconcile your records with the statements, making sure the respective balances agree. It can be useful to print a *Cash Journal Listing* from the program. This report contains all the cash transactions within a time frame that you specify, and then you can use it to compare account statements to make sure you've entered all the transactions.

Running the audit utility

If you're using NAIC Club Accounting Software, run the *audit utility* to ensure that all mathematical calculations carried out by the program are correct. If the utility reports errors, you may need to make adjustments to data that you've entered.

Occasionally, you may receive notice of a transaction that occurred in a month gone by. Once you enter this transaction, you automatically need to run the audit utility in the accounting software. The audit uses the updated information to recalculate the club's total value, unit value, and units purchased by members. You'll find that all reports that have been printed after the adjustment for the error may contain slight discrepancies. Generally speaking, reprinting past reports isn't necessary, unless the oversight was quite significant. Make sure to educate your club members about these sorts of small inconsistencies, which are common and, once corrected, not a problem.

Updating security valuations

As of the designated valuation date each month (such as the closing day of the month or other date set in your operating agreement), enter the prices for all the securities in your portfolio. You can find them in your local newspaper, or from a number of Web sites. When you enter ticker symbols for your stocks, newer versions of NAIC Club Accounting automatically retrieve prices from the Internet. You can visit Yahoo! Finance (www.quote.yahoo.com) for the most recent day's prices.

If you don't enter the valuations right away, you may need to search for prices for the proper valuation date. Saving the business section of your newspaper that contains the prices for your valuation date helps, or you can visit BigCharts.com on the Web. (www.bigcharts.com). BigCharts has a Historical Prices feature that enables you to look up prices on any date. You need to be consistent with the date that you choose to enter stock prices for your monthly valuation statement. Some clubs choose the last business day of the month as their designated valuation date. That enables them to easily match their accounting records with their brokerage statements. If you conduct your meeting in the middle of the month, however, those prices may be two weeks old and less meaningful to the club. Try making your valuations as current as possible for each club meeting.

Printing a Member Status Report

At each club meeting, you need to distribute copies of Member Status Report (see Figure 10-1) to each member. This report includes totals of each member's contributions to the club to date, along with the current number of units owned by each member and the current valuation. The report also includes the members' recent payments, their total payments, and their total payments plus any distributed earnings reinvested in their capital account from years past.

At your club meeting, have each member check the Member Status Report to make sure their most recent contribution was properly recorded.

Printing a Valuation Statement

At every club meeting, the treasurer also needs to print a Valuation Statement (see Figure 10-2). The Valuation Statement reports the balances of each account, listing every security the club owns, along with the number of shares, cost bases, and current prices of each one. As an option, the software also can calculate the total and compound annual returns of each holding and of the portfolio as a whole.

```
              Blue Chips and Salsa Investment Club 11/30/00
              Members Status Report as of November 30, 2000
```

NO.	NAME	PAID IN SINCE 10/30/00	TOTAL PAID IN TO DATE	PAID IN PLUS EARNINGS	UNITS SINCE 10/30/00	UNITS OWNED	CURRENT VALUE	PERCENT OWNRSHP	TOTAL RETURN SINCE 06/14/93	COMPOUND ANN RET
1	Eckroate, M.	100.00	1200.00	1192.77	4.082898	51.093601	1278.38	3.21%	14.01%	7.09%
2	Gerlach, D.	0.00	5251.00	5236.96	0.000000	381.711070	9550.55	23.99%	216.13%	19.73%
3	Hikida, K.	30.00	2025.00	2031.20	1.224870	131.913332	3300.52	8.29%	165.92%	16.53%
4	Judge, J.	0.00	1890.00	1903.18	-0.199862	131.130781	3280.94	8.24%	171.27%	16.89%
5	Knox, S.	100.00	2915.00	2911.40	4.082898	188.175220	4708.21	11.83%	164.79%	16.45%
6	Laurence, A.	30.00	3287.00	3369.50	1.224870	235.086175	5881.94	14.78%	159.87%	19.99%
7	Panchekha, A.	30.00	710.00	704.75	1.224870	29.073571	727.43	1.83%	4.40%	2.55%
8	Schaeffer, W.	0.00	4400.00	4491.37	0.000000	365.702061	9150.00	22.99%	212.81%	19.53%
9	Su, S.	100.00	1492.00	1498.13	4.082898	70.829711	1772.19	4.45%	42.01%	13.27%
10	Udov, L.	30.00	190.00	190.00	1.224870	6.147105	153.80	0.39%	-28.40%	-57.14%
	TOTALS	420.00	23360.00	23529.26	16.948312	1590.862627	39803.98	100.00%	171.90	16.94

Figure 10-1:
A Member
Status
Report.

Printing a Transaction Summary

Some clubs also distribute a Transaction Summary, listing all the transactions that have occurred since the last meeting. You can print one set from your computer printer and then photocopy them for distribution, or you can print them all from your printer. Alternatively, you can save the reports to a text file and then either distribute them via e-mail to club members or post them on your club's Web site. That way all members are responsible for printing their own set to bring to the meeting. Some clubs prefer this approach because it means that each member shares directly in the expense and neither the treasurer nor the club's kitty bears the cost of paper and printing.

Backing up your data

After you've finished entering data, printing reports, and double-checking figures for accuracy, make sure that you save a backup copy of your data file. You can save a copy on your computer's hard drive or on a floppy diskette.

Blue Chips & Salsa Investment Club

Valuation Statement as of May 28, 2001

SECURITY	TS DRP	FIRST BUY OR VALUATN DATE	SHARES OWNED THIS DATE	COST PER SHARE	TOTAL COST	PRICE PER SHARE THIS DATE	TOTAL VALUE THIS DATE	PERCENT OF TOTAL
Con Agra	CAG	12/31/96	127.508	12.0900	1541.58	20.2700	2584.59	2.9%
JLG Industries	JLG	02/10/97	366.311	12.5851	4610.06	12.0400	4410.38	5.0%
McDonald's	MCD	12/31/96	78.628	10.7323	843.86	30.5100	2398.94	2.7%
Merck	MRK	12/31/96	159.255	18.3747	2926.27	72.6000	11561.93	13.1%
Motorola	MOT	10/24/97	150.848	21.3299	3217.57	15.6700	2363.79	2.7%
Sprint Corp PCS	PCS	11/30/98	60.000	1.8058	108.35	22.5600	1353.60	1.5%
Synovus	SNV	12/31/96	5.123	7.2870	37.33	30.0800	154.09	0.2%
Walt Disney	DIS	12/31/96	100.520	13.6308	1370.17	32.6400	3280.98	3.7%
Washington REIT	WRE	12/31/96	220.281	15.8997	3502.40	23.3700	5147.96	5.8%
Wind River Systems	WIND	07/16/99	415.000	18.9645	7870.25	25.0300	10387.45	11.7%
Total Securities this Date					32270.93		66922.46	75.6%
Cash on Hand - Bank					0.00		0.00	0.0%
Cash on Hand - Broker					21563.29		21563.29	24.4%
Cash on Hand - Suspense					0.00		0.00	0.0%
Total Cash Accounts this Date					21563.29		21563.29	24.4%
Total Securities and Cash Accounts This Date					53834.22		88485.75	100.0%
Petty Cash					$ 0.00			
Total number of Valuation Units to Date					2866.547493			
Value of Each Unit This Date					$ 30.868			
Number of Units Each $10.00 will Purchase					0.32			

Figure 10-2:
A sample Valuation Statement

Tasks during each meeting

During your club meeting, the treasurer must be ready for action! Your members look to you to find out everything that's going on with the club's portfolio and accounts, so take the time to be well prepared.

Giving the treasurer's report

During a meeting, the treasurer needs to provide copies of recent Valuation Statements and Member Status Reports to all members and be prepared to offer a brief verbal report, highlighting those reports. The treasurer may perhaps offer some additional data not found in the reports, such as the percentage change in the club's unit value since the last meeting.

The treasurer should report on the details of recent transactions made by the club, such as purchases or sales of stock, expenses paid, or income received. A Cash Journal Listing can be printed from club accounting software as a reminder of all the recent activity, and although copies of this report don't have to be distributed to members, you can refer to it at the meeting.

If you can't attend a meeting, providing the reports still is the treasurer's responsibility. Clubs also rely on their treasurers' reports to inform them about how much money they have to invest and point out significant changes in the club's financial condition. If your club has an assistant or co-treasurer, that individual can fill in during your absence, making the report to the club and providing a short written report to your club president with the printed reports.

Answering member questions

The club treasurer must be prepared to answer any questions members may have during the meeting. Having copies of recent account statements and historical reports on hand for reference always is a good idea.

Collecting dues — even when members are absent

Although collecting dues from the members during a meeting is pretty easy, collecting them from absent members often is a hassle. Clubs have come up with a variety of ways of making sure their members pay their dues regularly. Some clubs implement direct deposit of member contributions, so members can automatically transfer money from their personal bank accounts to the club's account each month. Other clubs have members each write 12 checks at the beginning of each year, one for every month. The treasurer then simply deposits each month's batch of checks without having to worry about collecting them from delinquent members. If members want to make a larger payment in a certain month, and club bylaws enable them to do so, they simply contribute a second check for the additional amount at the meeting when they want to purchase additional club shares.

Receiving member contributions

Every month, your members need to be prepared to pay their dues to the club. Some treasurers bring along a simple worksheet listing the names of all members, so they can note the amount and check number of all dues payments as they are made. Other treasurers record the checks and amounts on a bank deposit form as payments are made, noting the member's name on the slip along with the amount.

Most members pay by check, and the check serves as their record of payment. Occasionally, members may forget their checkbooks and want to pay in cash. Some clubs don't accept cash, however. If your club treasurer mails your deposits to the bank or brokerage firm, trusting cash in the mail isn't such a great idea. If your club treasurer doesn't have a problem accepting cash, then providing the member with a receipt and noting in the treasurer's records who made the cash payment and in what amount are good ideas, particularly when more than one member pays dues in cash. An inexpensive pad of cash receipt forms, purchased at any stationery or office supply store, serves the purpose. Remember a receipt pad that provides a duplicate copy helps you keep things straight, too.

Some treasurers bring a *Treasurer's Kit* to club meetings. It includes copies of past reports, a complete cash journal, a calculator, bank deposit forms and envelopes, a cash receipt pad, and other useful items.

Recording portfolio actions

During the meeting, the club may decide to purchase or sell shares in its portfolio. Although the secretary records ballots and results in the minutes, the treasurer must carefully note all instructions. The secretary may not provide a draft of the minutes until some time after the meeting, or as late as at the next meeting, but the treasurer should take care of the transactions in a timely fashion. By writing down the specific action on issues as the club votes on them, you can promptly take care of them.

Tasks after each meeting

After the meeting, the club treasurer has a number of tasks to accomplish prior to the next monthly meeting. Although taking care of all the business immediately may not be necessary, some actions, such as buying a stock for the portfolio or depositing checks, shouldn't be put off for too long. In the days following each meeting you need to set aside some time for the things described in the following sections.

Recording and depositing member contributions

The treasurer should aim to get all member dues into the club's bank or brokerage account as quickly as possible after the meeting. The longer checks sit around in a desk drawer, the greater the chance for one to be lost or misplaced. The sooner the money is deposited, the sooner the checks clear and cash becomes available for the club either to earn interest or purchase a stock.

Before making the deposit, you record each payment in the club's books, verifying that the amount received is the same as the amount being deposited. If possible, photocopy all checks and the accompanying deposit slip for the files. Doing so is useful when verifying records later on, or when you're tracking down a discrepancy in the club's books.

Collecting from deadbeat members

Depending on your club's policies, you may need to track down members who miss meetings to collect their member dues. The more likely scenario is that you'll collect a double payment from that member, plus any applicable late fees, at the next meeting. Requiring payments that are made after the meeting date, or a grace period of two or three days after the meeting, to be recorded on the following month's valuation statement is good policy, because (it is hoped) your unit value will increase during most months and not decrease. Enabling chronically late payers to buy units at the previous (often lower) valuation isn't fair to the prompt members of your club. Late depositors can use tardiness to track how your club's stocks perform during the days after the meeting, and thus decide whether to make a large late contribution (if your stocks went up) or wait until the next meeting (if your stocks went down).

Recording and depositing member fees and petty cash

In addition to dues, the treasurer also records and deposits any fees paid by members, as well as any payments to the petty cash account. A fee differs from a payment because a fee isn't used to buy units for the member but still is recorded on the books. Fees often are levied when members make late payments ($5 is a common late fee), and some clubs have initiation fees for new members. Other clubs charge members an annual fee of $20 or $30 to spread around the club's expenses a bit more equitably. Fees are recorded in club books and deposited in its account. They're also reported in the status report as part of the total of a members' contributions, so they have the effect of raising the members' cost bases in the club.

Recording and depositing other income

Most of the time, dividends, distributions, and sales proceeds from investments are directly deposited into your club's brokerage account, without receiving a separate check. However, when you participate in a company's DRIP, or if you close or transfer your brokerage account, you may receive separate checks for certain transactions. Record and deposit these checks promptly.

Writing checks for expenses

If the club authorizes payment of any expenses, write and deliver checks for those items to the appropriate parties. Your club's bylaws may set a limit on the amount of a check that can be paid with only one signature, thus the treasurer may have to track down the president or another officer to complete the transaction.

Transferring funds from account to account

Many clubs have brokerage and bank accounts, so the treasurer must coordinate the flow of funds from one account to the other. Member contributions often are deposited in the bank account and then transferred to the brokerage account either as soon as checks clear or when money is needed for an approved purchase. Monitor the accounts and move funds as needed.

Brokerage accounts with check writing privileges are a fairly recent innovation that may enable clubs to bypass the need for a club bank account. Using a single account simplifies the treasurer's job and keeps paperwork to a minimum. If you go with this option, make sure that your brokerage checking account doesn't have a minimum withdrawal amount (for example checks that say "not valid for less than $500"). You may need to write checks in smaller amounts to pay for many club expenses.

Executing all authorized transactions

The treasurer usually is the agent authorized to place trades in the club's accounts. When the club votes to buy or sell a stock in its portfolio, making the trade is your job. Make sure that you double-check the specific details before confirming the trade, especially if you're trading online. And make sure that you have enough money on hand or in the account to pay for any purchases that you make. If your club has a cash account, money must be in the brokerage account before you place an order to buy; otherwise, you have three business days to *settle the trade*. That means you have three days to get the money into the account to pay for your purchase. (There is a movement in the brokerage industry to reduce this to just one day.)

Some clubs aren't completely comfortable with the treasurer being the sole point of contact with the brokerage firm. If the treasurer is the only member receiving statements, then it may take a long time to uncover any troublesome practices or outright fraud. Your brokerage firm may offer to send duplicate statements to another club officer, which provides a check on the treasurer's behavior. When using an online brokerage that enables all members to view the account, any member can see whether stocks started disappearing from your account just by logging in.

Occasional tasks

Some events occur relatively infrequently, such as a member withdrawal or addition to the club. This section discusses some of the occasional tasks the treasurer is called upon to perform.

Recording information on new securities

Whenever your club buys a new security, you need to record identifying information about that security, such as the correct spelling of its name and its proper ticker symbol (especially if you want to download price quotes from the Internet).

Recording information on new members

When new members join your club, be sure to collect all the information that you need, such as their full names, addresses, telephone numbers, e-mail addresses, and Social Security numbers. You'll need this information to pre-pare tax filings at the end of the year, so make it a habit to collect the infor-mation as soon as a member joins. You can create a form with blanks for all the required information and have new members complete it when they join.

Handling full and partial member withdrawals

One of the more complicated chores that a treasurer must handle is the withdrawal of a member from the club. Depending on your club's rules, a member can withdraw holdings in the club either partially or completely. Your operating agreement also specifies how a member is paid when making a withdrawal (all in cash, all in stock, or a combination of cash and stock) and any fees that are charged to the withdrawing member.

If you want to transfer stock to a withdrawing member, transfer only the shares that have gone up greatly in value since the club purchased them. That method has tax advantages because it enables the club to offload tax liability for the stock's gain to the withdrawing member without causing any additional tax liability to that member. Never transfer stocks that have gone down in price; instead, sell those shares and pay the member in cash. Doing so reduces your club members' taxes by recognizing their share of the loss. Passing a loss off to a withdrawing member in no way benefits that member or the club.

Chapter 8 includes details about handling withdrawals by transferring stock to the member or by paying the member in cash.

Fortunately, accounting software simplifies the process of member withdrawals. The procedures for processing a partial and a full withdrawal are exactly the same. Carefully following these steps helps you to accurately complete the withdrawal:

1. **Create a club valuation.**

   Your club rules spell out when a withdrawal must be recorded on the books. Typically, a withdrawal is valued on the date of the meeting after the meeting at which the withdrawal is submitted on paper to the membership. If the withdrawing member is receiving shares of one or more stocks, you can determine the number of shares to transfer by using the price of the stocks on the date of the meeting. You shouldn't record the withdrawal prior to establishing a current valuation for the club.

2. **Determine the number of the member's units to be withdrawn.**

   For a full withdrawal, all units that a member has purchased will be taken off the books. For a partial withdrawal, divide the dollar amount of the withdrawal by the current unit value to determine the number of units. (Accounting software does this automatically when you enter the withdrawal.) Withdrawn units are retired from the club's books.

3. **Deduct any withdrawal fees.**

   Before issuing a check or transferring stocks, make sure that you deduct any fee your club charges for withdrawals from the value of the cash and/or securities to be withdrawn.

4. **Record the withdrawal transaction in the club's books.**

   If you pay the member in cash at some later point, say after your next club meeting or upon the settlement of a sale of stock, charge the withdrawal cash to the suspense account first. When you issue the actual check, use funds from the suspense account. If the withdrawal includes securities, specify the stock, the price of the shares on the current Valuation Statement, and the number of shares. If your brokerage allows you to sell shares from specific lots, you can record the block from which the shares are to be transferred; otherwise, you must use the *first-in, first-out method* of disposing of the shares, transferring shares that the club purchased first.

As part of any withdrawal, a distribution of earnings is made in that member's capital account with the club. The share of the withdrawing member's income, gains (and losses), and expenses that have accrued since the last distribution date (most likely at the end of the previous year) is noted in the club's books. (More information about distributions is included in the discussion of year-end tasks later in this chapter.)

5. **Prepare and print a Withdrawal Distribution Report if it's a full withdrawal.**

   The Withdrawal Distribution Report is the primary report related to full withdrawals, showing the earnings, dividends, and capital gains since the last distribution, for which the member may experience tax liabilities. Make sure the member knows to keep this report for tax purposes. Having a complete history of their club participation also is helpful for the withdrawing member, particularly when he or she is completely withdrawing from the club. Prepare and print copies of the member's Individual Valuation Units Ledger and Cash Contributions Report, providing all the reports to the withdrawing member along with a check.

6. **Write a check to the withdrawing member.**

   Even if the bulk of a withdrawal is to be made by transferring stocks to the member, a cash component usually is necessary. Write the check according to the provisions of your operating agreement, making sure enough funds are in your account so the check doesn't bounce!

7. **Transfer shares of stock to the withdrawing member, when appropriate.**

   You can transfer shares by either of two methods. You can request that your brokerage issue a share certificate to the club (a fee for this is likely), and then transfer the certificate to the member. The transfer agent for the company whose shares are being transferred can provide details about the procedure for legally transferring the shares. Contact the company's investor relations' office or visit its Web site for details. You usually can ask the withdrawing member to open an account at the same brokerage firm (even if it's on a temporary basis) and then instruct your brokerage to transfer the shares to that account. Most brokerages won't transfer shares from an account in your club name to an account in a member's name unless they're at the same firm.

8. **For a full withdrawal, change the member's status from active to inactive in your accounting software and records.**

   Newer versions of the software automatically designate a fully withdrawn member as inactive. However, don't delete any of the past transactions or the member's records from the software, because doing so causes the software to make incorrect calculations from that point forward.

Year-end tasks

Most clubs are set up on a calendar-year basis, so the club treasurer faces some additional tasks at the end of the year and beginning of the new one. Although we refer to these as *year-end tasks,* in reality some may not be completed until April of the new year. This section discusses these year-end tasks.

Collecting and recording annual dues

If your club assesses an annual fee to defray some of its expenses throughout the year, now is the time to collect them. Your members may need a reminder to pay the additional fee on top of their normal monthly contributions in December, so make a point of reminding them at the November meeting. Annual dues like these are recorded as member fees in the books, not as payments that are used to buy units.

Reviewing files

The end of the year is a good time to make sure that your files for the year are in tip-top shape. You need to have all the account statements and trade confirmations received throughout the year, along with copies of all the reports you distributed to members. If you find any discrepancies or missing reports, take care of them now before your financial providers begin sending tax reports to their customers. Your club's audit committee also needs all this information to conduct its annual review of the club's books.

Recording recent transactions

You may have to wait until the end of January before you receive final year-end statements for all the club's accounts. You may be able to obtain details of the last interest credits, money market dividends, and other transactions for the final quarter of the year earlier by going online. Once you have all the information in hand, record the transactions in the club's books. Using the audit task in the club accounting software, make sure all the information is consistent in the program's database.

Reconciling account statements and Form 1099s

Check the balances and security information in the club's books to see that they match up with your bank, brokerage, and DRIP account statements. When you receive Form 1099 reports from all your accounts, make sure that the amounts on them match what you've recorded. Club accounting software offers a Transaction Summary Report that lists all the dividends and income received. Print a copy of this summary — with the option subtotaling all taxable distributions selected — and you can easily match your records to the company-reported figures.

Recording year-end prices for all securities

Record the prices for all the securities in the club's portfolio as of December 31. When the 31st falls on a weekend, use the last business day of the year but still label the prices as being from December 31.

If you didn't save the newspaper from the valuation date, you can retrieve historical prices from BigCharts (www.bigcharts.com). BigCharts reports the actual price on any date and split-adjusted prices if the company experienced a stock split at some point after that date. Be sure to use the actual price, not the split-adjusted price, when you enter the valuation. You enter the stock split transaction on the date it occurs.

Creating and printing a year-end Valuation Statement

Once you've entered the prices of all your stocks, you need to prepare a year-end Valuation Statement, similar to the ones that you do every month.

Distributing club earnings

Following IRS regulations concerning partnerships, your club needs to distribute club's earnings to members at the end of every year. Remember that as a partnership, members are individually responsible for taxes on their share of the club's earnings each year. At the end of the year, the treasurer conducts a *distribution of earnings,* allocating all the club's earnings to members who own units. Investment club members face the same tax liabilities as individual investors, so all of the following have tax consequences, either because they are subject to taxes, exempt from further taxes, or can reduce your taxes:

- ✔ Dividends
- ✔ Interest
- ✔ Capital gains and losses
- ✔ Investment expenses
- ✔ Tax-free interest received
- ✔ Foreign taxes paid

If you keep your club's books by hand, you determine each member's share of all these transactions by allocating each category based on the number of units owned by each member at the end of the year. This is a non-time-based distribution, because it doesn't matter whether a member joined the club in October or was a member at the beginning of the year.

Club accounting software offers a fairer way of distributing earnings known as a *time-based method.* The computer can do the myriad calculations necessary to allocate the tax-related transactions to each member based on their units owned throughout the year. This method is more equitable because a member who joins later in the year doesn't share any of the burden for taxable transactions incurred before he or she became a member.

Using club accounting software, you can run the Distribution of Earnings utility, quickly taking care of this task. However, make sure that you've completed all the other tasks in this section before generating a distribution.

When you create a distribution from your club, no cash changes hands. Your club members do not receive a check for the amount of their share of gains or dividends throughout the year, nor do they have to write a check to cover the club's expenses and losses. According to NAIC's recommended club accounting guidelines, whenever a distribution is made, the club's net income (earnings) is passed out to the members and no longer is part of the assets of the club. The club's earnings don't include unrealized gains on stocks still held in the club's portfolio at the end of the period, only the gains or losses from stocks that were sold during the year.

When the net income for the year is positive, the total value of the club decreases because all that income is removed from the club. As a result, the club's unit value is recalculated and decreases as well. When the club's net income for the year is negative, a liability is subtracted from the total value of the club causing the total value of the club to increase. If you think hard, you may remember math class from fourth- or fifth-grade and what happens when you subtract a negative number from a positive number — you get a bigger number. The unit value increases with the increase in the club's total value.

Once the new unit value is calculated, the club "reinvests" the distributed earnings (whether positive or negative) in the accounts of each member. If the distributed earnings are positive, then more units are "bought" at the new unit value. If the club had negative earnings (losses, in other words), then negative units are bought and each member's total number of units would be reduced.

The end result is that when the club's net income is *positive,* the number of units *increases* while the value of a single unit *decreases. Each member's current value and percentage ownership of the club remains constant.*

On the other hand, when net income is *negative,* the number of units *decreases* while the value of a unit *increases. Each member's current value and percentage ownership of the club remains constant.*

So why reinvest earnings? This practice keeps the current value and percentage ownership of each member exactly the same before and after the distribution. Although this bit of bookkeeping can confuse many club members (and many treasurers for that matter), it's the same as a mutual fund that makes an annual distribution to shareholders and then reinvests the proceeds in each shareholder's account.

When club members wonder why the unit value declined at year-end, ask them to look at their total account values before and after the distribution. When they see they match, they should be satisfied! The bookkeeping entries enable members to report their share of taxable transactions as required by law.

After you've distributed earnings, all future Member Status Reports that you print for your club will reflect the adjustment in units. The "Paid In Plus Earnings" column shows each member's tax basis in the club adjusted for all previous distributions.

You need to distribute earnings to the entire club only once a year at the end of the calendar year. When members withdraw from the club, a distribution estimate is prepared only for those members' earnings. Completing distribution for withdrawals isn't necessary. When the withdrawal is a complete withdrawal, the withdrawing member will not appear in the year-end distribution. To ensure that the distribution takes into account any transactions modified during the club's audit, reprint the Withdrawal Distribution Report after the books are closed at the end of the year. Give that copy to the withdrawing member as his or her official list of tax liabilities.

Preparing and distributing final year-end statements

After completing the year-end distribution, you'll print copies of the Distribution of Earnings Statement for every member of the club. You also must print and distribute an Income and Expense Statement and a Balance Sheet Report. In conjunction with the year-end Valuation Statement, these reports give your members a complete picture of your club's financial condition.

Preparing annual IRS and state partnership filings

Although investment clubs generally don't have to pay taxes, they usually must file an annual informational return with the IRS. Many states also require clubs to file a partnership return. Contact your state taxation department to see whether a return is required.

Investment clubs must file Form 1065, the federal partnership tax return, with the IRS every year. All your members must also receive a Schedule K-1, which itemizes their respective shares of the club's earnings for the year. A copy of each member's K-1 must be included with Form 1065. Taking care of these tax issues by April 15, the deadline for filing the return and for providing K-1s to your members, is the treasurer's job.

Now, you can imagine how your club members will feel if you don't deliver the information they need to prepare their tax returns until the day their own returns were due! To avoid being drawn and quartered by your fellow members, resolve to have K-1s prepared by early March. Financial institutions must provide Form 1099s to account holders by the end of January, so you have a bit longer than a month to prepare your club's tax documents, which is more than enough time.

For users of NAIC's club accounting software or online accounting site, a special add-on program is available each year to automatically prepare the Form 1065 and Schedule K-1s. The nominal fee for the service is worth it, because it makes the preparation of proper documents a snap. Simply run the program, and the details are pulled over from your accounting records. Voilà, the form is completed right before your eyes.

Print two copies of Form 1065. One must be sent to the IRS, and the other is for the club's permanent records. Print three copies of Schedule K-1 for each member. One is given to the member, one is attached to the copy of Form 1065 sent to the IRS, and the third is for the club's permanent records.

Send Form 1065 and the accompanying Schedule K-1s to the IRS, postmarked by April 15 and marked with "Return Receipt Requested." File the receipt with the year's tax records. Nonfiling and late-filing penalties are assessed, so don't miss the deadline. Fines are often assessed per month, per member, so they can add up fast!

IRS Publication 541 deals directly with the various tax issues related to partnerships, so it's your best reference if you have any questions as you prepare your club's return. You can instantly access the publication on the IRS Web site (www.irs.gov). In addition, NAIC usually provides instructions in its magazine, *Better Investing*, each February, and on its Web site (www.better-investing.org) to help clubs complete Form 1065.

Arranging annual audit

You're almost done with the year-end tasks, but you must take care of one more chore — the annual audit of the club's books. Your club should appoint an *audit committee* each year to review the club's books. If your club has purchased NAIC's Fidelity bond insurance, you're required to conduct an audit every year according to NAIC's specifications.

The best time for performing the audit is as soon as all the year-end tasks are completed. The committee's goal is making sure that all the bank and brokerage statements match the club's records, and that there's been no hanky-panky with the financial figures.

As treasurer, you need to prepare the club's records for the audit. Using accounting software, you can print copies of these reports for the entire year:

- ✔ Complete Journal Listing
- ✔ Cash Journal Listing
- ✔ Cash Contributions Report
- ✔ Transactions Summary Report
- ✔ Individual Investments History (for each stock in the club portfolio)
- ✔ Individual Valuations Units Ledger (for each member)
- ✔ Petty Cash Journal (if used in your club)

If it seems like you're printing every report in the software's catalog, you're almost right! But the information in these reports is exactly what the audit committee needs to reconcile all the transactions.

The treasurer also needs to provide the files for the year, including:

- ✔ Brokerage, bank and DRIP statements
- ✔ Photocopies of deposit slips and deposited checks
- ✔ Canceled checks
- ✔ Tax statements
- ✔ Stock certificates held by the club

When the committee meets, it should review each transaction, making sure that the account statements match the club's records. The committee should make sure that the number of shares of each stock held by the club is correct, and that all payments and fees have been properly recorded as payments and fees, respectively. Finally, the committee needs to check the beginning and ending balances of each account, making sure they match the club's records.

The entire process may take up to two hours to complete. In some clubs, the treasurer is asked to be on hand for the verification meeting to answer any questions that may arise. The audit committee must complete its work and provide a written report to the club secretary by March 31.

Software Makes Accounting Easy

Although using accounting software either online or on your personal computer isn't an absolute requirement, doing so is one way that technology can really make a difference for your club. Compared with manual bookkeeping, club accounting software is so much easier to use, so much more accurate, and so much faster, that the decision to go electronic is a no-brainer. Figure 10-3 shows a software-generated member deposit form, for example. An investment in software goes a long way toward ensuring that your records are accurate and that you're complying with all the applicable tax and partnership regulations.

An overview of NAIC Club accounting software

NAIC's Club Accounting software is recommended for clubs of all ages, sizes, and levels of experience. It's available for purchase as a Windows program for your personal computer, or as a Web-based version (www.naic-club.com). If you use a Macintosh computer, you can use the online version of the program. To evaluate the software yourself, you can download a demo version of the program at www.iclub.com.

The club accounting program stores all your transactions, including member contributions, investment sales and purchases, dividends, interest payments and expenses. It instantly calculates the number of units, your club's unit value, and the total value of your portfolio. In addition, it keeps track of all the information that you need to prepare your club's annual tax filings, including short-term and long-term capital gains and losses and dividend and interest income.

The software performs some calculations that are nearly impossible to calculate by hand, and some of its technological enhancements are fairer to your members. For instance, software can calculate the compound annual return of the securities in your portfolio and of the portfolio as a whole. The program can use something called a *time-based method* of distributing each member's share of the club's income, losses, and expenses at year-end or when withdrawing. When keeping the books by hand, by comparison, the treasurer distributes the earnings at year-end based on the number of units owned by each member at the end of the year. It doesn't matter whether the person was a member at the beginning of the year or joined the club in November. The software-driven time-based method ensures that all tax liabilities are allocated to members according to their ownership throughout the year. Members who join later in the year won't have to share in tax liabilities that accrued before they became club members.

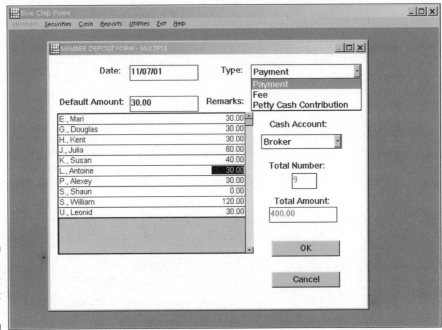

Figure 10-3:
A member
deposit
form.

When tax time rolls around, separate add-in software (available at a reasonable price) can generate and print all required tax reports and filings, including the club's Form 1065 return and Schedule K-1s for all members.

Taking care of your data

Take care of your important data by creating a regular backup of your club's computer files. You can fit years of club accounting data onto a single diskette, so be liberal in your use of that inexpensive storage. Every year, back up your club's files onto several floppy diskettes. Keep one near your computer (preferably someplace safe). Keep another in a separate location, such as at your office, or in a safety deposit box. Give a third copy to someone in your club to keep for safekeeping. When you have three copies, your chances of catastrophic loss become much smaller. And if you lose your current data because of a fire in your home or a computer hardware crash, you know you'll only have to reconstruct several months' worth of data, and not years of history.

Online accounting alternatives

If you've been reading this chapter and wondering "can't I just do this online," we've got good news for you. ICLUBcentral, the company that makes NAIC's Club Accounting Software, also offers the NAIC-approved online version of the same program (www.naic-club.com). Figure 10-4 shows a Valuation Statement, for example. Besides offering the same reports and functions of the desktop software, the Web site adds other features, such as message boards for your club to use to communicate and a file storage area so your club can easily share meeting agendas, SSG files, and the like. You can even move data back and forth from the online version to the desktop software if you like, because they're compatible.

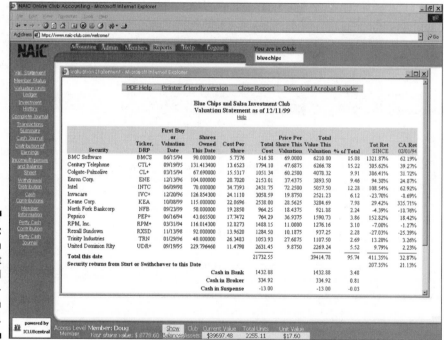

Figure 10-4:
A Valuation Statement produced by software from ICLUBcentral.

NAIC-Club.com even offers the same tax-filing functionality, so you can prepare your Form 1065 and Schedule K-1s right online. Check out the Web site for information about fees and registration.

ICLUBcentral also plays host to another online club accounting site, ICLUB. com (www.iclub.com). This site features other, advanced capabilities, but also offers the same compatibility with the company's club accounting desktop software.

Doing it by hand (if you must!)

If by now you've decided, for one reason or another, to keep your club's books by hand, or to create your own system of linked spreadsheets to manage all the tasks we've described in this chapter, all we have to say to you is this: Good luck! You'll need it! When NAIC first introduced its club accounting software in 1990, hundreds of existing clubs switched from manual to computerized bookkeeping. In the process, many of these clubs learned that their books were riddled with errors spanning many years. The books of some clubs looked like treasurers had scrambled all the numbers like eggs in a skillet. Other clubs discovered that their treasurers never retired the units of withdrawing members, so they had thousands of extra units on the books. Your club is fortunate, because you can start out on the right foot from the beginning.

If you are still convinced you want to do it all by hand, get a copy of NAIC's *Club Accounting Manual* and follow it to the letter.

Keeping Good Records

In addition to keeping the books for your club, the treasurer also should be responsible for maintaining other important records of the club's operations. Some of the paperwork you can expect to pass through your treasurer's hands are tax returns, brokerage statements, Form 1099s from your financial institutions, canceled checks, trade confirmations, account applications, and company annual reports.

An inexpensive file storage box makes a good home for all equipment and records you need to keep on hand. Use it to store boxes of blank checks from your bank, blank cash receipt forms to issue to any members who pay in cash, check deposit stamp and inkpad, and other related items. You'll also keep your club's current statements and other files in this box.

A few simple file folders also go a long way toward keeping your club records in shape. Start by labeling one folder "CURRENT," and keeping it someplace handy, maybe near your desk or computer. As you receive statements and confirmations during the month, you should put them into this folder for safekeeping until you produce reports that include such information for the next meeting. When you do sit down to create the club's Valuation Statement and prepare the reports, you'll have all the information you need to update the software with recent transactions. After you enter stock transactions, staple the paper trade confirmations (if your broker sends them) to that month's account statement. Do the same with canceled checks, stapling them to the bank statement.

Greenback Investors, Inc.

Members of *Greenback Investors, Inc.*, of Pine Bluff, Arkansas, formed as a corporation in 1983 rather than use the partnership format that most investment clubs choose. The 18 members are business acquaintances who each contribute $100 a month toward the club's portfolio, which is valued at more than $1,100,000. Club members meet monthly for lunch, followed by a one-and-a-half-hour business meeting. Regular attendance is required of all members. Once a year the club schedules a stockholders' dinner meeting to which members' wives and the widows of the two deceased members are invited.

The Greenback Investors' portfolio includes 73 stocks. Members are required to research potential stocks, make presentations to the group, and follow stocks the club already holds. Officers are selected alphabetically to share the responsibility of operating the club. The only exception is the office of treasurer, which is a permanent position.

The Greenback Investors are selective when choosing new members to replace outgoing members. Each potential member must be unanimously approved by the current membership and pays in an amount equal to what the departing member is withdrawing. Because of this careful deliberation when bringing in new members, each change has gone smoothly and membership turnover is extremely low.

Once you've entered all the transactions, file the monthly statements in a single file folder labeled "ACCOUNT STATEMENTS — 20## (write in the current year)." If you have separate brokerage and bank accounts, you can file them chronologically, or sort them by provider, holding them all together with jumbo paper clips — it's your choice. But you don't need separate folders for each financial account.

After you've printed out the monthly reports, put a copy of each report in a third file folder labeled "TREASURER REPORTS — 20## (again, whatever the current year is)." Are you catching on to the pattern here? Stapling each month's reports together is a good idea, as is printing them on both sides of a single sheet of paper and filing them chronologically. The audit committee's report also needs to be included in this folder.

You'll need one more file folder, this one labeled "TAX RETURN — 20##." You can probably guess what gets filed here. Put copies of your completed Form 1065 Partnership Return, Schedule K-1s for each member, and all your other tax-related information into this folder.

As you start a new year, create three new folders labeled with the new year, and repeat. Pass the old year's folders on to the newly elected treasurer, who may find them helpful for reference purposes.

The new treasurer can reuse the "CURRENT" folder until it wears out!

Chapter 11

Creating Your Education Program

*O*ne trait that nearly all successful investment clubs seem to share is that member education is at the top of their lists of priorities. Although being a member of an investment club can be an enlightening and informative experience in its own right, you nevertheless need to formally put an educational topic on the agenda for each club meeting. Use a portion of your time together each month to expand the knowledge of each member. And you don't have to stop at learning about stock analysis and portfolio building. Many clubs consider any personal finance topic to be fair game for their educational efforts and they schedule lessons about estate planning, retirement accounts, and saving for their children's college education.

Your club's educational component also serves another important function — it helps preserve your members' interest in the club. Guest speakers and fun yet informative presentations keep your members stimulated while adding a sometimes much-needed break to your club's regular meeting routine.

An old adage says that we learn best as we teach. Members who volunteer to make presentations about a particular topic often find that, in the process of researching and developing their presentations for the rest of the club, they learn more about the subject than they expected. The benefits of gaining all that additional knowledge just can't be beat, so don't worry about straining your brain when it's your turn to present.

Taking Charge of Education

Regardless what form your investment club's educational effort takes, or how formal or informal it may be, you'll want to designate one club member to be in charge of the initiative. That keeps your educational offerings organized and, it is hoped, ensures a solid program that moves logically from beginning topics to more advanced ones as your club members gain confidence in their investing skills. Keep in mind that your club's education officer doesn't have to actually *provide* all the education; he or she just has to be the one in charge of coordinating it.

Choosing an education officer

In many clubs, the vice president serves as the education officer, so it's his or her duty to create a program, assign tasks, develop presentations, come up with creative ways to keep members interested, research potential and identified topics, recruit guest speakers, and take care of any other aspects of the effort. Some clubs create an education committee made up of several members who serve in the same capacity.

Regardless of whether your club chooses to have just one education officer or a whole committee, you need to be on constant watch for burnout. Educating your entire club is quite a responsibility, so be sure to rotate the education leadership role on a regular basis. One way to ensure educational contentment is passing the buck to *all* your club members. Ask everyone to write down three or four things they still want to learn about. You can ask them to submit the topics anonymously so no one feels self-conscious about his or her knowledge level. These suggestions can easily form the basis for a year's worth of lessons and give those in charge of education a better idea of what topics to focus on. Besides, that way no one can complain that the education officer or committee is ignoring the club's needs, because all club members helped choose the curriculum.

Adding education to your agenda

Once you have an educational plan in place, your club needs to include some form of education on each meeting's agenda. This can be a quick 10-minute tutorial about reading the stock market tables in the daily newspaper during a month when you have a great deal of business, or a more involved, hour-long presentation about researching a stock from scratch. Your club can prepare these lessons on its own or rely on educational offerings from other sources that can be adapted to its needs.

For instance, when your club joins NAIC, it receives a 12-lesson study guide designed for new clubs with the recommendation that each month's lesson be read to club members during each of the first year's worth of meetings. Although the study lessons cover the basics of investing, reading them to your members is a surefire way to induce drowsiness. Ideally, the education officer needs to try adapting this valuable information to liven things up a bit while still conveying lots of knowledge to the club membership. Not only is it *possible* to have fun while learning about investing — we highly recommend making fun a top priority!

Making the most of your resources

Technology can help you in your quest to invigorate your club's education program. If you or other club members have access to an LCD projector, for example, you can hook it up to a personal computer during your meetings and project the display onto a screen or wall. Then you can talk through a slide presentation created in Microsoft PowerPoint, take a tour on the Internet to some useful financial sites, or work through an analysis of a stock using software tools. If your club is small, gathering around a computer may be just as easy for you and your members. Even a simple overhead projector and printouts on acetate sheets can be useful for demonstrating concepts in an educational presentation.

Never underestimate the power of handouts. People usually respond better to presentations when they have a printed outline or illustrations on paper in front of them. They can make notes in the margins and follow along as the presenter speaks. Regardless of who actually writes them, the education officer should be in charge of coordinating handouts for each lesson and distributing them to each member at the meeting. You also can mail or e-mail them in advance, but handing them out at the meeting is much better so members don't forget to bring them.

Planning Your Education Agenda

As your club starts out, you'll probably spend a considerable amount of time discovering the basics of investing. The education officer can prepare brief presentations on fundamental terms and concepts of investing. Here's a hint: You can use Chapter 13 as an outline for explaining investing basics to your club. Once the basics have been covered, remember that you still have plenty of other investment-related topics to tackle.

Learning to analyze stocks

Your club wants to spend plenty of time showing members how to complete and understand a Stock Selection Guide. The SSG is the tool that NAIC recommends for stock analysis. It's a two-page paper form that highlights the more important items to consider before investing in a stock. (Check out Chapter 14 for many more details about the SSG.) Your education officer needs to personally get up to speed on the mechanics of the SSG as quickly as possible.

A number of resources are available to help you learn how to use the SSG. NAIC's official SSG manual (which you'll receive when your club becomes an NAIC member) provides in-depth instruction on the SSG. The organization also sells an SSG instructional video, and local NAIC chapters (www. better-investing.org/regions/regions.html) conduct regular SSG training classes. The NAIC also offers a comprehensive Stock Study Course, complete with instructor's manual and student workbooks. Another alternative is the SSG Tutorial online at www.douglasgerlach.com/ssg/, which describes the basics of the SSG.

During your first few club meetings, focus strongly on getting all members familiar with the SSG. Provide blank SSG forms and company reports from Value Line or Standard & Poor's (available at your local library or online from a number of discount brokers) to your members, walking them through one page of the form at a time. In subsequent meetings, have your club break into groups of three or four members, asking each group to complete an entire SSG on a stock and then report the results of their analysis.

One presentation aid that is useful in teaching this method of stock analysis is an enlarged display-sized SSG sold by NAIC (www.better-investing.org). The plastic wipe-clean surface enables the board to be reused again and again. The large size is useful for showing groups how to use the SSG and for analyzing a stock during a meeting. Once your club discovers the basics of the SSG, you can use the oversized form as a visual aid for discussions about the stocks that your club is considering.

Your objective during these first few meetings isn't necessarily to find the first stock for your portfolio, but rather to establish a common base of investing knowledge for all your members as you become better acquainted with one another. Of course, if you happen to find an interesting stock or two, that's great! But rushing to purchase anything, no matter how promising it looks, isn't necessary. You have plenty of time to become more familiar with our recommended methods of stock analysis before you start loading up your portfolio. So take it slow and have some fun while you learn.

Not all your club members will become familiar with the SSG at the same pace. If a few members are having trouble, schedule a special training session that begins an hour before your regular meeting. Any members who require additional help need to attend those classes so they'll be able to catch up with others as quickly as possible. And if your whole club is having problems, don't forget to turn to your local NAIC chapter for help. A volunteer may be available to help get your club over its first few educational hurdles.

This same tactic of working in small groups during your club meeting can be used later on for finding out how to use other NAIC analysis tools, such as the Stock Comparison Guide and Challenge Tree forms. Sometimes finding out how to use these tools is easier in these small groups, but be open to whatever works best for you and your fellow club members. In some clubs, workgroups meet between club meetings, completing homework assignments for presentation at the next meeting. For more about small workgroups, see Chapter 15.

Choosing other topics of interest

As committed as your education officer may be, the burden of the club's educational focus doesn't lie solely on her shoulders. Each member should contribute something to the endeavor. As your club matures, every member needs to provide regular presentations on stocks for consideration in your portfolio. But members also need to consider other ways of expanding the education of the entire club.

Some ideas for member presentations include

- ✔ **A review of an investing book.** Your club members will likely take it upon themselves to learn more about investing. As they read books on the subject, why not ask them to present short reports about them to the club? This can spark great discussions about various investment philosophies or money management strategies.

- ✔ **A report on an investor event that he or she recently attended, such as an investor's fair, investment conference, or company annual meeting.** Some clubs even reimburse some or all of a member's expenses or registration fees for attending such events, as long as the member reports back to the club. Club members who can't attend events will appreciate a glimpse into their fellow member's experiences, so encourage this kind of sharing.

- ✔ **A presentation on a financial topic related to a member's personal experience.** For example, if a member refinances his home, he can report on the process of finding, applying for, and selecting a new mortgage. A member who recently opened an account at an online brokerage can report on her research and how she compared brokers before actually choosing one.

- ✔ **A report on the state of a particular industry group.** Understanding more about a specific industry as a whole can help your club members to better analyze companies in that industry. An interested club member can give a presentation on the key concerns and considerations to keep in mind when investing in companies in that industry.

An added bonus of having members give presentations on topics such as these is that they don't need to have a great deal of special expertise or research to be effective. No matter how much or how little a member knows about investing, he or she can put together a presentation that will be appreciated by the entire club. And don't overlook the educational value to the presenter. Members who prepare these kinds of reports for the club gain valuable experiences that will be most helpful as discussion turns to the stocks in your portfolio.

Inviting guest experts

Inviting a local expert to serve as guest speaker is another tactic for spicing up your club's education program. Guest speakers offer particular expertise about financial topics and bring new perspectives to your club. Finding willing guest speakers isn't as hard as you might imagine. Many professionals who work in the financial industry are well practiced at speaking before groups and are more than happy to speak to your club.

Of course, don't forget that generally the reason they're so willing is because there's something in it for them — the potential to drum up new business. Still, most experts are happy to make a fairly straightforward educational presentation to your club, as long as you give them the chance to provide business cards or informational packets to your membership. You can set the guidelines by asking the speaker to share those sales materials only at the conclusion of the club meeting and stressing that an aggressive sales pitch is neither welcome nor appropriate.

When you schedule a speaker, make that presentation the last item on your agenda, following the conclusion of your club's usual business. That gives the speaker a chance to talk directly with members about their personal needs after the meeting and to become a bit more familiar with how your club operates and observe a few of the club personalities. That can help the speaker tailor a presentation to better fit your club. You should probably schedule a light agenda for the meeting, so that you don't get bogged down in other business and can devote more attention to your guest speaker.

While most speakers will be happy to speak without charging you a fee, offering a small gift at the end of their presentations is a nice token of your appreciation. Even if (or maybe even especially if) it's home-baked cookies, your speaker will appreciate the gesture.

Here are some ideas for guest speakers whom you can find in your community. You or your fellow club members may already have business relationships with many of these professionals, so don't hesitate to inquire or extend an invitation.

- **Accountants** can discuss taxes and tax planning, or how to read financial statements.
- **Brokers and financial advisors** can address broad topics of interest about investing and securities.

- ✔ **Attorneys** can explain wills and estate planning basics.

- ✔ **Insurance representatives** can describe the differences between whole and term life insurance, annuities, disability, and long-term care policies, and other related topics.

- ✔ **A trust officer from a local bank** can discuss trusts and how they work.

Once you start thinking about everyone you know, you probably can come up with other appropriate and interesting speakers for your club. After you've scheduled a speaker, make sure that all your members know in advance that a guest speaker is attending. You'll want to honor your guest with a full turnout. Besides, you wouldn't want your members to miss out on the festivities.

Although guest speakers can provide a great boost to your club's education program, don't become too dependent on them just because they seem like an easy way to fill up your education schedule. One or two guest speakers a year add a little variety to your club's education program, but unless your speakers are focused solely on investing in the stock market, you're going to need more than just a basic overview of financial topics. So take advantage of this great resource, but remember to choose your expert guest speakers wisely and judiciously.

Finding other guests

Besides financial professionals, many other people can make great speakers for a club meeting. When you discuss your club with friends and family, keep your ears open for people they know who may have interesting insights for your club. Here are some places where you may find guest speaker candidates:

- ✔ **Publicly traded companies in your community.** Call their investor relations offices and invite an executive to speak to your club. Even the smallest companies are willing to speak to groups of interested investors of any size. It never hurts to ask. (If a company representative agrees to come, make sure that your club does a comprehensive study of the corporation first. That way you'll be able to ask intelligent questions and make the most of your time with the company rep.)

- ✔ **Privately owned companies in your community.** A local executive may be willing to discuss the business and industry, offering you unique insights that can help your club invest in similar public companies.

- ✔ **The local newspaper.** A business reporter or editor from your local newspaper may be able to provide a perspective on economic trends or public companies in your area.

✔ **A college or university near you.** Perhaps a business or finance professor from that institution would be willing to speak to your club. Most academics are involved in research of one kind or another, and they're already well versed at speaking before groups, so they may be great candidates.

✔ **Another investment club.** When you're just getting your club off the ground, inviting an experienced member of another investment club to speak to your club on the mechanics of starting a club as well as stock analysis techniques can be useful. A joint meeting with another club, either more or less experienced than your own, can be a fun social experience and can expose you to the operations and philosophy of the other club.

✔ **The local NAIC chapter.** It may have a club visit program, where they'll send a volunteer to help your club with problems if you've hit some hurdles.

Finally, while we'd love to come visit every club that reads this book, that could be a full-time job all its own. But if you have access to a speakerphone during your club meetings, you can get the next best thing — a teleconference! One of the authors of this book will join you for 20 minutes during your regular club meeting, answering questions that you may have about this book or about investment clubs in general. For details, visit `www.douglasgerlach.com/clubsfordummies/`.

Don't Forget the Fun!

As you can see, your club's education program doesn't all have to be about lectures and tests, because plenty of great ways of learning exist without being too academic. You can take advantage of a variety of stock market games. You can create your own stock-picking contest. You can have enthusiastic discussions based on online investment resources. You can venture out of your regular meeting and go on a field trip. Or, you and your club members can lightheartedly compete against each other with some formal (but still fun) tests of your investment knowledge.

Pop quiz, anyone?

As hard to believe as it may be, a quiz or two can be a fun way to help a few investing concepts sink in — especially when your members won't have to worry about being graded or have it affect their permanent academic records. Your education officer can create a few simple multiple-choice tests of ten or more questions, focusing each quiz on a different topic.

Test your investing knowledge

1. This legendary stock picker managed the most successful mutual fund in history.

  a) Warren Buffet

  b) Peter Lynch

  c) John Bogle

  d) Sir John Templeton

2. You can potentially decrease the risk in your portfolio by:

  a) Investing in companies of different sizes

  b) Investing in companies in different industries

  c) Not investing too much, even in companies that you're convinced will perform well

  d) All of the above

3. Earnings per share are:

  a) The share of a company's profits paid to investors

  b) Useless in most forms of stock analysis

  c) A measure of a company's cash flow

  d) A company's after-tax profits allocated to each outstanding share of stock

4. A stock's yield is:

  a) The stop price set when you place a trade.

  b) The percentage of its dividend compared to its current price.

  c) The interest rate paid by that stock.

  d) All of the above

5. A stock in the club's portfolio has just declined 20 percent in price. What do you do?

  a) Convene a special emergency meeting of the club to get agreement to sell the shares.

  b) At your next meeting, sell half your shares and hold on to the rest in case it comes back up.

  c) At your next meeting, re-evaluate the stock and consider buying more, if appropriate.

  d) At your next meeting, buy enough shares to double up on your investment, regardless of the reasons for the decline

6. The most important factor that demonstrates the skill of management is the:

  a) Historical growth rate of the company's sales and earnings.

  b) Stability and growth of the company's pretax profit margins.

  c) Stability and growth of the company's return on equity.

  d) All of the above.

7. According to NAIC, its average member will hold a stock in its portfolio for how long before selling?

  a) 18 months

  b) 2 years

  c) 6 years

  d) 11 years

1b, 2d, 3d, 4b, 5c, 6d, 7c

ANSWER KEY:

For example, you can create quizzes on topics such as financial statements, the Dow Jones Industrial Average, growth stock investing, or using a broker. Have fun writing the questions and answers, and come up with some funny or silly, yet tricky, choices for each. Spring the quiz on your club members during a meeting. Take 10 minutes for everyone to complete the quiz, and then review each question and the correct answer as a group. Allow time for discussion of the answers, too, and keep the focus on the discussion and not on how many questions each member got right or wrong. See the sidebar, "Testing your investing knowledge," for a sample quiz to get you started.

Once your club has a portfolio of stocks, you can create quizzes based on the companies that your club owns. Come up with a dozen questions about the products, management, and histories of those companies. Seeing how well you and your club members really know the companies in your portfolio can be quite interesting. Here's a sample of a quiz you can easily personalize for your club.

First, create a worksheet with six columns across the top and these headings:

✔ Name of Stock

✔ Ticker Symbol

✔ Exchange (NYSE, NASDAQ, and so on)

✔ Industry Group

✔ Company Size (small, mid, large)

✔ Dividends?

Down the left side, create a number of rows — the same number of rows as stocks in your portfolio — then a few more to throw off your members a bit. Do not, however, fill in the names of the stocks that your club owns. That will be your club members' jobs. Give each member of your club a copy of the quiz at your meeting to see how well they know just what companies your club owns. (Be sure to do it before the treasurer's report is distributed!) Ask them to fill in the name of each stock in your club portfolio, its symbol, the industry group it belongs to, how big the company is (if it's a small, mid-sized, or large company), and indicate whether it pays dividends.

Once everyone's done, go over the answers as a group. You may want to let everyone know upfront that they're not going to score 100 percent. The point isn't so much to get every question right as it is to spark your fellow members' interest in your club portfolio and hopefully start an interesting discussion as you go over the answers.

Games and puzzlers

Another way to increase your club's familiarity with financial terms and phrases is to create word-search or crossword puzzles that can be completed during a meeting. Choose a theme for each puzzle, and then come up with appropriate terms and clues. A number of inexpensive software programs are available that can help you create word puzzles, and they often provide trial versions or demos so you can evaluate the programs. Here are a few of the available programs:

- ✔ Crossword Compiler (www.crossword-puzzle-maker.com), Windows.
- ✔ Crossword Express (www.crauswords.com), Windows and Macintosh.
- ✔ Crossword Weaver and 1-2-3 Word Search Maker (www.varietygames.com), Windows.
- ✔ CrossWorks (www.homeware.com), Windows.
- ✔ Word Search (www.word-search.org), Macintosh.
- ✔ Word Search Construction Kit (www.wordsearchkit.com), Windows.
- ✔ Word Square Builder (www.kagi.com/scattersoft/), Macintosh.
- ✔ WordSheets (www.qualint.com), Windows.
- ✔ WordSplash (www.chronasoft.com/software/), Windows.

Trivia contests also are fun ways to convey information about little-known facts about the stock market. You can create quizzes about the history of the market, current events, or the philosophy of a well-known stock picker such as Peter Lynch or Warren Buffet. The Web is a great research tool for finding interesting facts and trivia about the markets.

Many clubs conduct ongoing stock picking contests of their own. Each member picks a single stock, and the performance of all the picks are tracked over a specific period of time. Because your club should be focusing on the long-term, setting the term of your contest for one year or longer makes sense. Some clubs require members to complete an SSG for their picks and be able to explain the reasons they chose those stocks. Each month, you can review the standings of each member in the contest, and at the end of the year, reward the winner with a prize.

Speaking of prizes, you probably don't want to go to any big expense just to acknowledge your club's contest and quiz winners. Fun gifts and homemade prizes can serve just as well. Some clubs collect the free items handed out by companies at investors fairs and conferences, and then use these pens, coffee mugs, key chains and other items to create a fun prize package for use by their club.

Hitting the road, not the books

Your education program doesn't have to be confined to the hours and location of your regular monthly meeting. Plenty of opportunities exist for your club to take field trips, either visiting local organizations or attending a financial event. Not all members have to attend to make it a club-sanctioned activity. In fact, in many cases, those members who do attend a particular outing can report back to the club at your next meeting. Here are some of our favorite ideas for educational club outings:

- ✔ **A local company.** In your own community, a publicly traded company may have a facility or headquarters that may welcome visitors. The investor relations office of the corporation usually is the best place to call to find out whether the company will offer your club a tour.

- ✔ **An NAIC class.** If you have a local NAIC chapter, sign up for a class that focuses on the SSG or some other aspect of investing. Your club members will enjoy the change of scenery as you expand your collective knowledge. Be sure to chat with others in attendance; they may be members of their own investment clubs, willing to share some tips with you.

- ✔ **An investor fair.** In addition to regular SSG classes, most local chapters of NAIC conduct an annual investors' fairs and other educational events throughout the year You can check online at `www.better-investing.org/regions/regions.html` to see whether a chapter meets near you. With more than 115 chapters across the U.S., chances are good that one is in your area. And even if the nearest chapter is some distance away, many clubs find it worth the effort to take a carload of club members on a road trip to attend an investors fair, staying overnight in a hotel and sharing the driving duties.

  A typical investors fair is an all-day Saturday event. Attendees hear presentations from several corporate representatives on the activities and achievements of their companies. A keynote speaker may also address the audience during lunch or at the conclusion of the day. Other companies may take part by staffing booths in the fair's exhibit hall, or the chapter may schedule other educational seminars during the fair. Admission costs usually are quite reasonable and may include a discount for a group of members attending from the same club.

- ✔ **An NAIC national conference.** NAIC also plays host to several major national conferences each year. The NAIC's National Congress and Expo features hundreds of corporate exhibitors and dozens of educational workshops, along with many nationally known featured speakers, all in the course of three information-packed days. CompuFest focuses on computerized investing. It helps your club members learn to use software and the Internet to become better investors. Members of your club who want to attend events like these can share hotel rooms and other expenses to help keep down the costs.

- ✔ **Other financial conferences.** Other organizations conduct financial conferences in major cities across the U.S., often in cooperation with local newspapers. Keep your eye out for events in your neck of the woods and either attend as a club or have any members who go share the details with your club at its next meeting. Some clubs even pay any registration fees for members who attend as long as they report back, educating fellow members about what they found out at the event.

✔ **Regional stock exchange.** Clubs that operate near major cities may encounter opportunities for taking a day trip to a regional stock exchange or other financial institution. Stock exchanges are in Boston, Chicago, Philadelphia, and San Francisco, and branches of the U.S. Mint are in Denver, Philadelphia, and other cities.

✔ **Big Apple, anyone?** Some even more ambitious clubs plan trips to locales like New York City, the center of the financial world. New York is home to Wall Street and the New York and American Stock Exchanges as well as Nasdaq. All accommodate visitors. Besides the exchanges, you can also visit the Museum of American Financial History, an arm of the Smithsonian Institution, or the Federal Reserve Bank, whose vaults have more gold than Fort Knox.

Taking Education Online

With each passing year, more and more educational resources become available online. Even if not all your club members are online, your club still can benefit from the Web bounty. Members who *have* Internet access can print out the materials, sharing them with the rest of your club during an educational presentation. Another option, if you have an Internet connection where you meet, is to access some of these resources with a laptop computer so that all your members can see them live. This, it is hoped, will show any technophobic members what an amazing tool the Internet can be for investors.

We provide a list of online resources to consult for investment club information in Chapter 4. These same sites are great places to go to look for material to incorporate into your club's education program. Your education officer can look for items related to what your members are interested in, print out what's most useful, and use it to plan lessons for the entire club.

A particularly rich source of investment education is NAIC Online's Investor's School. Dedicated NAIC Online volunteers regularly create and present live, interactive investment lessons on a variety of topics. The transcripts of these classes are archived at NAIC's Web site. You can find more information about the Investor's School at:

```
www.better-investing.org/chats/chat.html
```

Some of the subjects that the school has covered include in-depth analyses of many of *Better Investing* magazine's Stocks to Study, classes on analyzing bank and pharmaceutical stocks, and classes on investment club operations. Regardless of the level of your club's education, you'll find more than enough potential lessons just waiting to be presented. Quite a few clubs regularly discuss the monthly Stock to Study class after the transcript is posted online, and a few clubs even attend the live chat as a group so they can participate in the discussion in real-time.

NAIC's Sample Club even meets on line. The online, "model" club functions just like a real club, making buy and sell decisions on previously researched stocks. No real money, however, is involved, and any person who shows up at the online meeting is eligible to vote on the stocks being considered. You can see the club's portfolio for yourself and learn how to attend a meeting at the Investor's School page mentioned earlier in this section.

The more time your club spends online, the more you'll come to appreciate the tremendous, mostly free opportunities that abound for club education. Make it a point to ask all your online club members to regularly search for useful information from reputable sources to bring to your meetings.

University Place Investment Club

One founding member of the *University Place Investment Club* (UPIC) got the ball rolling by playing host to a meeting for friends and acquaintances who simply wanted to learn more about investment clubs. She encouraged each invitee to bring a friend to the introductory meeting. This no-pressure method of finding club members was successful and soon this group of friends and co-workers in University Place, Washington, joined together to form their club. With 20 members ranging in age from 35 to 65, UPIC has built a portfolio of 18 stocks that is worth almost $79,000. The club invests online through discount brokerage TD Waterhouse and considers club accounting software an absolute must.

UPIC meets for two hours every month. A rotating list determines alphabetically who's in charge of bringing the treats to the next club meeting. The monthly minimum contribution is $50, although members *are* permitted to contribute more. Potential members are required to read the UPIC new member packet and attend at least two meetings in a six-month period before they can ask to join the partnership. The member packet includes an explanatory letter, clearly spelling out the club's goals and expectations. One expectation is that all members serve a six-month rotation on the stock selection committee every two and a half years. Each member also tracks two stocks in the club portfolio.

Believing strongly in the necessity of a strong education program, UPIC expands its collective investment knowledge with 15- to 30-minute educational presentations by the club's junior partner at each meeting. UPIC also invites guest speakers and sometimes listens to audiotapes of seminars from national NAIC education events.

UPIC has lived up to the challenge of helping new members feel like they're truly a part of an active club that's been together for years. To help with this acclimatization, UPIC members take the social aspect of their club seriously, knowing this informal interaction enables members get to know each other and work together even better. UPIC occasionally schedules a meeting at a restaurant, but the senior partner also extends an open invitation to all club members to join her for dinner at a restaurant two hours before each monthly meeting. UPIC opens its social activities to family members of the entire club with an annual barbecue/ swimming party.

Chapter 12

Dealing with Special Club Problems

··

In This Chapter

▶ Applying the Law of Reasonableness

▶ Coping with negative portfolio performance

▶ Handling accounting problems

▶ Sorting through membership difficulties

··

*E*very club has its share of problems, big and small. But some problems loom larger, the kinds that are overwhelming and threaten your club's existence. Fortunately, whatever ails your club can be treated in most cases, even if the treatment isn't always so pleasant. We suggest in this chapter a number of formal guidelines for dealing with conflict, but our best advice for handling any kind of trouble in your club is to remember what we call the *Law of Reasonableness*. Here it is:

People generally want to get along, and they want their club to thrive. Sometimes, however, people need a little reminder that reasonableness and cooperation take them further in the world than antagonism and aggressive behavior.

Even if differences of opinion exist among members of your club, you always need to gain a consensus or put items to a vote. Sometimes, you may not get your way in a club — overall, the will of the club is the letter of the law. Remember that constant bickering and ever-present animosity can lead to your club's certain death. Invoke the Law of Reasonableness, thus reminding everyone of your shared purpose and that you ought to be able to find a common ground on most issues that arise in your club. In the end, you'll all be winners.

Settling — or Avoiding — People Problems

Your club's monthly meetings may last only two hours, but they can turn out to be the most exciting two hours of your month! Here's hoping they'll be exciting in a good way, understanding that the potential for conflict and strife can be great. Coping with argumentative members or playing referee during the meeting may not be your favorite part of club life, but it's a job that must be done when circumstances demand.

Dominant and bossy club members

Nobody likes a bully. In the democratic world of your investment club, a dominant member can defeat the whole reason for a dozen people working together once a month and using their best ideas to build a successful portfolio. If the club always defers to one or two members when it comes to making decisions about the club's portfolio, whose portfolio is it, really? Is it the club's portfolio or the portfolio of its more assertive members?

As Eleanor Roosevelt once said, "No one can make you feel inferior without your permission." But for various reasons, some clubs get caught up in the webs of one or more dominant personalities. Sometimes, these members are the more experienced or knowledgeable investors in the club, and less experienced members feel intimidated and hesitate to disagree. But the green-horns in your club never will gain knowledge or confidence if they're never given a chance to participate, and that can lead to the eventual mass departure of many of those members.

During a meeting, the club president's job is maintaining order and preventing personal flare-ups and sharp retorts. If a member's remarks during a meeting take an ill-spirited turn, then it's time for the president to restore civility. Usually a suggestion, such as "Let's keep the discussion focused on the issues," guides your club's members back on track. If a domineering member simply won't back down from argument for argument's sake, then perhaps your club can resort to running your meetings according to strict parliamentary procedure (*Robert's Rules of Order* is discussed in Chapter 9). By requiring members to follow a specific discussion protocol, you may better be able to maintain a sense of decorum. Your president may need to be strong-willed and able to stick to his or her guns for this to work.

But what if the club president is the problem? Sometimes clubs end up with a real take-charge personality at the helm. That's fine as long as the president doesn't turn into a dictator. If the leader of your club continually bullies members into agreement on stock purchases, or, as has happened in some clubs, pressures members to continue to re-elect that person as president, then a coup may be called for. A bit of behind-the-scenes maneuvering prior to your club's annual elections may enable you to build a majority consensus for a new candidate. Although that helps solve part of the problem, chances are your ex-president will continue the same behavior once out of office. Egotism is a tough habit to break, but it can kill an investment club.

The importance of teamwork can't be stressed or praised enough. As smart as we believe we, as individuals, are, when we work together as a team, we can be even smarter. In your club, regardless of how savvy each member may be about the market, your collective opinion can actually be savvier than any one individual. Don't let one member spoil the teamwork.

Differences of opinion about the portfolio

Many of us are programmed to avoid conflict at all costs, while others seem to thrive on contentious discussions. In your club, differences of opinion can be a good thing — the diversity of viewpoints can help all members to see issues from all perspectives. Too much conflict, however, can deteriorate your meetings into monthly grudge matches or stymie your efforts to build a portfolio.

No matter what happens, you must never tolerate personality attacks on any members of your club. Disagreeing and discussing are good, but keeping the debate focused on the issue at hand — and not on personal issues or blaming anyone for past decisions that went wrong — is necessary.

The interesting thing about investing is that two people often can have opposing opinions about a stock at the same time and yet neither one of them is completely wrong. But at any specific point after you buy a stock, one of those opinions likely will be right. That opinion may not be right forever, but pointing the finger at and laying blame on the person who nominated the stock is all too easy. Remember, however, that making the purchase was the club's majority decision and not the decision of just one person.

Your club may have regrets, saying "We should have sold that stock a year ago," but you can't get caught up in history. As any old hand in the market can tell you, you learn as much from your mistakes as you do from your good calls. Focusing on the educational aspect of your club can direct your attention away from your errors and remind you that handling a badly performing stock in your portfolio can teach you a great deal.

Although you won't always get "your way" in a club, you'll feel better by keeping these points in mind when your opinion differs from that of other members:

- ✔ Always remain civil to your fellow club members.

- ✔ Your club is a democracy — agree to disagree when necessary.

✔ The results of all votes are binding but not forever. If a member doesn't like an action the club has taken, she can take the matter up again at a future meeting.

✔ Don't sweat the small stuff. Becoming overwrought about decisions that your club makes is counter-productive, so keep the big picture in mind.

Partners who want to be "silent"

The time may come when a member of your club is unable to regularly participate in club operations and asks that he or she be considered a "silent" or "inactive" partner, contributing dollars each month but nothing else. This generally is a bad idea for two reasons:

✔ First, one of the tests that the SEC uses in determining whether an investment club is subject to SEC registration is whether it has any silent partners. The SEC considers other tests, such as the number of members and whether a single member makes all the investing decisions, but silent partners put you one step into the gray area.

✔ The second reason is even more important to consider. If your club was formed with education as its goal, silent partners aren't being served when they're not participating in club activities. If the club's portfolio is successful, the inactive member may gain a financial advantage from being a member, but a mutual fund certainly is more liquid and probably offers about the same financial benefits.

The club itself also may gain some advantage from having a greater amount of capital to deploy, because commissions and expenses would be a smaller percentage of each investment. However, those benefits are likely to be only slight, particularly if the club uses a deep-discount brokerage.

Likewise, your club may be hesitant about cashing out a withdrawal for that member and believe that carrying an inactive member on the books is a better alternative. However, if more of your club members decide to become inactive, who then will do the work?

Having said that, certain cases may exist in which your club can agree to carry an inactive member on a temporary basis. In some clubs, members come from highly mobile or seasonal professions. For example, many accountants and tax preparers give up most of their lives during January through April busily taking care of their clients' tax returns. In these cases, granting a member *inactive status* for a certain amount of time is quite reasonable, particularly with the understanding that those professionals will return to the fold at some point down the road. Members may also be granted temporary leaves for family or school-related reasons.

Political-social beliefs influencing stock selection

Everyone has beliefs and personal values when it comes to certain controversial issues, regardless of whether it's gun control or labor rights, tobacco or animal testing. Many investors incorporate their politics and social beliefs into their investment portfolios by refusing to buy shares in corporations with practices that run contrary to the investor's beliefs. This behavior often is called *socially responsible investing, green investing,* or *ethical investing.*

Some clubs practice socially responsible investing as part of their charters. They screen all potential holdings according to a preset list of criteria, eliminating companies in certain industries (such as defense contractors or alcohol producers) or companies that do not subscribe to certain policies. Other clubs may take a less formal approach but find that their members naturally tend to avoid certain companies.

Even if your club doesn't screen stocks for social responsibility, you still can remain true to your convictions. Your club, after all, is a democracy. When you're unwilling to buy a stock because it goes against your personal beliefs, you're free to vote against it. You can also introduce an amendment to the club's bylaws addressing the issue of socially responsible practices and whether your club should consider them before investing. Of course, a majority of members must approve the amendment before it becomes part of the club's operating procedures.

In the end, if you and your club frequently disagree about social or political issues and that creates a problem, you may decide to resign so that you're free to find a club that better suits your beliefs — or start your own. No matter what, though, you and your fellow club members need to make it a policy to respect each other's beliefs, even when you have to disagree.

Taking Control When You Face Financial Problems

Money can make or break your club and something about dealing with financial issues brings out the worst in people. Your club members may become anxious about an underperforming portfolio, angry about a bad decision they've made, or panicky about a decision they'll soon have to make. And sometimes, financial problems arise that test your club's mettle. We hope you won't have to deal with many major troubles when it comes to your club's finances, but if you do, the following sections offer some pointers.

Coping with negative returns in your portfolio

Although the hallmark of most successful clubs is their focus on member education and not so much on making lots of money in the market, if your club seems to be faring exceptionally poorly in the market, an adjustment or two may be called for. But just because your club's portfolio isn't performing as well as you hoped doesn't mean that you must take immediate action. As hard as it may be when your club's portfolio goes down in value, temporary downturns can at certain times be perfectly acceptable. At other times, though, you need to take action to fix your portfolio. The following five subsections describe some common reasons that your club portfolio may not be up to par.

Your club is young

When your club is less than 2 years old, high start-up expenses may be dragging down your club's return. You can look at your financial statements each month and see that your club's total value is less than the total of your members' monthly contributions. Expenses such as registration fees, NAIC membership and software all are essential, but it takes time for your club to earn enough to offset those costs.

If you're using NAIC's Club Accounting Software, you need to be aware of one quirk in the program that affects your club's unit value. For new clubs, the program tracks the starting unit value that you establish until you make your first investment. If your club has only expenses and no gains from investments, then you'd normally expect your unit value to decline. But if expenses take a bite of 30 percent to 50 percent of all member contributions in the first few months, your unit value will fall drastically.

This can be disheartening to club members. Even though they understand the cause of the depressed unit value, coming to meetings month after month when you're trying to get a club off the ground and seeing that your investment is worth less than when you started definitely isn't fun. By not recording expenses in the books until your club makes its first investment, thus enabling your collections to accumulate, your expenses will make up a much smaller percentage of your capital. As a result, your unit value won't fall as far when those expenses eventually are recorded.

Once your new club starts investing in the market, you cannot expect to see results overnight. Stock prices tend to rise and fall in spurts, not on an evenly consistent basis throughout the year. You can own a stock for months and its share price may never seem to stray far from its purchase price. And then, in a few days, the price can climb 10 percent or 15 percent. For your burgeoning club portfolio, the results of your research will take some time before they begin to pay off.

That's assuming you even have a *real* portfolio. It may take your club two or three years before it owns enough stocks to begin realizing the benefits of diversification. If you own only three stocks, and the price of one falls by a few dollars, your entire portfolio takes a big hit. If you own ten stocks, and one falls in price, your portfolio won't hurt nearly so badly. Be patient, and continue building your portfolio with an eye toward proper diversification. (Chapter 16 describes strategies for diversifying your portfolio.)

The overall market is down

Another case where a slow-growing portfolio may be acceptable is when the entire stock market is depressed. While your club's goal may be to generate a return of 15 percent a year, that's an average performance that you'll shoot for over a number of years. You won't likely gain that much every single year. Keep your club portfolio in context and understand how the overall market is performing. In the U.S., a bear market is a period of generally declining stock prices that can last for a few months or even a few years. You can also expect the value of your club portfolio to decline during a bear market.

Ideally, your club's portfolio will outperform the market in good times and bad, doing a bit better than the overall market when the market is up, and not as badly as the overall market when it's down. Look at the performance of the Standard & Poor's 500 Index, the most common benchmark used to measure the overall stock market. The S&P 500 is a group of 500 stocks that represent a broad spectrum of U.S. companies of many sizes in many industries, and its value is reported every day the market is open. When your club's portfolio always trails the S&P 500, in good and bad times, then you may need to reconsider your investing strategy. But if your club's portfolio is marching in step with the S&P 500, that's better than the performance of most mutual funds and you should be proud.

Your portfolio is overweighted in one stock

You feel great when your club picks a winning stock. Unfortunately, one good apple can spoil the entire bunch. Whenever a stock that you own goes up greatly in price, it can overwhelm the rest of your portfolio. As long as that stock is doing well that's definitely good, but when that stock takes a nose-dive, your entire portfolio suffers. If so, you'll need to take action to fix the imbalance.

How much is too much of a good thing? Or, rather, how much is too much of a good stock? If one stock makes up more than 25 percent or 30 percent of your total holdings, your portfolio may be at risk of overexposure. If one stock drags down your club, look at expanding your other holdings. Watch carefully as your portfolio grows by making sure that you keep your holdings in reasonable balance. You can find out more about portfolio management in Chapter 16.

Your portfolio is not sufficiently diversified

Similar to problems caused by having too much of your club invested in a single stock, your portfolio can be put to the test when your club's stocks are not properly diversified. Ideally, your holdings need to be spread out, invested in many different industry groups. Stock prices often move in tandem with the prices of other stocks in the same industries, because they often are similarly affected by changes in consumer spending, raw material costs, or other factors. If you own stocks that are in similar businesses, they all may be at risk even if only one stock has problems. That situation can lead to losses in your entire club portfolio, so work hard on keeping your holdings diversified. Diversification is discussed in greater depth in Chapter 16.

Your club expenses are too high

If your club is beyond the start-up years but still hasn't turned the corner toward profitability, it may be time to look inward at your club's operations. One place to check is commissions and other expenses that your club pays on a regular basis. Keeping your commissions at around 1 percent of your total investment every time that you buy a stock is one rule to go by. If you're paying much more than that, you should either look for a less expensive broker or invest larger amounts less frequently.

For example, if you've been buying stocks in $500 increments at a brokerage firm that charges $29.95 per trade, that commission is 6 percent of your total investment. You're starting out in a pretty deep hole — your stock must grow 6.4 percent just to cover the cost of the commission and get back to even. Even when if you raise the amount of each investment to $1,000, that same $29.95 commission eats up 3 percent of your initial investment, which still is far above our maximum recommendation. You'll need to do better. By comparison, paying a commission of $9.99 to buy $1,000 worth of shares in a stock is only 1 percent of your total investment. In those circumstances, your new stock holding now needs only to grow a little more than 1 percent before your purchase moves into positive territory. Lower commission costs are only one reason that we recommend discount brokerages over full-service brokerages in Chapter 7.

Other expenses also can weigh down your returns. Clubs should be lean organizations, with no overhead and little in the way of expenses. A pricey subscription to an investing newsletter or an expensive data service may not be the best use of your club's capital. Think hard before laying out cash for any nonessential items, and spend money only where it counts — and where you can quantify the gains from those expenses. If expenses are weighing down your returns, you should reconsider any unnecessary expenses. You can find more on club expenses in Chapter 10.

Discovering bungling and fraud, inside or outside the club

We certainly hope you never have serious problems with theft in your club, and that your relationship with your bank or brokerage firm is satisfying. But whenever your club runs into either of these financial shenanigans, take action fast, using the guidelines described in the following subsections.

A member rips off your club

Fortunately, cases of embezzlement in investment clubs are rare. When you follow the procedures laid out in this book, you'll have plenty of checks and balances in place to prevent any such mischief. For instance, NAIC's fidelity bond protects your club in the unlikely but nonetheless possible event of fraud. But the bond works like any insurance policy — you must purchase it in advance; otherwise, it can't protect you. We give more details about the fidelity bond in Chapter 7.

Warning signs that your treasurer may be in trouble

In many cases, the treasurer is the culprit when fraud arises. Here are a few telltale signs to watch out for when you're concerned that your treasurer may be practicing "creative accounting." Just remember that although it does happen, treasurer fraud is fairly uncommon. If your club notices any of the following potentially suspicious treasurer behaviors, however, an immediate audit of the club's books may be in order.

- ✔ Monthly valuation statements for every member or other portfolio updates aren't provided on a timely basis, and excuses are given as to why they can't be quickly provided.

- ✔ Your treasurer skips meetings without explanation or is impossible to contact.

- ✔ Other club members aren't allowed to inspect bank or brokerage statements, even for the annual audit.

- ✔ Member withdrawals or check dispersals are chronically delayed or never completed.

- ✔ Your treasurer has unexpectedly taken early retirement in a country without a U.S. extradition treaty.

So what do you do when you suspect — or discover — fraud in your club? If you determine that funds are missing from your bank or brokerage accounts, and your treasurer has disappeared from the face of the earth, your president or other officers need to take immediate action. Of course your club doesn't want to wrongly accuse your treasurer, but don't think that you owe the treasurer a chance to explain. You must stop the outflow of funds as quickly as possible.

Quickly get in touch with the financial institutions where your club has accounts, changing the authorized contacts on the accounts (removing the treasurer), changing the passwords or PINs for the accounts, and changing the address on record with the institution. The bank or brokerage may require all partners to sign a resolution or file other paperwork before making changes to the account, so convene a special meeting of your club, if you must, and then hand-deliver, fax, or overnight these forms to the appropriate financial institutions. If you're in an online club, you may be allowed to have each of your members submit their own, signed form to prevent delays.

Institutions aren't liable for any transactions made by an authorized person in your accounts, so you can't blame them for any problems. But they should be amenable to helping you fix the problem — keep a log of all conversations, documenting the time and date and the name of each person with whom you speak, and take careful notes about their instructions.

If you're reasonably sure that a member has absconded with the club's money, then call in the cavalry. Consult an attorney to determine the club's best course of action. Remember that this is business, not personal. If the treasurer is indeed at fault, the club need not feel obligated to let the treasurer attempt to make things right. You must, first and foremost, protect the club's assets.

Problems with your brokerage or bank

Occasionally you may have a problem with your bank or brokerage firm — funds disappear from your account, trades are improperly made, transfers aren't recorded in a timely fashion. Addressing these issues quickly is important. The longer that you wait after the problem appears, the tougher it may be to satisfactorily resolve.

When resolving problems with your brokerage firm, keeping good records of all conversations is important. Note the time and date and the name of the representative with whom you speak. Brokerage firms routinely record telephone calls, so they can check the tape in case of any conflict, but they need to know when and where to look.

When you speak to customer service representatives on the telephone, try to get a concrete resolution of your problem each step of the way. If that isn't possible, ask the representative to let you know when someone will get back to you or what action will be taken to solve the problem. Continue working your way up the chain of command until the issue is resolved.

When you can't get any satisfaction, you may need to take the next step — arbitration. When you open an account with any brokerage firm, you agree that you won't sue the company in a court of law in case of any disputes. Instead, both sides agree to present their case to an arbitrator and abide by the arbitrator's decision. You may still need an attorney to help you prepare your case, so arbitration may be an option only for large claims. In addition, the vast majority of securities industry arbitration cases are decided in favor of the brokerage firms, not the customers, so proceed with arbitration only when you have good cause.

 If you're unsuccessful in resolving your problem, and you still feel wronged by your brokerage firm, you can take the matter up with the appropriate regulatory agency, the Securities and Exchange Commission. Although you can easily file a complaint on the SEC Web site (www.sec.gov), don't expect regulators to help you solve your problems. They can take enforcement actions to prevent future problems, but they probably won't intervene on your behalf.

Your state securities commission may be more approachable and amenable to helping you resolve conflicts. Every brokerage firm must be licensed in every state where it does business, so your own state's regulators may take a greater interest in your troubles with a particular firm.

 When all else fails (or when the eventual resolution takes far too much effort), vote with your feet. Move your club's account to a new institution, and don't look back.

Problems with the club audit

Every year, your club needs to appoint a committee to audit the books. The audit process described in Chapter 10 is an important step in preventing problems with your club's finances. The audit committee's objective is to make sure that the books all are in order and that all transactions have been properly recorded.

But what happens when the committee discovers a discrepancy? Chances are the error actually is the result of a simple bookkeeping problem. Perhaps the treasurer missed a transaction, or entered the wrong amount. A careful review of the club's account statements can turn up these kinds of problems, and the treasurer can easily correct the club's books.

However, when a problem is found at the beginning of the recordkeeping year, the treasurer may need to delete and then re-enter the club's year-end distribution. And when the error is more than a few cents, and your club already has submitted its Form 1065 return and Schedule K-1s to the IRS, you'll also have to file a corrected return. That's why conducting your audit *before* you carry out your year-end distribution and tax reporting tasks is so important. That way you'll know the club books are in good shape.

 Your audit committee can discover yet another kind of problem in its review of the club's books, particularly where new clubs or inexperienced treasurers are concerned. Club accounting can be a complicated subject for some people. Your treasurer may not grasp the concepts and practices, or master the use of accounting software. As a result, transactions may be improperly recorded. Fees may have been recorded as payments (or vice versa), or money may have been deposited into the petty cash account instead of the bank account. In all likelihood, your club would catch these errors on your monthly reports; but if not, better late than never with an audit.

When your club has an experienced former treasurer, that person can assist in fixing the transactions, or the current treasurer can bone up on proper methods of club accounting by reviewing Chapter 10. Another option is sending the treasurer back to school — having the treasurer attend an instructional class conducted by your local NAIC chapter (`www.better-investing.org/regions/regions.html`). If more assistance is required, your nearest NAIC chapter may also be able to send a volunteer to lend a hand or advice.

It is hoped that you'll never have to deal with malfeasance, but it is one reason why an audit is so important. Although unlikely, an audit can turn up evidence of this problem — hundreds or thousands of dollars that appear to be missing from the club's books, with the treasurer apparently to blame. Quick action is called for, so follow the instructions regarding member fraud and theft that are outlined earlier in this chapter. Just be sure not to jump to conclusions. In the United States, people are considered innocent until proven otherwise, and negligence is an entirely different matter than outright theft.

Managing Membership Situations

Your club's membership will likely be fluid, with members moving, departing, and joining on a regular basis. In addition, your members will face changes in their own lives, and sometimes those changes impact their membership in the club. This section talks about some of the membership issues that may arise in your club's lifetime.

Transferring a club account

Occasionally, a member of your club may want to "transfer" his or her account to another person, either to an existing member or someone outside the club (who then would become a new member). Members usually are interested in making a gift because doing so helps the giver avoid capital gains taxes. The cost basis and holding period of the club account transfers to the recipient, who then would be responsible for any tax liabilities. While it seems like accomplishing a transfer should be easy, in reality, a number of obstacles must be overcome.

First of all, your club has policies regarding who can become a member. A member who wants to transfer his or her club account to someone outside the club is, in effect, trying to make that person a member. The club first must agree to accept the new member, which it may or may not want to do. General partnership law generally prohibits passing an ownership interest outside the partnership, so the recipient must be accepted as a member before the account can be transferred.

Other factors also must be considered. Because a club member's account has tangible cash value, it may subject the original owner to a gift tax liability or a reduction in his or her lifetime gift tax exclusion. Beginning in 2002, you can make gifts of up to $10,000 a year to any number of recipients without triggering any taxes or liabilities. However, any gifts in excess of that amount count against your lifetime $1,000,000 gift tax exclusion. Once you use up your exclusion, any gifts in a year that exceed $10,000 per person are subject to the gift tax. You may wonder why you need to be so concerned about giving away $1,000,000 — shouldn't we all be so lucky to have such concerns! However, it means additional paperwork for the giver to file with the IRS to report gifts in excess of the annual exclusion.

Unfortunately, no club accounting software or online service supports the transfer of member accounts to another person (but there's always a chance that such a feature will appear in future editions). The alternative may not be desirable, either. The recipient would have to be completely withdrawn from the club, and then the new member would be added with an initial contribution to the amount of the withdrawing member's payout. No checks would have to change hands — this can all be done on the books; however, the giver would unnecessarily trigger a taxable loss or gain from the withdrawal.

One thing you definitely should not do is have your treasurer simply change the name and other information of the member to reflect a transfer, because doing so changes the history of the member so that all past transactions will show as being made by the recipient. That is against IRS rules that prohibit *income shifting,* so it's inappropriate (except perhaps on the first day of the year when no income or loss has been generated in the club).

Coping with a divorce

Most clubs have a rule against jointly held capital accounts. Although some couples may function as a perfectly cohesive unit in a club environment, voting on matters and acting as one mind, your club can hit a snag when that happy couple's relationship disintegrates. Who gets control of the account? Do you split the account in two?

When both members want to remain in the club, dividing the account into two halves and properly recording the tax liabilities is nearly impossible. Withdrawing half of the account to split up the jointly held account is a bad option, because doing so unnecessarily generates tax liabilities — but that may be your only option. Simply avoiding jointly held accounts in the first place is far better for your club.

Even if you don't allow jointly held accounts, when a member of a club gets a divorce, his or her club account still may be subject to division according to the divorce settlement. That may create problems with your club if half of the member's club account has been earmarked for transfer to the spouse. The spouse probably won't want to be part of the club, so a withdrawal may be the only choice, despite the tax liabilities.

Missing-in-action members

It may seem unbelievable, but some clubs have had members simply disappear. Maybe the member starts missing meetings without any excuse, and when a club officer tries to contact the member, the phone has been disconnected and there's no forwarding address. Attempts to track down the member at work or through friends are unsuccessful. He or she has vanished without a trace.

Believing that someone would just walk away from their club holdings is difficult, but stranger things have happened. Circumstances can change drastically in someone's life, and if that member moves away or is under great pressure, the investment club membership may become a low priority.

So what does your club do if this happens? What is your club's legal obligation to the absent member? After all, your club can't just "take over" this abandoned portion of your club portfolio — it still belongs to the missing member even if he or she is nowhere to be found. Your club's first concern obviously is for the missing member's physical and emotional well-being. But you're still legally bound to them, which adds a more business-like feeling to your club's search. Some guidelines to follow if one of your members goes AWOL include

✔ Asking for alternate contact information (a close friend, co-worker, or relative, perhaps) when members first join your club. Doing so gives you other places to turn for a lead on your missing member's new contact information.

✔ Sending a letter of inquiry from your club president to the member's last known address if the member doesn't respond to phone calls or e-mails. Request notification of any forwarding address from the postal service.

✔ Investigating the process of a forced member withdrawal if the member doesn't respond to the president's letter after one month. You may also consider other ways to try to track the member down, including (but not limited to) contacting his or her place of employment or worship, contacting any known family or friends, placing a personal ad in the local newspaper, or, as a last resort, hiring a private investigator.

✔ Following your club's operating agreement and procedures to the letter, withdrawing the member in absentia because of inactivity after the appropriate amount of time. The withdrawal needs to be made in cash, rather than a transfer of stock, to limit complications. Your club treasurer should make the check out to the missing member, then put the check in a safe place in case the missing member eventually turns up.

✔ Contacting your state for guidance on turning over the missing member's funds to the state's *unclaimed property* department, after a full year passes with no updates. You may never hear from this member again. After the specified amount of time has passed, or if your club disbands before then, turn the member's withdrawal check over to the state.

Settling accounts when a member dies

If you follow NAIC's sample partnership agreement, the death of a member triggers an immediate withdrawal of that person's account. Following your operating agreement, the club should process a withdrawal and prepare a check or securities transfer to the deceased member.

Making the check or securities transfer payable in the name of the deceased member is important. Never should such documents be made out to a spouse or other family member. You can deliver the check or other documents to the family of the deceased, but steer clear of any estate problems that can arise from writing a check to the wrong party. The estate of the deceased member shouldn't have any problems receiving funds payable in the member's name.

Avoiding problems with beneficiaries

For the same reason that you pay off a deceased member by the member's name, your club probably shouldn't establish procedures to pay designated beneficiaries upon the death of a member. Some clubs ask all members to complete a beneficiary statement with instructions for payments. But because the *beneficiary* may not be recognized by the courts, if you were to pay out the value of a deceased member's account to that person, you'd be leaving the partnership open to potential claims from other heirs. If issues in the deceased's estate are contested, the partnership can be held liable for the amount wrongly paid to the beneficiary. Or what if the deceased partner's will provided other instructions for the disposition of the proceeds from the investment club account?

This is a matter best left for the probate system — a mistake made in this situation can be an expensive proposition for the remaining partners.

NAIC's club accounting software has a field in which you can enter the name of a member's beneficiary. However, just entering a name here isn't enough to warrant paying out the member's account to that beneficiary. You can use this field to maintain contact information in case a member passes away. Just don't consider this to be the person to whom a deceased partner's account must necessarily be paid out.

Even if a member of the deceased's family wants to take over the club account, trying to transfer the account is pointless, because, when you die, the cost basis of assets (like the value of your club account) are *stepped up* to their value at the time of your death. Thus, you have no capital gains or losses to worry about. Estate tax considerations may exist, but no benefit results from transferring the account within the club to an heir of the deceased member's family. Just withdraw the member, and let his or her estate decide what to do with the proceeds.

Buying out a departing member

Often, clubs talk about "buying out" a departing member. This actually is a misnomer, because no procedures exist for doing what the phrase implies. Member withdrawals must always be processed according to your operating agreement, and even when other members contribute additional cash to the club to cover the amount of the withdrawal, no real advantage is gained by any member. Making additional contributions may help the club to avoid selling securities when it doesn't want to divest any of its holdings, but because the contributing members' payments are recorded at the current unit value, remaining members receive no discount for kicking in the extra cash. In other words, buying out another member isn't tied in any formal way to the value of the withdrawing member's account.

Terminating a member

Ask anyone who's ever been a boss or run a business whether they enjoy firing employees, and you won't see many raised hands. Officially telling someone to get lost is tough, and it may be even more difficult in a club made up of friends and colleagues. In a family club, you may find it even more difficult to have to ask someone to leave.

Sometimes, however, you just have to bite the bullet. So when your members decide that another member must be terminated, here are some things to keep in mind:

✔ Find out whether the member will voluntarily withdraw as outlined in Chapter 8. Often, the member is as disgruntled with the club as the other members are with that person. A little diplomacy and frank discussion may persuade the member to request a withdrawal voluntarily and prevent all-out war from breaking out.

✔ Follow your operating agreement to the letter. Your club's agreement should lay the groundwork for terminating a member, and you shouldn't deviate from them at all.

✔ Be fair. Your agreement, it is hoped, is even-handed and enables for the process to be carried out with dignity.

✔ Be courteous. Acting like a machine-gun toting cyborg from the future isn't necessary when you're terminating a member. Be respectful and tactful, even when you have to be firm.

Part IV

Finding the Right Investment Approach

The 5th Wave
By Rich Tennant

In this part . . .

One of the biggest reasons you chose to join an investment club was to enjoy the tasty treats at every meeting, right? Okay, maybe the chance to actually learn to invest was a little higher on your priority list. Investment education is key to your club's success, and it needs to be a group effort. This part presents everything your club needs to know to start down the road toward investment success, including choosing your first stocks and tracking your club portfolio. So, call the meeting to order!

Chapter 13

Deciding on a Basic Plan: Buy and Hold Stocks, Reinvest Profits

In This Chapter

▶ Choosing individual stocks over mutual funds

▶ Focusing on the long term

▶ Deciding on your club's investing strategy

*W*hat's alluring, mysterious, occasionally fraught with peril, and equally able to empty your pockets as fulfill your dreams? No, the answer isn't "buying a fabulous, and fabulously expensive, sports car." We're talking about the stock markets here, about investing in the thousands of corporations that trade on the United States stock exchanges. Some of these companies have familiar names like Microsoft, Intel, Wal-Mart, and Coca-Cola; others you've probably never heard of, like Textron, Cintas, Millipore, and Rohm & Haas.

Of course, investing doesn't always have to be about investing in the stock market. You can invest in bonds, or real estate, or even gold bullion (if you have a safe place to keep it). But investing directly in stocks is about the only way for an investment club to become profitable. As a result, our introduction to investing focuses on the stock markets and how they hold the keys to your club's success, all from the perspective of a patient, long-term, buy-and-hold investment strategy that's perfect for investment clubs.

The Great Debate: Stocks versus Mutual Funds

Already, it's easy to see that you have questions. "Maybe it's all well and good to invest in stocks," you're probably thinking, "but what about mutual funds?" After all, according to the Investment Company Institute, 87.9 million Americans own mutual funds, a total of $5.5 trillion worth. Every other

American household owns at least one mutual fund. By comparison, the New York Stock Exchange found that 33.8 million Americans owned stocks directly at the end of 1998. So why shouldn't your investment club own mutual funds like the majority of investors? Wouldn't investing in mutual funds be so much easier?

The biggest of the reasons why your club should stick to buying only individual stocks is that once your club has built up a portfolio of stocks, you'll have created, in effect, your own miniature mutual fund. At that point your club's holdings will feature many of the same attributes as a real mutual fund, so investing in actual mutual funds would be redundant.

For example, your stock holdings will be diversified and include companies of many sizes and from many industries, just like the holdings of a mutual fund. Even if your investment club doesn't own hundreds or thousands of stocks like a real mutual fund, you'll still get the benefits of owning a diversified group of stocks. Another way investment clubs are similar to mutual funds is that you and your fellow club members invest relatively small sums of money in your club, while still taking advantage of the benefits of holding a diversified portfolio.

Where mutual funds fall short

So if mutual funds offer a way to invest in a diversified group of stocks with small amounts of money, why not cut out the middleman and just focus on buying funds for your investment club? It turns out mutual funds are more complicated than what you'd think upon first glance. Some of the reasons why funds aren't the best way to invest your club's money are discussed in the following sections.

Paying extra for advice

Mutual funds are managed by one or more financial professionals. Funds usually tout the superiority of their "professional management" as a reason why investors should own the mutual funds rather than individual stocks. Although having a professional at the helm of a mutual fund that invests in a specific sector or region can be advantageous, remembering that pros don't always measure up when it comes to investing in American stocks is just as important. Take the track record of broad-based domestic equity funds (that's another way of saying funds that invest in a wide cross-section of U.S. stocks — just like your club portfolio), for example. In any given year, fewer than 20 percent of these funds outperform the Standard & Poor's 500 (Stock) Index. Or, putting it another way, every year 80 percent of these funds are below average. Ouch.

Your club will be choosing its own stocks, so you won't need to pay for professional management. And, with mutual funds, pay for it you will. Even without paying commissions (or a load or a transaction fee, which are essentially the same as a commission), the average expense ratio for a mutual fund is about 1.4 percent. It may not seem like much, but that comes out of your holdings year after year after year. That's how mutual fund managers and their staffs earn their salaries, along with the rent, postage, and printing of statements and materials.

Although it may not seem like much, those fees can really add up over time. Your club's expenses are likely to be a much smaller percentage of your holdings, especially after a few years of operation. So even if your club portfolio performs "just average," you'll still come out ahead of most mutual funds.

Taxing matters

Another big advantage of buying individual stocks, as opposed to mutual funds, is that your investment club members can save on taxes. Funds don't worry about taxes — they can buy and sell stocks at whim, and any taxes that are incurred are simply passed along to shareholders. (A few tax-managed funds aim to minimize the impact of taxes.)

When a fund distributes long- and short-term gains and losses at the end of the year, shareholders pay the taxes. Often they pay at higher short-term rates than they would if they'd held the same stocks directly and minimized short-term gains in favor of long-term capital gains — or sold a stock at a loss to offset gains. Your investment club can use portfolio strategies that reduce the tax liabilities of its members.

Always an exception to every rule . . .

In a few instances, a club may opt to invest in mutual funds. Your club may want to invest in bank stocks, but finds it incredibly difficult to learn the best way to analyze those kinds of stocks. (Bank stocks have "issues" that can make them tricky to analyze. Just understanding that a bank's main business is selling money is tough enough, not to mention figuring out loan-loss provisions, efficiency ratios, and net noninterest income.) In that case, a mutual fund that invests only in bank stocks might be a good addition to your portfolio.

The same can be said about mutual funds that invest in particular regions or countries in the world, or any other industry group (like real estate or high technology) where the expertise of a professional manager may be a good thing because of the potential difficulty in analyzing these particular investments. Just remember that these kinds of funds are nondiversified by nature, and they tend to run hot and cold faster than the water in a cheap apartment.

Most clubs decide that they can do without mutual funds in their portfolios. You probably have plenty of opportunities to invest in funds in your 401(k) at work, or in your own investment accounts, so what's the point in chasing hot funds in your club's portfolio? After all, the whole point of being in an investment club in the first place is learning how to choose individual stocks, right?

That said, recognizing that mutual-fund investing is a fact of financial life for many people who have no other choice in their retirement accounts, you'll be happy to know that your investment club experience also can help you when it comes time to buying mutual funds. Surprisingly (or maybe not), understanding how to analyze stocks makes you a better mutual fund investor.

Sure, investing in stocks and investing in mutual funds are two completely different things, requiring different skills and analysis techniques. But by becoming a savvy stock investor, you'll gain the confidence to find out everything that you need to know about a mutual fund in the same way that you'd analyze an individual stock. The more you learn about investing in general, the easier it is to learn about new types of investing. Financial empowerment is exactly what we hope you gain from your investment club experience.

Making the Case for Buying Individual Stocks

We've told you why mutual funds aren't the best choice for most club portfolios. Now here's our case for why stocks *are*.

Publicly traded stocks are one of the cornerstones of capitalism, the basis of the American economy. Once you and your club members understand how the stock market works, you'll be able to recognize the many different kinds of stocks, and identify industry groups and sectors. You'll also find out how to build a solid group of growth stocks in your club portfolio.

The most important benefit of being in an investment club is the knowledge that you'll gain. You can take that education from your club experience and become a better investor in your own personal portfolio. Thus you need to learn how to choose superior stocks for your club's portfolio.

Clubs invest in stocks because using sound, time-tested principles of portfolio management and stock analysis is possible in a club that meets and makes decisions once a month. In fact, these methods and strategies thrive in the low-maintenance world of an investment club.

Investors aren't traders

People who buy stocks can be divided into two general categories: *traders* and *investors*. Traders buy and sell stocks on a regular and active basis, looking to make many relatively small profits rapidly, often by trading a high volume of stocks. Traders may hold a stock for a few days or weeks but usually no longer than a year, before selling it.

At an extreme end of the spectrum are day traders who buy stocks and hold them for only a few seconds or minutes before selling them, often tens (or even hundreds) of thousands of shares each day. Day traders hope to make profits of just pennies per share on each trade so that each day's take adds up to thousands of dollars.

Traders usually don't care about the business that a company is in, or its management, or even whether it's profitable. They're only looking for opportunities to make money fast by moving in and out of the market quickly, and focusing on short-term trends.

Investors, on the other hand, look at a stock as if they were buying part of the company itself. They consider themselves as part-owners of a business — which they are. Before buying, they look at the fundamental reasons why the business is successful and why its success will continue in the future. They understand that solid, well-managed companies ultimately deliver profits to their owners.

Most business owners aren't looking to make a quick buck, but rather to grow their business along with its profits. As a result, investors think about the long-term and how their stocks will perform years down the road.

Four reasons to 'buy and hold'

Investors (as opposed to traders) commonly approach the stock market with a *buy-and-hold* strategy. Investors buy stocks and then hold on to them — often for years at a stretch. In fact, according to NAIC, investment clubs hold stocks in their portfolios an average of six years before selling them. Why do they hold on so long? The following are the four main reasons why the buy-and-hold approach works so well:

- ✔ You pay less in transaction costs, which enhances your club's return.

- ✔ You get greater tax efficiency (we explain this term in the "Greater tax efficiency" section later in this chapter) from your portfolio, which reduces your taxes and, again, enhances your return.

- ✔ You don't need to worry so much about the natural short-term gyrations of the stock market.

- ✔ You spend only a few hours a month managing your portfolio, not a few hours a day.

Sound reasonable? A closer look at these points reveals even more.

Lower transaction costs

Whenever you buy and sell a stock, you almost always pay a commission to a brokerage or to the company itself if you're buying direct. So, keeping transaction costs low is simple: The less you buy and sell, the less you pay overall in commissions. In the olden days of Wall Street, transaction costs were much larger, because investors had to place trades through full-service brokers with expensive commissions. But even in the age of the Internet, rock-bottom commissions still take a bite out of each investment you make.

Transactions costs for frequent traders can add up rapidly, putting a sizeable dent in their profits (or making their losses even larger). Buy-and-hold investors keep a lid on transaction costs because they aim to buy carefully, hold on to a stock for a long time, and then sell after the stock has gone up significantly in price. As a result, buy-and-hold investors avoid paying out too much in transaction costs.

Greater tax efficiency

The current United States Tax Code recognizes two kinds of investment profits (and losses) that you can make when you sell a stock, based on how long you owned the security before you sold it. These profits are known as capital gains; losses are similarly known as — no surprise here — capital losses.

Short-term gains (or losses) result from selling a stock that you've held for less than a year. They're taxable at the same rate as the taxes you pay on your other personal income. If you're in the 28 percent federal tax bracket, for example, you'll pay taxes of 28 percent on your short-term gains.

Long-term gains (or losses) come from selling a stock after owning it for longer than a year, and usually are taxed at a much lower rate than short-term gains, depending on your income tax bracket. The difference in short- and long-term tax rates can be tremendous, so keeping up-to-date on any tax code changes that affect capital gain and loss tax rates and holding periods is important. Whenever possible, at least from a tax perspective, holding stocks for at least a year before selling them is best.

Because of the way they do business, traders may have a hefty tax bill to pay each year, nearly all of which is likely to come from higher short-term gains tax rates. Investors, on the other hand, don't sell as frequently, so they generally won't have as much to pay in taxes each year. Plus, the taxes that they do pay usually are assessed at the lower long-term gains rate. Higher short-term gain taxes, as well as more frequent transaction costs, simply gobble up profits in your portfolio.

Taken together, the twin demons of taxes and transaction costs tip the balance away from the hyperactive trading strategies of the day trader in favor of the buy-and-hold approach of the investor. While your investment club won't directly pay taxes on its gains, you and your fellow members certainly will. Every dollar that you *don't* spend on brokerage commissions or taxes is one more dollar that goes into your portfolio.

Filtering out the noise that surrounds the market

We have a name for much of the stock market news that you hear on television or radio, or read in newspapers, magazines, or on Web sites. We call it *noise*. Noise is what drives many investors to make uninformed, hasty decisions about their investments. Noise is irrelevant information that can distract you from the important things you need to focus on.

You must realize that most of traditional Wall Street is built upon encouraging investors to buy and sell frequently. But this persuasion isn't always friendly in nature. Brokerage firms earn money from the commissions investors pay, and so the more you buy and sell, the more they make. Unfortunately, the more your investment club buys and sells doesn't necessarily mean the more *you* make.

Human nature often is the enemy of sound investment decision-making, too. When a stock that you purchased falls in price a week after you bought it, that hollow feeling in the pit of your stomach can invade your brain. Looking at your account and all that money you've lost (on paper, at least) is hard.

Fear and anxiety shouldn't drive you to sell hurriedly, the way inexperienced investors often do. Riding out the storm often is a more prudent decision, and you'll find that your stock will rebound (and then some). Focusing on the long-term and buying stocks you intend to hold for years can help you prevent making short-term decisions you may later regret.

Time-efficient investing

Although buying stocks that you can forget about once you own them is a good idea in practice, your club needs to spend at least a little time watching your portfolio for the inevitable under-performers. Most people, however, can't spend their entire workday watching a portfolio. (Even the most understanding of bosses generally aren't open to having day traders as employees — all that online trading tends to get in the way of that work you're getting paid to do!)

With a long-term approach that focuses on buying sound, profitable companies, you and your fellow club members need spend only a few hours each month (or even each quarter) on the necessary tasks to manage your portfolio. After all, your time is worth something, and a buy-and-hold philosophy gives you above average returns without making your portfolio a full-time job. Go spend time with your family or friends instead.

Making growth your goal

You can use plenty of different yardsticks to measure stocks. These methods can be divided into two camps, *fundamental analysis* and *technical analysis.*

Technical analysis: Determining whether the price is right

Technical analysis is primarily concerned with the movement of a stock's price throughout a particular period. Technicians attempt to find indications of a stock's future price movement by tracking factors such as price and *trading volume* (the number of shares that are traded each day). They generally aren't interested in the company's business and don't usually care much about what a company does or who its management is.

Within the technical camp, *momentum investors* watch how quickly a stock moves up or down in price and try to buy while that stock is showing strength or sell before the tide turns. *Chartists* look for patterns in a stock's price chart that signal its future direction. Other market technicians may seek out certain indicators in a stock's price or volume that may predict where the stock is headed.

Fundamental analysis: Where is this company going?

Fundamental analysis, on the other hand, is the study of a company's underlying business, how it fits in the overall economy, and how efficiently it is run. The two main schools of thought regarding fundamental analysis are *value investing* and *growth investing.*

Value investors look at what a company's underlying assets or its future prospects for income are worth. From that they determine if that stock is underpriced. Growth investors look for stocks that have been growing their sales and profits faster than other similar stocks, or faster than the stock market in general. Companies that are getting bigger and more profitable generally see their share prices rise as they grow, which is what growth investors hope for. Fundamental analysis also includes other components, including *income investing.* Income investors look for strong companies that pay higher dividends, such as utility and real estate companies.

Some investors combine these different kinds of analysis. Some even use technical and fundamental criteria in making investment decisions. But most investment clubs and their members look for growth stocks to fill up their portfolios.

We recommend that your club and its members focus on a fundamental, growth-based approach to stock analysis. Investing in growth stocks enables investment clubs to successfully manage a portfolio when meeting only once a month. It also provides all the other benefits of a buy-and-hold philosophy — lower transaction costs and higher tax efficiency yet still avoiding the tendency to make reactionary short-term decisions.

Growth investing isn't just for investment clubs. Legendary fund manager Peter Lynch primarily used a growth-stock approach in managing Fidelity's Magellan mutual fund, turning in one of the best fund performance records in history. When you invest in growth stocks, you'll find that your portfolio becomes filled with established, well-managed companies that *can* be held for many years. Companies like Coca-Cola, IBM, and Microsoft have demonstrated great growth through the years and are cornerstones of many investment portfolios.

Investment clubs tend to find that when they go for growth stocks, they'll also see their portfolios grow.

Making the Stock Market Work for You

Several principles of financial management go hand-in-hand with investing in growth stocks. Your club needs to understand all these principles, and how they work together, to help your club portfolio be as successful as possible.

Staying fully invested in stocks

The term *asset allocation* describes the process of dividing up a portfolio among many types of investments (stocks, bonds, cash, real estate). Many full-service Wall Street brokerage firms recommend that their customers adjust their asset allocation plans depending on conditions in the overall market. The chief analysts at these firms regularly issue reports that detail the percentages that investors need to invest in different assets.

If the analyst foresees tough times ahead in the stock market, he or she may reduce the percentage of stocks in a *model portfolio* and increase the amount of bonds or cash. Similarly, an analyst who believes the stock market is poised for an upswing may recommend that investors increase their stock holdings. This approach is known by the fancy name of *tactical asset allocation*. Despite its impressive name, this technique unfortunately is tough to put to work in a club portfolio.

Don't try to time the market

Those who try to figure out the best times to jump in and out of the stock market (or from asset class to asset class) often are known as *market timers*. Market timing, however, is one of the more futile exercises in investing.

You'll likely encounter two problems with trying to put tactical asset allocation and market timing to work in your club's portfolio. First, if your club's crystal ball is wrong about the future direction of the market, you can inflict great damage to your portfolio — moving out of stocks too soon or too late.

And if you don't have a crystal ball, well, you can join the crowd. Not even the pros on Wall Street can say with even the slightest bit of certainty exactly where the market is headed in the coming days or weeks.

The second problem with tactical asset allocation and market timing is that circumstances in the market can change quickly. Changes may lead your club to take frequent action, buying and selling securities to align your asset allocation with some recommendation. Although that's a pretty convenient scenario for brokerage firms making money every time their clients buy and sell securities and never worrying about the tax concerns that come with excessive trading, the story is different for individual or club investors.

Nothing's wrong with staying in one place

The solution to these problems is simple: Stay invested in the market. The stock market goes up, and the stock market goes down, and having enough faith in your investment decisions to ride out the turbulent times can make the difference between making profit or losing your shirt in your club's portfolio. That doesn't mean that you must hold on to a stock even while its earnings are hemorrhaging and its share value is waning fast. (You can discover more about handling under-performing stocks in Chapter 16.) But keeping a level head while everyone around you panics during a market (or portfolio) crash or correction can help you improve your return. No matter what happens to the market in the short term, your club portfolio can prevail over the long term if you just exhibit a little bit of stick-to-itiveness.

Investing Regularly

To be sure, there *are* times when the stock market seems to be climbing upward to new heights, while at other times it seems to have trouble just getting out of bed in the morning. Sometimes the stock market looks like a great place to invest your money, but at other times it looks like a lousy place to put your dollars. Even so, keep in mind that your club is buying individual stocks — not the stock market.

Regardless of general market conditions, you can always find interesting candidates for your portfolio among thousands of publicly traded stocks. With the right approach to analysis and a faithful long-term perspective, you can certainly find bargain stocks to buy regardless of what market pundits are saying. By regularly investing, you take advantage of down markets, instead of letting them take advantage of you.

Harnessing the power of dollar cost averaging

Another important principle of long-term, buy-and-hold investing is *dollar cost averaging* (DCA). DCA is a remarkable technique that helps protect you from overpaying on purchases of a single stock over a period of time. By investing a fixed dollar amount of a particular stock on a monthly basis, you automatically buy more shares when the price of your chosen stock is low, and fewer shares when it is priced high. As any bargain hunter knows (and your club members should be working hard to be bargain hunters), any time you buy more of a product for the same amount of dollars, it's a good thing!

Letting market volatility work for you

So how does DCA work in practice? Through the years, as all those monthly purchases help keep down the average cost of the shares you buy, DCA also helps you take advantage of the stock market's natural volatility. One study shows that the average stock that trades on the New York Stock Exchange will see a 50 percent difference between its high and low share prices in any given year. When you use DCA, you get some protection when the price is in the low range, because you automatically buy more shares. When the price is high, you're also protected because you automatically buy fewer shares. So, you don't have to worry so much about knowing the right time to buy. Automatic DCA purchases keep you investing on a regular basis.

In January 1998, a study about dollar cost averaging conducted by *Money* magazine and the Value Line Investment Survey looked at how investors would've fared if they'd invested $100 a month in domestic stock mutual funds during the previous five- and ten-year terms. They discovered that investors would've received an average annual return of 25.7 percent over five years and 23.7 percent over ten years, if they used the DCA method of investing. On the other hand, if they had invested a lump sum from the start, they would've received average annual returns of only 17.4 percent and 13.3 percent, respectively.

That doesn't mean DCA *always* works. Buying a troubled stock month after month only worsens your returns. It won't improve them. You still must be diligent portfolio managers even with the stocks you buy regularly.

If you have either a 401(k) or 403(b) account at work, you may be using DCA without even knowing it. A little bit of money is taken out of each paycheck and then invested in your retirement account each month. Over time, that can help your retirement fund grow in value.

Taking advantage of your monthly investment schedule

A big advantage of investment clubs is that they invest every month, regardless of how the market is performing. Doing so provides benefits similar to those of dollar cost averaging and enables the club to continually build wealth over a long period of time. When the market falls back, clubs keep investing, even though it may hurt in the short term. When the market eventually begins to climb once again, the club's portfolio will be driven to new heights. That is why we keep saying how important it is to invest regularly and not try to "time" the market.

When you use DCA, watching out for the cost of commissions is important. Many investment clubs keep commission costs in check by using DCA to buy small amounts, say $100 or so, of a handful of stocks each month through dividend reinvestment plans (DRIPs) or automatic investing services like those offered by Sharebuilder.com (www.sharebuilder.com) or BuyandHold.com (www.buyandhold.com). These services charge low fees for regular investments, so you won't have to pay larger commissions other brokers charge. (We tell you more about DRIPs and brokerages in Chapter 7.) That way, clubs keep their portfolios fully invested while making the most of DCA. Other clubs shy from DCA, preferring to make lump sum investments on their own terms. Either way, understanding how DCA can help your portfolio become profitable is important.

Reinvesting your profits

One of the first financial concepts you ever learned probably was the power of compound interest. When you put money in the bank, it earns interest. If you don't withdraw the interest from your account, it also earns interest. Over time, the interest that you earn on reinvested interest grows and grows, creating a phenomenon known as compound interest. Eventually, the amount of interest that you've earned in your account will grow even larger than your starting principal. But if you withdraw that interest each month, your account gets stuck in the no-growth lane.

The same idea applies to an investment account. As you receive dividends from companies, or make money by selling shares that increase in price, you have a choice about what to do with that income. You can take it out and blow it on a shopping spree at the mall, or you can keep that money in the account and reinvest it in new assets. Naturally, if your club wants to maximize its returns and enable the power of compounding to grow your portfolio, you'll keep your winnings in the pot.

Saying that you should reinvest all the earnings in your portfolio, doesn't necessarily mean that you must reinvest them immediately. Or, if a stock pays a dividend, you don't have to reinvest it in the same stock. In Chapter 7, we discuss dividend reinvestment plans (DRIPs) and direct stock plans (DSPs), which are company-sponsored programs that enable you to invest your dividends in the purchase of additional shares of stock in those companies. This, indeed, is a great way to reinvest your profits and take advantage of dollar cost averaging, but it isn't the only way. Whatever you do, if you want to make the most from your portfolio, don't make plans to pay out profits to your club members, even on an annual basis.

Sticking to your guns

One advantage of investment clubs is that they help you maintain a disciplined approach to the stock market. Of course, your club has to agree on a unified approach in the first place (we talk about choosing a club investing philosophy in Chapter 4), and then follow up with the education that can turn your club members into smart investors.

GaAs Valley Group

The *GaAs Valley Group's* unusual name was inspired by the chemical compound gallium arsenide, which is thought to be a replacement for silicon. The club was started in 1993 in Sunnyvale, California, in the heart of Silicon Valley. Club members wanted a name that subtly alluded to the technological expertise that's abundant in their region. Nearly all of the club's 30 members belong to the same extended family, which spans four generations, and they range in age from 1 to 85. Because members are scattered across multiple states, the club operates completely online.

The GaAs Valley Group makes good use of its Web site, which contains a new member prospectus and fills in prospective members on every aspect of the club's organization from the investment philosophy to member responsibilities. Prospective new members must be recommended by a current member before their applications are voted on. Once accepted, they make an initial contribution of $500 plus their first month's minimum $25 contribution. One

major club issue has been how to get younger members more involved, but the club has accepted that the situation will improve once the junior set grows older.

The GaAs Valley Group invests its $169,000 portfolio online through Schwab, which also provides online research resources. Club members use stock selection software when completing a Stock Selection Guide (SSG), and the treasurer uses club accounting software to track the club's 23 stocks and other transactions. Regular meetings are conducted online and typically last an hour and a half, but club members routinely communicate via e-mail between meetings. Meetings are open to observers as long as they're guests of current members. Club members analyze and present potential stocks to the club on a quarterly basis (at least the members who are old enough to read do!). Members aren't expected to know anything about stock analysis when they join, so the entire club works together every month to learn new techniques and improve old ones.

Sticking to the long-term, buy-and-hold philosophy we've described here is vital to your club. If some of your members want to chase hot (and risky) biotech stocks and others want to chase hot tips whispered by some talking head on television, then your portfolio is going to have problems.

Successful clubs have a common methodology of investing, one that's shared by all members, and they follow it religiously. Mark Hulbert, publisher of *The Hulbert Financial Digest,* tracks the performance of investing newsletters. He's often asked which methodology works best. His answer? The top-performing newsletters come from many different strategic viewpoints: technical, fundamental, momentum, contrarian, value, and so on. The only common characteristic of all these newsletters' approaches is that their publishers consistently stick to their ideologies. His conclusion is that a disciplined approach is one of the most important factors in determining investment success.

In the beginning years of your club, you may find that profits are elusive. Keep the faith and stick to your guns, even in the face of a showdown (or is that a slowdown) at high noon. You'll soon find success.

Chapter 14

Finding and Studying Stocks

*B*efore your club can actually purchase a stock, you need to identify a few decent prospects. There are good ways and not-so-good ways to find stocks to analyze. Sure, the "bad" ways are much easier, but when selecting stocks, you don't want to take the easy way.

Once your family, friends, and co-workers find out that you're a member of an investment club, the likelihood that you'll soon be the recipient (willing or not) of dozens and dozens of *hot stock tips* increases. Everyone wants to share some rumor they've just heard about a stock, or some advice they saw on television, or a tale of some super financial achievement of their own.

Although some tips may pan out, blindly accepting this kind of advice and basing your investment portfolio on someone else's opinion can cause problems. We call these *brother-in-law stocks*. Oh, we're sure that your brother-in-law is a nice guy, but it still may be better if you steer the conversation back to the Chicago variety of "da Bears" and "da Bulls."

Don't worry, you can find plenty of sources where your club can discover ideas for investing that match up with your own mind-set and strategies. By using them you won't end up shopping for stocks in all the wrong places. And the cardinal rule to always follow is that you must conduct your own research on an idea before your club puts *any* of its money on the line.

That rule should be clearly spelled out in your club's mission statement (see Chapter 4), and you should never allow exceptions. If members get super-hot stock tips that they want to present to the club, more power to them. But they first must do their own research before you even begin thinking about putting the stock up for a purchase vote.

Finally, an excuse to ignore your relatives

Here's the scenario. At some family function, your brother-in-law tells you a *hot tip* about a stock, the Worldwide Widget Company, that he got from a friend of his who's "really into the market." Your relative by marriage appears to know all sorts of inside details about Worldwide Widget, and how the company soon will dominate the widget industry with its advanced new product.

The story sounds so great — how could this stock be a loser? You're convinced, you convince your club, and so at your next meeting you place an order and buy a few hundred shares. Everything goes okay for a while; the price of Worldwide Widget even goes up a bit, giving your club a nice bit of profit in your portfolio. Your fellow members adore you and make sure at each meeting that you get seconds on the tasty treats before anyone else.

But then disaster hits. Worldwide Widget experiences problems in its supply chain. The widget market falls apart internationally, and Worldwide Widget feels the pinch. Stories begin to surface about deeper problems within the company, and speculation says that sprockets may soon replace widgets as the component of choice. As you read all these news items in the paper, you remember your brother-in-law's words: "This

one is a sure thing." So your club holds on, while your portfolio is awash in red ink and somehow the tasty treats don't seem to make it down to your end of the table anymore.

Finally, you catch up with your brother-in-law at a family reunion, and you casually ask what's up with Worldwide Widget. "That old stock?" he replies. "I sold it months ago. Made a nice tidy bundle, too."

As you stand there dumbfounded, jaw dropping to your chest, you may figure out the problem with blindly taking advice from others. They have lots of ideas about what to buy, but even if the idea turns out to be a winner, there's no guarantee they'll be around to tell you if or when to sell.

Investors come in many different varieties, and investing strategies exist for one and all. You could've saved yourself and your club a few bucks if you'd known that your brother-in-law was a short-term trader, not a long-term investor like yourself. Or, if you and your club had done your own homework on Worldwide Widget and figured out whether the stock was even appropriate for your portfolio style, you might never have bought it.

Making Sense of the Media Deluge

Drop by the magazine rack at your local newsstand or bookstore and check out the number of financial publications that are now being published. Here's a sampling of what you're likely to find: *Money, Smart Money, Kiplinger's Personal Finance, Bloomberg Personal Finance, Forbes, Fortune, Mutual Funds, Worth, Green,* and *Technical Analysis of Stocks and Commodities.* You'll also find national newspapers like *The Wall Street Journal, Barron's,* and *Investor's Business Daily* over on the newspaper racks.

Should you trust that guru?

Besides these publications, hundreds of investment newsletters often entice readers to pay annual subscription prices in the hundreds of dollars. Television networks like CNNfn and CNBC have made stars of Maria Bartiromo and Joe Kernen, and have introduced terms like *squawk box* into the lexicons of many Americans. You'll also find dozens of other financial programs on commercial and public television, like *Wall Street Week with Louis Rukeyser* and *Nightly Business Report.* No matter where you turn these days, you're apt to find someone spouting off advice about the stock market.

In most cases, the problem with taking advice from any of these sources seriously is much the same as the brother-in-law problem. When some guru says to "buy" a stock, or some magazine includes a stock in its cover story on "The Best 10 Stocks to Buy for the Next 10 Minutes," do you understand the reasons behind that advice? Do you know if the expert is talking about *momentum stocks* or *long-term picks?* Is the magazine just trying to hype sales by creating a sense of urgency about its stock selections? If you follow their advice and buy, will they also tell you when to sell?

Of course, you may get some great ideas from watching television or reading magazines. Just remember that the talking head with the best hair isn't always the one who makes the best stock picks. If you hear about an interesting stock, definitely do at least a quick study to see whether it's worthy of bringing to your club. You can also expand your financial education and keep up to date with changes in laws and regulations that affect your portfolio by being a committed reader of the best investment magazines. But you may also have to wade through plenty of other useless stuff before finding the treasure (and even then you still have to figure out if it's treasure or just some old junk in a fancy box).

Helping club members become better investors

Another magazine that investment club members can put to good use, uncovering stock study ideas and expanding their investment education is *Better Investing,* the monthly magazine of the National Association of Investors Corporation (NAIC). Its title is an ideal descriptor of the publication's goal — helping readers become better investors. You can read more about the benefits of NAIC membership for investment clubs, including subscriptions to *Better Investing* magazine for NAIC members, in Chapter 1.

Besides articles geared toward helping investment clubs operate, *Better Investing* features two monthly columns profiling specific stocks that are solid candidates for inclusion in long-term growth stock portfolios (after your club completes its own study, of course). Each month's "Stock to Study" is chosen because of its potential to double in value (including market appreciation and dividends) during the next five years. Growth is the primary investment focus of these stocks, so the companies they represent have growth-oriented management, projected double-digit earnings growth, a solid record of past performance, and strong fundamentals.

Better Investing's monthly "Undervalued Stock" is selected because its current market price is depressed by what may be near-term considerations that have little to do with the company's underlying value to longer-term investors. These stocks all share short-term concerns that influence price, including uncertainty about near-term results and depressed fundamentals that are expected to improve. The potential for an increase in value of 20 percent during the next 18 to 24 months is the magazine's focus where these stocks are concerned.

The magazine is careful to remind readers that these stocks are only candidates for further study, and definitely not absolute recommendations that every investor should automatically buy. *Better Investing* does not provide on-going review of these selected stocks. If your club *does* decide to purchase any of them after your own extensive study, you'll also need to monitor the stock for future signs to sell, just like you would with any stock in your portfolio (see Chapter 15 for more on tracking the stocks in your portfolio).

Whether or not your club ends up buying any of these stocks, two monthly suggestions such as these are at least a good place to begin looking for prospective stock study ideas. Many NAIC-based investment clubs have their members take turns doing their homework on these picks, determining whether those featured stocks fit into their club's portfolio.

One NAIC member that we know uses these stocks as his only source of investment ideas. He conducts research and studies of each issue's featured stocks, and although he may buy only one or two picks every year, he maintains a watch list of all the stocks mentioned in past months and their current prices and outlook. If the price of a one stock falls, he is able to quickly re-evaluate it and make a decision about purchasing it. His approach works great for any club interested in studying stocks with strong fundamentals and good growth prospects.

You can find a listing of all recent Stocks to Study and Undervalued Stocks on the NAIC's Web site, along with reprints from the magazine (www. better-investing.org/bi/bi.html). Some portions of the site are available only to NAIC members.

Joining an Online Community

The online world provides plenty of opportunities for conversation, idle chitchat, and productive discussion. It's no surprise that when it comes to your club's portfolio, productive discussion rather than gossip or speculation offers better opportunities for gathering stock ideas from fellow investors.

Welcome to the I-Club-List

On the Internet, you can communicate with people in many ways. The easiest is via e-mail. If you can master sending messages and opening e-mail, then you can participate in an Internet *mailing list*. You don't need any special software other than your e-mail program. Mailing lists enable groups of people to discuss common topics. As many as 5,000 people can be on a particular discussion list, all eager to talk with other like-minded individuals.

One place that investment club members naturally gather to discuss club operations and the best stocks for clubs to study is the I-Club-List, which also is sponsored by NAIC and administered by a team of volunteers. The I-Club-List has been around since 1994, and its participants include club members and individual investors from around the world.

Once you *subscribe* to the list (don't worry, it's free), you'll start to receive messages in your e-mail inbox. You can elect to receive individual messages (Warning: Expect up to 75 per day) or a daily digest that consolidates all of that day's messages into one large e-mail. I-Club-List members discuss new ideas for club stocks, analysis methods and tools, and problems with their investment clubs. Although list traffic can be fairly heavy, list members generally are helpful, friendly, and responsive to newcomers brimming with questions.

If the I-Club-List sounds appealing, but you're not sure about the volume of e-mail, then you're in luck. You can read I-Club-List messages on the NAIC Web site, or even by using newsgroup reader software. To sign up for the e-mail or Web versions of the list, visit NAIC's mailing list Web page (lists.better-investing.org), which provides you with plenty of helpful information to bring you up to speed on how the I-Club-List works.

Dropping in for a friendly chat

Unlike e-mail, online chat rooms enable you to have a discussion in real time, just as fast as you can type. The NAIC holds regular chats on its web site (www.better-investing.org). Drop in during one of the chats and you can participate in discussions about individual stocks and specific industries, investing strategies and portfolio management.

If you don't feel like raising your hand to answer a question during these online tutorials, you're under no pressure to do so. You can sit in the back and listen quietly. Regular transcripts also are provided in case you can't attend a class live and you want to review the insightful discussions after the fact.

Using a message board

One of the more popular ways for investors to meet online is using Web message boards. On a message board, you can post a question or comment and get responses from other users — in time. Depending on how popular the message board is, it may take only minutes, or it may take days, or at times even weeks, before you see any responses. If you don't have a lot of time to spend online, message boards may be the perfect place for you because you can come back later, at your convenience, to see whether someone has posted a reply to your question.

Web message boards that focus on investing can be wild and woolly places. Tempers flare, words fly fast and furious across the board, and reasoned analysis often takes a backseat to inflamed opinion. Some of the worst examples can be found on boards like the Yahoo! stock message boards (biz.yahoo.com/co/). Beneath all the name-calling and irrelevant advertisement messages, finding any interesting information about a particular stock is tough.

You can never really trust that what anyone posts about a particular stock on boards like these is true. Unfortunately, countless times unscrupulous investors have posted misleading or completely false information about a stock, hoping to profit by manipulating less savvy investors into buying or selling it. You should always be suspicious of any poster's motivation and conduct your own research before acting on a stock tip you read on these message boards.

The stock message boards on the Motley Fool (www.fool.com) and Raging Bull (www.ragingbull.com) Web sites are much more reasonable. Although investors with all sorts of approaches to the market pay visits to these boards, you can occasionally pick up a few good stock study ideas by visiting these sites.

Finally, the NAIC Forum on CompuServe is accessible to anyone with a CompuServe, AOL, or AOL Instant Messenger user ID (go.compuserve.com/NAIC). If you don't have one, you can register for free on the spot and pay the forum a visit. The Forum is more than 10 years old and is home to more than a few savvy, experienced investors who are happy to share their thoughts and answer questions. Forum members carry on plenty of informal discussions on the merits of particular stocks they may be studying, and they're always open to questions from even the beginning investor.

Remembering your manners

We hope we've convinced you to go online in search of stock study ideas and investment education in general. Once you get there, however, you need to follow a few rules of the road when participating in online discussions. Here are the basics of online etiquette to keep in mind:

✔ Don't write messages on message boards or mailing lists using all capital letters. THIS IS THE ONLINE VERSION OF SHOUTING, and it's just plain rude when you're trying to have a conversation.

✔ Don't excessively quote a message you're responding to. You can include a piece of the original post in your reply to help maintain a sense of the ongoing discussion, but prune your use of the original message to the bare minimum.

✔ Keep all messages appropriate to the topic of the list or bulletin board, keep idle chatter to a minimum, and fight *thread drift* — the tendency for discussions to disintegrate until they've nothing to do with the original topic.

✔ Be nice! And a corollary: Just ignore people who aren't. Don't let anyone attract you into an online shouting match. You'll both end up looking like morons.

Screening Stocks

Every investment club loves to find just one terrific stock that no one's ever heard of — some small company that you can buy cheap and then sit back and watch as it rises into the stratosphere. More than 10,000 stocks are traded publicly, so chances are good that at least a handful of pearls are out there just waiting to be found. But how can you pinpoint your search to find the best candidates, those overlooked and undervalued stocks that might have bright futures?

Searching for gems with your computer

We've already given you plenty of places to look for stock study ideas. And you never know when a stock mentioned by a friend, in a magazine, or online will turn out to be a real winner after your investment club completes its study. But you can rely on other, less random ways of finding stocks that you know will fit your club's investment criteria before you even start your study.

With your personal computer, and either special software or the Internet, your club can use a methodical technique of finding your needle in a haystack. *Stock screening* is a term that describes the process of sifting through the universe of 10,000 publicly traded stocks, eliminating those that *don't* fit your predefined criteria. By getting rid of stocks that you'd never buy in a million years, you can end up with a few reasonable candidates worthier of your club's further research.

In the days before computers, screening stocks was hard. Can you imagine the time involved in opening the newspaper and looking at the data for each stock one at a time until you found one that looked interesting? Certainly, investors in the past (who didn't have access to the tools we have now) used this strategy to build successful portfolios. But we doubt that most investors today would even get out of the letter A stocks.

Computers make the job painless, because you can screen stocks in two ways. You can either buy software and a subscription to a database of stocks, or you can use Web-based stock screening tools that are available on a handful of Web sites. Whichever you choose, you can come up with plenty of great ideas for your club's portfolio once you master the art of screening.

Among the better software screening programs are STB Prospector (www.stbinvestorsoftware.com), which requires a separate subscription to datafiles, and AAII StockInvestor (www.aaii.com), which includes data updates in its subscription price. On the Web, you can find great free stock screening programs at StockScreener.com (www.stockscreener.com) and Multex Investor (www.multexinvestor.com). StockScreener.com provides an easy to use interface with 20 variables that you can select, while Multex Investor is a full-featured application with more screening variables and the ability to create complex, customized screens.

The process of screening a database can be broken down into two main steps:

1. **Identify your goals.**

   What kinds of stocks you are looking for? Are you looking for undervalued stocks, growth stocks, or income stocks?

2. **Select your criteria.**

   Once you know your goals, you can begin the process of determining the exact criteria upon which you can build your screen.

Looking for stocks with good revenue and earnings growth? Enter 15 percent for the minimum growth of sales and earnings during the past few years. Stocks that haven't grown at 15 percent or better disappear from the screen. Or maybe you're searching for small companies, so you can eliminate stocks that have revenues or market caps greater than $1 billion.

As you enter criteria, you can pause after each step, and test the results. If you get no results, then use your browser's back button to return to the screen and adjust your criteria. Once you've finished entering your criteria, you end up with anywhere from 10 to 100 stocks that may fit the bill. Any more than that and you need to tighten up your screening parameters by whittling that number down to something more manageable.

The particular criteria you use for your screens depend on your own needs and objectives. But a basic growth stock screen consists of nothing more than these few parameters:

- Earnings per share (EPS) growth greater than 12 percent (for most recent one, three, and five years and the most recent quarter)

- Sales growth greater than 12 percent (for most recent one, three, and five years and the most recent quarter)

- Projected EPS growth greater than 12 percent

After you build a stock screen, companies that appear in the results are not guaranteed buys. The purpose of screening is to build a short list of stocks so that you can move on to researching those companies. Stocks may pass your screen yet be undesirable candidates for other reasons. You can't simply buy any old stock that passes a screen and expect it to go up in price.

Sidestepping some sources

At first glance, many investment newsletters and Web sites appear to offer a plethora of investment picks, often of *microcap* or *undiscovered* companies. While these glossy publications and sites may look impressive, they aren't always exactly as they seem.

You may be surprised to discover that many, if not all, of the featured companies paid to be included. By law, however, these sites and newsletters must disclose whether they've been paid to highlight a stock, and, if so, tell readers how much they've been paid. You may have to search to find the fine print for this disclosure, but doing so is worth it. The research report on a stock may be completely accurate, and the analysis worthy of Wall Street's best and brightest minds, but it may not be 100 percent objective.

Analyzing Stocks

Once your investment club identifies a few potential candidates for your portfolio, the real work of investing begins. Now you must research and analyze your most promising candidates and then make a decision about which stock fits best into your club's portfolio.

A personal computer is almost essential for today's investor. With your computer, you can research stocks online and use investing software to scrutinize them to find their strengths and weaknesses. Even so, there is no "black box" solution that promises you big returns on any stock. Learning how to successfully select stocks takes practice, and it may take some time before you and your club members feel completely confident in choosing stocks on your own. Don't give up, however — the benefits of sound investing are measured in dollars!

Most clubs start off with a goal of doubling the value of their portfolio every five years. That means you need to generate a return of 15 percent a year from your investments. That isn't an easy trick, because the stock market's return is generally between only 11 percent and 12 percent annually during the past century.

It's possible to be above average if you:

- ✔ Keep your eye on the long-term and buy stocks with the intention of holding them for years.
- ✔ Search for stocks of well-managed companies that are growing at a healthy pace.
- ✔ Buy stocks that are reasonably valued.

Fortunately, there's a tool available that can help you meet those objectives — NAIC's Stock Selection Guide.

Using the NAIC Stock Selection Guide

Now it's time to introduce you to what we consider the best stock analysis tool available for long-term, buy-and-hold investors and investment clubs. It's called the Stock Selection Guide (SSG), and the National Association of Investors Corporation developed it back in the 1950s. (See Figures 14-1 and 14-2.) In those days, it was a two-page paper form, and investors scratched numbers and calculations on their SSGs with well-sharpened pencils.

The SSG definitely looks complicated at first glance, but you'll find it indispensable once your club gets up and running. The SSG is designed to show you how well corporate management is running a company by looking at a few key numbers. Once you've found a solid, well-run company, the SSG helps you figure out whether it's a good time to buy the stock or its shares are perhaps overvalued.

The SSG requires five to ten years of historical data: revenues, earnings per share, income taxes, book value, net income, dividends, share prices, and so on. You can get this information from a number of sources, at a number of Web sites, from the company itself, or in publications like the *Value Line Investment Survey* or *Standard & Poor's Stock Reports,* which may be available at your local library.

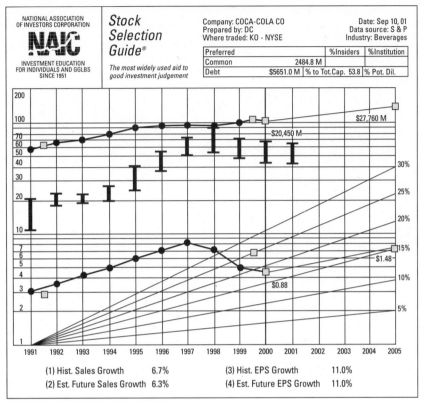

Stock Selection Guide®

The most widely used aid to good investment judgement

Company: COCA-COLA CO
Prepared by: DC
Where traded: KO - NYSE

Date: Sep 10, 01
Data source: S & P
Industry: Beverages

Preferred		%Insiders	%Institution
Common	2484.8 M		
Debt	$5651.0 M	% to Tot.Cap. 53.8	% Pot. Dil.

$27,760 M

$20,450 M

$1.48

$0.88

(1) Hist. Sales Growth	6.7%	
(2) Est. Future Sales Growth	6.3%	
(3) Hist. EPS Growth	11.0%	
(4) Est. Future EPS Growth	11.0%	

Figure 14-1:
Page 1 of
the Stock
Selection
Guide.

How are the earnings and sales?

Here's a quick tour of the SSG and how it works. On the first page (Figure 14-1), you'll see a chart of the company's earnings per share (EPS) and revenues or sales during the past ten years. A picture is worth a thousand words, and if the EPS and revenues are growing nicely, you can instantly see the upward trend on the chart.

Even though your club may have an objective of earning a 15 percent return in your portfolio, every stock that you own doesn't necessarily have to demonstrate that it can grow its earnings and sales at 15 percent a year. Large companies tend to have much slower revenue growth rates than smaller companies. As a company grows larger, doubling revenues becomes progressively more difficult.

If going from $1 to $2 is a doubling of value, imagine how much harder it is for a company to double its sales from $1 billion to $2 billion. That's why expecting a company to continue to grow 50 percent or 60 percent or 70 percent a year over a long period of time is so unreasonable. For a large company (one with sales of several billions of dollars) to have a long-term sales growth rate higher than 5 percent to 10 percent is simply impossible. On the other hand, successful small companies (with sales of several hundred million dollars a year) easily can grow at a rate of 20 percent or even much more. In between those two extremes, you'll find mid-cap stocks.

2 EVALUATING MANAGEMENT

COCA-COLA CO   Sep. 10, 2001

	1991	1992	1993	1994	1995	1996	1997	1998	1999	2000	LAST 5 YEAR AVG.	TREND
A % Pre-tax Profit on Sales	20.6	21.0	22.8	23.1	24.0	24.8	32.1	27.6	19.3	16.6	24.1%	DOWN
B % Earned on Equity	36.6	48.4	47.7	48.8	55.4	56.7	56.5	42.0	25.6	23.4	40.8%	DOWN

3 PRICE-EARNINGS HISTORY as an indicator of the future

This shows how stock prices have fluctuated with earnings and dividends. It is a building block for translation earnings into future stock prices.

Current Price: $46.19   52 Wk High: $64.00   52 Wk Low: $42.37   Dividend: $0.72

	Year	A PRICE HIGH	B PRICE LOW	C Earnings Per Share	D Price Earnings Ratio HIGH (A÷C)	E Price Earnings Ratio LOW (B÷C)	F Dividend Per Share	G % Payout F÷C x100	H % Hi. Yield F÷B x100
1	1996	$54.25	$36.06	$1.40	38.8	25.8	$0.50	35.7%	1.4%
2	1997	$72.63	$50.00	$1.67	43.5	29.9	$0.56	33.5%	1.1%
3	1998	$88.94	$53.63	$1.43	62.2	37.5	$0.60	42.0%	1.1%
4	1999	$70.88	$47.31	$0.98	72.3	48.3	$0.64	65.3%	1.4%
5	2000	$66.88	$42.88	$0.88	76.0	48.7	$0.68	77.3%	1.6%
6	TOTAL		$229.87		292.7	190.2		253.8%	
7	AVG.		$45.97		58.5	38.0		50.8%	
8	AVERAGE PE		25.0		9	CURRENT PE		52.5	

4 EVALUATING RISK and REWARD over the next 5 years

Assuming one recession and one business boom every 5 years, calculations are made of how high and how low the stock might sell. The upside-downside ratio is the key to evaluating risk and reward.

A HIGH PRICE-NEXT 5 YEARS
Avg High PE ~~58.5~~ 35.0 X Est. High EPS $1.48 = Forecast Hi Pr $51.88

B LOW PRICE-NEXT 5 YEARS
Avg Low PE ~~38.0~~ 15.0 X Est. Low EPS $1.00 = $15.00
Avg Low Price of Last 5 Years = $45.97
Recent Severe Market Low Price = $36.06
Price Dividend Will Support = $45.40

C ZONING
$51.88 High Frcst Price- $15.00 Low Frcst Price = $36.88 Range X 1/3 = $12.29
Buy Zone = $15.00 to $27.29
Hold Zone = $27.29 to $39.59
Sell Zone = $39.59 to $51.88
Present Market Price of $46.19 is in the SELL zone.   Selected Zoning = 33/33/33

D UP-SIDE DOWN-SIDE RATIO (Potential Gain vs. Risk of Loss)
$$\frac{\text{High Price - Present Price}}{\text{Present Price - Low Price}} = 0.2 : 1$$

E PRICE TARGET (Price appreciation over the next five years in simple interest rate)
$$\frac{\text{High Price}}{\text{Present Market Price}} \times 100\text{-}100 = 12.3\% \text{ Appreciation}$$

5 5-YEAR POTENTIAL

This combines price appreciation with dividend yield to get an estimate of total return. It provides a standard for comparing income and growth stocks.

A PRESENT YIELD
$$\frac{\text{Present Full Year's Dividend}}{\text{Present Price of Stock}} \times 100 = 1.6 \text{ Present Yield or \% Returned on Purchase Price}$$

B AVERAGE YIELD OVER NEXT 5 YEARS
$$\frac{\text{Avg. Earnings Per Share Next 5 Years X Avg. \% Payout}}{\text{Present Price of Stock}} = 1.6\%$$

C ESTIMATED AVERAGE ANNUAL RETURN OVER NEXT FIVE YEARS

	Simple	Compounded
Avg. 5 Year Appreciation Potential	2.5%	2.3%
Average Yield	+ 1.6%	+ 1.6%
Average Total Annual Return Over the Next 5 Years	= 4.1%	= 4.0%

Figure 14-2:
Page 2 of the Stock Selection Guide.

Now it's your turn

Once you've identified on the first page of the SSG that a company has seen sufficient growth in the past, you can use that information to project how quickly the company will grow in the future. You'll need to decide whether growth will slow in the future as the company gets larger, or whether it can continue at the same pace as it has in the past. Your estimates of a company's future growth will enable you to estimate the earnings per share five years from now, and thus helping you to decide whether this is a stock worth purchasing.

Even if the company you're studying is growing at a rate much greater than 15 percent a year, you want to be conservative in your estimates of future growth. For most mature growth companies, the highest you ever want to estimate growth, without being overly optimistic, is 20 percent, if you choose to go even that high. If, on the other hand, you find that the company is barely growing or in fact has negative growth, why continue on with this particular stock study? You can find plenty of better prospects to spend your time on.

Zeroing in on the profits

Next, turn your attention to the second page of the SSG (see Figure 14-2). Section 2 helps you identify how well a company's management is maintaining the company's pretax profit margins. *Profits* (also known as earnings or net income) are what's left after subtracting a company's expenses for such things as raw materials, supplies, salaries, advertising, office rent and taxes, from its sales. The *profit margin* is the percentage of each dollar of sales that's left after paying all these expenses. Well-run companies generally have stronger profit margins than their competitors, and the SSG helps you see how the company's margins have performed over time.

Section 2 of the SSG also looks at a company's *return on equity* (ROE). Stockholder equity is the amount of capital that the company has raised from issuing shares of stock, perhaps from its initial public offering (IPO) many years ago. Each year that a company earns profits, it pays dividends to shareholders (if authorized by the board of directors) or it keeps earnings and reinvests them in growing its business. Return on equity measures how well the company uses its retained earnings to generate returns on the investment of its shareholders.

Well-run companies will usually have a higher and more stable return on equity than their competitors. If you can find a company with stable profit margins and a ROE that compares favorably to other similar stocks, then you've likely found a stock that has exceptionally strong management.

Keeping an eye on the prices

Sections 3 and 4 of the SSG help you identify past price trends of the stock, particularly its *price-earnings ratio* (P/E), and then project what the likely high and low prices will be during the next five years. The P/E often is used in place of a stock's price to determine whether the stock is over- or undervalued, when compared with the stock's historical patterns, with the market in general, or with other stocks in the same industry group. You can see how much a stock's P/E has fluctuated during the past five years, and then use that information to help estimate a range of high and low P/E's that you expect the stock to sell for during the next five years.

Multiplying your EPS estimate from Section 1 of the SSG, by the high P/E estimate provides an estimated high price for the stock during the next five years. Multiplying your EPS estimated by the low P/E estimate gives you an estimated future low price. With future high- and low-price estimates in hand, you can compare them with the current price in Section 4 of the SSG.

Ask yourself if the difference between the current price and your target high price makes it possible to earn your target rate of return. And, if the target low price is too far beneath the current price, the stock may be too risky to purchase now — you have too much to lose on the downside. By comparing the current price with your estimated future price, you can see whether the stock is a reasonably good value right now, and whether it is likely to yield your targeted rate of return in your portfolio.

Finally, Section 5 of the SSG shows you how much a dividend (if your stock pays one) can boost your total return.

Our quick overview of the SSG doesn't begin to get under the hood of this important stock analysis vehicle. For a more detailed explanation, visit Doug's SSG Tutorial on the Web (www.douglasgerlach.com/ssg/). NAIC's Web site also has a great deal of information about using the SSG (www.better-investing.org, search on "SSG").

By following the three benchmarks of growth, quality, and value, you can successfully invest in common stocks and watch your portfolio grow. NAIC's Stock Selection Guide helps you determine whether a stock is worth purchasing based on these criteria. You, of course, can do more research on a stock beyond what's on the SSG, but many successful investors find the SSG to be the perfect tool on its own. As you and your club members become more experienced investors, you can learn more about a company, if you choose, by analyzing the information that you can discover in its financial statements.

Harnessing software for the tedious stuff

One of the biggest advantages of using your computer in investment analysis is that software programs make short work of complicated calculations and tedious graphing. Fortunately, several SSG programs (with NAIC approval) are available to help your club in its quest for a successful portfolio.

STB Investor Software offers two SSG programs, NAIC Classic and Stock Analyst Plus. NAIC Classic (see Figure 14-3) focuses on teaching step-by-step stock evaluation using a *wizard,* a comical sorcerer character who speaks and points out important judgment items on the SSG form as you work. Once you're comfortable working through all the areas of the SSG on your own, or anytime he begins to drive you bonkers, you can turn the Stock Wiz off and use the program directly.

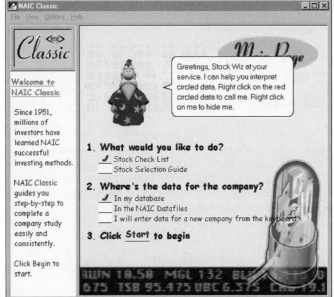

Figure 14-3:
NAIC
Classic
offers
analysis and
education
in one
package.

Stock Analyst Plus enables you to complete the SSG as well, but it also contains many advanced features including balance sheet analysis, retirement planning, and portfolio management.

You can download demo versions of NAIC Classic and STB Investor Software on the STB Web site (www.stbinvestorsoftware.com), so evaluate them for yourself!

Another program that offers SSG analysis is Investor's Toolkit, developed by Investware Corporation (www.investware.com). Investor's Toolkit faithfully follows the exact format of NAIC's Stock Selection Guide, and thus helps you determine whether a stock is a reasonable candidate for your club's portfolio. You can download a free demo version of the program from the Investware Web site, so you can also try it out before you buy.

Remember that computer software usually is licensed for use on a single computer, so you won't be able to purchase one copy for your club and share it with all your fellow members. However, many software providers offer discounts on multiple purchases; so ask the provider whether you're eligible for a club discount.

Even if you pay full price, the software is likely to pay you back in spades just in the time that you'll save by not having to manually fill out the form and draw the graphs. You'll also see faster improvement in your investing skills and gain valuable experience while using SSG analysis software, because you'll be able to complete more stock studies in less time. Few investors who learned to do the SSG by hand ever return to pencil and paper after trying the software!

Digging Deeper

While the SSG is a terrific aid to judgment, it isn't a *replacement* for judgment. Your own analysis is only as strong as your understanding of a particular stock, its history, management, competitors, and operations. Fortunately, more sources than ever are available to research stocks and gather all the data, news, and information that you need to be an informed investor. If you're hooked up to the Internet, your job of research is even easier.

Turning to the company for help

Your first stop for company research is the company itself. Publicly traded companies are required to publish certain specific information about their operations and financial conditions on a regular basis. In fact, larger companies have entire departments dedicated to responding to questions from shareholders and potential shareholders. Just call a company and ask for the investor relations department and they'll send you a copy of their annual report, recent press releases, and other background information about the company.

Most companies now provide much of this information on their own Web sites. You can search for a company's site by using Google (www.google.com) or another Internet search engine. Once you're there, look for a link on the corporation's main page to financial, company, or investor information. Chances are excellent that you'll find recent press releases, a history of the firm, current financial releases, management biographies, company contact information, and even the company's annual report in Adobe Acrobat format. (The free Acrobat reader is available from www.adobe.com. With this reader, you can download a copy of a publication that looks just like the printed, glossy version.) Plus, if you have questions, you can often e-mail them straight to company representatives right from their site.

Don't be shy about asking a company's investor relations staff any questions that your club may have. They are trained to respond to new and experienced investors and are happy to help you out. Companies usually are responsive to investment clubs and provide whatever information they can to help you with your stock study.

Tapping government data banks

If the company doesn't have a Web site, you still can find information about any public company at the Securities and Exchange Commission's EDGAR site (www.sec.gov/edgar.shtml). EDGAR is an acronym for Electronic Data Gathering, Analysis, and Retrieval, and it's the SEC's database of corporate filings. Public companies in the United States must file quarterly (10-Q) and annual (10-K) reports that detail their financial circumstances, notices of their annual meetings and the business that will be conducted at those meetings, and many other documents of interest to shareholders.

Filings are made available at EDGAR 24 hours after the SEC receives them, so you've got nearly instantaneous access to news and information about any public company. If you'd rather, you can telephone a company and ask them to mail you these reports; if you're a shareholder, you'll automatically receive them. In addition to information that you'll glean from the financial statements, you can learn plenty from reading management's discussion of their company's operations in their 10-Q and 10-K reports.

Besides the SEC's own site, you can download EDGAR filings from a number of other sites. EDGARScan (www.edgarscan.com) offers some interesting tools that graph a company's financial history and present many years or quarters of data on one page. 10-K Wizard (www.10kwizard.com) also makes it easy to read and download EDGAR filings (not just Form 10-K!).

Other places to look

Your local library may have Standard & Poor's Stock Reports, two-page reports that detail a company's financial history and describe its business operations. Many libraries also carry the Value Line Investment Survey, a weekly publication that provides analysis and data on 1,700 stocks.

While a Value Line subscription is expensive, you may want to try the reasonably priced three-month trial offer at www.valueline.com. Value Line is a popular resource for many clubs. Besides regular analysis, Value Line provides all the financial data a club needs to fill out a Stock Selection Guide, except for the current price. Most club members use their library's copy of Value Line, but some clubs subscribe for the convenience of quicker access to the reports.

A few other sites on the Web provide the historical fundamental data and share prices that you'll need for the SSG and your analysis of a stock. They include

- ✔ Daily Stocks (www.dailystocks.com)
- ✔ Wall Street Research Net (www.wsrn.com)
- ✔ Microsoft MoneyCentral (www.investor.com)
- ✔ Quicken.com (www.quicken.com)

Although Yahoo! Finance (finance.yahoo.com) has plenty of great research information for investors; its news story archives are particularly strong. News stories from the Web, magazines, and newspapers, along with press releases issued by the companies, all are archived on the site for several months. These stories can reveal much about a stock, particularly if you're in search of information that's emerged since the company's last quarterly or annual report.

Your club members can spend hours and hours researching stocks online. Many of the sites mentioned in this section provide links to help you pinpoint specific information about stocks elsewhere on the Web. But don't become discouraged that there's so much more available than you can ever use. Becoming overwhelmed is easy, so remember that too much time spent doing research is just as bad for your club as too little. Grab what you need to do your Stock Selection Guide plus a little extra, and then get to it!

Comparing Stocks to Find the Real Winners

Once you've found a terrific company that's selling at an attractive price, you may think you're ready to make the purchase. But you need to undertake one more important step before you do. After all, you want to build a portfolio of the strongest stocks out there, and you'll never know whether your company makes the grade unless you compare it with its competitors in the same industry.

NAIC has a tool that helps you compare a group of stocks to find the best of the bunch. Aptly called the Stock Comparison Guide (SCG — see Figure 14-4), it's a simple one-page form that helps you identify the winner (or winners) from among a listing of stocks from the same industry group.

You can get a list of any company's competitors from its investor relation's department. Pick one or more of them to study and complete a Stock Selection Guide for each. Using information from the SSGs, you can quickly fill out the Stock Comparison Guide. The criteria on the form are grouped into three basic categories:

- ✔ **Growth comparisons.** How does the historical growth of the companies' revenues and earnings compare? Which company has grown the fastest?

- ✔ **Management comparisons.** How do the profit margins compare? Which company has generated a greater return on equity? Which company has greater ownership of shares by insiders (management)?

- ✔ **Price comparisons.** How do the companies' prices and P/Es compare? Which stock has a higher dividend yield? Does one stock have a higher upside and lower downside?

Once your club sees how your chosen company stacks up against the competition, you can decide whether you're still interested in buying it. You may be surprised to find out that one of the original company's competitors is a much better buy. That's exactly why you always need to compare any potential stock purchase to other strong stocks in its industry.

Be sure to stay within the industry. If you try to compare a slow-growing regional bank with a high-flying telecom company, your comparison will be worthless. P/Es and growth rates can't be compared with any relevance between companies that aren't in a similar business.

| NATIONAL ASSOCIATION OF INVESTORS CORPORATION **NAIC** INVESTMENT EDUCATION FOR INDIVIDUALS AND GGLBS SINCE 1951 | *Stock Comparison Guide®* | Prepared by _____ DG _____
Date _____ 10 Sep 2001 _____
NAME OF COMPANY | | | | |

GROWTH COMPARISONS (From Section 1 of the NAIC SSG)	JOHNSON & 2	MERCK & CO 10	SCHERING -PLOUGH 10		
(1) Historical % of Sales Growth	10.4	10.4	10.4		
(2) Projected % of Sales Growth	10.4	10.4	10.4		
(3) Historical % of EPS Growth	13.3	13.3	13.3		
(4) Projected % of EPS Growth	9.7	9.7	9.7		

MANAGEMENT COMPARISONS
(From Section 2 of the NAIC SSG)

(5) % Profit Margin Before Taxes (2A) (Average for last 5 years) Trend	20.1	27.9	29.7		
(6) % Earned on Equity (2B) (Average for last 5 years) Trend	25.4	40.1	46.9		
(7) % of Common Owned by Management					

PRICE COMPARISONS
(See Sections 3-5 of the NAIC SSG)

(8) Estimated Total EPS For Next 5 Years	6.26	5.03	2.85		
(9) Price Range Over Last 5 Years High(3A) Low(3B)	106.9-41.6	96.7-28.3	60.8-12.6		
(10) Present Price	96.48	75.97	38.54		
Price Earnings Ratio Range Last 5 Years	(11) Highest (3D)	39.5	36.7	48.1	
	(12) Average High (3D7)	31.6	31.7	36.3	
	(13) Average (3-8)	27.0	26.2	28.5	
	(14) Average Low (3E7)	22.3	20.6	20.6	
	(15) Lowest (3E)	19.2	17.6	15.3	
(16) Current Price Earnings Ratio (3-9)	28.0	25.7	23.4		
Estimated Price Zones	(17) Lower-Buy (4C2)	77.0-109.1	60.9-117.3	34.0-55.6	
	(18) Middle-Maybe (4C3)	109.1-141.1	117.3-173.8	55.6-77.2	
	(19) Upper-Sell (4C4)	141.1-173.2	173.8-230.2	77.2-98.8	
(20) Present Price Range (4C5)	BUY	BUY	BUY		
(21) Upside Downside Ratio (4D)	3.9	10.2	13.3		
(22) Current Yield (5A)	1.3	1.8	1.7		
(23) Combined Estimated Yield (5C)	14.1	27.6	22.7		

OTHER COMPARISONS

(24) Number of Common Shares Outstand	1390.9M	2307.6M	1453.0M		
(25) Potential Dilution from Debentures Warrants, Options					
(26) Percent Payout (3G7)	36.7	44.8	35.7		
(27)					
(28)					
(29) Date of Source Material	4/30/01	4/30/01	4/30/01		
(30) Where Traded	NYSE	NYSE	NYSE		

Figure 14-4:
NAIC's
Stock
Comparison
Guide.

And you'll be happy to know that if your club members buy SSG software, you won't have any good excuses for not making your chosen company stand up to its competitors. With the software, you'll automatically be able to complete a Stock Comparison Guide with the click of a mouse (once you've done the necessary SSGs). Comparing potential stock purchases can't get much easier than that.

Primetimers' Investment Club

The *Primetimers' Investment Club* started out in 1998 as a group of former neighbors from Vancouver, Washington, who invited other friends to join them in their investment endeavor. The 15 members, ages 50 through 65, enjoy coffee and snacks at their monthly two-hour meetings, rotating the tasty-treat responsibility by keeping a hostess list. Because their membership limit is 15 and none of the founding members have left the club, they have yet to need their new member packet or admission requirements.

The Primetimers place a strong emphasis on their education program, and each member must learn how to complete NAIC's Stock Selection Guide (SSG). The club currently is working on learning the Portfolio Evaluation Review Technique (PERT) Worksheet as well. Primetimer members take investing courses at local community colleges, take advantage of NAIC seminars conducted in nearby Portland, and plan to make good use of the extensive educational resources offered online through NAIC's Investor's School. Past guest speakers at their meetings have included brokers, an accountant, and club members with expertise in specific industries. They've also conducted meetings at the local library to better investigate research resources there. They plan to arrange joint education sessions in the future with other clubs in the area.

Through this emphasis on education, the Primetimers learned that by presenting SSGs a month before the actual vote on stocks under consideration for purchase, members have a chance to do their own research. Each member tracks one of the eleven stocks in the club's $14,500 portfolio and is required to prepare a quarterly SSG update for that stock. Members invest $25 a month (plus $2 that goes into their petty cash account). The Primetimers use NAIC's club accounting software and online club accounting resources to track their portfolio. They make their stock investments through a brokerage that can be accessed either online or in person at its local branch office, depending on the club's needs at the time.

Chapter 15

Managing and Tracking Your Portfolio

In This Chapter

▶ Diversifying your stock portfolio

▶ Managing your stock holdings as a whole

▶ Keeping tabs on your portfolio performance

*A*fter your investment club purchases a few stocks, you find that you've got yourselves a portfolio in progress. And that means that you have to start paying attention to your portfolio in new ways, keeping tabs on how your club's stocks fit together to help you prosper in the market. With online tools, tracking and managing the stocks you own has never been easier, but you have to understand the underpinnings of portfolio management first.

Rule One: Diversifying

The idea behind portfolio diversification can be summed up in one tired, old, but nevertheless accurate expression: "Don't put all your eggs in one basket." If you own only one stock, your entire investment in the stock market is completely dependent on that one security. If the stock goes up in price, your investment goes up; if it falls, then the value of your investment falls. But when you own equal dollar amounts of two stocks, and one falls in price, your portfolio's overall value falls only half that amount. Because it's well documented that a group of well-chosen growth stocks tends to rise in price over time, you can smooth the near-term bumps in the road by owning a number of different stocks.

Reducing risk — smoothing the bumps

Any investment carries with it some risk. A stock that you buy can fall in price and conceivably even become worthless (although we're working hard to show you how to invest in stocks so that won't ever happen to you). Risk is unavoidable, however, when you want to achieve decent returns. The good news is that you can reduce the risk in your portfolio — making all those bumps just a bit smoother — by buying a number of different stocks. The more your stocks are different, the more diversified your portfolio will be.

In portfolios worth less than $100,000, no single stock should account for more than 20 percent of total value of the portfolio. In larger portfolios, no stock should account for more than 10 percent of total value of the portfolio. If a stock exceeds these thresholds, you don't necessarily have to immediately sell that stock. You need, instead, to be making plans to balance that investment as best you can with the addition of new club funds and purchases of other stocks.

Don't take diversification too far

Over-diversifying your investment club portfolio is as easy as owning too few stocks. So your club shouldn't own an excessive number of stocks, either, especially if you're buying only new stocks to reduce your risk by diversifying. You can build a well-diversified portfolio with only 12 to 18 stocks. If your club owns more than that, your returns may begin resembling the average returns of the overall market.

In addition, you may have more stocks than your members can reasonably manage. Each of your club members needs to be responsible for keeping up with a stock or two in your portfolio and making regular reports to your club about those companies. If you own too many stocks, handling the necessary oversight for each holding may be too difficult for your members.

A diversified portfolio doesn't protect you from losing money in the market, but it can limit your downside while enabling you to achieve your target rate of return.

Adding Some Variety to the Portfolio

You need to look at diversifying your club portfolio in two ways: by industry and by company size. You want to own companies that are involved in a mix of different businesses, and you want companies that are large, small, and in between, too.

Diversify by industry and sector

Choosing stocks that represent many different kinds of businesses is one way to help diversify your club portfolio. Companies are classified into industry groups according to their primary business. Those industry groups are then grouped together with other similar industries into sectors. Although different data providers may use slightly different classification systems, the Dow Jones industry and sector groupings are among the most common. The ten sectors used by Dow Jones are

- ✔ Basic materials
- ✔ Consumer cyclical
- ✔ Consumer noncyclical
- ✔ Energy
- ✔ Financial
- ✔ Healthcare
- ✔ Industrial
- ✔ Technology
- ✔ Telecommunications
- ✔ Utilities

Within each sector are dozens of industries. For instance, the industries included in the technology sector include

- ✔ Hardware and equipment
- ✔ Communications technology
- ✔ Computers
- ✔ Office equipment
- ✔ Semiconductors
- ✔ Software

Dozens and even hundreds of companies are considered to be within each industry. Dow Jones includes 175 companies in the semiconductors industry, for example.

Plenty of great companies are involved in the semiconductor business, to be sure, but the semiconductor business is classically cyclical and subject to wild swings in supply and demand that can make their share prices change dramatically throughout the year. If you invested only in semiconductor stocks, your club might become queasy following the roller coaster ride of up and down performance that your portfolio would likely embark upon.

The same factors that affect the semiconductor business also affect other industries in the technology sector, so the share prices of many technology stocks can rise and fall in tandem with semiconductor stocks. So when you buy stocks in the semiconductor, software, and computer industries, your portfolio value still may experience wild up-and-down swings. You can imagine what would happen to all three of those industries if people just stopped buying new computers.

Buying stocks from six or so different industry groups, in several different sectors helps protect your portfolio from the problems that accompany wildly changing values. That way when problems affect a certain industry, your entire portfolio won't be affected.

No hard-and-fast rules define the maximum percentage of any one industry that your club portfolio should own, so you'll have to play it by ear. Your portfolio diversification efforts thus will be in constant flux as your club buys and sells stocks and as the stocks that you own go up and down in price. Remember that as soon as you think you've achieved the perfect mix, your next club purchase can tip the scales out of balance again.

Don't go crazy trying to keep precise percentages of ownership in each industry. Just remember to discuss how each new purchase fits in with the range of industries you already own so that your club isn't too heavily invested in any one area.

Diversify by company size

Besides buying stocks from different industries, you also need to buy companies of different sizes. Although the overall stock market has grown over time by about 10 percent or 11 percent, small companies generally grow rapidly, mid-sized companies generally grow moderately, and large companies generally grow slowly but surely. What's more, when large companies as a group are having trouble, smaller companies often are moving ahead briskly — and vice versa. Experts call this *noncorrelation,* which is a fancy way of saying that the prices of large and small company stocks have a strong tendency to move in opposite directions at any point in time.

When you mix small, medium, and large companies in a single portfolio, the benefits of diversification help keep the total value of your investments growing, even when small-, large-, or medium-sized companies, as groups, are under-performing or outperforming.

Measuring size by market cap — maybe

Many investors classify the size of a company by looking at its *market capitalization* (or market cap for short). Market cap is determined by multiplying the number of outstanding shares of stock that a company has issued by its current share price. For example, Yahoo! may have 555.8 million shares outstanding with a share price of $19.75, giving it a market cap of $10.9 billion (555.8 million × $19.75 = $10.977 billion). By comparison, the market cap of General Electric may be $491.8 billion or more. A company's market cap changes every day as its share price changes, and less frequently as the number of shares outstanding changes. So, taken as a whole, these numbers can be quite different at any given point in time.

Right now, Yahoo! and General Electric are considered large-cap stocks. Large-caps usually are defined as companies with market caps greater than $10 billion. Small-cap stocks, on the other hand, have market caps that are less than $1 billion. Care to guess the market cap range of mid-cap stocks?

The problem with defining company size this way, however, is that market cap includes the share price in its calculation. Share price can be significantly affected by investor sentiment. When many investors really and truly like a stock, they can push up its share price, thereby pushing up its market cap and making the stock seem bigger than it really is. Defining a company's size by its revenues is a viable alternative that puts it on equal footing with all companies.

Mid-sized companies commonly are defined as having revenues of between $500 million and $5 billion a year. Small companies have revenues of less than $500 million, and large companies have revenues greater than $5 billion. When you look at General Electric this way, it's still a large company, with revenues of $130.3 billion in the year 2000. By contrast, Yahoo! had revenues of $1.06 billion during the same year, barely making it out of the small-company category.

NAIC recommends some simple guidelines for managing the mix of stocks by size in your portfolio. They advise you to shoot for 50 percent in mid-sized stocks, 25 percent in small stocks, and 25 percent in large stocks. This recipe gives your club's portfolio the pleasing combination of the stability of owning large companies, the faster growth of smaller companies, and the well-paced growth of medium companies.

Managing Your Club Portfolio

Once you've put all the building blocks of your portfolio into place, you'll need to make sure that it's holding up as well as you expected. Not only do you need to keep a watchful eye on the balance of investments in your portfolio, you also must make sure that each of the stocks that you own are still on track. The tasks of portfolio management work hand-in-hand with your stock analysis skills, and as your club matures, you'll find that you're spending more time overseeing your portfolio as a whole than you are finding interesting new stocks to purchase.

Keeping on top versus just keeping records

Whatever you do, don't confuse recordkeeping with portfolio management or portfolio tracking. Your club's accounting software is its most important tool in helping you keep good records of your holdings and registering each purchase and sale of stock and every other transaction in your portfolio. The software also helps you measure the return that your portfolio generates, as you'll find out later in this chapter. Portfolio management, however, is the constant weeding and feeding, if you will, of your holdings, selling losers, finding replacement stocks, analyzing stocks that have hit some speed bumps, and making sure your diversification plan is still holding strong.

Tracking your portfolio is how your club keeps up with changes in your stocks, including the growth or decline of share prices and other fundamental information. These days, portfolio tracking often is accomplished online. But Web-based portfolio trackers can't tell you whether your club should buy more shares of a stock that's stumbled or its diversification plan is out of whack. That's where portfolio management takes over.

Tracking your club's portfolio

Keeping tabs on the changes in all your club's stock holdings is important. You'll want to know about important news that affects your stocks and their industries when it happens so that you can determine its potential impact on your investment.

Tracking online, just for clubs

Web portfolio trackers make periodically checking stocks easy for your club members. A handful of sites are specifically designed to make watching an investment club's portfolio more convenient as a whole. At Iclub.com (www. iclub.com), you can find links to news, other research, and current share prices for all the stocks in your club portfolio.

Because this site is geared for clubs, only a designated administrator (one of your club members) is allowed to make changes to the club portfolio. Other club members can view the portfolio but, for your club's protection, won't have access to areas where club data can be modified. That way a well-meaning but clueless club member doesn't accidentally delete all the information another club member so painstakingly entered.

General tracking sites

Other Internet-based portfolio trackers, such as the ones in the following list, are designed for use by the individual. However, they still can be useful in your club research. You can probably even create a unique user ID so that your club members can share access to these sites, but beware, every member can make changes, either inadvertently or on purpose.

- ✔ Yahoo! Finance (finance.yahoo.com)
- ✔ Microsoft MoneyCentral (www.moneycentral.com)
- ✔ Quicken.com (www.quicken.com)

Using PERT: Portfolio Evaluation Review Technique

While you keep up to date with all the news about your stocks, you can gauge their financial impact and determine trends by using NAIC's portfolio management technique called PERT, an acronym for *Portfolio Evaluation Review Technique*. PERT helps your club monitor its holdings for changes in earnings per share, revenues, and pretax profits (PTP). If you need a quick review of these investment terms and why they're important, check out the discussion about investing in Chapter 13.

PERT has many components, but you start with a single-page form, the PERT Worksheet A (see Figure 15-1), entering a company's quarterly data. Then you calculate the rate of change from quarter to quarter, and again from one 12-month period to the next. When a company's growth rate is slowing, you'll be able to see it on the PERT worksheet — a good thing to know as you begin following your stock after you buy it.

You can also chart the rates of change in earnings per share (EPS), pretax profit (PTP), and revenues so that you can visualize the short-term trends. (See Figure 15-2.) If you're using Investor's Toolkit or STB Stock Analyst software programs, graphs automatically are created for you (yet another reason for recommending the use of this stock selection software). Seeing a downward trend in a stock's key fundamental data should raise a red flag, marking the need for your club to return to that stock and conduct a new analysis in case you decide it's time to sell. (See Chapter 19 for more about deciding to sell.)

PERT Worksheet-A

Company __MCDONALDS CORP__ __(MCD)__

| | QUARTERLY DATA | | | | | | | | | | LAST 12 MONTHS DATA | | | | | | | | |
| | EPS | | | PRE-TAX PROFIT | | | SALES | | INCOME TAX RATE | | EPS | PRE-TAX PROFIT | | SALES | INCOME TAX | | % CHANGE | | |
PERIOD	$		% CHANGE	$ MIL	% SALES	% CHANGE	$ MIL	% CHANGE			$	$ MIL	% SALES	MIL	$ MIL	% RATE	EPS	PRE-TAX PROFIT	SALES
03/94									35.1%							35.3			
06/94									35.1%							35.3			
09/94									35.1%							35.2			
12/94	0.22			471.60	20.8%		2,270.10		34.5%							34.9			
03/95	0.19			435.10	20.1%		2,161.30		35.5%							35.0			
06/95	0.26			584.90	23.7%		2,467.60		35.1%							35.0			
09/95	0.28			609.50	23.6%		2,580.10		34.4%		0.95	2,101.10	22.2%	9,479.1	732.4	34.9			
12/95	0.25		18.6%	539.60	20.9%	14.4%	2,585.50	13.9%	32.0%		0.99	2,169.10	22.1%	9,794.5	742.6	34.2			
03/96	0.21		7.7%	452.10	18.6%	3.9%	2,426.00	12.2%	33.3%		1.00	2,186.10	21.7%	10,059.2	736.5	33.7			
06/96	0.29		13.5%	625.50	23.5%	6.9%	2,665.10	8.0%	32.8%		1.04	2,226.10	21.7%	10,256.7	737.4	33.1			
09/96	0.31		10.7%	649.90	23.4%	6.6%	2,773.80	7.5%	32.2%		1.07	2,267.10	21.7%	10,450.4	738.6	32.6	12.6%	7.9%	10.2%
12/96	0.29		13.7%	523.50	18.6%	-3.0%	2,821.60	9.1%	31.7%		1.10	2,251.00	21.1%	10,686.5	675.1	30.0	11.6%	3.8%	9.1%
03/97	0.25		16.7%	515.70	19.7%	14.1%	2,617.60	7.9%	33.2%		1.14	2,314.60	21.3%	10,878.1	693.7	30.0	13.4%	5.9%	8.1%
06/97	0.31		6.8%	643.10	22.7%	2.8%	2,832.60	6.3%	31.9%		1.16	2,332.20	21.1%	11,045.6	693.5	29.7	11.5%	4.7%	7.7%
09/97	0.32		3.2%	659.10	21.9%	1.4%	3,006.00	8.4%	31.9%		1.17	2,341.40	20.8%	11,277.8	694.4	29.7	9.3%	3.3%	7.9%
12/97	0.29		1.7%	589.40	20.0%	12.6%	2,952.60	4.6%	30.3%		1.17	2,407.30	21.1%	11,408.8	765.7	31.8	6.3%	6.9%	6.8%
03/98	0.26		8.2%	540.20	19.3%	4.8%	2,804.90	7.2%	33.0%		1.19	2,431.80	21.0%	11,596.1	772.0	31.7	4.8%	5.1%	6.6%
06/98	0.26		-17.5%	533.80	16.8%	-17.0%	3,180.80	12.3%	33.1%		1.14	2,322.50	19.4%	11,944.3	744.4	32.1	-1.7%	-0.4%	8.1%
09/98	0.35		10.9%	717.30	22.3%	8.8%	3,215.00	7.0%	32.8%		1.17	2,380.70	19.6%	12,153.3	768.3	32.3	0.4%	1.7%	7.8%
12/98	0.25		-13.6%	516.10	16.0%	-12.4%	3,220.70	9.1%	32.5%		1.13	2,307.40	18.6%	12,421.4	757.3	32.8	0.4%	4.1%	8.9%
03/99	0.30		13.2%	608.70	19.8%	11.2%	3,035.10	8.2%	33.0%		1.17	2,367.90	20.0%	12,651.6	777.2	32.8	-2.1%	-2.6%	9.1%
06/99	0.38		46.2%	772.80	22.7%	44.8%	3,407.10	7.1%	33.0%		1.29	2,606.90	20.2%	12,877.9	854.9	32.8	13.2%	12.2%	7.8%
09/99	0.40		12.7%	800.30	23.2%	11.6%	3,444.20	7.1%	32.4%		1.33	2,689.90	20.5%	13,107.1	879.6	32.7	13.6%	13.0%	7.8%
12/99	0.36		41.2%	710.30	21.1%	37.6%	3,372.90	4.7%	31.5%		1.44	2,884.10	21.8%	13,259.3	936.5	32.5	26.9%	25.0%	6.7%
03/00	0.34		13.3%	662.70	19.8%	10.3%	3,343.80	10.2%	32.0%		1.48	2,946.10	21.7%	13,568.0	949.2	32.2	26.5%	24.4%	7.2%
06/00	0.40		5.3%	773.00	21.7%	0.0%	3,560.60	4.5%	32.0%		1.50	2,946.30	21.5%	13,721.5	942.0	32.0	16.3%	13.0%	6.6%
09/00	0.42		5.0%	789.10	21.0%	-1.4%	3,749.00	8.8%	30.5%		1.52	2,938.10	20.9%	14,026.3	924.3	31.5	13.9%	9.1%	7.0%
12/00	0.34		-5.6%	645.15	18.0%	-9.0%	3,589.60	6.4%	31.0%		1.50	2,870.95	20.2%	14,243.0	900.2	31.4	4.2%	-0.5%	7.4%
03/01	0.29		-14.7%	563.29	16.0%	-15.0%	3,512.00	5.0%	32.8%		1.45	2,771.55	19.2%	14,411.2	874.9	31.6	-2.0%	-5.9%	6.2%
06/01									32.8%							31.8			
09/01									32.8%							32.4			
12/01									32.8%							32.8			
A	B	C	D	E	F	G	H	I	J	K	L	M	N	O	P	Q	R	S	T

Figure 15-1: PERT Worksheet A is where you enter a company's quarterly data.

NATIONAL ASSOCIATION OF INVESTORS CORPORATION — NAIC — INVESTMENT EDUCATION FOR INDIVIDUALS AND CLUBS — SINCE 1951

PERT

Portfolio Evaluation Review Technique

DATE 08/06/2001

Page:1
Portfolio: Blue Chips + Salsa Club
Prepared using The NAIC Investor's Toolkit

DIV	COMPANY	% YLD	EST EPS	EPS QTR END	EPS $	EPS % CHG	SALES MIL $	SALES % CHG	PRE-TAX MIL $	PRE-TAX % SALES	PRE-TAX % CHG	TRAILING 12 MOS EPS $	TRAILING % CHG	CUR P/E	PRICE	RV	5 YR HI	5 YR AVG	5 YR LOW	EST GROWTH RATE EPS	P/E AS % OF GROWTH RATE	US/ DS	% COMPD ANNUAL RATE OF RETURN	EST 5YR LOW PRICE	EST 5YR HIGH PRICE
0.00	NOVELLUS SYSTEMS INC	0.0	1.98	06/01 / 06/00	0.40 / 0.59	-32.2%	376.9 / 326.0	15.6%	85.8 / 109.7	22.8% / 33.6%	-21.7%	1.68 / 1.91	-12.0%	24.6	48.85 07/17/01	120.2	29.9	20.5	11.1	18.0	136.9	2.9	22.3	19.4	133.5
0.00	WIND RIVER SYSTEMS	0.0	-1.09	04/01 / 04/00	-0.32 / -0.48	%	110.2 / 91.6	20.3%	-38.9 / -27.7	-35.3% / -30.3%	%	-0.92 / -0.09	%	-13.7	14.90 07/17/01	-30.7	69.7	44.7	19.7	18.0	-76.3	4.3	21.3	9.2	39.2
0.21	DISNEY (WALT) CO	0.7	.31	03/01 / 03/00	-0.26 / 0.04	-750.0%	6,049.0 / 6,303.0	-4.0%	-296.0 / 320.0	-4.9% / 5.1%	-192.5	0.27 / 0.41	-34.1%	92.1	28.30 07/17/01	336.0	29.8	27.4	25.1	13.8	664.7	0.0	-1.2	13.7	25.6
1.36	MERCK & CO	2.1	3.36	03/01 / 03/00	0.71 / 0.65	9.2%	11,345.0 / 8,851.4	28.2%	1,638.4 / 2,254.2	14.4% / 25.5%	-27.3%	3.00 / 2.61	14.9%	19.2	64.48 07/17/01	79.0	29.6	24.3	18.9	12.0	159.9	3.2	16.7	45.0	127.3
0.04	JLG INDUSTRIES	0.3	1.42	04/01 / 04/00	0.25 / 0.41	-39.0%	219.5 / 291.6	-24.7%	15.6 / 28.6	7.1% / 9.8%	-45.6%	1.28 / 1.26	1.6%	8.3	11.83 07/17/01	70.6	16.4	11.8	7.2	11.0	75.7	4.8	22.9	7.5	32.7
0.22	MCDONALDS CORP	0.8	1.60	03/01 / 03/00	0.29 / 0.34	-14.7%	3,512.0 / 3,343.8	5.0%	563.3 / 662.7	16.0% / 19.8%	-15.0%	1.45 / 1.48	-2.0%	17.3	27.72 07/17/01	82.0	23.9	21.1	18.2	10.5	165.1	5.3	16.6	22.0	57.8
0.51	SYNOVOUS FINANCIAL	1.6	1.06	03/01 / 03/00	0.25 / 0.22	13.6%	516.6 / 450.9	14.6%	117.3 / 99.8	22.7% / 22.1%	17.5%	0.96 / 0.84	14.3%	30.8	32.57 07/17/01	129.0	29.7	23.9	18.0	10.0	308.4	0.2	4.1	14.4	37.0
0.90	CONAGRA INC	4.3	1.45	05/01 / 05/00	0.26 / -0.04	%	6,683.5 / 6,391.5	4.6%	217.7 / -31.5	3.3% / -0.5%	%	1.34 / 0.87	54.0%	14.5	20.96 07/17/01	73.1	23.5	19.8	16.0	8.0	181.0	3.4	18.7	15.1	41.0
0.33	SIGMA-ALDRICH	0.8	1.83	03/01 / 03/00	0.48 / 0.45	6.7%	305.6 / 284.0	7.6%	53.4 / 60.5	17.5% / 21.3%	-11.8%	1.69 / 1.66	1.8%	22.5	41.10 07/17/01	113.7	24.2	19.8	15.4	8.0	201.5	1.2	8.3	26.0	59.0
0.50	SPRINT FON GROUP	2.3	1.76	03/01 / 03/00	0.36 / 0.51	-29.4%	4,358.0 / 4,397.0	-0.9%	510.0 / 726.0	11.7% / 16.5%	-29.8%	1.63 / 1.88	-13.3%	12.5	22.03 07/17/01	67.6	25.2	18.5	11.8	8.0	156.4	6.5	30.1	13.8	75.2
1.25	WASHINGTON REIT	5.3	2.00	03/01 / 03/00	0.47 / 0.41	14.0%	35.3 / 32.1	10.1%	10.7 / 10.9	30.4% / 34.0%	-1.7%	1.85 / 1.21	53.8%	11.7	23.50 07/17/01	94.7	14.1	12.4	10.7	8.0	146.8	1.6	14.9	14.8	37.1
0.16	MOTOROLA INC	0.9	-.31	06/02 / 06/01	-0.35 / 0.09	-488.9%	7.5 / 9,255.0	-99.9%	-766.1 / 419.0	198.4% / 4.5%	-283.0%	-0.29 / 0.50	-158.4%	-59.3	18.11 07/17/01	-123.0	73.2	48.2	23.3	5.3	-1,116.3	1.6	9.4	12.6	27.2
B	C	D	E	F	G	H	I	J	K	L	M	N	O	P	Q	R	S	T	U	V	W	X	Y	Z	AA / BB

Figure 15-2: This PERT report tracks earnings per share, pretax profit, and other indicators.

The PERT form and Portfolio Trend Report (Figure 15-3) bring together onto one page the most important data about each stock in your club's portfolio. Besides quality issues (EPS, revenues, profits), you also can obtain an overview of value issues (P/E ratio, upside/downside ratio), which estimates the future rate of return that you can expect from the stock.

INVESTOR'S TOOLKIT

Portfolio Trend Report

Page:1
Portfolio: Blue Chips + Salsa Club

DATE _____ 08/28/2001 _____

TICKER	COMPANY	PERCENT CHANGE				EST. E/S GROWTH	PROJECTED AVG. RET	TOTAL RETURN	NUMBER OF SHARES	DOLLAR VALUE	% OF PORTFOLIO	PMGuide RECOM.
		QTR. SALES	QTR. PTP	QTR. EPS	12 Mo.EPS							
NVLS	NOVELLUS SYSTEMS INC	15.6% / 67.4%	-21.7% / 42.7%	-32.20% / 20.83%	-12.04% / 14.02%	18.0%	13.4%	22.3%	306	14948.1 / 48.85 / 07/17/01	25.6%	
WIND	WIND RIVER SYSTEMS	20.3% / 143.8%	% / -178.4%	% / -173.68%	% / -320.41%	18.0%	16.0%	21.3%	415	6183.5 / 14.90 / 07/17/01	10.6%	Buy
DIS	DISNEY (WALT) CO	-4.0% / 5.4%	-192.5% / -29.2%	-750.00% / 86.67%	-34.15% / 18.75%	13.8%	-5.1%	-1.1%	101	2844.7 / 28.30 / 07/17/01	4.9%	
MRK	MERCK & CO	28.2% / 27.9%	-27.3% / 9.1%	9.23% / 10.29%	14.94% / 17.13%	12.0%	11.9%	16.4%	159	10268.8 / 64.48 / 07/17/01	17.6%	Buy
JLG	JLG INDUSTRIES	-24.7% / 15.0%	-45.6% / 170.1%	-39.02% / 200.00%	1.59% / 15.20%	11.0%	14.9%	22.7%	366	4333.5 / 11.83 / 07/17/01	7.4%	Buy
MCD	MCDONALDS CORP	5.0% / 6.4%	-15.0% / -9.0%	-14.71% / -5.56%	-2.03% / 4.17%	10.5%	13.6%	16.4%	79	2179.6 / 27.72 / 07/17/01	3.7%	Buy
SNV	SYNOVOUS FINANCIAL	14.6% / 18.3%	17.5% / 10.5%	13.64% / 18.18%	14.29% / 16.25%	10.0%	0.2%	4.2%	5	166.9 / 32.57 / 07/17/01	0.3%	
CAG	CONAGRA INC	4.6% / 8.9%	% / -30.7%	% / -36.67%	54.02% / 70.49%	8.0%	13.5%	17.4%	128	2672.6 / 20.96 / 07/17/01	4.6%	Buy
SIAL	SIGMA-ALDRICH	7.6% / 4.2%	-11.8% / 38.1%	6.67% / 24.24%	1.81% / 0.61%	8.0%	4.2%	8.2%	102	4173.1 / 41.10 / 07/17/01	7.1%	
FON	SPRING FON GROUP	-0.9% / -0.3%	-29.8% / -10.1%	-29.41% / -18.00%	-13.30% / -3.26%	8.0%	22.0%	29.2%	122	2688.0 / 22.03 / 07/17/01	4.6%	Buy
WRE	WASHINGTON REIT	10.1% / 6.4%	-1.7% / 11.1%	13.98% / 65.52%	53.78% / 43.60%	8.0%	11.6%	15.2%	220	5176.6 / 23.50 / 07/17/01	8.9%	
MOT	MOTOROLA INC	-99.9% / -11.4%	-283.0% / -192.3%	-488.89% / -214.29%	-158.35% / -70.41%	5.3%	4.4%	9.0%	151	2731.9 / 18.11 / 07/17/01	4.7%	

Small: 8.9%   Medium: 51.1%   Large: 40.1%   Total Dollar Value: $58,367

Figure 15-3:
Portfolio
Trend
Report.

A trend report (like the one for McDonald's in Figure 15-4) is great for club meetings, because your members all can see the performance of each individual stock and identify any possible problem areas.

Mastering the principles of PERT can take time, but doing so is well worth the effort when it comes to building and managing a successful portfolio. Fortunately, software programs like Investor's Toolkit and STB Stock Analyst greatly simplify the data entry and paperwork, enabling you to focus on results and conclusions that you can observe.

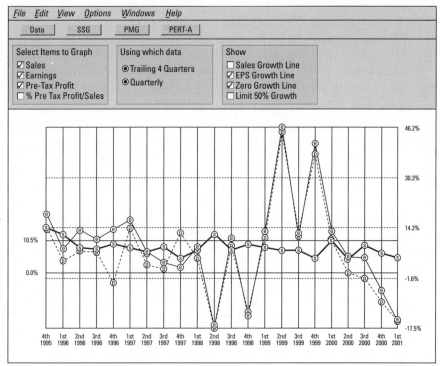

Figure 15-4:
Tracking
McDonald's
perfor-
mance.

Dealing with the Dogs of Your Portfolio

Every club must deal with its share of dogs, or stocks that don't live up to your expectations, the ones that go down in price the day after your club buys stay down for what seems like an eternity. Dogs drag down your returns and cause anxiety during club meetings.

Visiting the doghouse every now and then

Your club portfolio never is completely free of dogs, regardless of how experienced all your members become as investors, how much time you spend on research, or how big your portfolio gets. Acknowledging that things sometimes just don't work out between you and a stock is ever so important, because occasionally all your research about a stock just may be wrong.

NAIC offers some guidance when it comes to the dogs in your club's portfolio. The *Rule of Five* always comes true, as long as you're following the investing and portfolio guidelines that NAIC has developed (see Chapter 13). The Rule of Five indicates that out of every five stocks your club buys, one will outperform all your expectations, three will perform just about as you expected, and one stock will be a gigantic, big-L-on-the-forehead *loser* — a dog.

Put another way, when your club diligently does its research, it has a good chance of being right 80 percent of the time. And that's pretty good when it comes to investing in the stock market. But it's that other 20 percent of the time that causes plenty of problems.

Sending those dogs to the pound

When you think that a stock in your portfolio has fallen greatly in price and may be a dog, take action. Your mission is to determine whether the company is experiencing temporary, short-term problems, or facing bigger issues that will affect its performance for years to come. Often small problems are the tip of the iceberg, and you can't tell how big the problem is unless you go beneath the surface.

You can think of the process of examining a troublesome stock as analysis in reverse. You want to find out whether any of the fundamental reasons that attracted you to invest in the stock in the first place have changed. A few problems that can be good indicators that it's time to sell are:

- ✔ **Revenue growth is slowing.** When a company appears to be growing at a slower pace, it can mean that it's getting bigger and growth inevitably must slow. However, it also can mean that the company has problems. Perhaps it can't find markets for its products, or customers aren't interested in buying.

- ✔ **Profit margins are shrinking.** If a company's profit margins are steadily getting smaller, it means that making money is becoming harder and harder for the company.

- ✔ **An adverse change of management occurs.** When a dynamic company founder retires, does the company have a plan of succession? Or was the company's management forced out en masse? Will the new team have what it takes to keep the company growing?

- ✔ **Direct or indirect competition stands to affect the company's long-term prosperity.**

- ✔ **A company's success is too dependent upon a single product whose cycle is running out.** Pharmaceutical companies are susceptible to these kinds of problems. As drug pipelines dry up, these firms may have no more opportunities for growth.

- ✔ **Raw material costs increase significantly.** If a company can't obtain the materials it needs at good prices, and can't pass along higher costs to its customers, then its profits are adversely affected.

- ✔ **The company has been charged with fraud or "accounting irregularities."** Companies with these problems aren't quality companies, so you shouldn't feel bad about selling if major problems like these arise. Just sell quickly and move on to better quality companies.

- ✔ **You need to register a capital loss to offset capital gains that you may have incurred.**

- ✔ **You need cash for a member withdrawal.** Remember, don't transfer stock that has gone down in price to a departing member, because selling it, registering the loss, and using the cash proceeds to pay off that member is better.

Getting rid of the dogs in your portfolio often is prudent, but whatever you do, don't just sit around waiting for your dogs to rebound. You must understand the reasons why a stock has been touched by bad luck, because only then can you decide how best to proceed. If the stock's fundamentals have changed for the worse, and the future looks bleak, you'll probably want to sell — and soon.

But if the fundamentals still are great, and you can't find any real reason why the price has taken a nosedive, then the stock may be nothing more than a victim of circumstance. In many cases, your club may find that rather than selling, this may be a better time for investing more money in that same stock. The stock may be selling at a bargain basement price, so dig deep with your research first, then back up the truck and buy more shares on sale, if you think this dog might someday be a winner!

Selling winners

Warren Buffet, the chairman of Berkshire Hathaway and a legendary investor, maintains that if you've done your research properly, the best time to sell a stock is never. That's the essence of a long-term, buy-and-hold philosophy at work!

But for most mere mortals, holding on to a stock forever may not be practical or possible. Yet buy-and-hold investors rarely sell just to *lock in a profit* or because a stock has reached its predetermined *target price*. Selling the best performing stocks in your portfolio is just like cutting all the flowers in your garden as soon as they bloom — all you're left with is weeds.

Letting those stock flowers grow and cutting down the weeds is a better approach. In your portfolio, that means letting the winners continue to grow and dumping the losers. Your greatest returns may still lie ahead!

Nevertheless, you should recognize those times when it may be wise to get rid of a high performing stock. They include the following:

✔ **When your club needs to cash out a departing member.** Just don't make the mistake of selling an appreciated stock to do this. Instead, transfer shares to avoid capital gains taxes. Stock transfers are covered in more detail in Chapter 8.

✔ **When you have serious portfolio diversification problems.** For example, a stock that has performed exceptionally well for your club has grown to become too large of a part of your portfolio, and you need to scale it back. Ideally, however, you need to balance your portfolio by buying other stocks if possible, rather than selling.

✔ **When the stock is seriously overvalued.** The best judge for this is the stock's *relative value*. Relative value is determined by dividing the stock's current price-earnings ratio (P/E) by its average P/E for the past five years, expressed as a percentage. If the relative value is greater than 150 percent, the stock may be extremely overvalued and selling may be in order.

✔ **When you've found a replacement that offers better quality and a higher potential return for your portfolio.** Although hesitating before selling any high quality growth stocks is a good idea, you always need to be on the lookout for opportunities to improve your portfolio.

One last tip about selling stocks from your portfolio: Once your club votes to sell, don't look back. You sometimes may sell stocks for all the right reasons, but the stocks, nevertheless, proceed to go up or down in price contrary to all laws of reasonableness. Leave your regrets on the trading floor when you sell, and focus on the future instead.

How are you doing? Checking your returns

The bottom line of any investment portfolio is how well it performs over time. And nothing tells the story of your club's performance better than the numbers. By calculating your club's return during a particular period, you can see whether you're doing well compared to the market or falling behind. And even though your club's primary focus is education, it shouldn't come at too great a cost to your portfolio returns.

Running the numbers

Calculating the rate of return in your portfolio isn't always the easiest thing to do. Software and computers really come in handy. But even with help doing the calculations, the overall gains (or losses) of your holdings can be expressed in a number of ways. The following sections provide you with a brief primer on returns and how they're measured.

As an example, say that you put $1,000 into the bank on January 1 of this year. At the end of the year, you have $1,100. You've earned $100, or a 10 percent return on your starting balance for the year. That's easy enough to calculate, because you didn't deposit any more money throughout the year.

But what if you deposited an additional $1,000 at some point during the year? At that point, return calculations begin to get tricky. Calculating the returns on a fixed investment for a one-year period is easy enough, but when you have money moving in and out of an account, and when you're buying and selling stocks, calculating your club's overall returns by hand becomes difficult.

Total versus annualized returns

Your treasurer and club accounting software can calculate returns for each member's account, for each security, and for the club as a whole. The Valuation Statement and Member Status Reports generated by NAIC Club Accounting software (and its online counterpart) show the *Total Return* for each stock and each member since he or she joined the club. The calculation takes into account each individual transaction, such as purchases, sales, receipts of dividends from stocks, and monthly investments by all club members. The Total Return usually is quite different from a simple calculation of change from the starting value, because it takes into account each transaction.

The Valuation Statement also provides the *compound annualized return* for each stock, which is a number that assumes a stock will grow as it has in the past for a full year. If you bought a stock three months ago, and it goes up in price 25 percent, then the annualized return figure will be more than 200 percent, because the program assumes the stock will double in value every three months. This, of course, is highly unlikely, and if the stock's price remains at its current level, the annualized return begins to fall on each succeeding month's report.

We recommend that treasurers for clubs that are less than a year old turn off the display in NAIC Club Accounting Software for these annualized returns, because the numbers are fairly meaningless. After the first year, you can turn the returns display back on in each monthly report.

Unlimited Potential Investments

The eight members of *Unlimited Potential Investments (UPI)* are committed to keeping their club interactions as enjoyable as they are educational. This all-female club from the Atlanta area plans a social hour right before its monthly club meetings to ensure that members have a chance to visit and get to know each other even better before they settle in for their two hour business meeting. Club members, ranging in age from 26 to 40, take turns bringing food and drinks to their meetings or they'll occasionally meet at a restaurant or in a member's home.

This emphasis on forming a social bond doesn't detract from the club's mission of learning more about investing. Unlimited Potential Investments was formed in 1995 by a group of friends, co-workers, and family who share a similar investing philosophy and are willing to make a minimum five-year commitment to the club. New members also are asked to honor this long-term commitment and agree to member responsibilities, including active participation and stock watching duties.

The women of UPI contribute a minimum of $10 each month, and have grown their portfolio to more than $26,000. They use software for club accounting and stock selection purposes and online resources provided by Smith Barney, their full-service brokerage house. They invite guests, such as their broker, to speak at meetings and continue the club's education, and they conduct some of their meetings at the local library to make use of research tools there.

UPI members have learned some hard lessons about club operations through personal experience. In addition to member withdrawals and personality clashes, UPI has had to cope with tough financial situations. For instance, the club owned shares of ValuJet when one of its airplanes tragically crashed. The share price of the stock also crashed, and the club subsequently placed a market order to sell. When the order was filled, the club's shares had been sold at a much lower price than the club expected.

When the club first started, members were afraid to sell stocks because they'd become emotionally attached to their holdings. The savvy members of UPI now trust their research and educated opinions, working closely as a group on stock-purchase and portfolio-management decisions.

The returns in your club's portfolio during its early years may be low, and that's okay. Most clubs take a year or two to really become grounded in their investment philosophy, and many also have start-up expenses that eat into their returns.

At the bottom of the Valuation Statement, the NAIC Club Accounting Software displays a Compound Annualized Return of the current portfolio's overall performance, which doesn't include any securities that you've sold. The Members Status Report, however, does include the return from your club's entire history.

Putting your club's return in perspective

Once you know your club's rate of return over time, what next? Well, you need to compare each year's performance to a benchmark, such as the Standard & Poor's 500 index. Are you beating the market? Or are you still lagging behind? Underperforming the market in a single year isn't as significant a problem as failing to beat the market year after year. If your club has a goal of doubling its value every five years, then you need to aim for an average 15 percent return each year. Some years you'll do better, and some you'll do worse, but keep that target in mind as you compare your results.

If your club consistently has returns that fall far short of the market, then you need to refocus your members on education. Review your investment philosophy; overhaul your portfolio according to the investing principles that are described in Chapter 13, and try getting your portfolio back on track. Lackluster returns year after year, unless the market is in a sustained down period (which certainly happens from time to time), soon leads to a loss of enthusiasm among your members and can be your club's downfall. We're willing to bet, however, that you can improve your investing skills and your portfolio returns by paying more attention to your club's education program for awhile.

Chapter 16

Making Team Decisions to Buy Stocks

*O*n Wall Street, investment banks and brokerage firms employ teams of professional analysts to develop stock recommendations for clients. Each of these analysts typically is responsible for covering from three to 15 stocks in one or two industry groups.

The analyst's job is to come to work each day, learning everything possible about each of the companies he or she follows. Because analysts don't have dozens and dozens of stocks to analyze, they can spend their 60-hour workweeks getting down and dirty with each company, learning about their operations, their strengths, and weaknesses, how they stack up to their competitors, and the impact of the economy on the company's business. In short, they have time to check everything you'd ideally want to know about a company before you invested in it. That way these analysts can recommend that investors buy, sell, or hold shares in those companies.

Forming a Team of Specialists

As an individual investor, spending as much time researching stocks as professionals do may be hard for you. Oh sure, you still can conduct plenty of research, so you can find and manage a portfolio of a dozen or so solid stocks. You may even be more successful than many pros at picking great companies. But think how much more you can learn about a company if you have to research only one stock in that much depth.

With only one stock to follow, you can spend your time studying that company's press releases, scrutinizing its financial statements, poring over every Securities and Exchange Commission (SEC) filing, and poking into every nook and cranny of the company's operations. You periodically can call the company's investor relations manager with questions, and scour the Web for information about its competition. You can read trade publications to gain an understanding of how the company is perceived within its business segments. After digging so deep, you, too, become an expert on that single company.

And *that* is the essence of investing within an investment club. Your members each can take on the role of analyst for one or two stocks in the club's portfolio, immersing themselves in tracking each company's operations, and then reporting back to the club with regular updates and recommendations about their stocks. When a dozen members share their knowledge and research, the entire club benefits, and the portfolio you build often is better and stronger than the portfolios of any of the individual members.

This doesn't mean that if you have 16 members, you must have 16 stocks in your portfolio so that each member is responsible for tracking one. In most clubs, there's always plenty of work to go around, and some of your members and officers have other duties to manage. If a particular member (usually the club treasurer) has a number of other club-related responsibilities, asking him or her to follow one of the club's holdings on top of all the other work isn't in the best interest of the club.

But you need to remember where your portfolio would be if some of your members didn't contribute their time and experience to the club's efforts to build a portfolio. The rest of your club members should be required to regularly follow at least one stock, and if they won't, they should be asked to leave. The problem with club members who refuse to do their fair share of work is that your club will grind to a halt if everyone in the club behaves the way they do.

If a few members shirk their portfolio responsibilities, then your portfolio is being short-changed. Worse yet, those members are being short-changed, because they're not putting any effort into their own ongoing education. Like most things in life, you get out of an investment club about what you put into it. Even new members who have no investing experience need to be put to work on stock research tasks and assisting the club with its overall goals.

Many clubs have a specific requirement that members present a certain number of stock studies/progress reports in the course of a year. By formalizing this expectation in your club's bylaws, you emphasize how important it is for all members to be active participants in the process of building and managing a portfolio.

Applying the team approach to stock research

Although you can simply divide the work of stock analysis among all your members, many clubs find that flying solo isn't the only way to go. Your club members can work together in many productive ways, in pairs or small groups outside of your monthly meetings, with a goal of investigating promising stocks and then reporting back to the club.

Mentoring new recruits

Pairing an experienced member of your club with a rookie often works well in bringing neophytes up to speed. The mentor can offer guidance to the new member on the specifics of researching a stock — what items to look at, where to find information, what kinds of news is important, and what is useless noise. A mentor also can provide moral support when the rookie presents his or her findings to the club.

Breakout teams

Dividing up your club into several teams can help you accomplish a great deal of work without overloading any individual members. Breakout teams of three or four members can tackle specific industry groups, identifying four or five of the better stock candidates with each team member then analyzing, researching, and preparing reports on one or two of those companies. The team members then regroup, compare results, and select the best-looking stock from the bunch. At the next meeting, one member of the group presents its conclusions to the club, with backup from the other team members.

Official stock study committees

Some clubs appoint a standing stock-study committee that serves for six months or a year. The committee is responsible for finding new companies for the club to consider, researching and analyzing those stocks and then presenting their conclusions at each club meeting. Once a stock is purchased, a member outside of the committee takes over as its official stock watcher or analyst. The stock study committee's membership needs to rotate regularly among all club members so they can fulfill their club duties.

No matter how your club decides to split up the stock research duties, don't fall into the trap of presenting only "good-looking" stocks to your members. Some people hesitate before making a presentation about a stock that's overvalued or fundamentally flawed, thinking what's the point in telling them about it when club members never would buy its shares. This approach is wrong on two counts. First, you often can learn just as much from a bad idea as you can from a good one. Seeing and discussing the problems of a troubled stock can reinforce the important traits in the minds of your members. Second, a stock that's overvalued today may be undervalued six months later.

Once you've completed a stock study and determined that the company is strong and well managed, but the price is simply too high, don't forget about that stock. Review it again in six months, or keep a watch list of stocks that may be more attractive at some point in the future.

Buying your club's first stock

Buying your club's first stock is an exciting and usually scary thing. However, you don't need to be in any rush to start your portfolio. After your club has been together for six to nine months, and assuming that you've spent that time educating your members about investing in the stock market, you're probably ready to buy that first stock.

Unless your club is made up of experienced investing geniuses, you don't need to worry about making your first purchase until you've been together for at least six months. By that time you've collected enough cash to make a purchase in your brokerage account without seeing commissions eat up too much of your capital. And you've been studying, learning how to invest, and analyzing dozens of companies. So the time is right to pick a company or two and jump into the market feet first.

If your club has been together for a year and still hasn't bought a stock, what are you waiting for? Get your money working for the club! If your members are hesitating, then solidifying your educational efforts may be in order. Just remember that beefing up your educational program is better when you've got a stock or two in your portfolio, because your members then are more strongly compelled to learn once cold, hard cash is committed. Investing in the stock market gives you plenty of real-world lessons, and those, after all, are the most valuable kind.

Contrary to popular belief, you don't need to buy a hundred shares for your purchase. You may buy your first share through NAIC's Low Cost Investment Plan, and then later you can invest in more shares through the company's own dividend reinvestment program (DRIP). If the company offers a direct stock investing program (DSP), then perhaps you can invest directly without paying a large commission or having to set up a brokerage account. Chapter 7 describes these methods of investing in stocks in detail.

The first stock that your club buys may well turn out to be a *Loser* (with a capital L), but the education that you'll gain from the experience of figuring out what went wrong is priceless.

Managing Your Club Portfolio

In the same way that stock research tasks can be divvied up among all your club members, your members also need to share the responsibilities of monthly portfolio management. In fact, the real secret to a successful club portfolio is how well you follow through with each stock after you buy it. Sure, the idea behind a buy-and-hold portfolio is that you rarely have to worry about selling stocks, but it doesn't mean that you can just forget about those stocks after you buy them. Every month, your club should evaluate where each of its holdings stands — not just in terms of price, but also checking whether the company fundamentals still are sound.

Chapter 15 details the many components that go into constructing a successful club portfolio. The sections that follow explain how you can divide up the tasks to address all your portfolio's needs and the key building blocks that are part of portfolio management.

Duties of the stock watchers

A major part of an investment club's educational process is for each member to become a stock analyst, specializing in just one or two stocks in the club portfolio. These *stock watchers* are responsible for watching over their assigned sheep from the club's flock, making sure that they don't go astray. Every month (or on whatever schedule your club sets), stock watchers must be prepared to report to the club on any stock they track.

Choosing stock watchers

When it comes time to determine who will serve as the stock watcher for a particular stock, choosing the person who first presented the stock to the club isn't the best idea. Humans are a funny species with tendencies toward becoming emotional about the oddest things, including the stocks that we buy. Worse yet, club members tend to fall in love with stocks, so much so that the mere mention of their ticker symbols stirs their hearts. As a result, rationally examining the stocks that the club owns becomes harder and harder, looking at them as members sometimes do through misty, Vaseline-coated lenses. And don't even talk about the heartbreak that comes when a stock does you wrong.

In a club, members are susceptible to the stock love bug, which may even be compounded, because all eyes are on you and the stocks that you recommend for the club to buy. You may feel the pressure not let the club down, hoping that *your* stock pick isn't the one that bankrupts the club portfolio. Clubs need to avoid becoming a stock picking competition. The key is remembering that the club buys every stock with a majority vote and that stock then becomes the club's, not the individual's, holding. Be that as it may, you may not feel any more secure about the ideas that you bring to the club, and that can trip you up when it comes to reporting on your stock after it's been purchased. Your optimism may gloss over your view of a stock's shortcomings, causing you to have a bias toward that company.

To combat these tendencies, many clubs make it a rule that the member who presents a stock doesn't serve as the stock watcher for that stock. One of your fellow members may be able to maintain a more objective opinion about that stock, perhaps bringing a healthy skepticism to his or her follow-up reports.

Spreading around the stock watching assignments also ensures that everyone remembers that your club is a communal-type activity. No single member is personally responsible for the purchase of any stock. You all chose the stock together, so finger-pointing about "your stock" or foisting any kind of blame upon whoever brought the stock to the club — when it doesn't perform as expected — should never occur.

Making regular stock watcher reports

Your regular club meetings must include a time for presenting evaluations of your current holdings and descriptions of how they're holding up. Doing so requires much more than checking for net losses or gains recorded on the valuation statement since you bought each stock. It also means more than checking on how much the stocks' prices have changed since the last meeting.

Identifying big problems as early as possible and opportunities for reinvesting in a club-owned company are the stock watcher's goals, so that the club can take action. Remember, you can't simply buy every attractive stock that comes along. At some point your club will own all the stocks it can manage to follow, and to invest your cash contributions, you must either replace holdings or add to existing holdings. The stock watcher's job is to let the club know when a company's fundamentals have changed or are showing signs of a reversal in past trends, for better or for worse.

In some clubs, stock watchers are expected to report briefly each and every month on their assigned stocks. In other clubs, they're expected to report only when significant news is reported about the company or a change in its condition has occurred. If stock watchers give all-clear signals on stocks they track, then the club would rather spend time on other matters. Some clubs schedule quarterly reviews of all their holdings, and expect to hear stock watchers present a formal report following every quarterly earnings announcement.

Your club can choose a schedule that works best, but formalizing that arrangement is important so that all members know what's expected of their stock watchers and when.

Outlining a Stock Watcher Report

Chapter 15 discusses all that goes into managing a portfolio of stocks, and Appendix A includes a sample stock watcher form that your members can use when reporting to the club. The report outlines a systematic method for tracking each stock, thus helping your club understand a stock's current condition in light of the factors that led your club to add it to its portfolio in the first place. This section lists some of the points that stock watchers need to cover and explains some of the questions they need to answer in their regular presentations to the club.

Most of this information is available from the same sources and Web sites described in Chapter 14 for researching stocks. One primary source of information is the company's annual and quarterly reports filed with the SEC's Electronic Data Gathering, Analysis, and Retrieval System (EDGAR — www.sec.gov). EDGAR provides you with access to the **Form 10-Q** (quarterly) reports filed by the company about 45 days or less after the close of its quarter. **Form 10-K** (annual) reports are due to be filed within 90 days after the close of the company's fiscal year.

Stock watchers can make good use of press releases and news stories available from company Web sites or from Yahoo! Finance (finance.yahoo.com). Your club may also ask stock watchers to read business publications such as *The Wall Street Journal, Barron's, Business Week, Fortune,* and *Forbes,* searching for positive or negative stories about companies, their management, and their industries and competitors.

Sales growth

Over the long term, companies cannot grow their profits (earnings) without growing revenues. Stock watchers can explain to the club the results of sales or revenues from their companies' more recent quarterly reports and point to the reasons for any positive or negative changes. They should be able to cite any trends in a company's revenues or sales growth, whether it's introducing new products or services, or whether its division is experiencing a decline in sales.

Earnings per share (EPS) growth

Your stocks need to grow their earnings per share (EPS) on a consistent basis. Stock watchers must ask and answer many questions about EPS. How has the company fared in its most recently completed quarter? Are earnings up, down, or flat, compared with EPS from the same quarter last year? What trends are evident in the company's EPS growth? Are a company's increased earnings based on increased growth, decreased expenses, or a combination of both? Conversely, what are the reasons for a company's losses? What are its expectations for turning a profit in the future? Did the company have any one-time charges or extraordinary income that affected EPS?

Pretax profit margins and growth

Pretax profit margins are one of the best early warning signs for letting you know when companies are having trouble. A company with six consecutive quarters of declining profit margins is a prime candidate for replacement. From the company's most recent quarter report, describe how its pretax profits have grown or shrunk, and then identify trends in its pretax profit margin. You calculate the pretax profit margin by dividing a company's net profit before taxes by its revenues. If margins are shrinking, what is the reason for the contraction?

Management's ability and competence

Based on a company's recent performance, ask whether its management exhibits strength and competence. Has any recent turnover occurred in senior-level executive positions?

Breaking news

Summarize current news stories about the company, along with any press releases it has issued. What impact does this news have on the company's long- and short-term outlooks? Has the company launched any new initiatives, or is it having problems in one or more of its divisions?

Current valuation

Stock watchers must report their companies' current stock prices and P/E ratios. How do they compare with the stock's price and price-earnings ratio

(P/E) when the stock was purchased? A good way to accomplish this is completing NAIC's Portfolio Management Guide (PMG) every month with price, earnings, and P/E information. The PMG displays the relationship of a stock's current price and P/E ratio on a graph so that you can quickly see whether it's overvalued or undervalued. The PMG is discussed in more depth in Chapter 15.

Future outlook

What is the company's outlook during the next six months? What is its long-term outlook (during the next five years)? Has your outlook changed since the club bought the stock or since your last report?

Overall recommendation

Should the club sell all or a portion of its holdings, hold tight for now, or buy more shares? The stock watcher's job is recommending whether the club should take action or sit pat.

PERT update

Stock watchers should update a Portfolio Evaluation Review Technique, or PERT Worksheet A for their assigned companies after they report their quarterly results. (See Chapter 15 for details about PERT.)

Likewise, one member of the club needs update the main PERT form for the entire club portfolio. This form summarizes all the key data points for each stock, including EPS, sales, and pretax profits, and it includes several valuation calculations, such as relative value, P/E, and the upside-downside ratio. Knowing these factors can help you see whether the price of any stock is attractive and its other fundamentals are on track.

Some clubs assign a portfolio specialist to look at their overall portfolios, review their diversification, and manage their PERT forms based on information provided by stock watchers. When stock watchers distribute their PERT worksheets (see Chapter 15) to club members during their meetings, each member can track the portfolio as a whole on their own. By managing the worksheet yourself, you share your education and insights with the club.

Outlining a Yearly Stock Watcher Report

Once a year, stock watchers should present a full review of their assigned stocks. Although you can choose to review your holdings on the anniversary of their first appearance in your portfolio, completing your appraisal after the company has released its own annual self-evaluation in the form of its annual report and required filings to the SEC is a better time. That way you have plenty of details about the company, including any troubles it faced during the year. Understanding company issues is vital to presenting an accurate report to your club. Not all companies end their fiscal years December 31. You can find out when your company will release its annual report and filings by calling its investor relations department.

The next three sections discuss elements that should be part of your annual stock watcher report.

Overview of the annual report

Each year, the stock watcher needs to review the company's annual report and report on the highlights to the club.

The SEC requires all publicly traded companies to file Form 10-K each year. The 10-K reports the company's activities during the past year through complete financial statements and a discussion of its operations provided by the company's management. This simple text report usually is a treasure trove of details, especially because the company must report not only on the things that are going well but also on its problems.

Don't be over-impressed by the glitz

Traditionally, most companies go one step further, publishing the information contained in their Form 10-Ks in glossy annual reports accompanied by color photos (often of the smiling faces of the board of directors and senior executives), graphs, charts and illustrations. Fancy annual reports are meant to make the company look more attractive to investors, but the most important information usually can be found in the financial statements and footnotes in the back of the report.

In recent years, more and more companies are recognizing that the annual reports they are required to distribute to their stockholders are expensive to produce and print. Realizing that many investors would rather see money spent on growing and operating the business than on printing expensive promotional materials, many companies have begun placing a nice, shiny color cover on the plain text version of the Form 10-K for their shareholders. That's great for shareholders!

Reviewing the annual report

Companies in which your club is a shareholder should send your club treasurer (or whoever's address is used for your financial accounts) their annual reports in the mail each year, along with their proxy statements and notices of their annual meetings. Make sure that your treasurer distributes annual and quarterly reports to the respective stock watchers of those stocks. You also can download the Form 10-K of any company from the SEC's Web site (www.sec.gov), or you can ask the company's investor relations department to send you a copy of its Form 10-K and/or annual report by mail. Many companies now provide electronic versions of their annual reports on their Web sites, too.

The annual report is one of the most important sources of information about a company, regardless of whether you're researching a stock for the first time or reviewing its progress since you've become a shareholder. Companies create annual reports with the general public in mind, so the focus usually is on a straightforward, information-packed presentation. Annual reports generally give a basic overview of the company's business, products, and services, which is especially helpful when the company is involved in a sector — technology or industrial manufacturing, for example — in which you can't personally evaluate their products at the grocery or local shopping mall.

You'll find that most annual reports are organized in the same general way. The key components, and what you should be looking for as you prepare your report for the club, are

- ✓ **The letter from management.** Most reports begin with a letter to shareholders from management, written by the company's president, chief executive officer or chairman of the board. The company's top executives summarize the highlights of the firm's performance during the past year in the letter, bragging about their accomplishments all the while. Were there any low points during the year? A forthright company addresses them and tells shareholders what's being done to correct or improve upon the problems.

- ✓ **An operations report.** Next, the annual report reviews the company's operations. In most annual reports, this section may describe the company in terms of product lines or corporate divisions, and looks at its performance in a bit more detail. This report usually tells about new products the company launched during the year, outlines new plans and goals for the company year, and articulates the company's strategy for success.

- ✓ **The financial statements.** The third section of an annual report is the financial review. Often, this section is printed in small type on less expensive paper than the rest of the report, but don't let that lead you into ignoring it. The information you'll find here is usually the most important part of any annual report, including:

- **The auditor's letter.** One area to focus on is the report from the company's independent auditors. Publicly traded companies hire an outside auditor to verify that the company has followed accepted accounting principles and procedures. Most auditor letters are brief, indicating that no problems were found with the company's reporting.

  If the auditor's letter is longer than two or three paragraphs, you need to look at it more closely, because it can contain an indication that the company's practices are in question. Read the letter carefully, especially if the auditors qualify any of the observations they've made. Consider any such qualifications to be red flags that require further research on your part.

- **Management's discussion and analysis.** The management's discussion and analysis of financial statements is another required element of the annual report. These narratives describe the significant financial developments of the year and offer broad explanations and comparisons with prior years, giving company management the opportunity to explain why sales or earnings were less than impressive or how a new acquisition is affecting the company's profitability.

Management's discussion and analysis statements often are dense reading, but information that they contain is well worth your effort to read and understand. Gloss over the photos and pretty charts in the beginning of the annual report, if you must, but slow down and carefully and thoroughly read these statements!

Overview of the proxy statement

Upon receiving your annual report, you'll usually find that it includes a notice of the company's annual meeting, a proxy statement, and a proxy card on which you can cast your vote for business that may come before the board at its meeting.

A publicly traded company is owned by its shareholders. Each has a vote in the operation of the business. Once a year, the shareholders meet to elect representatives to the board of directors, the group that oversees the company on behalf of the shareholders. Other business that shareholders are required to vote on may come before the owners at the company's annual meeting.

The *proxy statement* provides details about all the business scheduled for discussion at the annual meeting, including the election of directors, approval of the company's auditors, and other matters such as changes in the company's common or preferred stock and employee bonus plans.

The *proxy card* is the ballot that shareholders bring with them to the meeting to record their votes, or, more likely, return to the company to enable management to cast their votes if they're unable to attend the annual meeting.

Your club should set a policy about voting its proxies for the companies held in its portfolio. Often, the proxy statement is just "business as usual," but occasionally important matters must be voted on by shareholders, such as a merger or acquisition. As the stock watcher, you need to be able make a recommendation on how the club should cast its vote on those matters.

As an owner of a publicly traded company, casting your club's ballot is the right and responsibility of its members, regardless of how few shares of the company they may own. Because you've chosen a well-managed, solidly run company (at least that's the assumption!), your club nearly always chooses to vote according to management's recommendations or authorizes management by the proxy to vote on your behalf.

Of course, you always need to let a corporation's management know when you disagree with their policies, but if the company has generated solid returns for its shareholders in the past, your club probably will be content to let management continue its exemplary leadership. Just remember that regardless of how your club votes, your vote still counts, and as responsible shareholders, you always should cast your proxy.

Besides describing the motions that are expected to be on the ballot at the annual meeting, the proxy statement also contains information that any business owner (that's your club, remember) needs to know. All proxy statements use the same basic format, so once you're familiar with it, gleaning the most important information from the statement shouldn't take more than ten minutes.

Many investors also make it a policy to review a company's most recent proxy statement before buying shares. Companies will send you a copy of their most recent proxy upon request, or you can download a copy from the SEC's EDGAR by searching on the company's name and look for Form DEF-14A.

Some of the key points that you can quickly derive from a Proxy Statement are about the election of directors, executive compensation, director compensation and a five-year performance chart.

Election of directors

The proxy statement describes each director's business experience, age, and length of service on the company's board. Check to see that most of the directors are outsiders — individuals who aren't affiliated with the company. Attorneys and investment bankers who receive fees from the company are considered insiders, as are retired employees of the company who may sit on the board.

Sometimes you'll discover that your company CEO sits on the boards of other companies, and those companies' executives sit on his board. This may be a sign of a "good old boys' network," and indicate that shareholders' interests may not be the first priority. Try to determine how many *independent directors* sit on the board — those who are neither employees nor affiliated in any other way with the company.

A summary of each director's stock ownership is provided in the proxy statement. You'll want to determine that each director owns shares in the company. Remember that it may take time for a new director to buy shares, and most directors probably won't hold a huge position. But a director who doesn't hold any company stock more than likely isn't committed to or convinced of the company's future success.

Executive compensation

The proxy statement provides details on executive compensation. Look to see that management is paid fairly and comparably to other companies of similar size within the same industry. (You may have to do some digging to find out.) Also check to see whether executives are being paid outlandish salaries. Many companies now include more stock options as part of company compensation packages, assuming that executives perform better when they're compensated as owners than they do merely as employees. Option awards also are included in the compensation table.

Director compensation

Check to see that directors are not excessively compensated for their service to the board. Ideally, directors should receive payment in whole or in part in company stock to help ensure that their interests are more closely aligned with the shareholders as a whole.

Performance chart

Every proxy statement contains a *Comparison of Five Year Cumulative Total Return* graph, which compares the stock's past performance to a group of its peers and to the stock index to which it best corresponds. Look to the chart for a quick, easy-to-understand snapshot of the company's past performance.

Updated Stock Selection Guide

The last part of your annual review needs to include an updated Stock Selection Guide (SSG). As described in Chapter 14, the SSG is your club's primary tool to understanding a stock before you buy it, but it also helps you keep track of a stock after it's part of your portfolio. You always should use the SSG to help your club decide to purchase more shares of a stock that you already own.

If you're using SSG software, updating a previously completed SSG shouldn't take much more than a few minutes. But it's amazing how a few minutes work can help your club make decisions that can mean thousands of dollars to your portfolio over time. So, don't try to wiggle out of doing it.

Heart & Soul Investment Club

In 1997, 15 friends, ranging in age from 25 to 38, shared with each other an article in *The Washington Post* about how little women know about investing. Determined not to let the same fate befall them, these African-American women decided to take their financial futures in their own hands and formed the *Heart & Soul Investment Club.* Food is an important part of the club's heritage — not only did they take their name from the restaurant in Washington, D.C., where they first met, but members offer even tastier snacks when it's their turn to provide meeting refreshments. The club also occasionally meets for brunch at a local restaurant.

As a group, they've visited the New York Stock Exchange, and they often travel together socially to plays or on ski trips. An annual spa day rejuvenates club members. Although no formal research has been conducted into the effects of spa treatments on investing prowess, we agree that it certainly can't hurt!

When it comes to investing, however, these women really mean business. Their portfolio, worth almost $10,000, contains ten stocks. They contribute a minimum of $35 every month and use club accounting software to track their investments. Each member follows at least one stock in the portfolio. Club members serve on rotating teams that are responsible for stock studies, industry studies, and educational presentations. These teams also take turns preparing educational presentations on subjects that are requested by club members.

Potential members must show an interest in finding out more about investing in stocks and a willingness to be an active member of the club. True to Heart & Soul's beginnings, culinary skills (although not required) virtually guarantee admission to the club. New members receive a detailed new-member packet that outlines member responsibilities, the club's attendance policy, its legal documents, and its history, giving newcomers the background they need. Although Heart & Soul members definitely enjoy the social and gastronomic aspects of their club, they're also sticklers for regular attendance and have even "invited" members with participation problems to leave the club, thus making room for more motivated new members to join.

The Heart & Soul Investment Club uses online resources to research and purchase stocks, working through online discount broker Quick and Reilly. Members communicate almost exclusively with e-mail, and consider online interactions absolutely crucial to maintaining a high level of interest in the club. Club involvement has made a huge difference in these members' personal lives: Only one had a stock portfolio when they formed the club, and now all but two have started investing on their own outside the club.

Chapter 17

Rescuing a Failing Club — Or Not

. . . .

In This Chapter

▶ Trying to keep your club going

▶ Knowing when it's time to fold your club

▶ Distributing the club's assets

▶ Closing the club's books and turning out the lights

. . . .

*E*veryone hopes that it never happens, but the time may come when, realistically, the outlook for your club has turned quite dreary. Member attendance may reach an all-time low, and no members are interested in serving as officers or want to do stock research for the club. The market may crash, taking your portfolio along with it and perhaps even your club's spirit and soul.

Although you hate the idea, it may be time to start thinking about ways to disband your club. Sometimes you just have to say goodbye, even though it may be painful or sad to admit. However, before giving up your club's ghost for good, you may try taking a few steps to keep it running in some fashion. Your last minute attempts at resuscitation may even get your club back on track, pulling it off the brink of disaster and then taking it to even greater heights than before.

Diagnosing Your Club's Ills

Investment clubs fail for many reasons, but generally they have

- **Unrealistic expectations.** If your club members expected to get rich quick or didn't understand the amount of work they'd be required to do, they've probably become disillusioned.

- **No shared investment philosophy.** If some of your members are ardent technical analysts who want to *day-trade* while the rest believe in buying on strong fundamentals and holding for the long-term, you've probably had your fair share of arguments about what stocks to buy.

> ✔ **Member burnout.** If the same few members are always the ones who volunteer to hold the officer positions and the only ones who do their stock study homework, they're probably exhausted and wondering why they ever wanted to join a club in the first place.
>
> ✔ **No interest in more education.** If your members balk at the idea of further learning and insist on just doing things the way they've done it since the club started, then your club is stuck in a time warp and probably is starting to stagnate.
>
> ✔ **Member laziness.** If many of your club members frequently miss meetings, pay dues late or not at all, and expect everyone else to do the work, your club probably has come to a virtual standstill with no money to invest and no ideas for stocks to invest it in.

How many of those maladies describe your investment club? If you're looking at all of them, you're more than likely right to be shutting down your club. But if only one or two apply, you may still be able to save the club. The following sections provide you with some ideas about investment club first-aid that you may want to try if you really don't want to close everything down yet.

Before Tossing in that Towel

Not so fast! Don't write all those member withdrawal checks yet! Before you throw up your hands and walk away for good, consider trying these last ditch strategies. Skim through earlier chapters in this book, looking for tips that discuss ways for handling many of the problems that, if left untreated, can send a club down the road to termination.

So if your club is having problems with attendance, institute an attendance policy that sets the minimum number of meetings that each member must attend during the year. Late fees can go a long way toward solving the problems of late dues-payers. Using e-mail can help improve communication between busy members. And stock study committees can help you put some fun back into your club research.

Rescue strategies for clubs in distress

If you've tried all these things, and they haven't had the results you'd hoped for, then your club may be on the brink of dissolution. So it's time to take more drastic actions to save your club.

Adjusting your meeting schedule and location

When members are finding it harder and harder to attend meetings, then maybe your meeting schedule and location are no longer convenient. Poll your fellow members and find out whether a better time and place to meet solves the problem.

And remember, nothing says that a club must meet every month. You may consider changing your schedule to meet every other month. That means your club's necessary business will more than likely take somewhat longer to accomplish than it would at monthly meetings, but less frequent meetings can be a better alternative than folding your club.

Terminating nonparticipating members

Many clubs fail because they lack member participation. Even when they're not around, nonparticipating members cause problems that reverberate throughout the rest of the membership. When members stop showing up for meetings, paying their dues, or following their assigned stocks, they create a vacuum that's difficult to fill. Other members become frustrated and disheartened, and, in turn, lose interest. For that reason, quickly dealing with nonparticipating members is important, even when you're considering the seeming drastic step of kicking them out. Two factors to consider are

✔ **Giving them one last chance.** Before moving to force anyone out of your club, you need to give all your absent members a chance to be more active again. If you've already tried to rope the strays back into your club, then you may need to take action. If things have gone so far that your club members are muttering about disbanding, then apply some tough love. Clearing out the deadwood often reinvigorates a club, so check your operating agreement for the procedures for removing nonparticipating members and then take action. Even when half of your club members end up voluntarily or involuntarily leaving the club, the remaining members still can successfully operate a club.

✔ **Following your operating agreement to the letter.** If your operating agreement or procedures (bylaws) don't specifically address the option of removing members who don't contribute, make sure that provision is added. You need to amend your bylaws to explicitly state member responsibilities and consequences for not fulfilling them (from late fees to expulsion). You'll have enough remaining members, it is hoped, to approve the amendments. After the changes are approved, you need to inform delinquent members that it's time to shape up or ship out.

As you begin cleaning up your club membership list, members who want to continue may need to ante up additional funds to pay off departing members. Or your club can sell a losing stock or two from its portfolio, or transfer appreciated shares to departing members, just like a regular member withdrawal. Look at cleaning house like this as an opportunity to prune your club's portfolio and align your holdings with your objectives.

Converting to an online club

If many members of your club still are interested but are moving away or simply can't find a way to make it to club meetings, consider converting to a purely online club. By using e-mail and the Web to communicate, your club can continue conducting business as it has in the past, but in a slightly different manner. Even if your club doesn't become a completely online club, you still can make better use of e-mail to maintain interest and participation between meetings. Chapter 9 includes details about all the online tools that you can use to operate a club.

Merging with another club — beware!

Occasionally, you may meet up with a member of another club that seems to have many of your club's same problems. While you commiserate, the idea will come to you — why not merge your two clubs and spark some enthusiasm?

Unfortunately, although no law or regulation prevents two partnerships or other entities from merging, a problem exists with accounting for the future gains and losses that eventually would be incurred by the new club. Any stocks brought into the new merged club portfolio can cause problems later on, because the gains or losses on those stocks would have to be allocated to members who belonged to the club that originally purchased those shares. In other words, merging two clubs creates a whopping accounting headache. We'll be blunt — just don't do it.

If you still like the idea of merging, members of one club can withdraw and then join the other club, or members can withdraw from both clubs and form a new, third club. Unfortunately, members who withdraw likely will incur tax liability for capital gains. However, if one club's portfolio has been doing poorly, then that club's members may be able to withdraw with little realized capital gains, and thus won't be penalized for leaving to join the other club.

Splitting your club in two

Some clubs suffer because club members have separated into two factions, and can't seem to agree on anything. Your club members may have considered just splitting the club into two new clubs, transferring half of all holdings into each club. Unfortunately, the accounting for such a split would be extremely cumbersome, not to mention impossible to accomplish with any currently available accounting software programs. Selling everything and then dividing up the cash would be far easier — but that's really no different than terminating the club in the first place or having several members withdraw.

Terminating when there's no other choice

Your club may find itself in an unusual position if a minority wants to continue the club while the majority wants to disband. If your operating agreement stipulates a withdrawal fee, the majority members may not be willing to pay it to remove their assets from the club just so the minority can continue the club. Similarly, those members who want to continue won't want to accept a withdrawal that incurs a tax liability only to reinvest those assets back into a new club.

Unfortunately, IRS regulations state that a partnership terminates when "at least 50 percent of the total interest in partnership capital and profits is sold or exchanged within a 12-month period, including a sale or exchange to another partner." So your club may have to terminate even when some members want to continue. That's okay, because they can form a new club, putting their experience to work in developing a club structure that avoids some of the problems inherent in the old club.

Sometimes it pays to be sneaky

Sometimes one or more club members just can't seem to get along with everyone else, and their bad behavior has a horrible effect on club operations and morale. If this is the case with your club, and you know things would improve without them, but you can't find a way to get them out of the club, a drastic and slightly devious option is open to you.

Assuming that you can handle any potential bad feelings that may come up later on, here's what to do. Ask other club members if they agree with your assessment of the *problem members.* If they do, and if they're willing to take on the tax liability associated with withdrawing from the club simply to get rid of these members, call for a club termination at your next meeting. When you have more than half the membership on your side, it won't matter whether the rest of the members won't agree to terminate. IRS rules mandate the termination of a partnership when "at least half of the total interest in partnership capital and

profits is sold or exchanged within a 12-month period." Your club will have to fold if you all leave.

Now here's the sneaky part you've been waiting for: As soon as you've agreed to terminate, conduct a meeting to start restructuring the investment club. But invite only the members that you really want in your new club. Yes, it may seem a little harsh not to let everyone know what you're doing, but the alternative is to continue with your dysfunctional club and miss out on the opportunity to be in a club with the members whose company you truly appreciate.

This option isn't for everyone, especially if you don't want to deal with questions or hurt feelings if the *uninvited members* find out about the new club. It can, however, work wonders rejuvenating your club, and you'll all breathe a sigh of relief when you get through an entire meeting without abrasive comments, annoying chatter, or contentious bickering.

Reinventing your club

Even if your club disbands, that doesn't mean it has to cease to exist. If you still have enough motivated members, your club can rise from the ashes and re-form under new and better circumstances.

The simplest way to reinvent your investment club is to do everything out in the open. Talk honestly about how your club has effectively quit functioning, and let your fellow members know that without a commitment to change by *all* the members, the lights must be turned out. Tell them that you're still interested in being a club member, just not in *this* club, and that if any of them *were* willing to be active members, you'd love to band together with them in a new club.

If the rest of the membership won't agree to terminate the club, then you can walk away with no regrets and start your new club, knowing that you did everything you could to make it work. You'll be more knowledgeable and wiser and can use your past club experiences to form an even better club. If any club members decide to withdraw with you, especially if they're dedicated and willing to make an effort toward forming a more successful club, your new club will be off to an even stronger start.

When All Else Fails . . . Shutting Down and Closing Out the Books

If you've considered all the options, and your club has decided to terminate, then what's done is done. The process of disbanding fortunately isn't too difficult. And, it is hoped, you and your members have learned something about investing from your club experiences, so it thus hasn't been a total loss.

Only a few differences in procedure exist between terminating a club and handling member withdrawals and year-end accounting. You can find much more information about withdrawals in Chapter 8. Just be aware of a few places where you'll need to pay particular attention when you're terminating the entire club. The checklist of items that need to be accomplished includes

 ✔ **Determining how to distribute assets, either by selling or transferring shares.** Like any withdrawal, don't sell appreciated shares unless you have to. Transfer shares of those stocks to departing members, either by requesting a stock certificate or transferring the shares directly to the members' brokerage accounts. Your members need to open accounts at the same brokerage where your club has its account. This greatly simplifies and accelerates the transfer of assets. If your club has DRIP stocks, you can easily transfer them to members' DRIP accounts.

Be prepared to wait two months or longer to receive stock certificates from the transfer agent when you opt to go that route. Your members can decide which stocks they're willing to accept as part of their withdrawal — as long as everyone in your club still is talking to each other!

✔ **Having all members withdraw in writing.** Regardless of your club's structure, whether partnership, corporation, or however it's set up, you'll need to ensure that the framework is legally terminated. Require all members to provide a letter that states that they no longer are members of the club. You may want to withhold payouts to any members who haven't provided this document, just as incentive.

✔ **Determining future potential income.** Check the ex-dividend dates of the stocks that you own, because you still can be entitled to receive a dividend even after you sell your shares. You can also receive money market dividends or interest in your accounts. If you receive these funds after you've already closed the books, you'll have to reopen them to distribute the funds. The amount may be so small that your members won't care about receiving their actual share of the proceeds, but these small payments still can mean additional accounting headaches. You often can check online account balances to determine what transactions have been posted to your account instead of waiting for the final statement to arrive in the mail.

✔ **Anticipating future expenses.** Is there a fee for closing your brokerage account? Are there costs for tax software or upgrades that you may need for closing out the books? Try to determine all these costs and account for them now. As is true of potential future income, these small amounts can be frustrating for your treasurer to account for, not to mention figuring out how to pay for them when no money is left in your club account!

✔ **Closing out your books well before the end of the year.** Disbanding a club can take time, often several months, but if you let the tasks linger past January 1, you'll be obligated to file tax returns for the new year. You definitely don't want to have to do extra work to account for a few dollars that were carried over into the new year. When you're terminating in November, however, you won't likely be able to close the books by December 31. In that case, don't sweat it; just take your time completing all the tasks of termination.

✔ **Creating a distribution report.** Using your club accounting software, create a distribution report for your club, just like your treasurer has done every year in the past. Mark it as the final distribution report on the top and distribute it to all members.

✔ **Filing final tax returns.** If the partnership is terminated before the end of the year, the IRS requires that **Form 1065** be filed for the short period. This return covers the period from the start of the year to the date of termination and is due on the 15th day of the fourth month after the termination. Because you'll be filing a report for a short period, using the current year's **Form 1065** is acceptable, rather than using next year's form, which won't likely be available. Mark "Final Return" on Line G of **Form 1065,** and mark "Final K-1" on line I of each member's **Schedule K-1.**

✔ **Keeping all your records.** The club needs to designate one member to keep all the partnership's records in a safe place. All tax returns, meeting minutes, bank and brokerage records, and other documents must be stored for up to seven years.

For more information about terminating partnerships, consult the *IRS's Publication 541: Partnerships,* which is available at the IRS Web site (www.irs.gov).

Closing down your club may be a sad affair, especially after all the hard work that you've put into it. But even the best and most dedicated club members sometimes find themselves in a difficult club situation, and termination turns out to be the only solution. The good news is that many of these club devotees go on to start or join other clubs. Instead of giving up on the investment club experience, they move on to find success and new opportunities elsewhere.

If you're interested in starting another club someday, keep notes on what worked and what didn't, what went right and what fizzled, so that you can take advantage of your experiences. Remember how much you've learned in the process. We're willing to bet that you've gained considerable knowledge about investing, confidence in picking your own stocks, and experience in useful group dynamics, all the while meeting some great new people and hopefully having a little fun along the way.

Part V
The Part of Tens

The 5th Wave   By Rich Tennant

"My portfolio's gonna take a hit for this."

In this part . . .

You're at the point of buying or selling a stock. But you want to make certain that you've considered all the angles. That's where the Part of Tens steps in as your friendly advisor — Chapter 18, "Ten Questions to Ask Before Buying a Stock," and Chapter 19, "Ten Questions to Ask Before Selling a Stock." It's all right here in quick summary form.

Chapter 18

Ten Questions to Ask Before Buying a Stock

*B*uying a stock is exciting. We're willing to bet that coming to a purchase decision and then actually buying a stock will be one of your club's favorite activities. All that education, all that analysis, all those tasty treats finally lead up to the big event, and you get to make your choice at last.

Before you're swept away by the enthusiasm of the moment, you must approach a purchasing decision logically. We cover stock analysis in detail in Chapter 14, so don't forget to check there to brush up on the full procedure. But here's a quick overview of what you need to pay attention to as you start your stock analysis adventure.

What does the company do?

You wouldn't buy a business without first understanding how that business works, starting with the products or services it sells. Buying a stock shouldn't be any different. Legendary stock picker Peter Lynch was once so impressed by the investing techniques of a class of seventh-graders that he borrowed one of their methods and cited their resourcefulness in his book *Beating the Street:* "Never invest in any idea you can't illustrate with a crayon." While you don't need to break out the Crayolas at your club meetings, the underlying principle is clear: Find out about the company's business before you buy its stock.

How has the company grown in the past five to ten years?

You want to make sure that the company you're analyzing consistently has been able to grow revenues and earnings per share and at a rate appropriate for the size of the company. *Revenues* are the money that a company takes in from sales and other sources, while *earnings* are the company's profits, the money that's left from revenues after all expenses are paid. *Earnings per share (EPS)* is the amount of a company's profits divided by the number of shares of stock that the company has issued.

What are the company's pretax profit margins?

Make sure that pretax profits have been stable from year to year during the past five to ten years, along with the more recent eight to 12 quarters. Similarly, you want to ensure that margins are better than average for the company's industry group. Profit margin is the ratio of a company's profits to its total revenues, and it measures how effective a business is at delivering results to the bottom line. Be sure to look at *pretax* profits and not profits after taxes. Companies have no control over the taxes they must pay to the government; so pretax profits are a better measure of the company's underlying ability to sustain excellence (if excellence exists in the first place!).

What is the current P/E ratio of the stock?

A stock's price-earnings ratio (P/E) is calculated by dividing its current price by the company's current annual earnings per share, usually from the last four quarters (known as the trailing P/E ratio). You can find the P/E ratio listed in the daily newspaper or on just about any Internet stock quote site.

The P/E ratio is one of the more common figures that investors look at when they analyze a stock. On the surface, the P/E ratio tells you how much investors currently are willing to pay for each dollar of the company's earnings. In practice, the P/E ratio is a matter of interpretation, and you need to be able to explain why a company's P/E ratio is what it is to your fellow club members. Check out Chapter 14 for help.

What's the dividend yield of the stock?

A *dividend* is a cash payment that is distributed among stockholders as a share of the company's profits, usually on a quarterly basis. The company's board of directors must authorize the dividend payments, which may be made in cash, stock, or property. Usually, only established companies pay dividends, because newer companies need to reinvest all their profits to grow their businesses.

Once you know how much a company pays each year in dividends, you can determine the dividend yield of its stock by dividing the annual dividends per share by the current price per share. For example, if a company pays $1.65 annually in dividends and its current stock price is $24.05, divide 1.65 by 24.05 to arrive at a dividend yield of 6.86 percent. You can then compare this dividend yield with the interest rate you may receive on a bond or a bank account. However, dividends aren't guaranteed, and stock prices change, so losing money on an investment is possible even if you receive dividends.

What is your target rate of return from the stock if you buy it today?

Buying a stock with the hope that it somehow will increase in price in the future isn't enough. You need to be able to quantify the average target rate of return that you can reasonably expect from the stock each year that you own it. If the company grows at your projected average annual earnings per share growth rate during the next five years, and trades at an appropriate P/E ratio, what is the projected high price that the stock will sell for? Although nothing guarantees that the stock *will* sell for that price, having the goal expressed before you buy gives you a benchmark to compare with the stock's capital appreciation.

Does the current price allow for your desired return during the next five years?

Finding a great company isn't enough, because hundreds of terrific companies trade on the market. You also must know the right time and price at which to buy a particular stock. Overpaying for a stock reduces your return. You can even lose money on such an investment. Too many times a club gets excited about a stock and jumps in with both feet, oblivious to the fact that the share price is too high to allow for a substantial return in the future.

So what happens if you find a great company and realize that its stock price is too high? If it indeed is a magnificent, well-managed business with bright prospects for the future, chances are that many other investors share in your positive assessment, and the share price will already reflect all these good vibes. But the stock's price can just as easily fall at some point in the next few months, or the company's earnings can *catch up* to the stock price, making it a more reasonable value. If you've already got it on your radar screen, pouncing once the opportunity arrives will be easier.

What's the worst possible likely outcome if you buy the stock today?

Every investment has a potential downside. Theoretically, any stock can fall in price to $0, causing you to lose your entire investment. The Over-the-Counter Bulletin Board (www.otcbb.com) and so-called "pink sheets" list hundreds of companies that have fallen to only pennies per share in price, so don't think it *never* happens. Even well-established, well-respected companies can sometimes be hit by unexpected and debilitating circumstances and never recover. So do your homework and find quality companies with great prospects for the future. Use Chapter 14 as your guide.

How does the company compare to its competition?

Some experts suggest that you invest only in the top one or two companies in any industry. By investing in the best, you better ensure that your portfolio is made up of good, solid businesses. As we mention above, comparing a company's profit margins to those of its competitors is important. Other important factors are return on equity, market share in product lines, total debt and the debt-to-capital ratio, and reputation in the industry. The company's SEC filings and annual report — and your research — will produce most of this information.

How does a new stock fit in your existing portfolio?

Every stock that you buy has an impact on your current holdings. Many important rules govern how you build a portfolio of stocks, such as maintaining diversification by company size and industry groups. You want to understand how a new stock fits alongside the other stocks you've purchased before. For instance, if you already own several technology stocks, then buying another in that sector can cause your portfolio to be overweighted, which, in turn, can be dangerous if tech stocks as a whole fall hard. Your club is better protected against bad news in one sector by being invested in many different areas. You can find more information about portfolio diversification in Chapter 15.

Chapter 19

Ten Questions to Ask Before Selling a Stock

*T*he day will come when your club must consider selling a stock from its portfolio. It may be that you're disappointed in a holding that hasn't performed as you had hoped, or maybe you've heard some bad news about a company, and you're thinking it's time to ditch the stock. Maybe the stock has beaten even your most optimistic projections, and you're wondering whether you should sell and lock in your profit while you can. Or perhaps a member of your club is withdrawing, and you need to raise some cash to pay her off. In Chapter 14, we cover the basics of buying and selling stocks in a long-term growth stock portfolio. This chapter gives you a quick list of questions to ask before deciding to sell.

Is the stock's future fading fast?

A company in your portfolio is having problems of one sort or another. Obviously your club needs to take a look to see whether you should sell or whether you'd be better off holding on and waiting out the troubles. If the company's problems are of a short-term nature, it can recover, and your patience may be rewarded as it hits even greater heights in the future. If the company faces far-reaching challenges that may have a serious impact on future growth and profitability, then your club may be better off selling now.

Unfortunately, determining whether a problem is short-term or long-term isn't always easy. You must definitely take a long hard look at the company to see whether any of its *fundamentals* are deteriorating. Ask yourself: Are profit margins declining? Look at the margins during the past five to eight quarters. Do you see any significant downward trends? That may be a strong signal that it's time to sell.

Are you being rash, emotional, or reactive?

Just because the company reports some bad news doesn't mean that you automatically should sell its stock. Often, negative news about a company surfaces and the price of its stock takes a hit. By the time the news is reported at your next club meeting, it's too late to protect yourself from any price declines triggered by the news. But the truth is that even if your club was diligently watching the stock each day, chances are good that you wouldn't be able to react quickly enough to sell shares before they fall in price anyway. The short-term damage is already done, so take your time to evaluate your options before selling.

Will your club's portfolio still be diversified if you sell?

The departure of one stock can upset the delicate balance of your diversified portfolio, or it can help bring your portfolio back into balance. Ironically, if your club is successful at picking winning stocks, that success may wreak havoc with the overall balance of your portfolio if only one or two stocks become overly large holdings. The objective of a balanced portfolio is spreading around the risk of each individual stock and tweaking your returns for the better. Selling a stock that's done well for your club can be a good thing.

What are the tax ramifications of selling?

Unless your club happens to sell a stock at exactly the same price at which it was purchased, your members will have to report either a capital loss or gain to the IRS at the end of the year. So before selling any holdings, make sure that you all understand the tax impact. Chapters 7, 10, and 13 cover tax topics, and take a peek at the last question on this list for an important warning.

Are you selling because of the stock — or because of the market or the industry?

Sometimes stocks are like lemmings — if one has problems, the whole group follows it right off the cliff. Often, if a company in a particular industry group has trouble, the prices of other stocks in that same group may also fall in sympathy, even though the other companies aren't affected. In that case, without any discernible impact on the stock that you own, selling wouldn't make sense. Some clubs will even purchase more of the stock after an irrational price drop like this, assuming that the stock falls into the club's buy range.

Is the stock overvalued or undervalued at its current price?

Sometimes stocks are cheap, and sometimes stocks are expensive. But the value of a stock has nothing to do with its price tag. A stock that sells for $10 may be expensive and a stock that sells for $1,000 may be cheap. It all depends on your club's estimates of how that stock is likely to perform in the future.

Are you 'cutting your flowers and letting your weeds grow'?

Many Wall Streeters spout rules about when to "take profits" from their portfolios, or when to sell stocks that have increased in price since they were purchased. Unfortunately, if your club follows these guidelines and sells all its winners just to take your profits, you'll soon find yourself with a portfolio of under-performers. The strategy of selling stocks when they reach preset price goals and holding on to your losers is known as "cutting your flowers and letting your weeds grow." Well-run companies can continue to grow for years and years, and their share prices will follow along.

Are you selling just because the stock's price hasn't gone up?

We can hear one of your fellow club members right now, trying to encourage your club to sell a stock with the complaint, "But this stock hasn't *done* anything!" Well, stocks don't *do* anything, anyway. What your member means is that the share price of the stock hasn't moved. It just sits there, month after month, neither increasing nor falling in price.

Actually, stocks with prices that haven't moved are far from abnormal. Stock prices tend to move up and down in bursts, rather than in nice, gradual sloping lines. The chart of a stock's price during the course of a few weeks or months usually looks more like an EKG printout. Occasionally, the chart even flatlines — but that's okay, a stock's price doesn't need to fluctuate for that stock to show plenty of signs of life.

Never sell on the basis of price alone. Take the time to study the reasons behind a stock's price movement or stagnation, and always remember that the market isn't a rational place.

Do you have a better use for the money after you sell?

Whenever your club sells a stock, you should have a plan for the proceeds from the sale. Do you have a replacement stock in mind to purchase? Or are you going to keep the cash in your club's bank account or money market fund? When you sit on cash in your portfolio, you lock in an interest rate of a few measly percent. Even when a stock has declined in price, it may still rebound and bring you out ahead of where you'd be by holding the cash. That's the thing about the stock market — you just never know whether a stock might rebound to your original purchase price or go even higher.

When selling to pay off a member withdrawal, have you considered all the options?

When it comes time to pay off a member who's withdrawing from the club, you may need to sell a stock or two to raise the necessary cash. In fact, being forced to sell a stock for this reason may be a good thing because it forces your club to confront some of the dogs that are dragging down your club's performance. But first, ask whether you have to sell at all. Along with your current cash, perhaps other members are willing and able to kick in extra contributions to pay off the withdrawing member.

If you must sell to raise cash, try to sell only stocks that have declined in value since you bought them. Club members can write off the loss on their tax returns. By all means, don't sell stocks that have risen in value because you'll trigger tax liability for everyone, including the departing member. But rather than selling holdings to settle accounts with a withdrawing member, a smarter strategy is to pay off that person by transferring to him or her the ownership of shares in the portfolio that have risen in value. The reason for this is somewhat complicated, but there is a provision of the IRS's partnership tax accounting that allows you to transfer an appreciated security to a member and then indefinitely defer the tax liability for that security. Chapters 8 and 10 cover member withdrawals in detail.

Appendix

Sample Documents and Forms

• •

*U*se this section as your guide to the language and style of documents and forms required by your investment club: bylaws, proxies, meeting agenda, meeting minutes, and Stock Watcher report. You can find the full text of a partnership agreement — along with our interpretation — in Chapter 5.

Bylaws

(Bylaws of the Blue Chips & Salsa Investment Club)

1. DEFINITIONS

A. "Club" means the Blue Chips & Salsa Investment Club, formed as a General Partnership on June 14, 1993 and reformed on June 14, 1999, and more fully described in the Partnership Agreement.

B. "Partner" or "member of the Club" shall mean a General Partner of the Blue Chips & Salsa Investment Club.

C. "Active partner" shall mean a General Partner of the Blue Chips & Salsa Investment Club who has fulfilled all requirements for membership as defined in Section III, and as shall be further defined by the Partners, and has not been deemed "inactive" as described below in Section IX, Paragraph E.

11. OFFICERS

A. The Club's officers shall consist of President, Vice-President, Secretary, Treasurer and Co Treasurer.

B. Duties of the Officers will include, but not be limited to, the following:

1. The PRESIDENT will appoint committees, oversee all Club activities, and preside over all Club meetings. The PRESIDENT will have the power to create and conduct an agenda for all meetings, and may enforce or waive formalities of such an agenda. The PRESIDENT will have the power to recommend disciplinary action to any Partner who, in the opinion of a member of the Club, is considered to have acted contrary to the provisions of these By Laws or has displayed negligence in the performance of duties or expectations.

2. The VICE-PRESIDENT will assume the duties of the PRESIDENT when absent or unable to serve the office. The VICE-PRESIDENT will be responsible for the activities, progress, and reports of all committees that are formed.

3. The SECRETARY will keep a record of Club business and issue a report of all meetings. The SECRETARY will be responsible for all correspondence pertaining to the Club, including the distribution of reports from meetings, officers and committees. Upon notification by the PRESIDENT or the CO-TREASURER; the SECRETARY will issue a notice to any Partner regarding any fines or disciplinary action, and include the reason and decision for the action.

4. The TREASURER will keep record of all Club financial activities; calculate and distribute valuation statements each month, and any other statistical reports required. The TREASURER will maintain records accounting for the Club financial operation; assets; and individual account value. The TREASURER will serve as agent for the Partnership to place BUY and SELL orders; and will distribute and collect funds.

5. The CO-TREASURER will assist the Treasurer and fulfill the duties of Treasurer in his/her absence or inability to serve, and shall maintain a backup set of accounting records, as well.

C. Officers will be elected by the total Partnership at the first meeting of the Club and to one-year terms at duly called Annual Meetings thereafter. Officers may succeed themselves in office upon re-election.

D. Annually, during the month of February, the current President shall call for nominations from the Club for all officer positions. The Club shall then elect the above officers following the voting procedures described below. The officers shall assume their duties upon the announcement of election results. Such announcement shall be prior to March 1 of each year.

E. Any officer position that becomes vacant during the year shall be filled as soon as possible following the same nomination and voting procedure described above.

F. A different person shall hold each office.

III. PARTNERS

A. All Club Partners shall participate in ongoing activities of the Club by:

1. Preparing and posting analyses or other assignments to further the investment endeavors of the Club;

2. Regularly contributing constructive comments about Club operations and investment opportunities;

3. Making regular payments to the Club;

4. Keeping a current mailing address on file with the Secretary at all times;

5. Reviewing monthly and year-end Club reports, including all financial and tax-information reports, and;

6. Voting in at least 50% of all Club elections during any four month period.

IV. PROCEDURES

A. Regular meetings will be held the second Monday of each month at seven o'clock p.m., or periodically as voted by the Club, at a time and location agreed upon.

B. February is designated for the Annual Meeting. At the Annual Meeting all Partners will be issued the Annual Report, and Club elections will be conducted. The Secretary will give notice to the Partnership as to the time, date, and location of the Annual Meeting and issue a proxy for the election of Officers to the entire Partnership.

C. Special meetings may be called by the President or any two officers of the Club upon verbal or written notice to the members of the Club.

D. The presence or duly executed proxies of one-half (1/2) the active members of the Club including at least one Officer of the Club will constitute a quorum sufficient to transact business.

V. FINANCIAL STATEMENTS

A. A monthly valuation statement shall list all assets, at cost and market values, and liabilities of the Club as of the last business day of the month. It shall also compute the Value of the Partnership, as defined in Paragraph 7 of the Partnership Agreement.

B. The Treasurer shall also prepare a summary statement of capital accounts maintained in the name of each Partner, as provided in Paragraph 8 of the Partnership Agreement.

C. The annual Club accounting shall show the distribution of dividends, interest, short and long-term capital gains, and expenses.

VI. VOTING

A. The right to vote is limited to active Partners.

B. Approved methods of voting are VERBAL, SIMPLE MAJORITY, TWO-THIRDS MAJORITY, POINT SYSTEM BALLOT, WRITTEN BALLOT, WEIGHTED BALLOT and PROXY. However, in the absence of a formal motion to conduct a given vote in another manner, all votes shall be carried by a simple majority of the active Partners.

C. The above notwithstanding, the general method of voting the BUY or SELL of two or more stock proposals is by the point system ballot followed by a voice vote of approval. Based on the number of proposals, each Partner assigns the highest number to the most preferred stock and then gives each remaining stock one less point, with the least preferred stock receiving one point

D. The above notwithstanding, any active Partner may request that any given vote be re-tallied on a weighted basis so that the value of a respective Partner's vote is in direct proportion to the value of his/her capital account measured against the aggregate value of all capital accounts comprising the asset base of the Partnership, as established in the most recent valuation statement duly prepared and presented by the Treasurer. Approval of such a request may not be unreasonably withheld, however, said request must be made during the meeting at which the vote in question has taken place.

E. If a Partner is unable to attend a meeting in person, said Partner is required to submit a proxy statement prior to the meeting.

VII. GUESTS AND NEW PARTNERS

A. Partners are permitted to invite guests to attend regularly scheduled meetings.

B. Guests are encouraged to actively participate in Club discussions and activities for two (2) months before consideration is given to adding the guest to the Club. Prospective members must make a presentation at a regular meeting of the Club of a stock study or some other investing topic before applying for membership.

C. The number of Partners shall be limited to twenty (20).

D. The acceptance of new Partners will be voted on by the Club as outlined in Section VI above.

VIII. BANK(S) AND BROKER(S)

A. The Club may maintain checking account(s) at the bank(s) that the Club deems necessary or desirable, or may operate only with the brokers' account or money market fund linked to the brokerage account.

B. The Club may engage one or more broker(s) as it deems necessary or desirable.

C. The Club shall request the bank or broker to send statements directly to both the Treasurer and Secretary.

D. The Club shall instruct the broker(s) that all requests for funds shall be made in writing and be signed by two (2) officers of the Club. However, only one (1) signature shall be required for trading purposes.

IX. PAYMENTS

A. Monthly payments in multiples of ten dollars ($10) and not totaling less than thirty dollars ($30) per Partner are due and payable at each regularly scheduled meeting (the second Monday of each month).

B. Any Partner may request from the President a temporary hardship waiver of the minimum monthly payment. Such request shall not be unreasonably denied.

C. If available and desired, Partners may arrange for automatic monthly withdrawal from the Partner's personal checking or other account to be deposited into the Club's account. Any expense for this shall be borne by the individual Partner.

D. There shall be no prepayment of monthly payments.

E. Non-payment for two (2) consecutive months shall cause the Partner to be designated inactive. The Treasurer shall notify the Secretary of any inactive Partners and the Secretary shall inquire by regular mail as to the reason for the non-participation of any inactive Partner.

F. Non-payment for four (4) consecutive months shall be deemed written notice of withdrawal in accordance with Paragraph 18 of the Partnership Agreement unless a waiver is granted by the Club.

G. The Club shall assess a fine against Partners for payments of monthly dues that are not received by midnight of the Friday immediately following the monthly meeting. This fee shall be $5.00 per occurrence. In the case of non-payment, the Treasurer is authorized to withdraw the fine from the delinquent member's capital account.

X. EXPENSE REIMBURSEMENT

A. From time to time, the Club may request a Partner to purchase goods or services for the benefit of the Club. Upon request of the Partner, the cost of such expenditure shall be reimbursed by the Club.

B. The President may authorize expenditures of less than $25. The total of such expenditures shall not exceed $125 in any calendar year.

C. Expenditures of $25 or more shall be authorized only by a Club vote.

XI. JOINTLY OWNED CAPITAL ACCOUNTS

A. There shall be no jointly owned capital accounts.

XII. PORTFOLIO

A. In keeping with the guidelines set forth by the NAIC, and to the extent practicable, the Club will strive to maintain an asset allocation in its portfolio consisting of the following:

1. Approximately 25% small companies (sales of $400 million or less), 50% mid-size companies (sales between $400 million and $4 billion), and 25% large companies (sales greater than $4 billion), by portfolio value.

2. Stocks of companies from a wide range of industry groups and sectors.

XIII. REMOVAL

A. Failure by a member of the Club to fulfill the duties as previously defined for four (4) consecutive months shall be deemed cause for consideration for removal in accordance with Paragraph 16A of the Partnership Agreement. A two-thirds majority vote of the remaining members of the Club shall be necessary for removal of a Partner. Such removal shall be deemed written notice of withdrawal in accordance with Paragraph 18 of the Partnership Agreement.

XIV. AMENDMENT OF THESE BY-LAWS

A. These By-Laws may be amended by a Club vote.

B. These By-Laws shall be construed in accordance with the Partnership Agreement and, in any conflict, the Partnership Agreement shall rule.

Sample Meeting Agenda

(Date)

Call to Order

Roll Call/Determining a Quorum

Introduction of Guests

Reading of the Minutes

Treasurer's Report

Portfolio & Stock Watcher Reports

Partner Presentations

Educational Presentation

Old Business

New Business

Announcements

Adjournment

Sample Proxy

(Mutual Investment Club of Detroit Limited Partnership)

TO: All the general partners attending the Mutual Investment Club of Detroit Limited Partnership meeting held on the date indicated below.

The undersigned does hereby constitute and appoint all those general partners of the Mutual Investment Club of Detroit Limited Partnership ("Mutual Club") who are present at a meeting to be held on ___(Date)___, or any adjournments thereof, attorney and agent for me, and in my name, place and stead, to vote as my proxies, at said meeting, with all powers I would possess if personally present. Each attending general partner is to be, and hereby is, entitled to vote my general partner's interest in the Mutual Club pro rata in proportion to each of the attending general partner's capital accounts. This Proxy is being given pursuant to Paragraph Ten (10) of the Limited Partnership of the Mutual Club, and all the terms and conditions of such paragraph and the other paragraphs of the Limited Partnership Agreement of the Mutual Club govern the use of this Proxy.

I have executed this Proxy on the date indicated below.

_____

(Signature)

_____

(Date)

Sample Meeting Minutes

(Blue Chips & Salsa Investment Club)

October 12, 200X

At Kent's Office:

Members Present: Kent H., Antoine L., Alexey P., Shaun S., Leonid U., Doug G., Bill S. (by proxy), Gary W., Susan K., Julia J.

Members Absent: Kathy F., Bill H.

Guests: Leslie S. (guest of Doug), Nikki T. (guest of Shaun).

Meeting Called to Order at 7:15 PM by Alexey, President.

Reading of the Minutes

The minutes from the September meeting were read. Kent moved to accept, Leonid seconded, motion carried by voice vote.

Treasurer's Report

Doug reviewed the member valuation status and valuation report. Our unit value is down from last month's $25.71 to $24.40.

He also reviewed the transactions since our last meeting. We purchased 50 shares of North Fork Bancorp at total cost of $964.25, and 11 shares of Keane at a total cost of $2,538.00. We also sold all shares of Motorola, netting $1,792.68.

We currently have $3,500 in cash available to invest.

Julia moved we accept the Treasurer's Report; Shaun seconded. The motion carried by voice vote.

Stock Watcher Reports

Shaun discussed BMCS, everything going well, improving products and double digit earnings growth. He recommends that we hold.

Alexey discussed RPM after reading annual report. Even though one of NAIC's favorites, company seems in trouble and cannot integrate well small companies that it bought. Having trouble serving customers with small orders. Honorable retirement of several key executives. Says needs complete reorganization and modernization of customer. It explains why the stock price has not moved in five years, and why it will not likely improve in the next few years. Alexey motioned that we immediately sell our current holdings at the market; Kent seconds. Motion carries unanimously.

Member Stock Presentation

Gary discussed McKesson HBOC. He stated that it has an interesting low valuation because of irregular earnings and accounting reporting problems. But the company is back on track and profitable, but very low margins on main business. There is no motion and the stock is dropped.

Educational Presentation

Julia presented "How to understand an annual report." She reviewed the important parts of an annual report, especially management's discussion of operations.

Next Month's Agenda

Gary will review RPM, Alexey will review Intel, and Antoine will present a study of Xerox.

Julia's educational presentation will be on the topic of the best stock research Web sites.

Adjournment

Kent motioned to adjourn at 9:05 pm; Antoine seconded. Motion carried by voice vote.

Thanks to Susan for the yummy hummus and pitas.

REMINDER: Our next meeting will be November 8, 200X at 7:00pm, at Doug's new office. Gary will handle refreshments (better bring a snack of your own if he decides to bake cookies again).

Sample Stock Watcher Report

Company Information

Stock Watcher's Name:

Current Date:

Company Name:

Ticker:

Recent Price:

Brief Company Description:

Date of Latest Quarterly Announcement:

Expected Date of Next Quarterly Announcement:

Company Fundamentals

Sales Growth & Trends:

Pre-tax Profit Margins Growth & Trends:

EPS Growth & Trends:

Management's Ability and Competence:

Summary of Recent News:

Valuation and Recommendation

Current Valuation:

Future Outlook:

Recommendation:

(See Chapter 16 for instructions on completing the Stock Watcher form.)

Index

Notes

Notes